AF352557

HEROIC AWE

The Sublime and the Remaking of Renaissance Epic

KELLY LEHTONEN

Heroic Awe

The Sublime and the Remaking of Renaissance Epic

UNIVERSITY OF TORONTO PRESS
Toronto Buffalo London

© University of Toronto Press 2023
Toronto Buffalo London
utorontopress.com
Printed in the U.S.A.

ISBN 978-1-4875-4536-9 (cloth)   ISBN 978-1-4875-4539-0 (EPUB)
                                  ISBN 978-1-4875-4540-6 (PDF)

Library and Archives Canada Cataloguing in Publication

Title: Heroic awe : the sublime and the remaking of Renaissance epic / Kelly
    Lehtonen.
Names: Lehtonen, Kelly, author.
Description: Includes bibliographical references and index.
Identifiers: Canadiana (print) 20220225400 | Canadiana (ebook) 20220225443 |
    ISBN 9781487545369 (cloth) | ISBN 9781487545390 (EPUB) |
    ISBN 9781487545406 (PDF)
Subjects: LCSH: Epic poetry, European – History and criticism. | LCSH: Sublime,
    The, in literature. | LCSH: Heroic virtue in literature.
Classification: LCC PN1303 .L44 2023 | DDC 809.1/32 – dc23

We wish to acknowledge the land on which the University of Toronto Press
operates. This land is the traditional territory of the Wendat, the Anishnaabeg, the
Haudenosaunee, the Métis, and the Mississaugas of the Credit First Nation.

University of Toronto Press acknowledges the financial support of the Government
of Canada, the Canada Council for the Arts, and the Ontario Arts Council, an agency
of the Government of Ontario, for its publishing activities.

For Jonathan

Contents

Illustrations

Acknowledgments

This project owes its inception to Patrick Cheney, whose graduate courses and scholarship encouraged my love of Renaissance epic poetry and inspired my interest in the sublime. His dedicated mentorship and support, numerous insights, and rigorous feedback on many drafts were crucial in giving the project a solid foundation – and in shaping my development as a scholar. Laura Knoppers, David Loewenstein, and Caroline D. Eckhardt were all instrumental in the project's early development, through their engaging courses and constructive comments. Unhae Langis Park volunteered invaluable rhetorical and translation suggestions in a closing stage of the manuscript, and with Julia Reinhard Lupton, offered ready encouragement and scholarly support, for which I am very grateful. Special thanks also to Sherry Roush for generous mentorship, astute guidance on Italian scholarship and translations, and enthusiastic support of the project's development from proposal to current form.

I am deeply indebted to Robert Goebel, my undergraduate advisor at James Madison University, for engaging classes that inspired my return to academia years later, and many subsequent years of mentorship and encouragement as I navigated the scholarly world. At Penn State, I was fortunate to find such brilliant and kind friends as Andres Amerikaner, Connie Bubash, Ted Chelis, Kristen Fisher, Izzy Liendo, Jayme Peacock, and Paul Zajac, who shaped my research in unquantifiable ways.

I am particularly grateful to The King's College for a generous financial contribution to subsidize publication of the book, and especially to Interim Provost Matt Parks, for confidence in the project and dedication to supporting academic scholarship. Ethan Campbell offered consistent encouragement and guidance on the transition from dissertation to book. I am also grateful to my Faculty Assistant, Gracie McBride, for her editorial assistance with the references.

In the early stages of the project, the Penn State Department of Comparative Literature provided a summer research grant to support archival work at the Biblioteca Angelica in Rome and the Biblioteca Nazionale Centrale in Florence.

I am grateful to the librarians and staff at these institutions for their assistance in consulting rare manuscripts and early print editions of Longinus's treatise.

The Folger Shakespeare Institute financially supported my participation in a year-long research seminar, "Renaissance/Early Modern Translation" colloquium, that was of enormous benefit to the development of the first chapter. I would like to thank the organizer, Anne Coldiron, and my fellow seminar participants for their helpful feedback and encouragement.

I am very grateful to Suzanne Rancourt and other editors at the University of Toronto Press for guiding the project so efficiently through the many stages of development and review. Robert Doran and another anonymous reader offered outstanding feedback that certainly improved the quality of the final book.

I am also grateful to the publishers who have given me permission to reuse earlier material here. Chapter 1 is derived from "Peri Hypsous in Translation: The Sublime in Sixteenth-Century Epic Theory," *Philological Quarterly* 95, no. 3–4 (2016): 449–66. The first half of chapter 5, and a few paragraphs from chapter 2, are adapted from "The Satanic Sublime in Paradise Lost: Tasso, Charisma, Abjection," *Modern Philology* 116, no. 3 (2019): 211–34. A few paragraphs from chapter 3 are derived from the Du Bartas subsection in "Heroic Adaptations of Genesis 3: Knowledge and Skepticism in Renaissance Biblical Epic," in *The Bible and Western Christian Literature*, ed. Elisabeth Jay, vol. 2, *Renaissance and Reformation*, ed. Sophie Read (London: Bloomsbury, forthcoming).

I would like to thank my parents, Ron and Debbie Baker, as well as Mark, Christine, Jeremy, Meg, Berry, and Sarah Baker, and Ben and Alice Davis, for many years of love and support. Special thanks to Kara and Ann Baker, Katie Willis, Kimberly Cornaggia, Emily Lavely, and Maria Greshock for their friendship and constancy in the most turbulent of seasons. My deepest gratitude goes to Jonathan, to whom this book is dedicated, for such abundant enthusiasm and endless love and support, and to Sam, whose natural orientation towards the sublime inspires me daily.

HEROIC AWE

The Sublime and the Remaking of Renaissance Epic

Introduction:
The Sublime in Renaissance Epic

Just after Satan first catches sight of Adam and Eve in *Paradise Lost*, Milton describes the fallen archangel "still in gaze," needing some time to recover his "faild speech" (4.356–7).[1] Satan confesses that the two humans inspire his "thoughts [to] / pursue with wonder … so lively shines / In them Divine resemblance" (4.362–4). The moment marks a fleeting, yet remarkable encounter that the poem's originator of evil has with the sublime – an emotional experience of helpless, speechless awe on facing something of shocking power or grandeur.[2] When Satan describes his response to this sight, he claims to "Melt" (4.389), a word defined in the *OED* as being "overwhelmed with dismay." This condition resembles what Longinus, the first major theorist of the sublime, calls *ekplexis* (astonishment and paralysis), the core emotion of sublimity.[3] Satan's sense of powerlessness is on high display, as the encounter comes just moments after he resolves to live forever in rebellion, declaring "all Good to me is lost" (4.109). Scarcely 200 lines later, this resolve nearly comes apart, as he is momentarily separated from his evil intentions at the mere sight of two human creatures who reflect God's image.

In this scene, Milton represents a paradigm that occurs regularly not only in *Paradise Lost*, but in the broader tradition of Renaissance epic from which he drew. In numerous passages of Renaissance epic, an aspiring epic hero faces a reflection of divine glory that compels him or her into an experience of ecstasy or terror. Heroes who welcome this unsettling compulsion enter a form of communication with the divine realm and solidify their heroic status. But as the above passage of *Paradise Lost* continues, Satan stubbornly rejects this impulse, willing himself away from the draw of divine love and towards the path of evil that he establishes for himself. For all the ways that Satan aspires to heroism in *Paradise Lost*, he is not the poem's hero, and this is in large part because he rejects the experience of the sublime: he refuses to pursue the enrapturing power that entices him towards heavenly glory.

This book illustrates the dependence of Renaissance epic on Longinus's philosophy of the sublime. The sublime itself is a notoriously slippery concept with numerous applications, but, understood (as it typically was during the early modern period as it is now) as an experience of being overcome with terror or ecstasy at someone or something greater than oneself, the Longinian sublime would play a role in the reconception of heroism in several Renaissance epic poems. Consequently, in early modern epic, heroism was often depicted as an individual *participation* in being emotionally, psychologically, and spiritually overwhelmed. As the culminating work of Renaissance epic poetry, *Paradise Lost* has been widely acknowledged as an exemplary work of sublime literature for its power to produce the sublime in readers;[4] but what has not been recognized is how closely Milton integrates sublimity into his model of epic heroism, and how earlier versions of Renaissance epic also make the sublime central to their own heroic models. Nearly a century before *Paradise Lost* (1674), several Italian, French, and English epics assign the willingness to experience the sublime – the readiness to be overwhelmed and even terrified – both spiritual and heroic significance. And in developing a concept of heroic spirituality in Longinian terms, these poems reimagine the relationship between epic, religion, and politics in the early modern world.

Longinus's first-century treatise, *Peri Hypsous* (*On the Sublime*, first printed in 1554), was once thought to be of little influence before Nicolas Boileau's popular 1674 translation, but we now know otherwise. As Caroline van Eck's 2012 edited collection *Translations of the Sublime* demonstrates, *Peri Hypsous* was circulating widely across philosophical, religious, and literary circles by the sixteenth century. Through numerous avenues, the treatise shaped aspects of early modern culture from art and architecture to rhetoric and theology (fields of particular importance to epic), long before Milton first mentioned Longinus as an important theorist in his 1644 treatise *Of Education*.[5] As Patrick Cheney's recent monograph shows, moreover, the Longinian sublime was crucial to early modern literature – Cheney argues that the sublime energized a new concept of authorship during the Renaissance that gave rise to the modern English canon.[6]

The early modern recovery of Longinus's text was especially timely for the development of epic. During the Renaissance, epic poets were under particular pressure to celebrate the greatness of their own nation, and to make the accrual of worldly power a heroic quality.[7] This pressure was of course political, but it was also literary, stemming in large part from the poetic authority of Virgil. As the great Roman epic, the *Aeneid* developed a concept of epic heroism based on absolute devotion to nation, as well as to the deities.[8] Furthermore, the *Aeneid* conflated national service and religious commitment in ways that threatened to be especially problematic if transposed onto Renaissance epic, being largely Christian and monotheistic. As Tobias Gregory notes in his study of epic and religion, monotheism could create a powerful "'us' vs. 'them'" mentality that was "enduringly serviceable for political ends."[9] In effect, Virgil's influence not only threatened to make epic a genre of excluding and villainizing a religious "other," but it offered a literary precedent that could open the door for religious and political leaders to manipulate their subjects' religious devotion for nefarious purposes, corrupting politics and faith alike. This manipulation has occurred throughout history and continues in multiple forms today. Given the particularly close collusion of political and religious institutions, along with the rapid growth of religious sectarianism, the traditional Virgilian approach to epic posed an especially potent threat to early modern Europe.

Beyond the *Aeneid*, the literary theory most prominent during the Renaissance created a stimulus towards civic duty that could indirectly further the pressures on poets to prioritize nationalism. Horace, one of the most influential classical theorists in the early modern era, argued that poetry is finally about service to society: it has a moral purpose to "form ... character" and be of "use to the city," a maxim that could translate easily enough into promoting a commitment to nation.[10] Reflecting both Horace and Virgil, Spenser sets out, in the Letter to Raleigh accompanying *The Faerie Queene*, to "fashion a gentleman or noble person in vertuous and gentle discipline," who serves as a representation of "the most excellent and glorious person of our soueraine the Queene."[11] Accordingly, many studies of Renaissance epic have emphasized the genre's investment in supporting and celebrating political authorities.[12] Epic heroism, consequently, has been largely understood to be *external* – exceptional action that a hero performs; and it was understood to be *horizontal* – service to earthly institutions.[13]

But alongside the Virgilian and Horatian influences on epic, Longinus's theory of the sublime offered an antidote to the rising pressures of nationalism, supporting an *interior* and *vertical* dimension to epic. As a theory of literature and of the emotions, *Peri Hypsous* offered a radical alternative to the predominant philosophies of poetry by Horace and other classical theorists. As Cheney shows, Longinus was distinctive in holding that the highest forms of literature were not about promoting civic duty at all, but about cultivating the "vehement emotions" of the sublime – ecstasy, terror, and astonishment.[14] In effect, Longinian philosophy was more concerned with psychology and affect than it was with action, and as explored below, with a specific type of psychology and affect that aligned with concepts of religious faith prominent during the Protestant Reformation. For Longinus was deeply invested in emotions that he associated with divinity, theorizing that the sublime itself was a particularly *heroic* expression of humanity's longing for immortality. Whether Longinus understood divinity literally or metaphorically is unclear, but his theory aligned in fascinating ways with Christian views (of a variety of perspectives) about the importance of cultivating a particular psychological and emotional orientation towards God. In doing so, *Peri Hypsous* offered a compelling literary model to support shifting concepts of heroism onto the dynamics of individual spirituality and away from civic duty, and thus, away from nationalism.

While acts of exemplary service to community and nation are undeniably important to early modern epic, Longinian theory therefore supported a move towards interiority seen in a major strain of European epic poems, including works traditionally tied to nationalism, such as *The Faerie Queene*.[15] Scholarship by Colin Burrow and, more recently, Christopher Bond and Christopher Warner emphasizes the importance of the emotions to epic, including pity, love, and remorse.[16] In recognizing Longinus's contributions to epic, direct and indirect, we can see how the passions of *ekplexis* were crucial to ideas of spiritual heroism. As this book argues, several Renaissance epic poets across Europe – in particular, Torquato Tasso, Guillaume de Salluste Du Bartas, Edmund Spenser, and of course, John Milton – used concepts of the sublime to redefine epic heroism as the pursuit of individual spiritual encounters; and in prioritizing these personal sublime experiences, they urged readers to resist cultural pressures to place their faith and hope in institutions. This is not to suggest that Renaissance epic was one homogenous unit, but to identify a series of major, internationally relevant epic poems that represent different theological perspectives and literary traditions, all working to separate religion and politics in ways that have not been fully acknowledged.

Longinian Affect and Heroic Spirituality in the Renaissance

Longinus, unlike most classical theorists, maintains that literature's (and humanity's) most fundamental purpose lies not in civic ends, but in emotional and spiritual ones. Commending the experience of being psychologically and emotionally overwhelmed, Longinus offers an unabashed celebration of the peaks and devastating lows of spiritual experience, a celebration that resonates with many Christian concepts of spirituality prominent in the early modern period.

Although Longinus's personal religious beliefs are unknown, he repeatedly suggests that human beings possess in their very nature a longing for something beyond ordinary mortal life. Humanity, he writes, has an innate desire to pursue "whatever is great and more divine than ourselves" – echoing the biblical idea that humans are created in the image of God and have the mark of eternity in their heart.[17] They thus have an innate need to connect to the divine realm. According to the author of *Peri Hypsous*: "The whole universe is not enough to satisfy the speculative intelligence of human thought; our ideas often pass beyond the limits that confine us. Look at life from all sides and see how in all things the extraordinary, the great, the beautiful stand supreme, and you will soon realize what we were born for."[18] Longinus's emphasis on connecting to the divine realm anticipates Calvin's highly influential Geneva Catechism, which maintains that the "summum bonum hominis [greatest good of man]" and "humanae vitae praecipuus ... finis [pre-eminent purpose of human life]" is not virtue or sanctification or good deeds, but "Deum ... nouerint [coming to know God]."[19] For Calvin as for Longinus, humanity's greatest purpose is therefore personal and vertical in nature. For both writers, humanity not only has a need, but an innate design for divine communication. This is at least in part why Longinus theorizes that "transport" is a more valuable end than "persuasion," resisting the Horatian idea that poetry is fundamentally about virtue, and that virtue itself is the chief end of humanity.[20] Instead, Longinus's chief purpose for humanity is to come "near the mighty mind of God," into a condition of psychological and emotional ecstasy and astonishment, celebrated in turn during the Renaissance.[21]

Seeing the sublime as humanity's highest end, Longinus energized a distinctive concept of spiritual heroism that would emerge in epic. Stephen Halliwell notes that the Longinian sublime entails an "aspiration of the human towards the conditions of the divine," with the term "aspiration" suggesting heroism.[22] Several times, Longinus describes the sublime poet as a noble soul (*megalophuḗs* or *megalophrosynê*), as someone with a proper orientation towards the most important things.[23] For Longinus, those who pursue the transcendent experience of the sublime possess the discipline to pursue matters of highest importance, bypassing the temptation to become caught up in the pleasures and duties of everyday life. Couching his illustration of heroism in spiritual terms, Longinus notes that those who pursue the elevated state of the sublime approach the "mind of God," while those who fail thereby "neglect … their immortal part," causing their inherent "greatness of soul" to "waste away."[24] In making the pursuit of heavenly glory and rapture noble and heroic, Longinus anticipates the emphasis not only of Calvin, but of early modern theologians of multiple persuasions who maintained that religion is first and foremost a matter of the heart and soul rather than an institutional affiliation.[25] He thus offers a substantial theory of emotion as well as literary model for epic poets to celebrate strong passions as a mark of sincere spirituality.

As explored in the first chapter, many Renaissance poets and theorists give lip service to traditional expectations for epic, but, in fact, endorse a heroic form of sublimity in their poems. As if acknowledging the expectation that epic should cultivate the sublime, Milton himself insists that readers of epic expect a Longinian emphasis on strong emotions rather than a celebration of virtuous deeds. In the opening of Book 9 of *Paradise Lost*, he maintains that his "Argument" will be "Not less but more heroic" than the "wrauth / Of stern Acchilles," or the "rage / Of Turnus for Lavinia," or "Neptun's ire or Juno's" (9.14–18). In these comparisons, Milton imagines that his readers will think first of heroism as the heightened emotions that epic describes (and makes them feel as a result), rather than the noble acts of service that make good citizens: he finds the "ire" and "rage" of Aeneas's antagonists more compelling than Aeneas's renowned *pietas*. Milton, of course, is questioning whether "ire" and "rage" are the right *kinds* of emotions to celebrate, for later in the same passage he suggests that the emotions surrounding "Patience and Heroic Martyrdom" (9.32) are the true elements of epic heroism, which do have an aspect of virtue. But throughout *Paradise Lost*, he himself emphasizes that "Heroic Martyrdom" is more than an act of virtue – it is sublime. In Book 12, following Michael's prophecy of Christ's crucifixion of redemption,

Adam reacts with speechless amazement – he is "replete with joy and wonder" at the effects of this sacrifice (12.468). In the *Gerusalemme Liberata*, Tasso also associates heroic martyrdom with the sublime, in an even more "heroic" passage that would be influential on Milton. In canto 2, the pagan knight Clorinda is stunned by the sight of the captive Sofronia, who has offered herself as a martyr to save the rest of the Christians from the pagan King Aladino. In her astonishment, Clorinda's eyes are opened to the fact that Sofronia herself is innocent, acknowledging a truth claim that, as argued in the second chapter, marks the beginning of her own individual journey towards salvation. In many related instances, the Renaissance epic tradition commends the heroic character of the vehement passions of sublimity – including not only those of deep joy, but those of terror and astonishment – for their role in building connection to God.

In observing epic's orientation towards fervent emotions, moreover, Milton finds support among multiple readers of classical (particularly Homeric) epic, from Longinus himself to many who followed.[26] In 1753, Thomas Blackwell saw the "Marvellous and the Wonderful" as the very "nerve of the epic strain," while Thomas M. Greene, in his classic *Descent from Heaven*, identified heightened emotion as the pulse of classical epic.[27] Greene found in Homeric epic a "superabundant vitality" that he associated with both the genre and the heroic ethos of characters like Achilles, who possesses "measureless reserves of living power, [an] inexhaustible capacity for fury." For Greene, classical heroism is based on a spirit of magnificence that makes heroes not only capable of great deeds, but deeply rousing, larger than life.[28]

Yet there are major differences between the sublimity of classical epic and that found in Renaissance epic, as they draw from different aspects of Longinian theory. Perhaps because Homeric epic tends to emphasize human mortality, Homer's model of the sublime is largely a tragic one, deriving from a Sisyphean resilience to the overpowering feelings of futility and/or absence. When Longinus discusses the sublime in Homeric epic, he takes his most striking example from Book 11 of the *Odyssey*, when Ajax shuns Odysseus in the afterlife, still outraged by the dishonour of seeing Achilles's armour awarded to Odysseus rather than himself. Ajax's resolute commitment to the cultural code of glory, even after death, is at once futile, extraordinary, and devastatingly final, evoking a powerful sense of loss.[29] Longinus also cites Ajax's calm prayer to the gods in Book 17 of the *Iliad*, as darkness descends on the Greek army: admiring the "true feelings of an Ajax," he locates sublimity in the magnificent courage and dignity the warrior exhibits in spite of his desperate circumstances.[30] In both instances, Longinus considers Ajax's actions to be sublime because they showcase the *megalophrosynê* of someone who has long passed away – these deeds showcase the temporal limitations of transcendence and the terrible knowledge that they cannot last.

Reflecting this Homeric model of the sublime, Paul Fry argues that sublimity is located in "darkness, solitude," since for Longinus, "the sublime seems always to have been viewed as a trial confrontation with death."[31] This claim may be true of Longinus's concept of Homer, as well as modern and postmodern versions of the sublime, but it does not fully encapsulate Longinus's theory of the sublime or the way it was used in early modern epic. For Longinus theorizes not only the sublimity of absence, but the sublimity of (divine) presence. In between the two Homeric passages just mentioned, Longinus cites the "fiat lux" episode from Genesis – "'Let there be light,' and there was light; 'Let there be earth,' and there was earth."[32] This citation fascinated readers of Longinus from the sixteenth century onward, both rhetorical theorists as well as theologians, who, as Dietmar Till has shown, incorporated Longinian principles of language and style into Protestant hermeneutics.[33] Unlike the Homeric passages Longinus quotes, the sublime here is not a gaping loss, but a representation of the power of God, depicted as inconceivably great.

Echoing this depiction, Renaissance epic locates sublime heroism in a character's rapturous response to depictions of divine power – whether a heavenly vision, inspired word, or divine energy channelled through an ennobled character. From Clorinda being astonished at the stunning sight of Sofronia, to the Redcrosse Knight in ecstasy taking in the vision of the New Jerusalem, Renaissance epic heroes follow the promptings of the sublime to reach beyond the world of the five senses and access the spiritual realm, entering a condition of stunned, speechless communication with the powers of heaven. Built on the sublimity of divine presence, Renaissance epic heroism thus differs significantly from Homeric heroism in several ways: where Homeric heroes often shock and overwhelm others (characters and audiences) with their great feats, heroes of Renaissance epic as diverse as Clorinda and Adam are typically the ones *being* overwhelmed. In fact, Renaissance epic heroes are often *most* heroic and exemplary when they respond with amazement to a representation outside themselves. In their condition of *ekplexis*, they reveal a heart rightly oriented (or in the process of being oriented) towards divine promptings or intuitions, properly concerned with the spiritual condition of their own heart instead of the enemies they must defeat.

In the epic poems in this study, this aspiration for the divine entails humility in place of the hubris so often displayed by Achilles or Odysseus or Hector – the humility to acknowledge intellectually, emotionally, and spiritually the overwhelming magnitude of another being. Yet humility is just the starting point, with the *telos* being the ecstasy of contact with heaven. Renaissance epic thus features a version of the sublime similar to Dante's *Commedia*, where ecstasy and rapture are also central to the protagonist's movement towards God, but a version that more fully encompasses the "negative" emotions of terror and horror into the heroic model. In a study of the Dantean sublime, Piero Boitani notes that Dante regularly distinguishes between the "positive" and "negative" emotions of the sublime, associating joy and elation with scenes that anticipate the recognition of God and terror with the tragedy of eternal damnation.[34] Unifying two poles that Dante's medieval epic typically divides, Renaissance poets make the negative emotions of terror and paralysis core components of the relationship to God. For Renaissance heroes, both divine terror and divine joy prove important to keeping the mind and heart fixed on the promise of eternity, and to resisting the temptation to ally faith with worldly power.

This study, then, looks at four Renaissance epic poems that make the sublime especially integral to their model of epic heroism and exploration of spirituality: Tasso's *Gerusalemme Liberata* (1581), Du Bartas's *Les Semaines* (1578/1584/1603), Spenser's *The Faerie Queene* (1596), and Milton's *Paradise Lost* (1674). The status of *Les Semaines* as epic may be less apparent than the others, but its contributions to the genre remain important.[35] Du Bartas participates alongside his Italian and English rivals in celebrating as heroic the sustained, overwhelmed response to portrayals of divine power. I focus on these poets because of their known interaction with each other and impact on *Paradise Lost*, as well as their investment in the sacred purposes of poetry and the theological controversies embroiled within them. Together, they offer representative models from three different European literary traditions – Italian, French, and English – and multiple theological-religious contexts: in Tasso's case, the authoritarian regime of the Counter-Reformation; in Du Bartas's, a theologically divided France he wished to unite; in Spenser's, a recently converted Protestant England; and in Milton's, a site of limited religious freedom that threatened his own nonconformity. While it would be tempting to explore Ariosto's *Orlando furioso* (1516/1532), I exclude Ariosto because his work pre-dates the publication and broader circulation of *Peri Hypsous*, and because I do not believe Ariosto wrote the sacred model of the sublime that I am presenting here – perhaps a deflated version, but a version lacking the fascination with the divine that Tasso, Du Bartas, Spenser, and Milton would demonstrate in such great measure. Despite Pierre de Ronsard's aspirations to sublimity, discussed in chapter 1, I believe the same holds true of the *Franciade* (1572), a more Virgilian model of epic. Sublime spirituality is not a ubiquitous feature of Renaissance epic, though it is an important part of the genre's development.

In considering the impact of Longinian sublimity on these poems, this study thus attempts to contribute not only to scholarship on Renaissance epic, but also to the growing body of scholarship on the sublime. Despite van Eck's attention to how Longinus began to gain prominence in sixteenth-century Europe, many studies on the sublime continue to exclude the early modern period and overlook the impact of Longinus's text during this period of rapid growth; most commonly, they begin with Nicolas Boileau's popular 1674 translation of *Peri Hypsous*, with the work of Immanuel Kant or Edmund Burke, or with Milton (through the lens of eighteenth-century theorists).[36] In focussing on the period before 1674, this book builds from two foundational studies on the early modern sublime. As noted, Cheney argues that the sublime helps to explain the excellence of English Renaissance literature, while the other, by David Sedley, shows how the sublime dovetailed with scepticism in the philosophy and literature of six-teenth- and seventeenth-century Europe.[37] To these monumental efforts to show the importance of the sublime to the early modern world prior to the work of Boileau, I contribute an examination of Longinus's impact across the European epic tradition – in France, Italy, and England – leading up to Milton. Alongside the impacts described by Cheney and Sedley, the sublime becomes a vital but neglected means of challenging the longstanding connection between religious devotion and nationalism in the genre. Ultimately, the rise of the sublime helps to drive the development of a new form of heroic spirituality evolving rapidly from the controversies of the Protestant Reformation.

Longinus and Religious Faith in the Reformation

As *Peri Hypsous* circulated during the sixteenth century, it offered a literary the-ory with an interesting perspective on a pressing question that was at the heart of the Reformation, an issue epic poets had to grapple with as they confronted the pressure to celebrate their nation and institutional authority figures. This was the question of the role of institutions in human-divine relationships: whether believers needed to enter into a relationship with God in the context of official ecclesiastical structures, or whether they should view their relationship as primar-ily individual, with Christ as the only mediator between God and humanity. Did religious/political institutions have authority over individual spirituality? If so, how much, and what happened if those institutions proved corrupt? If not, how did a Christian find stable community when religious institutions were fallible? In *Peri Hypsous*, Longinus explores an analogous set of questions about how readers and writers experience the divine ascent of the sublime, as identified below.

The issues themselves did not always divide predictably across denominational lines. In general, Catholicism upheld the spiritual authority of pope and priest over the laity, famously excommunicating Martin Luther, the original Reformer, who insisted that Christ alone was mediator between sinners and God. But Catho-lics and Protestants alike questioned the authority of their political and religious leaders without necessarily questioning their own faith. In particular, the Catholic tradition of mysticism, a movement centred on the individual connection to God, was flourishing in both Spain and Italy during the sixteenth century – and would be influential on Tasso, as discussed in the second chapter. This movement, more-over, was seen as a direct threat to Counter-Reformation authority, who feared its emphasis on individual spiritual experience as a threat to the power of the Church.

The issue was also fraught within Protestant institutions. In England, Henry VIII led a national conversion from Catholicism to Protestantism over his own resistance to papal authority, only to form the Church of England. The Anglican Church then took over political and spiritual authority in the lives of citizens, while dissidents opposed the attempts to make private religious practices and beliefs a matter of political obedience. And even while many Protestants from Luther forward insisted that they must first follow the promptings of conscience and Scripture above institutional authority figures, ecclesiastical communities would divide and break off into new ecclesiastical units. Community remained a central part of religious experience, though its basis was constantly being questioned.

For his part, Longinus maintains that aspiration for the divine is a fundamentally individual experience: that the emotions of *ekplexis* arise from experiencing "wisdom or goodness," from tasting "true, abiding pleasure."[38] This experience stems from an inherent greatness of mind – thus, it is fundamentally vertical and individual, first and foremost to the divine rather than to other human beings. Yet he also theorizes an important communal element to the sublime. In the composition of poetry in particular, he states that one route to experiencing sublimity lies in the "zealous imitation of the great prose writers and poets of the past." By learning from a select list of the very best poets – Homer, Herodotus, and others – writers both enter and produce sublimity (for Longinus, writers must feel the sublime to create it) by following these poetic authorities. Through a communal process of imitation, poets "share the enthusiasm of these others" and enter the sublime, so that the "natural genius of those old writers there flows into the hearts of their admirers."[39] Longinus thus imagines a kind of alternative community of writers and readers who enter sublimity together, a community that is essential to the flourishing of sublime poetry.

As his influence on the Renaissance would grow, Longinus's theory about the mechanisms of the spiritual ascent of the sublime offered an interesting literary precedent to poets wrestling with these issues. Most importantly, he emphasized that even while poetic authorities existed, they represented just "one path" to sublimity. These authorities were not living figures with institutional power, but simply poets who had proved their authenticity. In effect, while sublimity often could be a function of community, it arose in the psyche, with an "unconquerable passion for whatever is great and more divine than ourselves," and expanded to a group who shared the same passions.[40] This principle corresponded with what Luther, mystics, and many other spiritual leaders advised about true religion: that it began in the condition of the heart, even while community remained an essential form of support to faith.

In very different contexts, Tasso, Du Bartas, Spenser, and Milton all use their epic poetry to explore this problem of institutional authority and community in the life of faith. Reflecting (consciously or not) principles of Longinian philosophy, each poet finds ways to qualify (sometimes explicitly and absolutely, sometimes indirectly and moderately) the authority of the institutions represented in epic poetry, ranging from Tasso's latent critique of Counter-Reformation authority, to Milton's ruthless condemnation of Charles I. In their place, each poet finds ways to centre heroic spirituality first on a vertical quest for divine rapture, in which the hero is oriented towards a divine goal, and supported by a group of like-minded souls who are on the same vertical quest. Similar to what Longinus describes in *Peri Hypsous*, the sublime serves as a kind of supernatural bond among those who would pursue divine glory, creating a linking point based outside of civic and religious institutions. This results in concepts of community that differ significantly among each other, but that all depart from the national concept of group identity that grounds Virgilian epic.

Longinian Theorists and the Network of the Sublime

Longinus serves as the focal point of this study on the sublime, even while I acknowledge significant contributions from writers who might not have had access to Longinus.[41] Longinus defines the sublime more extensively and influentially than any other theorist before Kant, and his circles of influence were expanding rapidly during the Renaissance. During the sixteenth and seventeenth centuries, Longinian ideas spread widely into literary theory and theology, yielding discourses on the sublime by a variety of writers – many of whom read Longinus or the work of scholars who had. The major poets in this study, in turn, had numerous avenues by which to derive and develop their ideas of the sublime, with multiple direct and indirect links to *Peri Hypsous*. At the same time, I do not necessarily mean to imply that an author who reflects Longinian principles was influenced by *Peri Hypsous*. Among the key sources of the sublime for epic poets were Protestant and Catholic authors – from Calvin describing the emotions upon facing divine judgment and grace, to Catholic aesthetic theorists discussing ecstasy in spiritual transformation – whose work in some cases reflects the diffusion of Longinian thought, but whose ideas in others may only reflect (important) resonances with *Peri Hypsous*.[42]

The Longinian sublime itself has several dimensions, but this project will focus on Longinus's concept of the so-called "natural" or psychological sublime, rather than the "rhetorical" sublime, a principle of high literary style. Though many early modern scholars showed interest in Longinus's comments on the technical details that create a lofty or "sublime" style, Longinus seems to view the sublime as a heightened psychological and emotional condition experienced through poetry, nature, or other means.[43] As Robert Doran argues, Longinus shares this understanding of the sublime with later theorists such as Burke and Kant, separating him from other classical and early modern theorists who were primarily interested in rhetorical style.[44] Moreover, as I will explore more fully in the first chapter, many early modern scholars, intrigued by Longinus's theory of the sublime, interpreted the concept as an ontological or metaphysical principle. As often as not, they describe sublimity as an external energy or force with divine origins that produces a heightened emotional state, thereby conceiving of sublimity as a principle of religious transcendence.

What Longinus and early modern Longinian scholars supplied to Renaissance epic poets, most of all, was a particularly useful conceptual and lexical framework for representing the emotional conditions associated with divine relationship. Although the sublime does overlap with other philosophies important to the Renaissance, like Neoplatonism, with a concept of *furor* that sometimes intersects with the Longinian experience of rapture, Longinus's text describes a greater emotional range – encompassing both "positive" emotions of rapture and ecstasy, as well as a set of "negative" emotions such as terror and horror.[45] While the blissful ecstasy of Pietro Bembo from Castiglione's *Il Cortegiano* – a quintessential Neoplatonic transport – could fall within the sphere of the sublime, the sublime often has a starker edge. According to Longinus, the concept of *ekplexis*, or astonishment, the core emotion of the sublime, is a state of such overwhelming surprise that it may involve excruciating pain.[46] Longinus does not describe the experience of the sublime as harmful – as seen above, he notes that the sublime puts audiences in touch with their divine nature; but the element of distress is important to note, especially since it corresponds to Christian descriptions of the human encounter with divine judgment.[47] For anyone feeling a sense of guilt before the presence of God, even the thought of his omnipotence and holy separateness would be terrifying. In this sense, epic poets found in Longinus's theory of the sublime a fitting framework for conveying the condition of frightened reverence and inspired awe underlying the experience of divine contact.

In looking at the negative dimensions of the sublime, this study will supplement work on Longinus with later theorizations of the sublime that elucidate elements he left implicit – theories that were themselves influenced by Longinus, though of course not available during the early modern period. Among these are Julia Kristeva's theory of abjection, which Kristeva connects explicitly to the sublime, and which offers a fuller theory of the terror that Longinus emphasizes in *Peri Hypsous*.[48] As defined by Kristeva, abjection involves feelings of terror and horror akin to the sublime, but transports the individual *inside* the self in a state of withdrawal. As we will see, this concept proves useful to exploring the period of sorrow and despair prior to the experience of grace that occurs consistently across the epic poems in this study, a phase of intensive awareness of human imperfection that each epic hero must pass through on the way to divine rapture.

Alongside Kristevan abjection, epic poetry also anticipates Max Weber's theory of charisma and charismatic authority, another theory that scholars have linked to the sublime. As Weber theorizes, charisma is a captivating power of personality – a spirit of magnificence – that has an enchanting effect comparable to sublimity.[49] The Renaissance poems of this study draw from early modern concepts that look forward to Weber, including Catholic principles of the mediating potential of images to draw viewers towards the divine, and Reformed concepts of the *charismata* (spiritual giftedness shared among community).[50] In some cases, charisma can be a demonic distraction – a false form of spirituality (idolatry) to be distinguished from true forms – but in others, it serves as a channel or reflection of divine glory that draws viewers to God.

Focussing on these theoretical and theological concepts of sublimity in the work of Tasso, Du Bartas, Spenser, and Milton, this project explores the role of the sublime in shaping heroic poetry of the Renaissance, beginning with a chapter on the historical rise of the Longinian sublime in the sixteenth and early seventeenth centuries and its reception in theories of epic poetry. The four subsequent chapters analyse specific models of sublimity emerging in the *Gerusalemme Liberata*, *Les Semaines*, *The Faerie Queene*, and *Paradise Lost*.

The first chapter argues that early modern rhetoricians and poetic theorists developed a Longinian concept of the sublime that repurposed epic poetry towards divine ecstasy instead of civic ends. As part of this contention, I challenge the still-common assumption that Longinus's earliest interpreters reduced the sublime to a stylistic or rhetorical principle, in line with traditional theories that the high or "sublime style" was most appropriate to epic poetry. Instead, beginning with the earliest print editions of *Peri Hypsous* in the sixteenth and early seventeenth centuries (beginning in 1554), scholars and translators read the Longinian sublime as a concept, something channelled through the noble mind and passions of an author, thus anticipating Boileau's interpretation of Longinus as well as the theories of Burke and Kant. Reflecting these early discourses, poetic theorists in Italy, France, and England – including Tasso, Ronsard, Philip Sidney, and several others – incorporated Longinian principles into their discussions of epic poetry. In so doing, they regularly presented epic as a genre fostering a vertical connection between the poet/audience and the divine realm, instead of centring epic on civic functions – a shift seen in theories by Catholics and Protestants alike.

The second chapter examines the reception of Longinian principles in the *Gerusalemme Liberata*, suggesting that Tasso challenges the civic-building principles of literature endorsed by the Counter-Reformation. In the poem, Tasso celebrates the role of charismatic figures who channel divine power to their onlookers by prompting the heightened emotional experience of the sublime. Commending heroes who pursue these charismatic figures instead of their duty to institutional forms of authority, Tasso rejects the Counter-Reformation's emphasis on devotion to official, hierarchical forms of power, while embracing Catholicism's emphasis on the sacred potential of mediating individuals and objects. This model of epic heroism ultimately demands great risk – personal and political – in the pursuit of divine ascent, and thereby builds an alternative community of faithful heroes oriented towards spiritual ends, whose purposes supersede those of Church authorities.

The third chapter examines Du Bartas and key parts of his expansive collection of biblical epic poetry known as *Les Semaines*. Though he has not regularly been associated with the epic tradition, Du Bartas develops a heroic model in his epic version of Genesis that complements Tasso's, by opposing the pursuit of sublime astonishment to the pursuit of political gain, depicted as a false form of spirituality. As an advisor to Henri de Navarre (later Henry IV) during the French

Wars of Religion, Du Bartas was especially concerned with the problem of religious dogmatism, leading to church leaders' efforts to secure political power at the expense of spiritual unity. Through Satan's role in the Fall of humanity, and Adam and Abraham's pursuit of connection to God, Du Bartas depicts heroism as a matter of keeping the focus upward, in awe and humility at the mysterious greatness of God, in connection with those who share the embrace of divine mystery. Celebrating a welcoming of the unknown as a catalyst of the sublime, Du Bartas insists that humanity's greatest, most glorious ends lay not in having one's own views affirmed publicly or politically, but in sharing heavenly glory with a community of spiritual equals.

The fourth chapter considers Spenser's portrayal of heroism in Book I of *The Faerie Queene*, the Legend of Holiness, a prototype for the entire epic. Unlike other poets in this study, Spenser takes on the challenge of representing the sublime to be simultaneously irresistible and heroic, making sublimity into an uncontrollable mechanism of salvation for the principal hero, the Redcrosse Knight. Writing in the officially Protestant nation of England, Spenser thus develops, in contrast to Du Bartas, a more sophisticated and staunchly Calvinist depiction of the sublime that privileges the believer's undeserved salvation by grace, rather than national allegiance, as the basis of Christian identity. In reiterating Redcrosse's powerlessness to resist various forms of sublimity, each representing a form of divine holiness, Spenser portrays holiness itself as more than a virtue to be acquired, but an aspect of God's presence that violently transforms the sinner with the support of Christian community, establishing the priority of the individual relationship to God. Meanwhile, in carefully distinguishing genuine sources of charismatic leadership (Una) from false ones (Lucifera), Spenser limits the role of charisma and underscores the dangers of idolizing charismatic leaders in national and ecclesiastical institutions, including his own Queen Elizabeth I. Centring the knight's community firmly on the followers of the Christian faith, a group extending beyond England, Spenser carefully limits the knight's expected devotion to national purposes to *only* those that serve divine ends.

The fifth chapter, focussing on *Paradise Lost*, examines how Milton uses the sublime to structure the poem's concept of heroism, in conversation with variants of epic heroism by Tasso, Du Bartas, and Spenser. In Book 5, Milton represents sublimity as the stated objective of the poem's human heroes, Adam and Eve, and explores the choices that hinder them from entering it, along with the choices that finally prepare both to be reunited to God in ecstasy after the Fall. Extending his predecessors' emphasis on community, Milton represents sublime heroism as fundamentally interrelational, based on mutual dependence and the heroic choice to subordinate the self. In Satan, Milton first develops a perversion of this heroic model, as the fallen angel tries to make himself into an object of worship – as a charismatic figure – above the other devils; Milton thus extends Spenser's warning about the power of authority that is not divine. In Adam and Eve, meanwhile, he celebrates the process by which the pair learns to identify with each other in sacrificial love, and, in humility, embrace the mysteriousness of God (like Du Bartas's heroes) to experience a sublime reunification with God. As Milton responds to the respective Italian, French, and (early) English models of sublimity, he creates in *Paradise Lost* an especially deliberate model of sublimity that aims to foster Christian unity across national borders.

The conclusion looks further at the unity the sublime supplies to Renaissance epic poetry, briefly considering the sublime in *Paradise Regained* (1671). In this minor epic, Milton uses Satan's unsuccessful temptation of the Son of God to reinforce the shift from Virgilian epic to Renaissance heroism. Through the dialogue between Satan and the Son, Milton critiques Satan's Virgilian pursuit of national power as cultivating an illusion of virtue and shallow glory. In its place, Milton reiterates a principle that holds within this major strain of Renaissance epic: that Christian heroism demands the spiritual and emotional humility to resist the temptation to ally itself with world power, yet seeks, at the same time, the eternal glorification of the individual self. The result is a palpably Longinian celebration of the value of the individual human soul, and an expression of hope for its fulfilment in spiritual community.

1 Longinus in Renaissance Theories of Heroic Poetry

As Longinus's first-century treatise, *Peri Hypsous*, began to circulate during the sixteenth and seventeenth centuries, it had particularly transformative and often surprising effects on theories of epic poetry, or heroic poetry, as it was often called. As a rule, theories of heroic poetry in early modern Europe – like epic itself – are understood to uphold the Horatian principle that poetry should build virtuous citizens and, in many cases, support the growth and glory of nations. In a prime example, Joachim Du Bellay's *Défence et illustration de la langue française* (1549) celebrates the literary and political potential of a forthcoming French narrative poem (presumably Pierre de Ronsard's *Franciade*) written in the model of the *Aeneid*. According to Du Bellay, this highly anticipated epic poem would produce "immortelle gloire, honneur de la France, et grande illustration de nostre langue [immortal glory, honor for France, and great enrichment of our language]."[1] Following the (apparently) Virgilian *Défence*, Tasso's *Discorsi del poema eroico* (1594) – the most renowned early modern theory of epic of all – has been recognized for its endorsement of a different institutional power, that of Counter-Reformation authority. In emphasizing the moral and pedagogical purposes of poetry, the *Discorsi* nominally reflects the strict guidelines for art set forth by Counter-Reformation leaders, and therefore has usually been assumed to support the moral aims of the institution itself.

Yet, despite various pressures to make epic a genre of virtuous service to institutions, these same writers found in Longinus an alternative theoretical model to subvert its "official" aims. In Longinus, theorists from France, Italy, and England – of multiple theological perspectives and contexts in Reformation history – discovered a distinctive theoretical model emphasizing that literature should promote an elevated psychological and emotional condition of astonishment (*ekplexis*), a state appropriate to humanity's natural desire for immortality. Under the influence of Longinus, epic theorists invoked concepts of the sublime to emphasize the sacred purpose of literature: its capacity to point readers upward in an individual spiritual encounter. In effect, epic theorists used the sublime to celebrate humanity's vertical relationship to God as a distinctive and superior end to that of its expected devotion to worldly institutions.

After a brief synopsis of the transmission history of *Peri Hypsous*, this chapter will explore the development of Renaissance epic theory in two main stages. First, I evaluate how Longinus's early editors, translators, and commentators from the sixteenth century onward engaged more deeply with *Peri Hypsous* than is typically acknowledged. Instead of reading the text as a rhetorical treatise – an instruction manual on the technical skill needed to write great poetry – as is often assumed in modern criticism, these scholars recognized the most central principles of Longinus's text in their commentaries and translations. In particular, they recognized the Longinian sublime as something manifesting itself in the mind and emotions of an author, rather than a feature of literary style. Above all, these scholars acknowledged Longinus's emphasis on a sublime poet's noble psychology – the natural facility and orientation towards the divine that allows poets to produce the emotions characteristic of sublimity.

Second, I explore a series of French, Italian, and English theorists who incorporated the Longinian principles being disseminated by translators and commentators, each in a manner inflected by a unique place in Reformation history. These theorists include Ronsard and Du Bellay, Tasso, and, in England, Philip Sidney, George Puttenham, and Milton, among lesser-known figures such as Giordano Bruno and George Chapman. Together, these scholars' theories of epic represent a broad shift away from civic ends and towards spiritual purposes, a movement that harmonizes with Longinian thought. The movement intensifies and diversifies throughout the evolution of sixteenth- and seventeenth-century epic theory, undermining the accepted connection between faith and politics across early modern culture.

Peri Hypsous in Early Modern Europe

In contrast to Chapman and Milton, who explicitly mention him, it is very possible that some of the epic theorists studied in this chapter never read Longinus themselves, but each likely had at least indirect access to Longinian thought through the diffuse network of editions, translations, lectures, and other sources that spread throughout Renaissance Europe. The first-century treatise, lost from the tenth to the fifteenth centuries, was rediscovered and made its way into Italy in manuscript form, before its publication by Francesco Robortello (1554) and Paolo Manuzio (1555).[2] Following the editions of Robortello and Manuzio, in 1570 Francesco Porto published a third surviving sixteenth-century Greek edition, which would become the basis of most seventeenth-century editions.[3] All three of these Greek editions include substantial Latin paratexts – prefatory letters and marginalia – that suggest a close critical engagement with the sublime.[4]

Meanwhile, even before the treatise's first printing, scholars were already invested enough in Longinus to begin translating his text into Latin. At least two Latin translations were completed in manuscript form before 1554, one by the French scholar Marc-Antoine de Muret and another anonymously, followed by the first Latin translation published by Domenico Pizzimenti in 1566 and a second by Pietro Pagano in 1572.[5] In 1612, Gabriele de Petra published the most influential translation to appear before Nicolas Boileau's 1674 French vernacular – a Greek-Latin scholarly edition with a Latin translation, marginalia, prefatory material, and appendices – which would be republished multiple times.[6] Shortly after the first Latin translation, Giovanni Niccolò da Falgano completed the only known sixteenth-century Italian translation in manuscript form in 1575; the first French and English translations were not completed until 1645 and 1652, respectively.[7]

Besides the full-length editions, Longinian theory was transmitted through the works of several intellectuals and literary theorists across Europe from the late fifteenth century onward, and more widely after Robortello's 1554 edition. As Marc Fumaroli maintains, one early scholar of the sublime was Erasmus, whose 1528 *Ciceronianus* would be instrumental to the first publication of *Peri Hypsous*. In the *Ciceronianus*, composed and distributed in France and later Italy, Erasmus offered groundbreaking and highly influential opposition to the "Ciceronian" view of rhetorical style and imitation practice, then dominant in rhetorical theory. While the Ciceronians favoured an ornate, courtly style, Erasmus and other "anti-Ciceronians" favoured a simple style ("sermo humilis") developed through a more eclectic, natural mode of imitation.[8] His view directly recalls Longinus's concept of the sublime: where the Ciceronians thought writing should aim for stylistic elegance, Erasmus endorsed the more Longinian *telos* of dazzling or stupefying – writing should be stylistically simple and conceptually profound, irresistibly captivating.[9] The *Ciceronianus* would likely be a factor in the development of an early form of sublime epic theory that emerged in France.

Following the 1554 publication of *Peri Hypsous* came a significant string of Longinian scholars who lectured and/or wrote explicitly on *Peri Hypsous* from the 1560s to the 1590s. Among these early scholars, the most prominent were Pietro Vettori, Francesco Patrizi, Lorenzo Giacomini, and Francesco Benci. In 1560, Vettori published a widely-circulating commentary on Aristotle's *Poetics* already reflecting the clearly growing interest in Longinus. Vettori demonstrates high regard for Longinus, introducing him as one who "plurimum judicio valuit [prevailed most in judgment]"; but he also speaks of Longinus in familiar terms, introducing his first quotation from *Peri Hypsous*: "Meminit tamen Longinus in libro peri hypsous, huius reditus Grecorum [You remember, however, that Longinus in the book on the sublime has spoken of these Greeks]."[10] Only a few years after the treatise's publication, Vettori expected readers to be well aware of Longinus and his guiding ideas.

By the end of the century, Patrizi, Giacomini, and Benci had done much to spread Longinian thought in France and Italy. Patrizi, arguably the most Longinian scholar of the sixteenth century, published a three-volume treatise, *Della Poetica* (1586), that quotes Longinus more frequently than any other theorist of the day.[11] Patrizi, moreover, had a connection to Tasso and may have been the one to introduce Longinus to him, as I will explore below. Shortly after *Della Poetica*, Giacomini lectured on Longinus and published the explicitly Longinian *Discorso del furor poetico* (1587), which emphasized the emotional condition of the author over technical skill.[12] Soon afterward, Benci, a professor of rhetoric at the University of Rome, published a lecture entitled "De stylo et scriptione" (1592), which paraphrased several of Longinus's ideas, and may have been responsible for disseminating Longinian thought to Montaigne and other French scholars.[13] The works of all four of these theorists demonstrate an important familiarity with Longinus and investment in publicizing his ideas, illustrating how well regarded the sublime was becoming in and beyond sixteenth-century Italy and France.

Because *Peri Hypsous* would not be printed in England or translated into English until the mid-seventeenth century, scholars have paid less attention to the movement of the text in sixteenth- and early seventeenth-century England, compared to elsewhere in Europe, with Patrick Cheney offering the only detailed study to my knowledge on English Renaissance authors preceding Milton.[14] Although the treatise did not circulate as widely in England, Cheney notes that Greek editions seem to have been available there by the early 1570s.[15] Meanwhile, John Rainolds, a close acquaintance of Philip Sidney, was lecturing on Longinus at Oxford in the early 1570s. Rainolds would later become the tutor of Gerard Langbaine, who was encouraged by Rainolds to publish what became the first and second editions of *Peri Hypsous* in England (both reprints of de Petra's parallel-text translation with additional appending material by Langbaine, published in 1636 and 1638).[16] Meanwhile, Protestant theology – which had an especially strong foothold in England – often overlapped with Longinian theory and language in striking ways, and would give the English sublime a distinct flavour, as I will discuss further below.

Early Readings of *Peri Hypsous*: Before Boileau

While Longinus was read, translated, and cited in the sixteenth and early seventeenth centuries, modern criticism still perpetuates a misconception about its early Renaissance reception, which has likely discouraged studies of the early modern sublime. Since Samuel Monk's 1935 monograph (republished in 1960), critics often maintain that before the Longinian revival sparked by Boileau, the sixteenth- and early seventeenth-century scholars who read Longinus were interpreting the Greek *hypsos* as a stylistic category applicable to literature written in the grand or high style.[17] Although a few critics, including Emilio Mattioli and Eugenio Refini, have argued that even the earliest sixteenth-century Longinian scholars recognized *hypsos* as a concept that goes beyond rhetorical style, Monk's position remains widely accepted in current scholarship.[18] The *Oxford Encyclopedia of Aesthetics*, for instance, maintains that the sublime was not finally uprooted from the categories of rhetoric until Boileau, as does Robert Doran's outstanding 2015 monograph, *The Theory of the Sublime from Longinus to Kant*.[19]

While it may be true, as Bernard van Huss has recently noted, that many sixteenth-century theorists merely attempted to "defuse Longinus by reading rhetorical meaning into him or to press him relatively forcefully into pre-existing systematised moulds of poetics based on style," the early editions and translations of *Peri Hypsous* indicate that a number of Renaissance scholars did engage deeply with the treatise, correctly recognizing that Longinus used the word *hypsos* to refer to a philosophical concept associated with transcendence, rather than a stylistic principle.[20] And while modern critics have noted that early translations of *Peri Hypsous* render the title using the adjective "sublimis" rather than the noun "sublimitas," suggesting a reduction of the sublime to a category of style, these titles do not tell the whole story.[21] For instance, in the body of his translation, da Falgano translates "hypsos" as "un concetto alto et pieno di vanto [a lofty concept and full of significance]," explicitly classifying the sublime as an abstract noun, rather than a stylistic quality.[22] And Pizzimenti introduces his translation by noting of Longinus: "Nam multa non tantum ex grammaticae rivulis, sed ex ipsis etiam philosophiae fontibus hausisse videtur. [For we see that much has been drunk not only from rivulets of grammar, but also from the fountains of philosophy themselves.]"[23] Both indicate that Longinus was just as interested in a philosophical principle of sublimity as he was in rhetorical concerns of language and style.

Across the early editions of *Peri Hypsous*, editors and translators recurrently highlight Longinus's interest in the sublime as a concept, often representing sublimity as a great force or divine energy mediated through the ennobled mental and emotional capacity of an author. This is particularly apparent in the translations and analyses of sections 8 and 9, in which Longinus outlines the five main sources of sublimity and elaborates on their significance as an organizing scheme for the treatise. In section 8.1, Longinus enumerates the five main sources as follows:

1) τὸ περὶ τὰς νοήσις ἀδρεπήβολον [the power of grand thoughts or conceptions];
2) τὸ σφοδρὸν καὶ ἐνθουσιαστικὸν πάθος [the inspiration of vehement emotion];
3) ἥ τε ποιὰ τῶν σχημάτον πλάσισ [the proper construction of figures];
4) ἡ γενναία λέχις [noble diction];
5) ἡ ἐν ἀξιῶματι καὶ διάρσει σύνθεσις [dignified and elevated arrangement].[24]

In sections 8.4 and 9.1, Longinus elaborates on this passage, noting that the second source, emotion, is an often neglected but critical aspect of sublimity, while the first, *noésis/megalophués* (power of great thoughts/greatness of soul, used inter-changeably), plays a greater role than any of the others:

Οὐ μὴν ἀλλ᾽ ἐπεὶ τὴν κρατίστην μοῖραν ἐπέχει τῶν ἄλλων τὸ πρῶτον, λέγω δὲ τὸ μεγαλοφυές, χρὴ κἀνταῦθα, καὶ εἰ δωρητὸν τὸ πρᾶγμα μᾶλλον ἢ κτητόν, ὅμως καθ᾽ ὅσον οἶόν τε τὰς ψυχὰς ἀνατρέφειν πρὸς τὰ μεγέθη, καὶ ὥσπερ ἐγκύμονας ἀεὶ ποιεῖν γενναίου παραστήματος.[25]

[Now, since the first – *megalophués*, I mean – plays a greater part than all the others, here too, even if it is rather a gift than an acquired quality, we should still do our utmost to train our minds into sympathy with what is noble and, as it were, impreg nate them again and again with lofty thoughts.]

In effect, Longinus privileges the first two sources – *noésis/megalophués* and vehe-ment emotion – as "natural" and primary, while subordinating the latter three sources – diction, arrangement, and figures – as learned and secondary.

Early modern editors and translators show particular interest in these core pas-sages. Robortello includes lengthy marginal notes across sections 8 and 9, which Pizzimenti and Pagano reproduce in their own editions, while even Porto – who is fairly sparing with his annotations – adds a note marking off section 8.1 as a fundamental part of the treatise.[26] Moreover, Robortello includes a marginal gloss loosely translating Longinus's discussion of natural greatness in section 9.1, call-ing attention to the importance of a poet's psychological condition:

Quoniam primum locum in distributione obtinet νοησις, monet, quam vis *megalophués* sit potius a natura, quam ab arte datum: assuefaciendum animum, ut concipiat res grandes.[27]

[Since *noésis* holds the primary position in the classification, he (Longinus) reminds us how much more *megalophués* may be conferred by nature than by art: habituating the mind, so that it may conceive great things.]

With this comment, Robortello directly associates the sublime with great concepts (*noésis/megalophués*). Though acknowledging the role of training on the part of the poet, Robortello, echoing Longinus, stresses that such training must be conceptual rather than technical: sublime poets acclimatize the mind and the imagination, ennobling themselves to think lofty thoughts.

Pizzimenti and Pagano continue Robortello's emphasis on the mental condi-tion of the author when they comment on one of Longinus's most central and renowned phrases, "ὕψος μεγαλοφροσύνης ἀπήχημα [sublimity is the echo of the noble mind]." In a marginal comment, Pizzimenti writes: "hypsos in oratione manare *ex animae* magnitudine [sublimity in speech emanates from greatness of soul]."[28] Notably, he preserves the Greek "hypsos" in noun form, representing sublimity as a substance, and uses "in oratione" incidentally, to modify its subject. Pagano, for his part, amplifies his translation of the same Greek passage as follows: "granditatem esse extremam mentis, ac animi magna, ac alta cogitantis conditionem [greatness/sublimity lies in the outermost condition of the mind, and the nobility of the soul, and profundity of thought]."[29] Significantly expanding the original, Pagano triply emphasizes the elevated psychological and spiritual state to which Longinus refers. With the phrase "granditatem … extremam mentis … conditionem," Pagano suggests that the sublime is something at the very limits of human capacity and understanding. He thus captures the key idea, noted elsewhere in *Peri Hypsous,* that the sublime is at the mind's outermost borders and on the spectrum of the divine, which Longinus implies in his enigmatic expression "τὸ ἐπ' οὐρανὸν ἀπὸ γῆς διάστημα [the space between heaven and earth]."[30] Pagano, like Pizzimenti, understands sublimity as a heightened psychological state or enigmatic force channelled through the mind of the author.

In their commentaries on section 8.1, furthermore, these early translators recognize that the sublime, as a natural principle, manifests itself in an author's display of vehement emotion, the second most important source of sublimity. Where the original Greek states simply "δεύτερον δὲ τὸ σφοδρὸν καὶ ἐνθουσιαστικὸν πάθος [the second is vehement and inspired emotion]," Pagano's translation elaborates: "secundum vero est animorum commotio, atque affectio, quae vehemens est, ac animi rapiendi, atque incitandi vim maximam habet [truly, the second is the agitation and affecting of souls, which is violent, and rapturing the soul, also maintains great power for stirring up]."[31] With this expansion of the original, Pagano emphasizes the *violence* of emotion, as if the sublime were an independent power that actively overpowers the soul of the author. Da Falgano's Italian translation also expands the original, claiming the second source of sublimity to be "uno affetto si vehemente che venendo da furore divino e atto à fare infuriare altrui [an emotional force as violent as one coming from divine *furor* and capable of inspiring (or inflaming) others]."[32] Here da Falgano accentuates an ontological concept of the sublime, specifying that this heightened emotion comes from a divine source, rather than technical training, and, like Pagano, emphasizes its violent potential. In translating the Longinian phrase to note that emotion will inspire or inflame *others*, da Falgano suggests that the sublime is a dynamic, unstable, and celestial force, transferring inevitably from the author to the reader as well.

The passages cited above demonstrate the innovative perceptions of sixteenth-century scholars: in establishing that the sublime *overwhelms* readers, the translators recognize that Longinus revises the Horatian *telos* of literature away from persuading to moral action. As Longinus writes, the sublime "οὐ πείθει τὸν ἀκροατὴν μόνον ἀλλὰ καὶ δουλοῦτα [does not only persuade the audience, but enslaves]."[33] Both Pagano and da Falgano offer relatively faithful translations of this passage, Pagano writing that the sublime "in seruitutem redigit [reduces to servitude]," and da Falgano that it "lo rende schiavo [makes one a slave]"; however, Pizzimenti takes liberties, writing that the sublime "non solum auditorum persuasum habet, verum etiam sibi emancipet [not only has persuaded the audience, but truly emancipates them from themselves]."[34] In fact, Pizzimenti's translation amounts to the exact opposite of the original Greek, but in fact may prove the most faithful to the spirit of Longinus. For Pizzimenti speaks to Longinus's key idea that the sublime creates *ekstasis*, or transport, in the reader, who is in one sense a slave (to the sublime), and in another sense free from the limits of human nature. With this unusual translation, Pizzimenti represents the radical and transcendent character of the sublime as not simply instructing, persuading, or moving, but *rapturing* unresisting readers.[35]

Early seventeenth-century editors, beginning with de Petra, prove to be equally attuned to Longinus's interest in the sublime as psychological condition and its operation through the ennobled mentality of the author. In the introduction to his translation, de Petra, like his predecessors, identifies section 8 as the centrepiece of Longinus's theory, diagramming its main ideas under the heading "Totius Doctrinae Περι Υψους Diagramma [Outline of the Entire Teaching of *Peri Hypsous*]".

In the far-left column, de Petra quotes Longinus's exact language from section 8.1, enumerating the five sources of sublimity. Below each enumeration, he translates the Greek into Latin, and adds a brief note (also in Latin) just next to it. In the three columns to the right, he highlights supporting points made elsewhere in *Peri Hypsous* and subordinates them under their respective headings from the left column. In this diagram, de Petra reflects Longinus's own emphasis on the first two sources of sublimity, rather than giving the five sources of sublimity equal weight. He devotes a disproportionate three-quarters of his commentary to greatness of mind and emotion, thereby echoing Longinus's emphasis on the psychological condition of the author.

Moreover, de Petra uses the enumerations on the right to further highlight the importance of the author's noble mind and emotions, exploring the creative processes by which sublimity becomes manifest. At the top of the third column from the left, he enumerates the five most prominent strategies (in his reading of *Peri Hypsous*) by which an author demonstrates nobility of mind and emotion, citing Longinus as follows: "ἄκρον λημμάτων ἐκλογῇ, καὶ ἡ πρὸς ἄλληλα ἐπισυνθέσις [selecting the greatest ideas, and combining them together; sect. 10]," "αὔχησις [amplification; sect. 11]," "χύσις [grandeur; sect. 12]," "μίμησις [imitation; sect. 13.2]," and "φαντασία [visualization; sect. 9.5; 15.1]." In his notations on each of these strategies, de Petra demonstrates focussed attention on an author's psychological condition – on the ability to conceptualize and otherwise demonstrate an instinct for the magnificent. Elaborating on the concept of *mimesis*, the fourth in the list, in section 13.2, de Petra leaves the simple comment "πάθεν καὶ τι μίμεσις [emotion and imitation]," thereby emphasizing Longinus's point that imitation and sublimity in turn result not from the formulaic replication of a great author's work, but from a more fundamental emotional investment in great art. In an in-text comment on another item above, *phantasia*, de Petra captures the

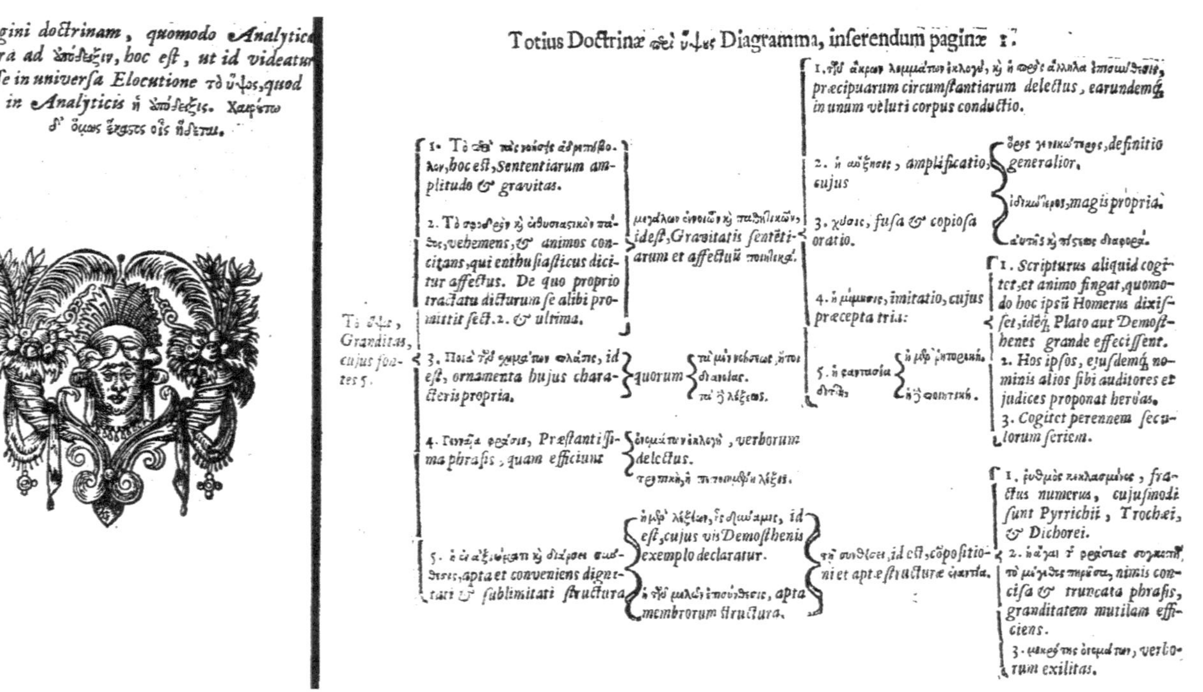

Figure 1. Totius Doctrinae Περι Ὑψους Diagramma

(Outline of the Complete Teaching of *Peri Hypsous*) Image published with permission of ProQuest. Further reproduction is prohibited without permission.[36]

vigour and uncontainable energy of Longinus's concept. He annotates the term as that which "[n]os sane visiones appellamus, per quas imagines rerum absentium ita repraesentantur animo, ut eas cerner oculis, ac praesentes habere videamur [we might call visions, by which images of things absent are represented by the mind, that they might be discerned by the eyes and we might perceive them as present before us]." When he defines "visions" as processes by which "absent" images appear realistically before the readers, he picks up on Longinus's concept of *phantasia* as an "enthralling" and even somewhat miraculous process of poetic creation.[37] Like Longinus, de Petra draws attention to the author's psychological and emotional vitality in producing vivid poetry, while gesturing to a supernatural quality that underlies the production of the sublime.

If de Petra leaves the supernatural dimension of sublime poetry implicit, Langbaine makes them explicit in his 1636/1638 editions of *Peri Hypsous*, the first published in England. While maintaining continuity with the emphases of earlier editors, Langbaine includes on the title page a stunning image by William Marshall that celebrates Longinus's interest in divine rapture and the sublime as psychological condition. Even if the title, "De grandi loquentia sive sublimi dicendi genere," or "great eloquence or the sublime kind of speech," suggests that the work is a manual for crafting a high style, the words and images in the background suggest an understanding of the sublime as something much more than artistic craft.

In this visual portrayal of sublimity, the representation of the vertical dimension is especially striking, echoing Longinus's reference to the divine as the "space between earth and heaven."[38] Among the intimations of transport and rapture, the upper-right corner depicts a Zeus-like figure saying, "Os Homini Sublime [the face of man is elevated]," while the figure below – Phaeton in his chariot – is suspended in the gap between the earth and the sky, suggesting a physical portrayal of Longinian *ekplexis* and *ekstasis*. Phaeton himself mouths the words, "Animos aequabit Olimpo [he shall bring souls up to Olympus]," referring to the motion of rapture. On the lower right, flashes of lightning and thunderclouds reinforce this impression, with the words "tonitura Mentes. / Humanas motura [thunderclaps will move human minds]" – a likely reference to the "thunder" of Demosthenes, one of Longinus's most prominent images of sublimity. On the left-hand side, an eagle says, "In sublime feror [I am carried into the heights/sublimity]." In its overall impression and in its smallest details, the engraving strikingly emphasizes the elevated spiritual and emotional condition that the sublime entails – for author as well as audience.[39]

From these passages, it is apparent that early editors and translators of *Peri Hypsous* had a great deal to say about an ontological principle of the sublime, a concept associated with transcendence and distinct from language. Although it may be true that many theorists before Boileau merely assimilated Longinian ideas into contemporary theories of style, a substantial number of earlier scholars did engage deeply with the treatise's core ideas. This in no way diminishes the significance of

Figure 2. William Marshall's cover page to the Langbaine edition of *Peri Hypsous*[40]

Boileau, whose role in the transmission of *Peri Hypsous* can scarcely be overestimated, but it does point to a highly significant role for earlier Longinian scholars, whose interpretations were foundational not only to the explosion of the sublime in seventeenth- and eighteenth-century aesthetic philosophy, but also to the transmission of Longinus into theories of epic across France, Italy, and England.

France: Sublime Theories of Epic by the "Pléiade"

It is somewhat surprising that the influence on epic theory itself was felt first in France. Early modern interest in Longinus generally travelled from East to West, from the Byzantine realm to Italy, where *Peri Hypsous* was first printed, and then to France and England. Yet the two chief writers of the French "Pléiade," Ronsard and Du Bellay, were the first European authors to show sustained interest in the sublime purposes of epic, a development already surprising for two writers so regularly recognized for their investment in French national identity.[41] Nonetheless, their sublime sensibilities are apparent by 1549 in Du Bellay's *Défence*, and sustained in lesser-known poetry and prose of both writers, including Ronsard's preface to the *Franciade*.

The sublimity of Ronsard and Du Bellay probably reflects Longinian influence from the fifteenth-century manuscript tradition. Ronsard and Du Bellay were likely exposed to the concept of sublimity through Erasmus, a major influence on French scholarship generally and on the two leading writers of the Pléiade themselves.[42] In their commentaries on epic, both Ronsard and Du Bellay take the anti-Ciceronian side of the quarrel that Erasmus championed a few decades earlier, downplaying the need for strict adherence to stylistic rules. The poet-theorists call instead for epic to have the same elements of poetic composition privileged by Erasmus, Longinus, and Longinus's early modern critics: greatness of mind channeling powerful emotions. Tracing this interest in the poets' later prose and poetry, we not only see a strain of sublime scholarship much earlier than critics typically recognize, but find a surprising emphasis on poetry's divine roots and spiritual purposes from a group known for its celebration of French national identity.

The *Défence*, first, contains several Longinian echoes; but one of the most striking is its emphasis on an author's psychological and emotional capacity. Like many rhetorical and poetic theorists, Du Bellay urges great writers to reproduce the style of literary masters, but for the specific purpose of channeling the original author's greatness of mind, soul, and spirit, rather than his (or her) skill. As great poets set out to "immiter les bon aucteurs Grecz et Romains, voyre bien Italiens, Hespagnolz, et autres [imitate the good Greek, Roman, even Italian, Spanish, and other writers]," they must, according to Du Bellay, seek out those who have "ceste ardeur et allegresse d'esprit qui naturellement excite les poëtes [this ardor and spirit of joy that naturally excites poets]," much like Longinus exhorts writers to be "carried away by the inspiration of another" and "share the enthusiasm of these others' grandeur."[43] Moreover, Du Bellay adds, writers must carefully avoid those who "admirent voluntiers les petites choses, et deprisent ce qui excede leur jugement [willingly admire petty things, and scorn what surpasses their scope of judgment]."[44] As for Longinus (who offers a similar critique in the concluding section of *Peri Hypsous*), for Du Bellay one of the greatest inhibitors to poetic greatness is enslavement to the love of pleasure. Thus, for both writers, careless imitation habits are not concerning because they inhibit technical skill, but because they dull the psychological and emotional capacity – Longinian *megalophués* – that constitutes for both theorists the source of literary excellence.

While Du Bellay repeatedly emphasizes that it is this excellence of mind, heart, and feeling that most marks the great poet, he notes, as Longinus does, that this excellence is only trainable to an extent – it is in-born. The great poet is "doué d'une excellente felicité de nature [gifted with excellent blessings of nature]," and "acquise premierement par la magnanimité de ton couraige [moved first by your magnanimity of heart]."[45] To the extent that poetic composition requires exertion, that effort is supplied by a basic "vigeur d'esprit [vigour of mind]."[46] Like Longinus, Du Bellay favours natural giftedness above technical skill to the point of collapsing the binary between talent and skill altogether, such that the natural great-mindedness of a poet fuels the passion to acquire skill – creating a positive cycle of talent fostering focussed effort. The result is a poet who greatly resembles Longinus's sublime poet, one who, Du Bellay writes, will

> me fera indigner, apayser, ejouyr, douloir, aymer, hayr, admirer, etonner, bref, qui tiendra la bride de mes affection, me tournant ça et là à son plaisir. Voyla la vraye pierre de touche, où il fault que tu epreuves tous poëmes, et en toutes langues.

> [make me angry or calm, fill me with joy, make me grieve, love, hate, admire, wonder – who will, in short, hold the reins of my emotions, turning me this way and that as he pleases. This is the true touchstone, by which you must test all poems, and in all languages.][47]

In his quest for the great-minded epic poet who can evoke the most powerful emotions, Du Bellay echoes Longinus's top two characteristics of sublimity, establishing both as the desired attributes of the anticipated author of French epic.

This poet was of course to be Ronsard, who shares several of Du Bellay's (and Longinus's) emphases in his preface to the *Franciade*, especially the poet's psychological capacity. He writes that the aspiring epic poet must have "les conceptions plus divines [the most divine concepts]" and the ability to channel "un enthousiasme et fureur d'un jeune cerveau [enthusiasm and *furor* of a young mind]."[48] He also maintains (however unpersuasively, given the actual content of his French epic) that he will write more in the model of "la naive facilité d'Homere que sur la curieuse diligence de Virgile [the innate facility of Homer than the attentive diligence of Virgil]" – reversing the typical early modern preference for Virgil's craftsmanship over Homer's native genius.[49] And like Du Bellay, he also emphasizes the ability to "esmouvoir les passions et affections de l'ame ... par des carmes qui t'esmouvront le premier, soit à rire ou à pleurer, afin que les lecteurs en facent autant après toy [stir up the passions and affections of the soul ... by charms that incite you first, whether to laugh or to cry, in order that readers may do the same after you]."[50]

The chief distinguishing marker of Ronsard's theory of sublime epic, however, is his emphasis on the supernatural aims of poetry. In this, his vision of the source and purpose of poetic "greatness" departs from the theory of Du Bellay, whose *Défence* focusses on the national ambitions of France. Taking a position even more reminiscent of Longinus, Ronsard finds the ultimate purpose of poetry – which the "poete heroïque" must stop at nothing to achieve – to "fai[re] entreparler les Dieux aux hommes et les hommes aux Dieux [facilitate communication between the gods and men and between men and gods]."[51] And in endorsing the connection between the natural and supernatural realms, he underscores that literature's purpose is not primarily for improving the self or society, but for enhancing human spirituality – to which the moral and civic functions of poetry are in service.

Although it might appear that Ronsard is merely paying tribute to epic's characteristic juxtaposition of human and divine realms – a feature applicable to classical pagan epic as well as Christian epic – he affirms a distinctively monotheistic approach to poetry elsewhere. In the lesser known *Abregé de l'art poetique françois* (1565), addressed to Alphonse d'Elbene, Abbé de Haute-Combe en Savoie, which sets out several important rules for poetic composition, Ronsard opens by asserting that poetry must, first and foremost, make every effort to honour the Christian God:

> Sur toutes choses tu auras les muses en reverence, voire en singuliere veneration, et ne les feras jamais servir à choses deshonnestes à risées, ny à libelles injurieux; mais les tiendras cheres et sacrées, comme les filles de jupiter, c'est à dire de Dieu, qui de sa saincte grace a premièrement par elles fait cognoistre aux peuples ignorans les excellences de sa majesté ... Et si tu entreprens quelque grand œuvre, tu te monstreras religieux et craignant Dieu, le commençant ou par son nom, ou par un autre qui représentera quelque effect de sa majesté, à l'exemple des Poëtes Grecs ... Car les Muses, Apollon, Mercure, Pallas et autres telles Déitez ne nous representent autre chose que les puissances de Dieu, auquel les premiers hommes avoient donné plusieurs noms pour les divers effects de son incomprehensible Majesté.[52]

> [Above all, you will hold the Muses in reverence, even with particular veneration, and never have them serve dishonesty, or mockery, or harmful libel; but hold them as dear and sacred, like daughters of Jupiter, that is, of God, who in his holy grace through them first made known the excellencies of his majesty to ignorant people ... And if you take on any great work, you will show yourself to be religious

and God-fearing, either starting with his name or with another who represents some effect of his majesty, in the example of the Greek poets ... Because the Muses, Apollo, Mercury, Pallas, and other such deities represent nothing else to us besides the power of God, to whom the first men gave many names for the different effects of his incomprehensible Majesty.]

In this introduction to one of his theories of literature, Ronsard defends the divine purpose of literature at considerable length and with surprising intensity for a poet so interested in French national identity. Twice he indicates that respect for the supernatural, even if accomplished through depictions of classical pagan religion, is the *most* important aspect of poetry. Anticipating the likes of Spenser and Milton, Ronsard holds that the Christian God is not threatened by or in competition with literary representations of other deities – he suggests that their very presence reveals the innate human orientation towards the divine, thereby glorifying and even illuminating the character and majesty of God, who cannot be perfectly represented in any one form. The effect is a powerful affirmation of the divine over the civic, especially read in connection with Ronsard's above statement from the *Franciade* about poetry facilitating communication between humanity and God. In this view of poetry, Ronsard Christianizes Longinus's view that literature offers a means of achieving the highest aim of human beings – the experience of being brought in touch with their divine nature, through the sublime.

But if Ronsard appears to surpass Du Bellay's commitment to spiritual purposes, Du Bellay's 1558 *Songes* (*Dreams*, or *Meditations*) goes further, rejecting the hope of a French national revival celebrated in the *Défence* and endorsing a higher-order desire – a deferred experience of the sublime. The *Songes*, a series of dream poems that read like a cross between Ecclesiastes and Revelation, repeatedly emphasize the vanity or inconstancy of worldly things, including the nation of Rome. They open with the poet-dreamer encountering a spirit or "Demon," an emblem of poetic inspiration, projecting visions of representations of the glories of Rome.[53] In doing so, they tap into the same sublime impulse that both Du Bellay and Ronsard develop elsewhere. In sonnet 5, for instance, the poet-dreamer is "ravy" [ravished] to see an image of Roman conquest before him; yet in all but three sonnets in the sequence, the images evaporate, ending the poem in destruction and ruin, as in the opening sonnet, where the Demon-spirit instructs the poet: "Voy comme tout n'est rien que vanité [See how all is but vanity]."[54]

In their emphasis on vapor, the *Songes* most obviously recall the biblical book of Ecclesiastes, but they also anticipate the writings of Montaigne, who in writing of the ruins of Rome, was one of the first early modern writers to be credited with producing the sublime.[55] While Montaigne's vision of sublimity is secular, however, Du Bellay celebrates the sublimity of an evaporation of worldliness that points heavenward. Acknowledging "la mondaine inconstance [the inconstancy of worldly things]," the first sonnet of the *Songes* concludes, "Puis que Dieu seul au temps fait resistance, / N'espere rien qu'en la divinité [since God alone resists time, hope for nothing but in the divinity]" (12–14). For Du Bellay, the glories of Rome are mere shadows of eternal heavenly glory in God himself.[56] The concluding sonnet is apocalyptic but similar in purpose, portraying the sister of Typheus, emblem of Rome, warring against heaven itself, before she is struck down by lightning just as the poet awakes. The image is startling in light of the endorsement of nation-building throughout the *Défence* and *Antiquitez* – here Rome is not merely a "vanity," a harmless entity foreshadowing what is to come, but a depiction of the Whore of Babylon of Revelation 17, the very emblem of evil. In this instance, the empire of Rome and the kingdom of heaven are no longer connected but diametrically opposed. The only proper response, the sequence implies, is to exchange nation-building impulses for divine purposes. The *Songes* defer the partial sublimity of Rome for the greater sublimity of heaven.

While it may be tempting to dismiss Du Bellay's references to Christian belief as nominal, given his strong emphasis on French national identity in the *Défence*, the *Antiquitez*, and elsewhere, the melancholic tone of the *Songes* suggests a belief that is sincere and profound. Together, these sonnets express a deep longing for intangible glory, fulfilled only by God after death, a longing that emanates a considerable sublime undertone – a Longinian emphasis on humanity's desire for divinity and immortality. Moreover, with the framing device of the Demon and dreamer-poet, the *Songes* are quite Longinian in citing poetry as the central expression of this sublimity, and quite Christian in their emphasis on the biblical God as the basis of the sublime. If Du Bellay demonstrates that humanity must yearn for its spiritual rather than its earthly home, his *Songes* make it the poet's role, in consultation with the Demon-spirit, to cultivate this sublime longing, shunning worldly glory in favour of divine.

Remarkable as it is that the French Ronsard and Du Bellay would arrive at a sublime theory of epic before Italian theorists, the French trailblazing is fitting, given that the first writer to popularize the sublime in the late seventeenth century would be Nicolas Boileau. At the same time, given the religious undertones of the early modern sublime, France represented a site as appropriate as any for theorists to begin to integrate Longinus's distinctive ideas about the ideal purpose of literature into a formal concept of epic. As modern critics have well noted, Longinus proved especially attractive to scholars who had ties to Calvinism or faced accusations of heresy (Francesco Porto, for instance, was an exiled Protestant).[57] This may be due to intersections between Protestant hermeneutics and Longinian theory, but it may also have been related to Longinus's emphasis on a poetics of spiritual citizenship and immortality, sometimes at the expense of literature's role in promoting moral and civic duty, in an era when literary theory advocated the use of literature to promote moral behaviour and citizenship. And in fact, Ronsard and Du Bellay have been identified as sympathetic to the aims of the Reformation.[58] Perhaps France, the birthplace of John Calvin and home to numerous persecuted adherents to Protestantism from the onset of the Reformation, was a destined hotspot for the sublime.

Whatever the case, the theory and poetics of Ronsard and Du Bellay show an underexamined interest in ideas significant to Longinus – especially the idea that great poetry points readers to their spiritual origins. As the writers of the Pléiade would be enormously influential particularly on English writers, their emphasis on Christian sublime poetics would likewise spread to poet-theorists such as Sidney and Spenser – as well as, perhaps, Tasso, who can be credited as the first to bring the concept of sublime poetry into a full-length theory of epic.[59]

Italy: *Meraviglia,* Risk, and the Tassoan Sublime

In Italy, Tasso extends the sublime vision of Ronsard and Du Bellay in the most developed theory of epic of the period – the *Discorsi del poema eroico* (1594; composed in the 1560s). In the *Discorsi*, Tasso develops his own model of sacred poetics that builds from key Longinian principles emphasized by Ronsard and Du Bellay, while intersecting with the thinking of other Italian poet-theorists, such as Giordano Bruno. These principles include Longinus's top two characteristics of sublime poetry – the noble psychology of the author, and the cultivation of *ekplexis*. Compared to the poet-theorists of the Pléiade, Tasso creates a more complex and provocative theory of sublime epic centred on his distinctive concept of *meraviglia* (alternatively spelled *maraviglia*), a concept that gives rise to a particularly Longinian (and, for Tasso, personally significant) principle of poetic risk-taking.

Because of the *Discorsi*'s centrality to Renaissance epic theory, Tasso's work will be given more attention than any other poetic theory in this chapter, especially given the fact that his claims to the sublime have been directly contested. In particular, Gustavo Costa has gone so far as to argue against any Longinian influence on the *Discorsi*, noting that Tasso never once references *Peri Hypsous* – a claim that may have inhibited scholarship on the Tassoan sublime.[60] Traditionally, scholarship reads Tasso's treatise on epic as conflicting in emphasis, but more or less a piece of poetic theory promoting the moral and pedagogical purposes of art, as suggested above.[61]

Like other artists in Counter-Reformation Italy, Tasso was subject to a notoriously strict set of restraints on artistic requirements intimated during the proceedings of the Council of Trent (1545–63) and codified by Catholic theorists. As described in *De sacris et profanis imaginibus* (1584) by Gabriele Paleotti, one of several influential Counter-Reformation theorists, the centre of Christian life was to pursue virtue and avoid vice, and thus artists, too, should focus on depicting the excellence of virtue, or open themselves to accusations of vanity and depravity. For Paleotti and many others, there was no alternative to this binary: artists either pursue sanctification and religious piety, or they must be "intent only on aggrandizing themselves, and on their desire to be thought excellent."[62] Literary theorist Agnolo Segni promoted a view of Aristotelian catharsis that was particularly extreme, distrusting poetic art that evoked extreme delight for any reason: he argued that art should bring about "la purgazione degli animi nostri da loro affetti [the purgation of the passions from our minds]," expelling the emotions rather than cultivating or intensifying them.[63] Artists and artwork pursuing beauty, delight, or elevation for their own sake were deemed dangerous.

What was often at stake in these theories (at least the most repressive), however, was not simply virtue, but institutional control of religious practice. Despite his well-documented connection to the Counter-Reformation, Tasso's natural instinct seems to have been more Longinian, a force emerging when his emotional and aesthetic sensibilities overcame his desire for conformity. As Lawrence Rhu notes, Tasso's early *Discorsi dell'arte poetica* (composed in 1560s, published in 1587) privileges the emotional over the ethical function of literature: Rhu maintains that the *Arte Poetica* "asserts without qualification … that delight is the aim of such works."[64] The subsequent *Discorsi del poema eroico* offers conflicting statements, at times affirming that poetry should be useful and inspire moral action in accord with Counter-Reformation doctrine, but elsewhere maintaining a position at least as committed to delight as the *Arte poetica*: "l'utile non si ricerca per se stesso, ma per altro; per questa cagione è men nobil fine del piacere, e ha minor somiglianza con quello ch'è l'ultimo fine [the useful is not sought for its own sake but for another end; for this reason, utility is a less noble end than pleasure, and bears less resemblance to the final objective]."[65]

Beyond delight, moreover, the *Discorsi* reveals the author's innate attraction to Longinian principles of astonishment, though the pressures of the Counter-Reformation, whose principles of literature were squarely at odds with those of Longinus, seems to have led him to omit any direct references to the sublime. Studies by Doran and Françoise Graziani suggest that *Peri Hypsous* may indeed have played an important, if uncelebrated role in Tasso's development as a theorist, since he could have encountered *Peri Hypsous* through sources such as Robortello's first edition, Pagano's Latin translation, Vettori's commentaries on Aristotle's *Poetics* or Demetrius's *On Style* (1562), or Patrizi's *Della Poetica*.[66] Doran even identifies Tasso's poetic theory, particularly his theory of *meraviglia*, as a precursor to Boileau's theory of the sublime.[67]

Whatever the reason for the omission, in the *Discorsi* Tasso develops an important but largely neglected discourse on the sublime that suggests an even greater debt to *Peri Hypsous* than has been previously acknowledged – whether to the classical treatise directly, or to the mediating influence of Tasso's contemporaries, who certainly did read Longinus. Centring this Longinian discourse on his concept of *meraviglia*, Tasso produces a poetic model that is perceptibly Longinian in character and emphasis, even while his discourse on sublimity sometimes strains against evident moralism.[68] In his concept of *meraviglia*, Tasso translates into his theory of heroic poetry concepts and even vocabulary emphasized by Longinus's early critics and translators, to develop a poetic theory that prioritizes emotions much stronger than pleasure and delight – ultimately theorizing rapture and astonishment, the violent emotions of the sublime, as the ends of great poetry. In doing so, he develops a highly Longinian concept of poetic risk that subtly challenges Counter-Reformation poetic principles, in prioritizing the poet's direct connection to the divine over duty to society.

Meraviglia and the Heroic Poem

In his defence of epic, Tasso identifies a particularly Longinian version of *meraviglia*, described below, as the genre's most important feature, arguing that heroic poetry possesses not only the full range of features found in tragedy and in lyric poetry, but also a unique ability to "muover gli animi con la maraviglia [move souls with *maraviglia*]" that is either absent or suppressed in other literary forms.[69] For Tasso, *meravaglia* is distinctive to epic and the feature that elevates it above other literary genres, representing a greater end than the catharsis that characterizes tragedy. In his portrayal, *meraviglia* not only sets epic apart as a genre but, as a noun with similar conceptual range to the sublime, becomes a kind of verbal substitute for it. By making *meraviglia* both sublime and central to epic, Tasso works to transform the conception of the genre.

Earlier Renaissance scholars such as Bartolomeo Maranta (who published in 1564) explicitly associate *meraviglia* with epic, but an Aristotelian version associated with *admiratio*, or a milder aesthetic pleasure along the lines of delight or curiosity.[70] In contrast, Tasso draws on a newer definition developed by Longinus's early translators and critics, who present *meraviglia* as a dynamic force associated with astonishment or violent transport, containing a mildly negative inflection characteristic of the sublime. In the 1575 Italian translation of *Peri Hypsous*, Da Falgano uses the word "meraviglia" to translate *ekplexis* [astonishment, terror, or paralysis], the Longinian *telos* of poetry, as well as variants of *thauma*, a synonym for *hypsos*. For instance, da Falgano renders Longinus's "ἐν ποιήσει τέλος ἐστὶν ἔκπληξις [the end of poetry is astonishment]" as "poesia ha per suo fine la meraviglia [the end of poetry is *meraviglia*]."[71] And in rendering Longinus's statement that "θαυμαστὸν δ ὅμως ἀεὶ τὸ παράδοξον [it is always the unusual that is marvellous (as opposed to the merely useful, which is ordinary)]," he writes, "quello che trapassa ogni pensiero, et ogni credere porta sempre seco meraviglia [that which surpasses every thought and every belief always carries with it *meraviglia*]."[72] Da Falgano amplifies the original slightly, defining *meraviglia* as "that which passes every thought" – a rendering far from Maranta's *admiratio*, instead using *meraviglia* to anticipate Kant's concept of the mathematical sublime.

Tasso's version likely draws as well from the theory of Patrizi, whose work he would certainly have been familiar with.[73] In short translations and discussions of Longinian passages, Patrizi defines the key term *ekstasis* as *meravaglia*, and in a separate passage defines *meraviglia* explicitly in terms of the sublime:

di sé levava negli animi degli uditori, come dice Longino: "οὐ μόνον πείθει ἀλλὰ καὶ δουλοῦται <non solo persuade, ma eziandio asservisce.>"[74]

[arises on its own in the minds of listeners, as Longinus says: "not only does it persuade, but enslaves as well."]

Elsewhere, citing section 36.3 of *Peri Hypsous*, Patrizi translates the Greek "ἐπὶ δὲ τῶν φυσικῶν ἔργων τὸ μέγεθος [θαυμάζεται] [with natural things, greatness (is what) astonishes/produces the sublime]" as *nelle naturali cose la grandezza si ha in maraviglia* [in matters of nature, greatness is found in *meraviglia*].[75] By transposing the verbal construction, θαυμάζεται [to astonish or produce sublimity], onto the noun *meraviglia*, Patrizi assigns the Italian word an active meaning, associating it with a dynamic verbal construction. He identifies *meraviglia* itself as a dynamic and independent force that actively overwhelms the reader, lending the word a sense of instability and incomprehensibility.

Tasso echoes these uses of *meraviglia*, allowing the Longinian resonances to supply a particular force to his version of the concept. He defines the term as that which "ci rende quasi attoniti di veder [makes us almost speechless to see]."[76] He thus assigns agency to *meraviglia*, putting it in the subject position and representing it as an animate power that paralyses the audience. Tasso maintains that Homer's greatness emerges most clearly when he "adolcisca l'auditore, e, riempiendolo di stupore, l'incanti con la meraviglia [weakens the hearer, and, filling him with astonishment, enchants him with *meraviglia*]."[77] By associating *meraviglia* with enchantment and "stupore" – paralysis – Tasso invokes an experience much more complex than aesthetic pleasure, pointing instead to the presence of a mysterious, overwhelming force actively transmitted to the reader.

In his connection of *meraviglia* and stupore, Tasso echoes a little-known dream vision narrative by Francesco Porta, *Castel Nuovo della Gargagnana* (1578), in which the narrator experiences "alta maraviglia" when he sees a celestial messenger descending from above. This encounter, he writes, is among those that "fanno altrui stupire: et fermi à prima vista del colore, chè fà di morte rimembrar la gente, / E qual si vede in huom tratto di Tomba [stupefy others: and at first sight remove their colour, reminding people of death, as seen in someone taken from the grave.]"[78] Particularly noteworthy here is the productive negativity of this conception of *meraviglia* – though discussing the presence of a divine being, he associates the experience not only with paralysis and stupefaction ("stupire") but with death and dying. Though Tasso's concept is not quite so negative, he too describes *meraviglia* as a powerful presence that can *fill* the audience with astonishment. When he writes, "Dee dunque ancora l'epopeia aver il suo proprio diletto con la sua propria operazione; e questa per aventura è il mover maraviglia [Therefore the epic should have its own proper delight and its own effects, and this is perhaps inducing *maraviglia*]," he cites unique and unorthodox ends of epic to establish the genre's supremacy: not instruction, but rapture.[79]

In defining *maraviglia* in Longinian terms, Tasso links the concept – and his theory of sublime epic – to another major idea from *Peri Hypsous*: the concept of *phantasia*, or the capacity to produce vivid images. Referring to this concept interchangeably as *enargeia* or *evidenza*, Tasso identifies this ability as central to producing *maraviglia* and sublimity, and in connecting *enargeia* with poetic astonishment, develops a concept that will re-emerge in other early modern theories of the sublime.[80] For Tasso, Longinus, and Longinian scholars, *phantasia/enargeia/evidenza* are the sign of the noble-minded poet. For his part, Tasso defines *enargeia/evidenza* as "quella virtù che ci fa quasi veder le cose che si narrano [that power that makes us almost behold the things narrated]."[81] For Tasso, *enargeia/evidentia* is itself remarkable – it is about much more than representing reality to instruct the reader, but about imagining scenes in such astonishing specificity that they visually transport their audience. In a discussion of classical poetics, he maintains that this is a skill proper to the very greatest writers:

> Ne l'espressione de le cose nondimeno, ed in quella che i Greci chiamano *"energia,"* fu meraviglioso ed eguale ad Omero, e co 'l suono e col numero l'imita in guisa che ce le pone innanzi a gli occhi, e ce le fa quasi vedere e udire.[82]

> [Nonetheless in the expression of things, and in what the Greeks call *energia* (*enargeia*), he (Virgil) was marvellous and equal to Homer, and with the use of sound and rhythm, he imitates him in such a way that he sets them before our eyes, nearly making us see and hear them.]

In celebrating the ability to produce image, Tasso recalls Vettori's 1560 commentary on Aristotle's *Poetics*, which defines *phantasia* as a capacity unique to the ennobled author: Longinus "celebrat quasdam eximias phantasies poetarum: cum enim locum ex *Oedipo Coloneo* mirifice laudasset, addit statim in reditu etiam illo summo ingenio a poeta excogitatum fuisse [celebrates the excellent imaginative capacity of some poets: for when he had splendidly praised the passage in *Oedipus at Colonus*, he immediately adds that it had been invented by a poet at the height of genius]."[83] Connecting poetic genius to the powers of imagination, Vettori recognizes that sublime poetry is not simply a stylistic construction, but is "excogitatum," originating "from the mind … of a poet at the height of genius." Tasso's theory of *enargeia/evidenza* reflects this idea, as he establishes these qualities as proper to only the most "meraviglioso" of poets.

Most importantly, however, for Tasso as for Longinus, Ronsard, Du Bellay, and the English theorists to follow, the poet who can produce such astonishment must write from a position of metaphysical and psychological elevation. As Graziani notes, Tasso's representation of *meraviglia* celebrates the epic poet's "altezza d'ingegno," a nobility of mind indicative of a divine vocation.[84] As Longinus emphasizes, Tasso's sublime poet, too, must be ennobled, with an innately powerful psychological and emotional capacity that reveals the fundamentally sacred purpose of his poetry. And Tasso specifically defines this purpose as vertical in orientation: the sublime poet "al supremo Artefice nelle sue operazioni assomigliandosi [mirrors the great Architect in his workings]" and "de la sua divinità viene a partecipare [participates in his divinity]" by writing poetry that becomes its own microcosmic space ("un picciolo mondo").[85] In particular, the idea of participating in the very divinity of God strongly suggests that for Tasso, the final aim of poetry is not virtue, but exaltation and transcendence.

Perturbazione and Heroic Risk

Tasso develops his concept of a sacred sublime poetics further in a particular emphasis of his epic theory – the importance of taking literary risks, a key Longinian principle with important application in his own time.[86] In his discussion of Homer's poetics, Tasso marvels at how the classical poet takes "grandissima libertà" in his writing: "né però gli lascia nel proprio paese o nella propria natura, ma questi allunga, altri accorcia, altri trasmuta e quasi volta sottosopra [does not allow words their own country or their own nature, but lengthens some, shortens others, and turns others practically inside out]." The end results of such risk-taking, Tasso claims, "riempiono gli animi di tumulto e di perturbazione [fill minds with turmoil and agitation]."[87] While *meraviglia* may be Tasso's most apparent principle of sublimity, his discussion of "perturbazione" – the emotionally unsettling disruption of poetic norms – offers another important link to Longinus and an underlying means of creating *meraviglia*. Francis Goyet notes Longinus's distinct preference for discontinuity and interruption, as a rhetorical means of producing the rapture characteristic of the sublime, while Mario Praz notes that Tasso associates disorder with sublimity. I would add that Tasso describes the concept of literary disruption as an authorial risk associated with a striking sense of violence, a violence that he uses to challenge the dominant Counter-Reformation poetic model itself.[88]

As a rhetorical device, *perturbazione* may involve several forms of disruption to the stasis of a poem – a broader, plot-based disruption, or a syntactical, linguistic disorder – but for Tasso each works to elicit emotional turmoil and Longinus's concept of *ekplexis*. At its core, Tasso defines *perturbazione* not simply as emotionally moving, but as effecting calculated disruption and chaos. His admiration of Homer recalls Longinus's admiration of Demosthenes's "violence and his speed, his force, his terrific power of rhetoric, (which) burns, as it were and scatters everything before him, and may therefore be compared to a flash of lightning or a thunderbolt."[89] Underlying Demosthenes's speech (and Homer's poetry) is a "rough [ἀποτόμῳ] sublimity" – a sense of harshness and severity that, for Tasso, grounds the ideal epic poem as well. Tasso emphasizes that syntactical "asprezza" [roughness] can produce an emotional disruption along the lines of the sublime, noting, for instance, that Dante's "asprezza," manifested in the running together of vowels, creates "un non so che di magnifico e di grande [a magnificent and grand 'I know not what']."[90]

As I explore in more detail in the following chapter, the phrase "un non so che" is one of Tasso's core markers of the sublime, the Italian predecessor of the "je ne sais quoi" that Boileau would later associate with Longinian sublimity. In the *Liberata*, Tasso repeats the phrase several times to indicate a mysterious sublime intuition that prompts several characters to pursue the compelling, but unconventional voice of divine inspiration. In the *Discorsi*, too, Tasso links the phrase directly with the unconventional and the irregular – with the emotional agitation that results from poetic disorder – and distinguishes the resulting sensation from the merely pleasing. The effects of "asprezza," he maintains, are ultimately *less* likely to be "piacevole a gli orrechie [pleasing to the ears]" and more conducive to the volatile emotional condition he associates with "la magnificenza."[91] In this description of the "rough" and perhaps threatening side of poetic astonishment, Tasso moves beyond a comparatively benign idea of curiosity or mild admiration, referencing the unsettling sublimity described by Patrizi, Pagano, da Falgano, and Longinus himself.

Of the various forms of *perturbazione*, Tasso finds one of the most compelling to be "il senso che sta largamente sospeso [the protacted suspension of meaning]," a stylistic disturbance intended to unsettle the reader, prompting a form of *ekplexis*.[92] As Tasso describes this disturbance,

> Ma nell'ordine artificioso, che perturbato chiama il Castelvetro, alcune delle prime deono esser dette primieramente, altre posposte, altre nel tempo presente deono esser tralasciate e riserbate a miglior occasione, come insegna Orazio. Prima deono esser dette quelle senza le quali non s'avrebbe alcuna cognizione de lo stato delle cose presenti; ma se ne posson tacer molte, le quali scemano l'espettazione e la meraviglia, avenga che il poeta debba tenere sempre l'auditore sospeso e desideroso di legger più oltre.[93]

> [But in sequences that are contrived, or disrupted, as Castelvetro calls them, some of the first (events) must be stated in the first position, others postponed, and others put aside for the present and reserved for a better occasion, as Horace teaches. Those without which we would have no understanding of the current state of things must be stated first; but many can be omitted – those that lessen expectation and *meraviglia* – since the poet must always keep the audience in suspense and desiring to read more.]

Tasso applies this strategy not only to the overall narrative design but also to the design of sentence and stanza; by delaying key ideas until the end of a verse, the author produces a tension and desire that urges the audience on, a strategy intended to heighten the sense of instability, suspense, and astonishment [*meraviglia*]. Tasso compares the reader's experience of narrative suspension to a traveller walking along a lonely road without a place to stop and rest, implying that the delay of key elements in a sentence can make the audience uneasy, and thus requires a certain discipline and commitment on the author's part: the poet must be willing to hold off until just the right moment, to generate heightened "expectations" and thus intensify the emotional effect.[94]

Tasso's advice echoes Longinus's point about the sublime impact of this strategy – how reordering sentence structures creates not only heightened emotions, but an aesthetically productive form of violence.[95] As Longinus notes in section 22.4, a poet should

> suspend the sense which he has begun to express, and in the interval manages to bring forward one extraneous idea after another in a strange and unlikely order, making the audience terrified of a total collapse of the sentence, and compelling them from excitement to share the speaker's risk: then unexpectedly, after a great interval, the long-lost phrase turns up pat at the end, so that he astounds them all.[96]

While Longinus emphasizes the terror experienced by the reader much more directly than Tasso, both theorists highlight the author's counterintuitive effort to create suspense and discomfort in the reader, to infringe on the reader's sense of security by violating poetic norms. According to both, the sublime poet must go so far as to risk the alienation of the audience, in order to entertain the possibility of producing sublimity.

Underlying Tasso's endorsement of *perturbazione*, then, is an authorization of creative risk-taking that marks off the sublime poet. For Tasso as for Longinus, sublimity depends on a willingness to aim for the heights at any cost; Longinus was adamant about the connection between risk and stunning brilliance, on the one hand, and caution and mediocrity, on the other: "Perhaps it is inevitable that humble, mediocre natures, because they never run any risks and never aim at the heights, should remain to a large extent safe from error."[97] Tasso, too, in claiming that the delay of key elements of a sentence makes the audience uneasy, suggests that great poetry requires a certain boldness and daring. He praises Plato's confident use of metaphor: "e per ciò fu tenuto arditissimo [and for this (he) was held most daring]" as well as Homer's and Dante's "l'ardire" and "licenza" in diction and use of imagery.[98] Tasso's sublime poet must show "un certo disprezzo de la soverchia diligenza [a certain disdain for excessive diligence]," boldly taking liberties, because excess concern for accuracy produces a certain pedantry and laboriousness that "al magnifico dicitore non si conviene [is not fitting for the magnificent writer]."[99] Against its Longinian counterpart, Tasso somewhat qualifies his concept of risk by his demand for prudence: "come io non biasimo l'ardire guidato da la ragione, così non lodo l'audacia senza consiglio [just as I do not reproach a boldness guided by reason, I do not praise audacity without reflection]." Yet for Tasso, courage remains an essential quality for the heroic poet – one of the central "passioni dell'animo" – however prudently the poet must apply it.[100]

Ultimately, as Tasso highlights the need for poetic risk – including willingness to violate poetic conventions and audience expectations – he intimates the subversiveness of his poetics. In theorizing a Longinian poetics that endorses a certain violence against the reader, Tasso suggests (without directly stating) that a poet might direct this risk-taking, this challenge, to features beyond strictly poetic style – towards content. To produce such strong effects on the audience, Tasso's heroic poet must write from a position of metaphysical elevation, as we have seen, a position that implies a certain separation from social custom and traditional authority. Tasso's model emphasizes that the sublime poet must allow nothing to stand in the way of the divine goal of producing stunning poetry, even, implicitly, the official guidelines of Counter-Reformation authority. While the neo-Aristotelian/ Horatian model emphasizes moral function and civic duty, or horizontal relations among earthly individuals and institutions, Tasso's model endorses emotions of all kinds – pleasure, delight, and the more disconcerting yet elevating emotions of the sublime. In privileging divine aims over civic-building aims, Tasso thus develops a poetic principle featured across theories of epic poetry, and in his implied resistance to Counter-Reformation officials, joins a list of early Longinian scholars previously noted for a degree of religious nonconformity.[101] As we will see in the following chapter, the idea that the vertical relationship supersedes civic action emerges more distinctly in the *Gerusalemme liberata*, becoming a defining heroic principle of the epic.

While Tasso is the core proponent of the sublime in Italian epic theory, he is not alone: he is joined not only by Patrizi but by contemporary poet-theorist Giordano Bruno (also a friar and mathematician), who connects sublimity and heroism in his *De Gli Eroici Furori* (*On the Heroic Frenzies*, 1585). Compared to other theorists in this chapter, Bruno describes a less orthodox version of divine transcendence, but as an acquaintance of Philip Sidney, his concept of the sublime may have helped to bridge the gap between Italian and English poetics.[102]

The "divine frenzy" celebrated throughout Bruno's text is a condition of Neoplatonic *furor*, here a state of divine inspiration that incorporates key aspects of Longinian thought, including the description of the process and emotions surrounding poetic inspiration.[103] While Bruno never mentions Longinus, he shows a strikingly similar investment in extreme emotion, connection to the divine, and in particular, authorial elevation of thought and risk, an investment that further suggests the diffusion of sublime theory.

In his dialogues on poetics, Bruno, like Longinus and Tasso, is adamant that poetry must privilege inventive originality, rewarding authorial risk. In a fictional dialogue on poetry, Bruno's speakers, Cicada and Tansillo, voice their disapproval of those who confine poetics to rule-keeping:

> CICADA: Son certi regolisti de poesia che a gran pena passano per poeta Omero, riponendo Vergilio, Ovidio, Marziale, Exiodo, Lucrezio et altri molti in numero de versificatori, examinandoli per le regole de la *Poetica* d'Aristotele.[104]
> TANSILLO: Sappi certo, fratel mio, che questi son vere bestie.
>
> [CICADA: There are some poetic rule-makers who have great difficulty accepting Homer as a poet, demoting Virgil, Ovid, Martial, Hesiod, Lucretius, and many others to the status of mere versifiers, evaluating them by the rules of Aristotle's *Poetics*.
> TANSILLO: You can be sure, my brother, that these people are real beasts.]

In emphasizing that poetry cannot be reduced rules, Bruno's dialogue implicitly celebrates the Longinian greatness of spirit – *megalophués* – that transcends regulations. Here and elsewhere, he prefers a high-mindedness lacking among poet "versifiers" and their "bestial" evaluators, suggesting that the desired originality comes from a condition of divine inspiration that resembles Longinian *ekplexis*.

Describing this condition through an account given by the fictional Cesarino, Bruno explains the position of the properly inspired hero, the "furioso eroico":

> [I]l proposito del furioso eroico penso che verse circa l'imbecillità de l'ingegno umano il quale attento a la divina impresa a un subito talvolta si trova ingolfato nell'abisso della eccellenza incomprensibile, onde il senso et imaginazione vien confusa et assorbita, che non sapendo passar avanti, né tornar a dietro, né dove voltarsi, svanisce e perde l'esser suo non altrimente che una stilla d'acqua che svanische nel mare, o un picciol spirito che s'attenua perdendo la propria sustanza nell'aere spacioso et inmenso.[105]
>
> [I think that the aim of the frenzied hero deals with the weakness of human ingenuity, which, intent on the divine enterprise, all at once finds itself plunged into the abyss of incomprehensible excellence, and hence the senses and imagination become confused and preoccupied, and, not knowing how to go farther, nor where to turn back, nor where to turn, he disappears and loses his being, just like a drop of water that vanishes into the sea, or a slight breeze that dissipates, losing its very substance in the great wide sky.]

While the "frenzy" described here operates on the margins of reason, it recalls the Longinian experience of being overwhelmed by something greater than the self – in this case, "eccellenza incomprensibile." The hero who experiences it must recognize, just as Longinus urges at the conclusion to *Peri Hypsous*, that there are desires far greater than the pleasures desired by animals, or of those who have so watered down their tastes that they can no longer desire the sublime.[106]

For Bruno, moreover, the condition of "frenzy" described here contains a Longinian emphasis on violence against the self. Bruno's hero must be willing to accept the risks and consequences of psychological transport, risking "losing its substance in the great sky" to enter a superior condition of transcendence. In celebrating the risks of poetic transport like Tasso had done, the *Eroici Furori* thus gives greater voice to a Longinian sensibility important to the *Discorsi* and implied by Tasso: that sublime poetry, being reliant on divine power and oriented towards divine ends, works to unsettle and provoke rather than restore through catharsis.

Given his high regard for provocation, it is perhaps unsurprising that Bruno held a variety of heretical beliefs, for which he would be examined by the Inquisition and martyred in 1600. Bruno thus joins the ranks of Porto, de Petra, and Tasso among scholars who share an interest in the sublime and a resistance to Catholic orthodoxy, though Bruno, in denying the virginity of Mary and the divinity of Christ, goes much further in his heterodoxy than the others. And though Bruno did not demonstrate the interest in Protestantism that Porto and de Petra had done, the English theorists heir to his work did, including Philip Sidney, to whom Bruno dedicated the *Eroici Furori*. The early stages of sublime English epic theory, beginning with the work of Sidney in the late sixteenth century, would yet again feature a connection between the sacred and the sublime – though, in this case, a distinctively Protestant version.

England: The Protestant Sublime from Sidney to Milton

Sixteenth-century English theory produces a version of the sublime that expands its predecessors' discussion of the divine source and sacred aims of epic poetry. Beginning with Sidney's *Defence of Poetry* (written in the 1580s and published in 1595), English literary theory invokes Longinian principles repeatedly and defends heroic poetry as an especially sublime genre.[107] Sidney may have been influenced by his acquaintance with John Rainolds, or his knowledge of French or Italian theory; but, like other English theorists of epic – George Puttenham, George Chapman, and Milton – he was especially impacted by the close connection between Longinus and Protestant theology, hermeneutics, and stylistics. Along with Puttenham's *The Arte of English Poesie* (1589), Sidney's *Defence* develops a Protestant conception of the sublime that sustains Tasso's challenge to humanism, but from a Reformed perspective; in the early to mid-seventeenth century, Chapman and Milton then extend their predecessors' emphasis on the sacred sublimity of heroic poetry by examining the ways that divine inspiration impacts the agency and identity of the sublime epic poet. The marriage of Protestantism and sublimity, I would argue, becomes a trademark of English epic theory in the sixteenth century, and continues to characterize English epic in the seventeenth.

The association between Longinus and Protestantism is especially important to England, as a nation that was especially militant in its Protestantism. Dietmar Till notes that during the Renaissance, most Protestant theologians departed from Roman rhetorical categories, which tended to emphasize elaborate style, giving preference to Hellenistic ideas such as those of Hermogenes and Longinus, which emphasized simplicity of style and lofty, elevated content over ornate phrasing. As Till notes, St. Augustine, one of the most foundational writers for the Protestant Reformers, held a theory of biblical style that radically reinterpreted Cicero's taxonomy of style, reorienting the classification scheme towards profundity of thought rather than elegance of phrase; this in turn, he argues, made Longinian principles especially attractive to Reformers.[108]

Further, Till maintains that Longinus, with his emphasis on simplicity, became "the most important authority for the sublimity of the Bible" – a guiding principle for Reformers, as described by Calvin himself:

> [T]he sublime [haut] mysteries of the kingdom of heaven have for the greater part been delivered with a contemptible meanness of words [paroles contemptibles]. Had they been adorned with a more splendid eloquence, the wicked might have cavilled, and alleged that this constituted all their force. But now, when an unpolished simplicity, almost bordering on rudeness, makes a deeper impression than the loftiest flights of oratory, what does it indicate if not that the Holy Scriptures are too mighty in the power of truth to need the rhetorician's art?[109]

A few decades later, Lutheran theologian Matthias Flacius, whose two-volume *Clavis Scripturae Sacrae* (1567) would be foundational to Protestant Biblical hermeneutics, claimed similarly that the Bible presents distinctive qualities of simplicity and succinctness that defy the Ciceronian association of grandeur with stylistic elegance. According to Flacius, these qualities are epitomized in the *fiat lux* – "let there be light" – at the opening of Genesis, which Longinus famously cites in *Peri Hypsous*.[110] As these Protestant theologians echoed Longinus's views about simplicity of phrase and profundity of thought, they would be instrumental in disseminating Longinian principles.

Moreover, the predominant Protestant view of justification and regeneration may also have created a favourable environment for the reception of Longinus, facilitating a major shift in literary theory. Under the influence of Calvin, many Protestants (particularly in the sixteenth century, before the rise of Arminianism) believed that the will was so depraved that virtue was not possible through human effort, but only through miraculous transformation by the Holy Spirit – a belief analogous to Longinus's core principle that sublimity was an irresistible force channelled through an ennobled mind, rather than cultivated through skill. Thus, while English theorists in the first part of the sixteenth century had traditionally emphasized the role of technical craft, towards the end of the century, English theory approached a model more reflective of Longinian thought, emphasizing innate genius and underscoring the miraculous, divine basis of great poetry. This shift is especially apparent in the sublime poetics of Sidney (and sometimes echoed by Puttenham), while taking on striking new emphases in the seventeenth-century in the work of Chapman and Milton.

The Sixteenth Century: Sidney and Puttenham

Like the *Discorsi*, Sidney's *Defence of Poetry* has traditionally been considered a work of neo-Aristotelian poetics, reflecting the Horatian maxim that the purpose of literature was "to delight and to teach," and like Du Bellay's *Défence*, a work with civic and nation-building aspirations; but the treatise also betrays a perceptible sublime subtext. While Sidney himself, like Tasso, Ronsard, and Du Bellay, never cites or discusses Longinus directly, his theory is full of Longinian vocabulary, speaking of literature as "ravishing," carrying readers to the "heights," and being "unresistible" – concepts similar to Longinian *ekstasis* and *ekplexis*.[111] Notwithstanding its continuity with earlier epic theory, Sidney's appropriation of the sublime incorporates a particularly Protestant notion of "greatness," reflecting an overlap between Longinian theory and the Calvinist doctrine of the regenerated will.

Although the *Defence* discusses literature in general rather than focussing specifically on epic, Sidney does create a particular emphasis on the heroic poem. In a systematic discussion of various genres, Sidney reserves his longest and most impassioned defence for "Heroical" poetry, which he names the "best and most accomplished kind."[112] Several of the most notable instances of sublimity appear in this section, while even in his general discussion of poetry, Sidney borrows a disproportionate number of examples – including several of those discussed below – from epic poetry, citing Homer, Virgil, Dante, Ariosto, and Tasso. This suggests that epic was foremost in his mind, as he developed an idiosyncratic discourse on poetics that periodically taps into the sublime.

In the *Defence*, Sidney, like Longinus, Tasso, and Du Bellay, emphasizes that inborn genius is a prerequisite to producing great writing. Qualifying his discussion of technique, he stresses that poetry "must not be drawn by the ears; it must be gently led, or rather it must lead; which was partly the cause that made the ancient-learned affirm it was a divine gift, and no human skill: since all other knowledges lie ready for any that hath strength of wit; a poet no industry can make, if his own genius be not carried into it."[113] By putting poetry in the subject position, as that which "must lead," Sidney assigns poetic ability ontological status, defining it as a dynamic force that moves independently through the author – comparable to Tasso's discussion of *meraviglia*. He anthropomorphizes poetry, describing it as an animate force with its own potency rather than a passive art to be learned as a craft. According to Sidney, the force of innate poetic ability manifests itself most clearly in a poet's emotional vehemence, or *energeia*: it is poetry's "forcibleness" – the authentic display of emotion, an inborn trait – that gives life to poetry, not that "honey-flowing matron Eloquence apparelled, or rather disguised, in a courtesan-like painted affectation." In fact, Sidney reserves some of his harshest criticism for poets whose verse lacks emotional vigour, and who have no "divine" gifting. Their minds are so dull and blind to "immortal beauty," he writes, that they instead feature "certain swelling phrases" that show no evidence that the poet can actually "feel those passions."[114]

On this point, Sidney is echoed by Puttenham, who similarly highlights the role of "divine instinct" manifested in the "excellency of nature and complexion" that the poet displays. Even in the discussion of the figures, forms, and rhetorical principles of style that dominates much of *The Arte of English Poesie*, Puttenham nonetheless underscores the psychology of the poet that underlies principles of style, noting, for instance, that a writer's language "showeth the matter and disposition of the writer's mind … and his inward conceits be the mettle of his mind, and his manner of utterance the very warp and woof of his conceits."[115] Although both theorists offer considerable discussions of *techné*, each emphasizes that *techné* will remain fruitless without a noble mind preceding and guiding it.

Sidney, however, puts a more distinctive twist on the idea that concepts must predominate. In linking poetic genius to the nobility of the poet's mind and emotions, he sounds much like Longinus, but he "reforms" the representation of authorial nobility by attributing it to the "heavenly Maker of that maker," who overcomes the poet's inherent weakness. To Sidney, poets are limited by an "infected will," which otherwise "keepeth us from reaching unto it" – that is, literary excellence. But the inspiration of the "heavenly Maker" has a regenerating effect that surmounts these limitations, "when with the force of a divine breath [the poet] bringeth things forth."[116] In effect, Sidney mirrors Longinus in subordinating a poet's technical skill; but in emphasizing human depravity, he presents a slightly more deterministic view of how that individual participation actually operates.

Further highlighting the importance of the author's conceptual power, both Sidney and Puttenham echo Tasso's discussion of *enargeia/evidenza* and Longinus's discourse on *phantasia* in their discussion of the poetic imagination – ultimately emphasizing that the end of literary greatness lies in rapture.[117] For Sidney, it is not "rhyming and versing that maketh a poet … But it is that feigning notable images of virtues, vices, or what else."[118] In arguing that poetic greatness is located in the noble "image of each action" an author creates, Sidney probably shaped the belief of Puttenham, who likewise argues that the key to great poetry is the ability to see with the mind's eye, to produce "beautiful visions" that reflect grand truths and concepts. Puttenham writes: "the fantastical part of man (if it be not disordered) [is] a representer of the best, most comely, and beautiful images or apparances [*sic*] of things to the soul and according to their very truth." For Puttenham, such images are attractive not for their lavish verbal representation but for their profound representation of reality. Ultimately, Puttenham notes that poets producing such images have access to a power and knowledge beyond human reason: their minds have been [divinely] "illuminated with the brightest irradiations of knowledge," a thought highly characteristic of Longinus.[119]

In this concept of the poetic imagination, Sidney further heightens the emphasis on the emotional and transformative (and redemptive) potential of poetry. Noting that "the lofty image of such worthies most inflameth the mind with desire," Sidney describes the epic poet accomplishing what even a philosopher cannot, creating images that "inflame" the mind, mysteriously drawing the reader right into the centre of a scene to "strike," "pierce," and "possess the sight of the soul."[120] Sidney's great poet has powers of imagination that aim not only to teach but to stupefy, to produce an effect much like Longinian *ekplexis*. Sidney, though, again inflects his theory with a characteristic emphasis on regeneration, for great poetry not only astonishes and overwhelms but produces "heart-ravishing knowledge" that transforms a person to the very core.[121] Poetry aims to "draw us to as high a perfection as our degenerate souls … can be capable of" – a transformation described in terms of ascending to the heights.[122] Literature thus plays a role in God's redeeming purposes, stunning the audience and leaving readers unable to resist divine grace channelled through poetry – Sidney's Protestant version of the sublime.

In the conclusion to the *Defence*, Sidney extends the Longinian and Tassoan principle that the sublime derives from authorial nobility, suggesting, in a more characteristically Reformed idea, that innate nobility is also prerequisite for the *reader* to experience poetic rapture. In the final paragraphs, Sidney lambasts ignoble readers, those "born so near the dull-making cataract of Nilus" that they "cannot hear the planet-like music of poetry," and those who have "so earth-creeping a mind that it cannot lift itself up to look to the sky of poetry."[123] In this critique, Sidney echoes the conclusion to *Peri Hypsous*, where Longinus laments that so many people "neglect the development of their immortal part" through addiction to vice, thus losing the ability to rise above their "mortal and foolish nature," which cannot appreciate the sublime.[124] In referring to the ignoble mind as "earth-creeping," Sidney recalls the dualistic distinction that Longinus makes between the "immortal," noble mind of the poet, and the "earthly," low-born mind of the philistine – echoing the metaphorical distinction drawn by the apostle Paul between those saved to eternal life and the unregenerate who are enslaved to the flesh.[125] While Longinus's comment is ambiguous and could refer to author or reader, Sidney refers explicitly to the reader – in effect, reversing the literary principle that poetry creates nobility. In Sidney's definition, not only does poetry instruct or reform a reader – although it can play a role in that end – but the very ability to appreciate and benefit from it requires the person to have already been psychologically and spiritually transformed.[126]

Like Tasso, then, Sidney invokes the sublime to challenge multiple tenets of Horatian approaches to literature: namely, that the quality of literature depends primarily on rhetorical training and technical skill, and that its highest ends are its abilities to delight, teach, and move to virtue. Sidney imagines epic moving beyond (without dismissing) these principles. Instead of viewing literature as a primarily horizontal interaction between the poet and his own (developing) ability, and the poet and society, Sidney, like the Longinian Bruno, represents greatness as a matter of vertical communication between society and the divine, in which divine power, not the poet, initiates this transcendence.

The Seventeenth-Century Sublime: Chapman and Milton

In the early seventeenth century, Chapman continues the Protestant sublime poetics of his predecessors, serving as an important, if neglected theorist of epic. Chapman is one of the first English scholars known to have read Longinus. In the introduction to his translation of the *Iliad* and *Odyssey*, Chapman offers a lengthy, impassioned defence of the sublimity of Homer that furthers his predecessors' assessment of the sacred aims of epic. Though he is known for his justification of difficult poetry – for making the somewhat elitist refusal to cater to the "profane multitude" – Chapman is not defending stylistic complexity but conceptual complexity, ultimately aligning with the Reformers' preferences for high thoughts. Believing that complexity best reflects divine truth, Chapman, stresses that great literature derives from "heaven-high thoughts of nature" and "radiant and light-bearing intellect," which should not be oversimplified for the sake of transparency without nuanced content.[127] Moreover, Chapman maintains not only his predecessors' admiration for the divinity of poetry, but also Sidney's Reformed emphasis on the radical transformation of the poet – emphasizing the miraculous dimensions proper to sublimity and to epic.

Celebrating the mythical elements of the *Odyssey*, Chapman defends the poem's divine greatness and, in doing so, brilliantly uses Longinian thought against itself, to reject the Greek theorist's famous criticism of the classical poem. Longinus famously maintains that, compared to the truly sublime *Iliad*, the *Odyssey* lacks vehemence, force, and thus sublimity, that it "wanders in the realm of the fabulous and incredible," such that "the mythical element predominates over the real."[128] To argue for sublimity in the *Odyssey*, Chapman first compares the poem to the vast "ocean, with all his court and concourse," recalling Longinus's comparison of a sublime work to the natural phenomenon of the "sea, often flooding a vast expanse of grandeur."[129] But he ultimately extends the comparison to that which supersedes nature: he pronounces Homer's lines to be "of such command to the voice of the Muse that they knock heaven with her breath, and discover their foundations as low as hell."[130] Within the *Odyssey*'s fantastic, mythical representations that Longinus finds distasteful, Chapman sees an incomparable power beyond what exists in the natural world. Just as Longinus carefully distinguishes sublime poetry for its "elevation," its defiance of limits, and expansive speculation, Chapman maintains that the majesty of the *Odyssey* lies in its possession of these very fantastic, supernatural qualities – its imaginative powers of ascent.

Following Sidney and Puttenham in his emphasis on the mysterious origins of sublime poetry, Chapman sustains his defence of the transcendent qualities of the *Odyssey* by highlighting the miraculous ennobling and transformation of Homer himself, once again invoking Longinus against himself. While Longinus stipulates that a sublime poet must have an ennobled mind, Chapman denies that Longinus has actually experienced the poetic rapture that he had theorized as crucial to the sublime poem:

> But this proser Dionysius [Longinus], and the rest of these grave and reputatively learned ... are not in these absolutely divine infusions allowed either voice or relish. For ... he that knocks at the gates of the Muses *sine Musarum furore* is neither to be admitted entry nor a touch at their thresholds, his opinion of entry ridiculous, and his presumption impious. Nor must poets themselves ... presume to these doors without truly genuine and peculiar induction, there being in poesy a twofold rapture (or alienation of soul, as the abovesaid teacher [Ficino] terms it): one, *insania* ... The other is *divinus furor*, by which the sound and divinely healthful *supra homini naturam eregitur, et in Deum transit* ... Of the divine fury ... your Homer hath ever been both first and last instance, being pronounced absolutely *ton sophōtaton, kai ton theiōtaton poiētēn*; the most wise and most divine poet.[131]

To Chapman, Longinus is merely a critic of occasional wisdom, "a man otherwise affirmed grave, and of elegant judgement," who yet lacks the proper sublime spirit to write sublime poetry himself, and therefore to recognize reliably, where he sees it, which poetry was actually sparked by *"divinus furor."*[132] In citing Ficino, Chapman echoes as well Longinian principles of poetic inspiration and rapture, particularly in pointing out that the sublime author must lose his very identity, becoming *"supra homini naturam eregitur, et in Deum transit* [elevated above the nature of man, and become God-like]." Chapman's point recalls Longinus's claim that "writers of genius ... are above all mortal range ... Sublimity lifts them near the mighty mind of God," so that the sublime poet must inevitably and mysteriously be transformed from mortal to superhuman.[133] In claiming such status for Homer, but not Longinus, Chapman does to Longinus just what Longinus had done to Plato: he uses Longinus's ideas of the sublime poem to defend the poem Longinus denounced, just as Longinus used Plato's own writing to defend the poetry that Plato criticized. Chapman thus maintains that sublime poets like Homer experience not only transformation and reformation, as Sidney and Puttenham had stressed, but alienation of self. To gain an infusion of divine power, Chapman's sublime poet must lose his/her identity: "dying to self" – recalling the biblical metaphor of regeneration.[134] More than his predecessors, Chapman highlights the extraordinary and disruptive nature of the process by which heroic poetry is composed – featuring the sobering costs and gains of writing.

Another English writer to develop a theory of sublime heroic poetry – and undoubtedly the greatest – is Milton. While Milton has long been recognized for his knowledge of Longinus (and, of course, achievement of sublime poetry), scholars have not fully considered his conscious application of Longinian theory to epic poetry in his own literary theory, or how he sustains his predecessors' emphasis on transcendence.[135] At least twenty-five years before the first edition of *Paradise Lost*, Milton incorporates a discourse on the sublime into discussions of poetry in several of his prose works, particularly *Reason of Church Government* (1641), *An Apology for a Pamphlet* (1642), and *Of Education* (1644). And like Sidney, Milton creates particular emphasis on epic throughout his poetic theory – and even more so, for underlying his entire theory is a lifelong ambition to write a great epic poem.

In his prose works, Milton describes epic poetry in a manner consistent with several principles of Protestant sublimity, particularly its emphasis on simplicity of style, complexity of thought, and emphasis on the pursuit of divine ends. In *Of Education*, Milton's depiction of poetry follows a discussion of rhetoric, "taught out of the rule of Plato, Aristotle, Phalereus, Cicero, Hermogenes, Longinus":

> To which poetry would be made subsequent, or indeed rather precedent, as being less subtle and fine, but more simple, sensuous, and passionate. I mean … that sublime art which in Aristotle's Poetics, in Horace, and the Italian commentaries of Castelvetro, Tasso, Mazzoni, and others, teaches what the laws are of a true epic poem, what of a dramatic, what of a lyric, what decorum is, which is the grand masterpiece to observe. This would make them soon perceive what despicable creatures our common rhymers and play-writers be, and show them what religious, what glorious and magnificent use might be made of poetry, both in divine and human things.[136]

While Longinus seems only incidental in this passage, a minor figure of rhetoric preceding the more important discussion of poetry, Milton's discussion bears the marks of Longinian sublimity. Immediately after referring to Longinus, he describes poetry as "that sublime art," pronouncing the latter to be "simple, sensuous, and passionate," rather than "subtle and fine," and thus emphasizing conceptual and emotional profundity as the essential elements of great literature.

Further, in charging the aspiring poet to demonstrate "what religious, what glorious and magnificent use might be made of poetry, both in divine and human things," Milton stresses that poetry has its *telos* in the divine. He echoes this principle in the *Reason of Church Government*, theorizing that one of the poet's most important objectives should be to "celebrate in glorious and lofty hymns the throne and equipage of God's almightiness," and stating that the final function of poetry is to depict "whatsoever in religion is holy and sublime."[137] Milton thus highlights poetry's vertical function of pointing the reader towards an understanding of the ineffable, which implicitly precedes its civic function.

Like his predecessors', Milton's concept of divine epic depends greatly on an ennobled author, though with an important variation. While Chapman's discussion of sublime poetry (extending Sidney's) emphasizes the alienation (or regeneration) of the sublime heroic poet, Milton's theory of epic poetry emphasizes the author's agency in the process of achieving it – not his or her agency in maintaining literary technique, but in aspiring for unity with God. Milton features an interpersonal dynamic to sublime poetry – a connection between the poet and God based on a combination of divine favour and human agency that is consistent with his Arminian beliefs. Milton's sublime poet acquires his/her abilities, which are "the inspired gift of God rarely bestowed," through "devout prayer to that eternall Spirit who can enrich with all utterance and knowledge, and sends out his Seraphim with the hallow'd fire of his Altar, to touch and purify the lips of whom he pleases."[138] In this description of divine inspiration, Milton goes beyond Sidney and Longinus himself – he is not content to identify a godlike agent who initiates poetic impulses, but notes that the poet actually makes a personal entreaty to receive divine power. And by referring to the Seraphim who "purif[ies] the lips," Milton identifies the agent behind sublime poetry as the very angel that touched the lips of the prophet Isaiah, who showed humility and deference in submitting to this purification.[139] By implication, Milton identifies an element of self-subordination in the process of poetic gifting, a recognition of personal weakness and dependence on divine mercy and restoration that precedes poetic inspiration. In effect, Milton distinguishes his concept of divine inspiration from the passive reception of divine favour by portraying it instead as an active pursuit of the divine that involves subordination of self – a model that will later shape his own concept of sublime heroism in *Paradise Lost*. Like Sidney's sublime poet, Milton's must be reformed and transformed through an *ekstatic* process of divine inspiration; but his sublime poet may actually choose to initiate that divine rapture.

While Renaissance theorists, then, differed in their nuanced applications of Longinus, the sublime consistently proved central to the theoretical development of heroic poetry from sixteenth-century Italy to seventeenth-century England. As diffused, Longinian thinking maintained a striking emphasis on heroic poetry's connection to the divine – from Ronsard's poet facilitating direct communication with God, to Tasso's transported poet performing a heavenly vocation, to Sidney's miraculously regenerated poet transporting readers, to Milton's active poet striving to participate in the celebration of divine magnificence. Inspired from above, heroic poetry aimed to rapture – and regenerate – the soul, an art not only of human ability and with civic aims, but of divine means and with eternal purpose. As epic poets transferred theory into practice, they continued to use the sublime to feature the sacred emphasis and transcendent aims of epic poetry. And this quest for transcendence, as we will see in the next chapter, becomes a distinctive marker of Tasso's *Gerusalemme liberata*.

2 The Tassoan Sublime and the Counter-Reformation: Charisma and Romance in the *Gerusalemme liberata*

In the previous chapter, I suggested that Tasso's concept of *meraviglia* in his poetic theory aligns with Longinus's concept of sublime *ekplexis*, reflecting the idea that poetry should move readers to astonishment. Whether influenced directly or indirectly by *Peri Hypsous*, Tasso's theory sometimes resists (though does not reject outright) the neo-Aristotelian and neo-Horatian principles that art should promote civic duty and virtue first and foremost, principles that had been explicitly endorsed during the Council of Trent, and that Tasso himself was expected to follow.

This tension between civic duty and *meraviglia* not only extends to the *Gerusalemme liberata*, but presents an even greater set of difficulties for Tasso's epic poetry than it does for his theory. Modelled in large part on the *Aeneid*, the *Liberata* conforms at least superficially to core Virgilian values – absolute devotion to religious and political authority. The *Liberata* might not reflect the nationalistic ambitions of the *Aeneid* per se, but the poem depicts in the Christian crusade a Virgilian fervour for a conquest that is simultaneously spiritual and political, bent on unifying followers of God under a single institutional authority.[1] The *Liberata*'s central protagonist, "pio Goffredo," is an obvious imitation of "pius" Aeneas and just as heartily devoted to the army's joint religious-political ambitions. The poem thus suggests an obvious binary between the devout Christian knights as servants of God, church, and state, and their implicitly faithless opponents.

Yet, while the poem seems to endorse Goffredo, its dedication to the forms of civic duty represented in the poem is less clear. Throughout the *Liberata*, many characters find themselves in the position of sublimity ("attonito," "stupefatto," or "conquiso") that Tasso celebrates in the *Discorsi*, even when they are directly defying the army leadership. An especially problematic occurrence appears in the thirteenth canto of the *Liberata*, when the knight Tancredi attempts to secure wood from a nearby forest, enchanted by the pagan sorcerer Ismeno to prevent the Christians from rebuilding their siege tower. After withstanding the initial horrors of the forest that had frightened away the knights preceding him, Tancredi, too, fails to accomplish his civic duty to destroy the enchantments, yielding in astonishment before an apparition of his beloved Clorinda. As a mysterious voice emerges from a tree, now oozing blood, the narrator exclaims, as if sharing the knight's condition, "Oh meraviglia!" (13.41.2).[2]

Tancredi's paralysis before the marvel raises questions about the kind of heroism Tasso celebrates, and more generally, about the relative role of institutional authority in epic. Although Tancredi had been harshly rebuked by army leaders in the previous canto for pursuing his passion for Clorinda over his military duty, the poem offers little condemnation of his inability to complete his mission, despite what might be considered a crucial failure of duty. Tasso leaves the individual failure unresolved, as the knight simply re-emerges to defeat Argante in canto 19. Alongside episodes such as Rinaldo's notorious romance with Armida, this passage appears to condone the defiance of spiritual authority in his poetry, while disregarding the expectations for art established by the Council of Trent.[3] How can we reconcile Tancredi's apparently condoned action with the kind of civically responsible heroism that Tasso celebrates elsewhere – and that we see in Rinaldo's successful destruction of the wood's enchantments in canto 18? To what extent does the poem support its representations of religious leaders and institutions?

These passages have sparked an ongoing controversy over the *Liberata*'s attitude towards Church authority in the Counter-Reformation context. Traditionally, the poem has been read as an endorsement of institutional Church authority; most scholars, including David Quint, maintain that the *Liberata* critiques the immoral pleasures of the romance episodes, validating Church authority and post-Tridentine aesthetics.[4] But a substantial minority, citing the many morally ambiguous events in the poem, contest this reading. For Jo Ann Cavallo, Tasso validates the pleasures of the romance passages to produce a subversive critique of the Counter-Reformation's "repression of individual freedom."[5]

In an effort to reconcile the two competing dimensions of the poem, Annabel Patterson identifies a strain of Neoplatonism underlying Tasso's poetry and theory that, she argues, unites a neo-Aristotelian emphasis on moral education with the enchantment of the romance episodes, making ethical development an inevitable consequence of the pursuit of beauty.[6] The *Liberata* certainly owes much to Neoplatonic concepts of beauty, and this scholarly approach does help to reconcile Tasso's competing commitments to civic virtue and pleasure in several instances, but it does not account for some of the most significant tensions. For instance, in the enchanted wood episode, the conclusion that Tasso equates morality with beauty may be overly idealistic, for Tancredi's aesthetic response to Clorinda peaks when his civic duty fails.

Tasso's use of the sublime, however, represents an additional means of integrating the poet's duelling commitments to civic morality and pleasure, though it remains almost entirely neglected in studies of the *Liberata*.[7] In my view, the sublime is even more central to Tasso's poetry than it is to his poetic theory, where it has been more frequently acknowledged. As we saw in the previous chapter, Tasso argues that poets must take rhetorical and stylistic risks to produce great, sublime poetry, so that they might resemble "al supremo Artefice" and participate in "la sua divinità."[8] Tasso extends this principle in the *Liberata* to celebrate apparent *moral* risks for the higher spiritual purpose (expressed in the *Discorsi dell'arte poetica*) of promoting "true religion."[9] Following the *Discorsi*'s claim that the aim of poetry is sublimity, Tasso incorporates into the *Liberata* spiritual and aesthetic principles from the rich tradition of Catholic mysticism (discussed in greater detail below), a tradition devoted to the pursuit of individual unity with God in strikingly Longinian terms.

In the *Liberata*, Tasso depicts several heroic characters in a similar pursuit of divine communication, but in very different contexts – when Goffredo leads the Christian army into battle, when Tancredi fails at his assigned task in the enchanted wood, and even when Rinaldo and Armida first meet. By celebrating the pursuit of sublimity in each passage, despite vastly different moral implications, Tasso produces a complex but generally unified heroic model that subordinates each hero's *apparent* aims – including Goffredo's pursuit of civic duty and Tancredi's pursuit of delight – to the greater goal of sublime connection to God, a model that aligns with Longinian theory. For while Longinus notes that sublimity has an ethical dimension as well as a dimension of pleasure and delight, he does not equate the sublime with either. For Longinus, sublimity transcends virtue, and at times it may produce feelings of terror that inhibit pleasure.[10] As Tasso invokes Longinus's concept of the sublime as an overarching component of his model of heroism, he qualifies the respective roles of civic-building and pleasure-seeking in epic, emphasizing that spirituality itself is first and foremost an individual and interior matter.

More specifically, Tasso represents two complementary types of heroes who participate in the sublime, each aspiring passionately for divine ascent, but in different ways. The first type includes *charismatic* figures such as Goffredo, who pursue God directly. Driven by their own virtuous, passionate, individual pursuit of divine truth, charismatic figures mediate divine glory in their appearance and actions, captivating their viewers and generating a condition of sublimity in those who see them. The second type includes *romantic* heroes such as Tancredi, who become ravished by the sublime image of a beloved, and pursue its sublimity, ultimately towards God – though they pass through an experience of *abjection*, a negative or dark sublime, that qualifies the role of pleasure in the experience. Thus, Tasso superficially associates charismatic heroes such as Goffredo with the pursuit of civic virtue, and romantic heroes such as Tancredi with the pursuit of pleasure and delight, but has each of these respective pursuits give way to the greater aim of transcendence.[11] With their mutual orientation towards the heightened emotional experience of the sublime, these two heroic modes are not in competition, but, rather, are both oriented towards divine union. In this way, Tasso reconciles epic's civic-building and pleasure-seeking functions by ranking both beneath the greater pursuit of sublimity and divine truth – the foundation, for Tasso, of spiritual authority and the final aim of epic poetry. What Tasso questions, I would suggest, is not Christianity itself, but the Church's claims to absolute power over individual spirituality and attempts to control aesthetic representation.[12]

In the sections below, I first consider principles of Renaissance aesthetic theory – including the mystical tradition – that may have contributed to Tasso's concept of sublime heroism, before looking at the charismatic and the romantic modes of heroism in the *Liberata* itself.

Tasso and Longinus: Catholic Aesthetics and the Heroic Passions

As suggested in the previous chapter, Tasso's own aesthetic sense seems to have been naturally oriented towards sublimity, though the sublime likely felt somewhat illicit in light of his well-known religious scruples. Tormented by worries for his own orthodoxy, he not only feared persecution, but turned himself over to inquisitors to have his faith examined. It seems likely that his own investment in spirituality was genuine, even as he struggled with its implications for his poetry.

One particularly complicating factor in Tasso's beliefs was his patronage by the Este family. Tasso's primary benefactor, Alfonso II d'Este, was the son of Renée de France (1510–74), a correspondent of John Calvin who turned the Este court into a refuge for Protestants. Renée eventually brought several of her visitors and the Este court under the condemnation of the Inquisition, particularly for the possession of prohibited material (ultimately, under compulsion, she would half-heartedly recant, before returning permanently to France).[13] Although Alfonso and his brother Luigi remained Catholic, with Luigi appointed Cardinal by Pope Pius IV, the religious persecution may well have been weighing on the family when Tasso came to join them several years after their mother's departure. It seems likely that this family legacy coloured Tasso's impression of the power that religious institutions held, leaving him with a latent fear in his younger years that grew into a paranoid terror of persecution as he grew older. In several respects, Tasso appears to have been caught between competing demands – a need for official affirmation of religious faith that conflicted with strong personal aesthetic tastes and spiritual instincts. Though he feared Church authorities, he also seems to have resented and wrestled against this very fear, particularly in his art.

Since his early years, Tasso, without leaving his faith, retained interest in a concept of the Longinian sublime, even as it was at odds with the Council of Trent's assertion of absolute spiritual authority, and far-reaching guidelines for art. In particular, the work of certain Italian rhetoricians and theologians – including several with associations to the tradition of mysticism – created a favourable foundation for Tasso's reception of the sublime without requiring him to renounce his faith. Mysticism, thriving in Italy and Spain during the sixteenth century, was centred on the individual pursuit of an experience of connection to God, not unlike Longinus's description of *ekplexis*. Giuseppe Mazzotta acknowledges Tasso's interest in the mystical tradition, including his adoption of an emerging aesthetic theory that endorsed the power of sacred images and art to connect believers to God.[14] As a movement, moreover, mysticism was seen in Italy and Spain as a direct threat to Counter-Reformation authority, who feared its emphasis on individual spiritual experience as a threat to the power of the Church.[15] Tasso, I suggest, found in mysticism both theological and aesthetic principles that overlap with Longinus's theory of the sublime, and that allowed him to uphold his commitment to the Christian faith and most Catholic doctrine. In short, Tasso would endorse the mediating role of sacred objects – including the role of sublime art – in facilitating the pursuit of God. Through mysticism, Tasso created a distinctive theory of heroic passion that celebrates the individual experience of transcendence.

In the most striking area of overlap between mysticism and sublimity, several theologians and aesthetic theorists associated with the Catholic tradition of mysticism emphasized the role of strong, sublime passions in divine knowledge, divine union, and spiritual transformation – often recalling Longinian principles.[16] Costanza Barbieri notes that mysticism fuelled an entire artistic movement during the sixteenth century designed to help viewers make the leap from earthly beauty to divine glory.[17] The work of painter and printmaker Federico Barocci (1535–1612), for instance, was acclaimed in its own time as "beyond the reach of human praise," for it "enraptures, tears asunder, and gently transforms us."[18] San Filippo Neri (1515–92), Italian priest and founder of the Congregation of the Oratory, was well known for his lavish artistic images of himself in ecstasy before the Virgin Mary, his art leading the viewer to make a "leap from the material to the immaterial," from mundane beauty to divine glory.[19] Such approaches to art were believed to offer a way to foster spiritual development that was more intuitive, less abstract, and ultimately more accessible than doctrinal arguments.

These artists' approaches reflect an idea supported by Longinus (and reflected in the *Liberata*) that the pursuit of ecstasy itself can be cognitively transformative, drawing the human mind outside its natural limits and towards a transcendent form of divine knowledge. While scholars have often emphasized how the sublime represents the limits of the knowledge – arguing that the experience of the sublime is marked by confusion and bewilderment, as it certainly can be – Stephen Halliwell argues that the sublime is a transformative mode of "deep cognition."[20] In the phenomenon Longinus calls *ekstasis* – a process of transport in which the mind literally "stands outside itself" – the sublime inherently draws the individual into a higher form of knowledge, or truth. In effect, the sublime, which Halliwell calls an "echo … of infinity," transmits flashes of intuition that connect the subject with a metaphysical vision of the grandeur of the cosmos. By following these intuitions, cooperating with the "compulsions" of ecstasy, the subject reaches beyond the material realm and towards a transcendent reality.[21] The Longinian sublime is therefore distinct from pure mania or lunacy, for participation is not compulsory, but involves a willing, conscious, enthusiastic embrace of the cognitive intuitions of the sublime. As Giordano Bruno does with his "frenzied hero," Tasso would make the passionate pursuit of sublime intuition an implicitly heroic action – and the final measure of epic heroism. And in keeping with mysticism's emphasis on the power of visual imagery, Tasso frequently represents sublime intuitions being channelled visually, through the cognitively transformative sight of an inspiring leader or beloved other whom the hero pursues directly towards God.

As early modern aesthetic theorists celebrated the pursuit of passionate cognitive transformation as a route to divine transcendence, they also supported Tasso's concept of risk – particularly as they subordinated moral teaching to the generation of heightened emotional experience. As Bette Talvacchia notes in a discussion of carnality in religious art, both writers and visual artists might actually "take advantage of a certain [moral] license in order to startle the reader back into serious consideration of [spiritual matters]." Because these artists believed that the appreciation of beauty of any kind would promote spiritual contemplation and divine ascent, some held, however controversially, that "sexual seduction was accepted as part of earthly experience" and, in artistic form, represented a "path of movement toward transcendence."[22] In an aesthetic theory that might be seen elsewhere as spiritually destructive, such artists saw morality itself as separate from spirituality, and subordinated it to the aims of divine exaltation. In privileging rapture over ethics, they invoked the principle of risk so central to Longinus, who subordinates the "rules" of literature to the high thoughts and passions that mediate the sublime.

Without taking the theory quite as far as some theorists, Tasso likewise adapts the principle of risk to the moral realm in his epic. Creating a challenge to church authorities, he uses features of sublimity and mysticism to show that spiritual practice is fundamentally individual, and that spiritual heroism is too transcendent, too dependent on intuition, to align completely with the codes of civic and moral authorities. In the *Liberata*, accordingly, as both charismatic and romantic heroes participate in the pursuit of the divine, they follow the intuitive promptings of the sublime, pursuing a spiritual quest over civic authority where the two conflict.

Charismatic Heroism: Goffredo, Clorinda, Sofronia

Tasso's "charismatic" heroes reflect each of these sublime features of Catholic aesthetic theory – heightened passion, intuition, risk, transcendence. Charisma, as intimated earlier, is the power of the sublime channelled through a human persona that brings viewers into a condition of enthrallment or captivation.[23] As Max Weber originally theorizes, charisma is akin to an aura: "a certain quality of an individual personality by which he is set apart from ordinary men and treated as endowed with supernatural, superhuman, or at least specifically exceptional powers or qualities."[24] These elusive qualities produce magnetic effects on viewers, drawing them into the person's field of forces, in a process much like Longinian *ekstasis*.[25] While charisma can have profoundly negative associations, as developed in other poems, in Tasso's epic, it serves as the basis by which numerous characters encounter representations of the divine and experience spiritual transformation. In channelling divine experience, charisma represents the sacred power of mediating objects between viewers and God, as a key component of Tasso's Catholic theology.

In the *Liberata*, Tasso uses charisma and charismatic heroism to represent a direct channel to divine power and divine beauty; charismatic heroes miraculously inspire and draw viewers towards a state of passionate and zealous love for God. In doing so, the *Liberata* reflects Weber's concept of charisma as notoriously independent (the "potential creativity of the human spirit"), operating in tension with existing institutional frameworks and often undermining them.[26] In the *Liberata*, charismatic heroes sometimes act outside civic norms and against traditional authority figures, pursuing divine aims above earthly ones where the two conflict. Thus, Tasso distinguishes charismatic heroes from the Virgilian hero centred on *pietas*; rather than pursuing civic duty, charismatic figures primarily follow the promptings of sublime intuitions, leading them to truth and transcendence.

Although a number of characters in the *Liberata* embody charismatic heroism, I focus on Goffredo, Clorinda, and Sofronia, all of whom are patently virtuous but driven by a passion for transcendence that is independent of institutional moral codes. In Goffredo, Tasso focusses especially on the role of risk-taking, considering the heroic potential of the leader's defiance of prudence and traditional authority structures when an instinctive passion for transcendence call for it. In Clorinda, a pagan, Tasso emphasizes the heroic value of pursuing sublime intuitions, highlighting the transformative and redemptive potential of pursuits that fall (perilously) outside traditional moral and religious authority. And in Sofronia, finally, Tasso considers the impact of charisma on viewers of art themselves, outlining their role in responding to representations of the sublime. Emphasizing the divinely oriented nature of charismatic heroes, Tasso ennobles the sublime as an appropriately heroic subject for epic poetry, challenging Tridentine suspicions about the role of extreme emotional experience in art.

Goffredo

In general, critics associate "pio Goffredo" with anything but charisma. He is most often seen as Tasso's quintessential figure of Virgilian *pietas* – of obedience, reason, and prudence, as Tasso himself proposes in the *Allegoria del Poema*. Yet the authenticity of the *Allegoria* has always been in question;[27] and while Goffredo is hardly the most appealing character to the poem's readers, he does manifest significant charisma when interacting with other characters. In the first canto, he calls the recent deeds of his own army "meravigliose" (1.26); correspondingly, Tasso describes him as having a noble passion or "zelo" for the divine, reflected in his charismatic appearance, which implicitly channels the divine glory to which he aspires. When a contingent of Christian soldiers rebels in canto 8, Goffredo instantly stops the rebellion with his mere presence ("di celeste / maestà, vi risplende un novo lume [strange light gleams (from his face) with heavenly grandeur]") and his voice ("né come d'uom mortal la voce suona [his voice does not sound like a mortal's]"), thereby leaving Argillano, the leader of the rebellion, "attonito e conquiso [astonished and conquered]" (8.78; 81).[28]

In canto 20, Goffredo makes another particularly charismatic appearance, as before the final battle, "[n]ovo favor del Cielo in lui riluce / e 'l fa grande ed augusto oltra il costume; / … altro che mortal cosa egli rassembra [new grace from Heaven shines in him and makes him great and majestic beyond the norm … [H]e resembles something beyond mortal]" (20.7.3–4, 8). In his final speech to the troops, Goffredo leaves those listening enraptured, an example of sublime *ekplexis*:

> è rapito ogn'uom ch'ascolte.
> Come in torrenti da l'alpestri cime
> soglion giú derivar le nevi sciolte,
> cosí correan volubili e veloci
> da la sua bocca le canore voci.   (20.13.4–8)

[every man listening was ravished, as when snow melts in torrents from an alpine peak, so the melodic sounds streamed swiftly and smoothly from his mouth.]

In this scene, Goffredo's ability to create amazement – among enemies and followers alike – is due less to his virtue than to his commitment to risk-taking, as he must defy the prudence and deference to civic norms that he is typically known for. In Goffredo, Tasso offers a qualified depiction of civic virtue, celebrating the passionate pursuit of divine transcendence even where such pursuits put communal interests at risk.

As early as canto 2, Goffredo's charisma stems from his risky approach to war, when the Egyptian ambassador Alete enters the Christian camp to request a truce, and warns Goffredo of all he stands to lose in pursuing the crusade. Acknowledging the charismatic effects of Goffredo's campaign, Alete argues that to continue would be imprudent:

> [G]ran cose in picciol tempo hai fatte
> [...]

> esserciti, città, vinti, disfatte,
> superati disagi e strade ignote,
> sí ch'al grido o smarrite o stupefatte
> son le provicie intorno e le remote.   (2.66.1, 3–6)

[great things you have done in little time … armies, cities, conquered, defeated, hardships and unknown territory overcome, such that the provinces near and far are dismayed or stunned.]

He adds: "'Ben gioco è di fortuna audace e stolto / por contra il poco e incerto il certo e 'l molto [It's the game of the brash and foolish to trade what is certain and great for what is uncertain and small]'" (2.67.7–8). In these statements, Alete affirms Goffredo's ability to astonish and amaze all who see him, but suggests that in continuing, he is transgressing civic duty by risking the lives of his men in a hazardous campaign. Dependent as it is on unreliable allies (the Greeks) and an unstable food supply, Alete insinuates that the campaign recalls Icarus's foolhardy flight: "ai voli troppo alti e repentini / sogliono i precipizi esser vicini [for rash flights that go too high / a steep fall is usually near]" (2.70.7–8). Goffredo's response is telling. While we might expect him – given his divine authorization – to deny that any risk actually exists, he acknowledges the uncertainty of the campaign, implying that God's "giudizi occulti [mysterious decrees]" (86.2) may include earthly failure, but "né mai grave ne fia per fin sí degno / esporre onor mondano e vita e regno [it is not so bad, for such a worthy end, to risk worldly honour and life and kingdom]" (2.82.7–8). Goffredo does not take lightly the prospect of losing life, honour, and dominion – not only his own, but his troops' – yet he insists that the risk is necessary (2.86–7). Tasso thus contrasts Goffredo's campaign with one of the *Liberata*'s likely models – the Israelite conquest of the Promised Land recorded in the Book of Joshua, in which those alert to the conquest are similarly stunned and dazed by the marvels enacted by the campaigning army.[29] While Joshua repeatedly encourages the Israelites to be courageous, because God has already delivered their enemies into their hands, Goffredo embodies a less assured kind of heroism, one that demands hazarding the success of civic purposes for the greater goal of divine transcendence. In this early scene, Tasso emphasizes that Christian heroism cannot finally be measured by the success of civic ventures, however significant they may be, but is revealed in the divine orientation and noble passions of the heart.[30]

Goffredo's justification for risk in canto 2 illuminates a problematic episode in canto 11, in which Tasso defends the charismatic heroism of even imprudent risk – and the defiance of civic authority – when motivated by noble passions oriented towards the divine. During the Christian army's first attack on Jerusalem, Goffredo leaves off his heavy protective armour to allow more freedom of movement, in an attempt to win the *Mural Prize* awarded to the first soldier to scale the walls of a besieged city. This decision is typically read as an act of rare imprudence, and thus a blemish on Goffredo's character, appropriately challenged by Raimondo as an act that jeopardizes the entire army:

> [C]he ricerchi tu? Privata palma
> di salitor di mura? Altri le saglia,
> ed esponga men degna ed util alma
> (rischio debito a lui) ne la battaglia.   (11.22.1–4)

> [What are you seeking? A personal prize for climbing the wall? Let others climb, and expose a less worthy and useful soul (a risk another must take) in battle.]

Since Raimondo is Goffredo's wisest counsellor, his argument against the "rischio" of climbing the wall might be read as a morally authoritative command that Goffredo is wrong to defy. Thus, Anthony Esolen notes that Raimondo is right to confront Goffredo for a blameworthy action to "fulfill an ill-advised vow" that the captain had made to God.[31] Although Goffredo fails in his aim of being first up the wall, I suggest that Tasso justifies the captain's attempt as an act of charismatic heroism that draws his troops into a comparably sublime condition – where they themselves are overwhelmed by the expression of courage they see and feel inspired to imitate it.

As Goffredo moves ahead with his plan, in an attempt to fulfil his vow, he inspires the Christian soldiers to follow his bold lead and embrace the hazards of fighting with renewed vigour: "da i ciechi perigli al rischio aperto / fuori se n'esce e sua virtú dichiara [open to unseen dangers and risks / (they) rush out to display their virtue]" (11.39.3–4). The soldiers thus imitate Goffredo, responding to his charisma. The army's intrepid charge severely shakes the Saracen side, inflicting heavy losses and causing many to flee (11.49); and although Goffredo incurs a calf wound that requires him to back down, his injury is miraculously healed (11.24.8).

Moreover, as Goffredo returns quickly to battle, his risky action both creates terror in the Saracens ("corse lor per l'ossa / un tremor freddo e strinse il sangue in gelo [a cold tremor runs through their bones and turns their blood to ice]"; 11.76.7) and intensifies his charisma, inspiring his troops to fight with renewed intensity:

> Conosce il popol suo l'altera voce
> e 'l grido eccitator de la battaglia,
> e riprendendo l'impeto veloce
> di novo ancora a la tenzon si scaglia.   (11.77)

[The soldiers recognize the lofty voice and the excited battle cry, / and quickly regaining momentum / yet again leap into the clash.]

In its sublime effects, Goffredo's risky decision creates unity among the troops, bringing them into the same zealous condition of devoted service as their captain – much more effectively than if Goffredo had more prudently held back. In featuring the stirring and unifying effects of his charismatic heroism, Tasso implicitly affirms the captain's privileging of his vow to God over his responsibility to the earthly wisdom of Raimondo. Rather than an act of foolish disobedience to the authoritative voice of a human, Goffredo's venture represents for Tasso a praiseworthy ability to take a major risk – achieving an astonishing feat. Thus, Tasso exposes Raimondo's counsel as excessively cautious, and an interference by earthly authority that threatens the expression of Goffredo's heroism. He presents adherence to the ethical codes of local custom as a secondary objective that must give way to sublimity, when inspired by an interior sense of divine calling.

In this episode, furthermore, Tasso transforms Goffredo's decision into a commentary on the problems of Counter-Reformation authority itself: Raimondo's cautious preference for conformity to official norms over openness to the intuitive promptings of God might be read as a critique of the leadership's preferences for moral security and established law over the flourishing of divine poetry. Just as Raimondo's words threaten to hinder Goffredo's charismatic heroism and the sublimity and glory it produces, Church leaders' fearful regulation of artistic creativity could threaten the flourishing of sublime art, their fears hampering the potential of artists to channel divine power and passion through their poetic vocations. In contrast to Raimondo, Goffredo figures a faith-based poetics courageous enough to take risks and achieve greatness, as well as a heroic ethos that, though not devoid of virtue, is willing to defy the prudence and dutiful obedience normally attributed to him. Cavallo has argued that Tasso uses the romance of Rinaldo and Armida to implicitly critique the Counter-Reformation hierarchy embodied by Goffredo.[32] Tasso's representation of Goffredo in canto 11 suggests that the captain himself may represent a subtle critique of Catholic authority in the domain of literary aesthetics, an example of the sublimity that authorities would keep out of poetic art. By depicting the Christian army profiting from Goffredo's intrepid military campaign, and redeeming the commander's seemingly "imprudent" battle strategy against the more reserved advice of Raimondo, Tasso espouses a heroic approach to art that sometimes sacrifices civic virtue for more elusive, and sublime, spiritual purposes.

Clorinda

Clorinda's brand of charismatic heroism offers an important complement to Goffredo's, for even though she does not convert to Christianity until late in the poem,

Tasso still represents her as a producer of *meraviglia* and, thus, a charismatic channel of divine power. While Clorinda's charisma is often distinctively erotic, unlike Goffredo's, Tasso links the two figures through their shared, heroic pursuit of divine rapture and the sublime, which allows both to become mediators of its elusive power. While I will reserve discussion of Clorinda's charismatic attractiveness to Tancredi for a later section, I focus here on the particular features that make her charismatic, and on her heroic orientation towards the intuitive promptings of the sublime.

Clorinda is noble and independent – both standard features of charisma. Tasso describes her as "d'alta sembianza" (2.38.2) and of "grande ... regal sembianza" (45.6), signifying the innate nobility of mind and passion – the Longinian *megalophués* – that orient her towards higher order pursuits, towards transcendence.[33] In Clorinda's independent spirit and passionate pursuit of sublime intuitions, Tasso shows – subversively – that participation in divine rapture can begin outside the confines of Roman Catholicism, though leading, as her conversion indicates, to a form of Christian faith. In Clorinda, Tasso highlights the importance of noble passions over and above that of obedience to earthly religious figures.

Clorinda's openness to sublime passion and intuition is apparent not only in the scene of her conversion, but in her earlier appearances in the epic. In canto 2, Clorinda is the only pagan to respond to the sublimity emanating from the figure of Sofronia, who offers herself as a martyr to King Aladino to spare the entire Christian community from slaughter, before she (Clorinda) goes on to release Sofronia from an unjust death sentence. Because of her orientation towards intuition rather than custom, she alone is able to see and value the truth of Sofronia's innocence over her allegiance to King Aladino's political authority, and she alone challenges him. Clorinda, gazing in wonder ("mira"; 2.42) at the sight of Sofronia tied to the stake, falls into a state of astonishment on hearing the account of her noble self-sacrifice:

> Stupissi udendo, e imaginò ben tosto
> Ch'egualmente innocenti eran que' due.
> Già di vietar lor morte ha in sé proposto,
> Quanto potranno i preghi o l'armi sue.
> Pronta accorre a la fiamma, e fa ritrarla.   (2.44.3–7)

[Listening, she was stupefied, and realized suddenly that those two were equally innocent. Already she has resolved to herself to prevent their death, to the extent that arms and prayers were able. Quickly she rushes to the flames, and puts them out.]

In these lines, Tasso emphasizes an important relationship between the sublime, knowledge, and heroic action. It is doubtful that the backstory recounted by the

guards could have provided Clorinda with certain knowledge of the pair's innocence, and indeed the verb "imaginare" suggests supposition rather than logical
deduction. Implicit in these lines, rather, is a mysterious and intuitive sort of
knowledge channeled by the sublime, to which Clorinda is attuned. Given that her
sublime condition (being "stupissi") coincides with her resolution to act ("Già …
ha in sé proposto"), it would seem that Clorinda's sublime condition serves as the
agent of her immediate action. In effect, Tasso represents sublime passions – stupefaction, amazement – as enabling rather than paralysing, prompting an intuitive
recognition of truth that motivates heroism.

Thus, while her conversion scene in canto 12 is sometimes viewed as a dramatic
transformation from proud, noble warrior to humble and unassuming Christian,
I suggest that Tasso creates a consistency to her character. Before and during her
conversion, Clorinda maintains the charismatic tendency to follow the intuitive
promptings of the sublime, which implicitly channel divine power, even when
they lead her to disagree with the civil authorities to whom, as a Muslim, she
would typically submit.

Attuned as she is to the intuitive promptings of the sublime, Tasso depicts
Clorinda as free to take important risks that pave the way for her conversion, a
conversion he depicts as fulfilling the noble passions that drive her. As we find in
the scene just preceding her death, Clorinda is inspired to destroy the siege tower
by a powerful intuition, an overwhelming impulse to "fèr [create] meraviglie"
(12.3.1). Even while this impulse leads to her death, Tasso defends her desire
as a noble and productive orientation for the sublime. In relating her scheme to
Argante, Clorinda confesses that "un non so che d'insolito e d'audace / la mia
mente inquieta: o Dio l'inspira / o l'uom del suo voler suo Dio si face … vogl'io
che questo / effetto segua, il Ciel poi curi il resto [Something – I know not what –
bold and unusual, unsettles my mind, either God inspires it, or man makes himself
his own god of his own volition … I want to follow this plan, let Heaven take
care of the rest]" (12.5).

As I mentioned in chapter 1, the phrase "un non so che" is an important
marker of the sublime, denoting an emotional experience with the ineffable.
The phrase had been used earlier by Dante and Petrarch, but Tasso was probably the first Italian to incorporate the phrase as frequently as he does – it
appears seven times in the *Liberata* alone, several to be discussed later in this
chapter – and the first writer to use the phrase consistently to denote the rise
of a particular emotional state resembling the sublime. Praz notes that Tasso is
likely responsible for transmitting the phrase to the French, whose corresponding version, "je ne sais quoi," becomes part of the formal vocabulary of the
sublime.[34] Nicolas Boileau adopts the phrase in his landmark edition of *Peri
Hypsous* to signify the ineffable, namely the gap between the human imagination
and the concept of infinity, rooted in the divine, that the imagination seeks (the
Romantics would later focus on the emotional longing for infinity prompted by

this gap).[35] Tasso, laying groundwork for both Boileau and the Romantics, uses "un non so che" to signify an individual's emotional response to the presence of sublime energy – in Clorinda's case, a powerful instinctive divine knowledge. This knowledge is intuitive and uncertain – Clorinda herself admits not knowing whether it comes from God or idolatry – but, in the context, Tasso portrays it as implicitly divine, in preparation for salvation via Christian conversion.

Thus, especially since the decision leads directly to conversion, Tasso celebrates Clorinda's choice to follow the intuitions of the sublime as an independent and heroic pursuit of spirituality – a pursuit that occurs off script, outside prescribed channels. And while she is fatally wounded by the unknowing Tancredi, Tasso represents her request to be baptized in the same terms, as the heroic result of a "new spirit" ["novo un spirto"] that invades her upon request (12.65.5): she thereby becomes "di gioia trasmutossi" (12.68.6), transformed by "fé, di carita, di speme [faith, charity, and hope]" (12.65.6). In Tasso's depiction, as she looks with passionate longing towards heaven – "gli occhi al cielo affisa [eyes fixed on heaven]" (12.69.3) – Clorinda anticipates a sublime union with the God that she sought and followed from the beginning without knowing it, by following the "thrillingly charged energy" of the sublime that points her towards faith and transformation.[36] And as she remains attentive to intuitions of divine truth and purposeful in following them at any cost, she retains the same nobility and independence she had shown in earlier episodes.

In this subversive depiction, Tasso broadens the representation of Christian heroism to suggest that the foundation of spiritual transformation is an orientation towards the noble passions of the sublime, not dutiful participation in prescribed institutional codes. Clorinda's unusual route to faith thus signifies the potential of the sublime to prompt spiritual transformation where earthly authorities lack the power to inspire. And in celebrating a heroine whose salvation occurs outside the guidance of Church authority structures, Tasso again assigns to epic the task of celebrating the passionate pursuit of sublimity over and above civic ends.

Sofronia

Like that of Clorinda and Goffredo, the portrayal of Sofronia complicates the traditional place of morality in epic. As a noble figure of Christian martyrdom, Sofronia, even more than Goffredo or Clorinda, might initially be read as exemplifying the ethical principle that art should teach, delight, and move the viewer to virtue; yet even Sofronia's virtue is ambiguous. Not only does she interfere with (King Aladino's limited) powers of civic authority, but she tells an outright lie about having burned the Virgin Mary statue. Sofronia, too, epitomizes the independent pursuit of divine truth – over and above the demands of local civic codes – that typifies charismatic heroism.

While tied to the stake in the public view, moreover, Sofronia supplies the basis of Tasso's most focussed examination of the relationship between virtue and artistic representation itself. In her courageous, passionate aspiration for divine glory, she becomes a public spectacle who captivates her observers and points them towards the divine alongside her. As Praz suggests, Tasso implicitly associates Sofronia with *sublime* art (and what Stephen Jaeger would call charismatic art) by suggesting that her appearance reflects the Longinian principle of dissimulation. For Sofronia is careless of her beauty ("sua beltà non cura") (2.14.3), and "Non sai ben dir s'adorna, o se negletta, / se caso od arte il bel volto compose [It's hard to tell if she adorns herself or neglects herself, if chance or art forms her lovely face]" – effects that enhance her appeal all the more (2.18.5–6).[37] Importantly, Sofronia does not simply delight those who see her; she captivates and transports, provoking the kind of strong emotion feared and censored in artistic representation by many Counter-Reformation authorities. In examining viewer reactions to the emotions Sofronia elicits, Tasso represents the response to sublime art as a choice resting with the viewer, suggesting that it is up to the individual to decide whether and how to be caught up in its mystique.

In perceiving Sofronia as a work of sublime art, Clorinda becomes a heroic *reader* of the sublime who, as we have seen, participates in its transformative power. Conversely, in King Aladino, who resists Sofronia's charisma, Tasso presents the rejection of sublime art as a plausible but unheroic decision. Following Sofronia's sacrificial confession of guilt, the king is left momentarily in the condition of the sublime: "[a] l'onesta baldanza, a l'improviso / folgorar di bellezze altere e sante, / quasi confuso … quasi conquiso [by her open boldness, by the sudden flash of her noble and sacred beauty, nearly confounded, nearly overcome]" (2.20.1–3). Yet even while the king is clearly affected by the force of her persona, Tasso portrays the confrontation as a battle, Sofronia's charisma mysteriously attacking him and allowing him agency in the way he responds. At the most critical moment, Aladino overhears Sofronia blissfully anticipating the prospect of divine rapture, saying to Olindo beside her: "lieto aspira a la superna sede. / Mira 'l ciel com'è bello, e mira il sole / ch'a sè par che n'inviti e ne console [aspire joyfully to the heavenly seat. Look at the sky – how beautiful it is; look at the sun that seems to invite you to it, and to console you]" (2.36.6–8). In several of the most fascinating lines of the poem, Tasso describes Aladino's response: "Un non so che d'inusitato e molle / par che nel duro petto al re trapasse. / Ei presentillo, e si sdegnò; né volle / piegarsi, e gli occhi torse, e si ritrasse [An 'I know not what', strange and soft, seems to invade the king's tough exterior. And he had a foreboding upon recognizing it, and became disdainful; he refused to yield, and tore his eyes away, and left]" (37.3–6). The text is explicit: Aladino himself senses the power of the sublime – "un non so che" – just as Clorinda feels before her scheme to destroy the siege tower. The sensation reflects an intuitive knowledge of the truth of Sofronia's innocence that would be transformative if he followed it. In the context of this passage, the source of this ineffable power is again clearly divine, channelled through Sofronia as she aspires for an experience of divine rapture. But Tasso makes clear that the king chooses not to follow it – he depicts the struggle between Aladino and this ineffable "non so che" in terms of physical warfare, as if the mysterious force actually attempts to pierce the king's skin while he stubbornly "refused to give in," literally wrenching his eyes and body away as if performing a feat of great heroic strength. In a scene that anticipates Satan's rejection of the sublimity of Eve, the passage affirms sublimity (and charisma) as universal forces, as Longinus suggests, while on the other, indicating that those caught up in sublimity remain free to respond or not to the presence of the divine implicit in it.[38]

Arguing for the importance of free will to the *Liberata*, Sarah van der Laan notes that Tasso "create[s] more room [compared to Homer] for human agency to shape history," a tactic that opposes the Reformation deemphasis on human freedom.[39] I would suggest that Tasso's emphasis on choice, while indeed supporting post-Tridentine theology against Calvinist theology, simultaneously resists post-Tridentine views of art. In Aladino's resistance of Sofronia, Tasso seems to suggest that forced resistance to a sublime poetic work reflects a narrow-minded, stubborn, and reprehensible choice – a denial of noble instinct and an adamant rejection of divine glory itself. In Sofronia's example, Tasso both encourages his own readers to choose the path of Clorinda, who, in allowing herself to be moved by the divine power of sublime art, participates heroically in its transformative power, while critiquing those who would reject it as prideful. And without denying the captivating potential of sublime art, he emphasizes that the overpowering effects of such artistic representations need not be feared, as they allow – indeed, require – viewers to make the choice for themselves.

But when sublimity leads to transcendence, Tasso makes this choice a surpassingly noble one. In the depictions of Sofronia, Goffredo, and Clorinda, he features a passionate orientation towards divine transcendence as the highest form of heroism worthy of celebration in epic. To participate in its divine power, the epic hero must have Goffredo's venturesome spirit, even at the cost of civic obedience, and Clorinda's willingness to pursue elusive intuitions, which may appear outside the realm of traditional religious instruction. And as Sofronia's example suggests, the divine presence channelled through sublime poetry invites readers to cooperate heroically in its mysterious power, not as pawns but as active participants. While all of these figures pursue forms of civic virtue in their own way – through their self-sacrificial offerings for their communities – Tasso represents civic-mindedness as being overshadowed by the zealous pursuit of God and passionate desire for divine rapture that inspires their heroic actions and produces charismatic effects on observers. This divine orientation, moreover, represents Tasso's ultimate defence against the claim that sublime poetry fostering deep delight is inherently corrupting. To read and write great poetry, indeed, may require a degree of moral risk, but to accept that risk, Tasso suggests, is to open poet and reader alike to the transformative power of the sublime, representing a reward far beyond the value of sober moral instruction.

Romantic Heroism: Tancredi, Rinaldo, Armida

If Tasso's charismatic heroes represent a challenge to Church authority, particularly over aesthetics, the romantic heroes of the *Liberata* emphasize how sublimity can advance individual faith outside institutional bounds. As suggested above, the pursuits of charismatic heroes are inextricably interwoven with those of romantic heroes, both of whom respond with passion to the intuitive promptings of the sublime. Compared to charismatic heroes, however, romantic figures (namely Tancredi, Rinaldo, and Armida) follow an indirect route to the divine, through the captivating (and sublime) image of the beloved. Rather than operating independently, they first become stunned by the sublime sight of the beloved, whose beauty offers a reflection of divine glory. Thus, they follow the promptings not of spiritual leaders, but of a sublime image, towards heaven.

In the *Liberata*, romantic heroism appears to celebrate the pursuit of individualistic, often immoral pleasures, yet in each instance, Tasso features a crucial interruption to these pleasures that qualify their role in the epic. Each romantic hero suffers an either temporary or permanent loss of the beloved that Tasso figures as a state of abjection – a violent and dark form of sublimity that terrifies and drives the individual *inside* the self in a state of withdrawal.[40] In Kristeva's psychoanalytic theory, abjection overlaps with the sublime, but takes the more specific form of a horrified crisis of identity (the likes of which Tasso must surely have been personally familiar, given his well-known spiritual and psychological struggles). In effect, the subject of abjection senses a threat to the coherence of the sense of self, and withdraws internally in a condition of fear and self-loathing.[41] As Tasso portrays it, this violent separation of self is a necessary precedent to the full experience of sublimity, akin to the contrition and self-denial that accompany repentance and spiritual renewal.[42] As romantic heroes become aware of their own faults and weaknesses, Tasso uses a concept of abjection to feature the importance of confronting the effects of evil, in preparation for unity with God. Private interests such as the pursuit of pleasure, he suggests, play a role in heroism and in the divine aims of heroic poetry; but, like civic virtue, they too must be subordinated whenever they interfere with the greater pursuit of transcendence.

In his portrayal of divine reconciliation, Tasso thus establishes the need for violent separation from the self as a crucial step, and a hallmark of the sublime in his epic – a feature that later poets from Du Bartas forward, and especially Spenser and Milton, will emulate in their portrayals of divine judgment. Following Tasso, these poets will use similar terms to explore the psychological extremes of spiritual transformation, from metaphysical terror to rapturous divine union.

Tancredi

For much of Tasso's epic, Tancredi in particular seems to be more of an anti-hero than a heroic figure, as his obsessive love of Clorinda often becomes an illicit and dangerous distraction from his spiritual and civic duty to the crusade, which he only truly performs in cantos 18 and 19. Douglas Biow argues, for instance, that in the enchanted wood episode, Tancredi's dedication to the image of Clorinda represents an illicit desire for privacy and individual pleasure, one that is simply incompatible with the communal emphases of epic.[43] And Tancredi's desire for Clorinda does prompt several noteworthy failures of civic duty, both before and after he accidentally kills her; even the narrator recurrently suggests that Tancredi's love is a weakness (1.9.4; 13.46.3–4). At the same time, neither Tancredi's failures of civic duty nor the narrator's comments need be interpreted as a definitive critique of Tancredi's heroism, for they suggest not weakness, but humility and ardent passion – the seeds of strong spirituality if rightly directed.

Tancredi finds in his romantic attraction to Clorinda a route to divine transcendence that Tasso implicitly affirms as heroic, despite the resulting diversions from battle. In canto 1, Tancredi's initial sight of Clorinda produces the telling condition of *meraviglia* – the same condition Clorinda hopes to *create* just before destroying the siege tower. As we saw, her interest in *meraviglia* at that moment reflects an intuitive recognition of God at work, eventually leading to her conversion. Tancredi's response to Clorinda has similarly redemptive potential, since, even at this stage of the poem, she represents a channel to the divine. In this key scene, Tasso writes:

> Egli mirolla, ed ammirò' la bella
> Sembianza, e d'essa si compiacque, e n'arse.
> Oh meraviglia!
>
> [...]
> Ma l'imagine sua bella e guerriera
> tale ei serbò nel cor, qual essa è viva
> e sempre ha nel pensiero e l'atto e 'l loco
> in che la vide, esca continua al foco.   (1.47.5–7, 48.5–8)

[He gazed at her, and admired her beautiful aura, which delighted him and he burned for her. Oh *meraviglia!* … the beautiful and warlike image was seared onto his heart, such that it lives on, and he always holds it in his thoughts, and the act and place in which he saw her continue to fan the flame.]

Tancredi is clearly in the condition of the sublime, falling into paralysis and intense passion, a condition repeated upon Clorinda's reappearance in canto 6, when he becomes "attonito quasi e stupefatto [nearly stunned and stupefied]" (6.28.5), as if transported from his earthly existence. Halliwell refers to this kind of transport as an *ekstatic* loss of self, in which ecstasy creates in the individual a transformed consciousness that points him/her towards a higher, intuitive form of knowledge.[44] In his attraction to Clorinda's *image*, which burns and lives on in him as a life-giving presence, Tancredi becomes drawn to the natural sublimity channelled through her, a power that draws her – and him with her – towards the transcendence she herself achieves in canto 12. Although Clorinda's beauty clearly poses a significant impediment to Tancredi's chivalric duties, Tasso implies that the knight's passion for her divine image may be in direct service to his spiritual development.

Following Clorinda's death at the end of canto 12, Tasso implies Tancredi's heroism as the knight recovers from his deep despair (I will return to the despair itself below). As Tancredi prays to Clorinda, he defies the admonition of Pietro, a figure of civic authority, who condemns the knight's love of Clorinda – "A Dio rubell[a] [rebel of the Lord]" – and urges the knight to "frena / quel dolor [restrain that grief]" (12.88.7–8), so he can return to military duty (12.87.4). In this defiance, Tasso represents Tancredi taking a significant risk necessary to spiritual renewal and transformation. In effect, Tancredi must choose between the voice of civic authority and the charismatic authority of Clorinda, just as Goffredo, in his decision to fight as an infantryman, had to choose between the moral admonition of Raimondo and the kind of intuitive promptings of the sublime described by Longinus. Although Tancredi momentarily restrains his grief, in obedience to Pietro, he makes no more than a nominal attempt. At last, he completely ignores the advice to forget Clorinda, praying to her with a passion devoid of the "restraint" advised by Pietro:

> Lei nel partir, lei nel tornar del sole
> Chiama con voce stanca, e prega e plora,
> Come usignuol cui 'l villan duro invole
> Dal nido i figli non pennuti ancora,
> Che in miserabil canto afflitte e sole
> Piange le notti, e n'empie i boschi e l'ora.
> Al fin co 'l novo dì rinchiude alquanto
> I lumi, e 'l sonno in lor serpe fra 'l pianto.   (12.90)

[With the setting and rising of the sun, he calls to her with weary voice, praying and weeping, like the nightingale – whose still unfeathered chicks the hardened peasant would not spare in the nest – which wails its mournful song alone through the night, filling the woods and air. At last, towards sunrise he closed his eyes, and sleep crept in among the tears.]

Despite his apparent weakness, even Tancredi's prayer is depicted as heroic. An intense, night-long struggle that leaves the knight exhausted, his prayer involves the agency, courage, and struggle of a warrior. Instead of fighting another person, however, Tancredi fights against himself: against his human frailty, which longs for sleep, and against the agony that leaves him longing for death, being prompted by a greater desire for the sublime presence of Clorinda. And as he hopes "che dal Ciel forse l'ascolta [that from Heaven she might hear him]" (12.89.8), he performs an act of desperate faith that is no less heroic for its display of noble passion for her sublime beauty.

As Clorinda responds in a vision to Tancredi's prayer, Tasso confirms the nobility of the knight's captivation by her sublimity. Clorinda not only encourages Tancredi to admire her as a channel of divine union but suggests that his ongoing efforts to do so fulfil a spiritual duty: "Mira come son bella e come lieta, / fedel mio caro, e in me tuo duolo acqueta / ... vagheggiarai le sue bellezze e mie [See how lovely and happy I am, my faithful dear, and still your sorrow through me ... gaze on His beauty and mine]" (12.91.7–8; 92.8). In acknowledging Tancredi's *faith*fulness in love, Clorinda invokes a concept frequently portrayed in the Bible in metaphors of military heroism to suggest that his extended devotion to her before and after death was an expression of spiritual heroism.[45] Her use of the verb "vagheggiare" also has significant sublime connotations, as it indicates both an act of gazing in admiration, as well as a sense of longing for that which surpasses understanding and representation – a culmination of the very sublime pursuit Tancredi had been performing.[46] Clorinda urges Tancredi, moreover, to continue to aspire for unity with her and with God as his ultimate end: "Faccian l'anime amiche in Ciel soggiorno [may our souls dwell together in heaven]" (12.99).

Tancredi's love of Clorinda, as a shadow of the divine, thus represents a heroism that supersedes civic pursuits. Although Tasso later celebrates Tancredi's acts of military heroism, namely the defeat of Argante and the defence of Raimondo (19.1–26; 20.84–6), such acts appear to be secondary to Tancredi's passionate, heroic, though indirect pursuit of the divine through his love of Clorinda. For Tasso, the sequence is crucial: only once noble passions are in place, and the individual aspires to heavenly pursuits, can that individual properly pursue civic ends.

While this portrayal of ennobled love effectively subordinates the pursuit of civic morality to the pursuit of the sublime, Tasso uses Tancredi's condition of abject despair to qualify the role of pleasure in this process. In the passage leading up to the knight's prayer to Clorinda, Tasso portrays his agony over her death in terms of abjection to feature the knight's discontentment with his own sense of self, his need to identify the "evil" part and reject it in preparation for spiritual transformation. The most explicit form of Tancredi's evil emerges in his ruthless slaughter of the disguised Clorinda earlier in the same canto – a fault that previous criticism has not sufficiently acknowledged. In this scene, Tancredi attacks Clorinda with a cruelty and brutality entirely inappropriate to a Christian knight, even for a poem intently imitating Homeric and Virgilian models. The vocabulary describing Tancredi's efforts suggests an illicit wickedness that he must be rid of: he fights with "l'orgoglio" and "l'ira," and becomes "geloso" (12.53) – embodying the three most serious sins, according to Dante; troublingly, Tancredi also "gode and superbisce [rejoices and exults]" as he watches Clorinda fall dead by his feet (12.58). In contrast, when he fights Argante in canto 19 – the highest-stakes combat of the war – he shows far more deference and humility in his victory. But during his fight against Clorinda, Tasso features a pre-repentant state, for the knight behaves no differently than the bloodthirsty Argante, fighting with a brazenness that even the narrator criticizes as "folle" (12.58.7). Thus, Tasso suggests that the knight needs to undergo a process of self-examination and contrition to properly loathe the evil within him, before he is finally ready for divine reconciliation and access to God's presence.

Although Tancredi, during his abjection, condemns himself only for the specific action of killing Clorinda, Tasso seems to represent the consequent psychological fracture as a broad repentance for sin. His psychological fracture is evident throughout his long lament, particularly in the lines: "Temerò me medesmo; e da me stesso / sempre fuggendo, avrò me sempre appresso [I will fear myself; and always fleeing from myself, will always have myself nearby]" (12.77.7–8). The repeated reflexive pronouns, "me medesmo," "me stesso," and "me sempre appresso," suggest that Tancredi sees his own identity as two-fold, with a "self" with which he identifies, and a separate, evil "Other" that is also inextricably attached to him and has acted through him, whose presence he fears and hates. He accuses the hated "Other" at length of evil, desperate to be rid of it:

> Io vivo? Io spiro ancora?
> […]
> Ahi! Man timida e lenta, or ché non osi,
> tu che sai tutte del ferir le vie,
> tu, ministra di morte empia ed infame,
> di questa vita rea troncar lo stame?　　　　　　　　(12.75.1, 5–8)

[Do I live? Do I still breathe? … Oh! Hand, timid and slow, how can you not dare – you that know everything about wounding lives, you, evil and infamous minister of death – to cut off this guilty life at the root?]

In these lines, Tancredi repeatedly turns against himself, speaking to his hand as if isolating part of himself, and attempting to quarantine the evil of which he wishes to be rid. In recalling a radical biblical metaphor, Tancredi both recognizes the extent of his own evil, as well as his helplessness to separate himself from it – which prompts him to turn to Clorinda in prayer and finally receive implicit absolution (12.91; 98).[47]

In featuring the agony of Tancredi's abjection, Tasso portrays the pursuit of sublime beauty as a treacherous quest that brings the individual to the brink of death, involving much more than an embrace of private delight, but also suffering, sacrifice, and painful transformation en route to divine glory. At the same time, he offers sublimity itself as a supremely powerful catalyst of repentance and transformation. Only Tancredi's passionate desire for Clorinda could make him desperate enough to undergo so drastic an experience, recognize and reject his own sin, and thus be able to soar to the heights, to Clorinda, and to God.

The significance of Clorinda's sublime image to Tancredi illuminates the episode of the failed arboricide. By the time Tancredi enters the enchanted wood, he has already reoriented his desire for Clorinda towards heaven and aspires for that end himself. Rather than suggesting that his love remains immature, or that his failure to destroy the enchantments represents a serious heroic failure, Tasso implies that Tancredi is justified in neglecting his civic duty to re-enact Clorinda's destruction. For in those enchantments, he perceives the same sublime force that connects him to heaven, and in responding to the promptings of the sublime, Tancredi performs an act of spiritual heroism that trivializes his civic failings.

As Tancredi prepares to destroy the wood's enchantments, he hesitates upon reading the enigmatic inscription on the cypress tree, an event that places him, once again, in the condition of the sublime. As he hears a melancholic sound among the trees, "un non so che confuso instilla al core / di pietà, di spavento e di dolore [a confused 'non so che' fills his heart with compassion, with fear and with pain]" (13.40.7–8).[48] With this telltale phrase, Tasso takes us back to Aladino's and Clorinda's responses to the intuitive promptings of the sublime – Aladino fighting his intuition, remaining uninfluenced by Sofronia's divine charisma, and Clorinda embracing her intuition to attack the Christians, thereby finding opportunity for salvation. In invoking "un non so che" as Tancredi senses the tree's enchantment, Tasso establishes that the knight's dilemma consists of whether to heed the intuitive promptings of the sublime – and the divine source it channels – or to stubbornly resist it; and in choosing the former, he follows the noble path of Clorinda herself.[49] This is not to suggest that Tasso sees the apparition as anything but demonic in origin, or that the act of destroying it would be inherently immoral, but that he validates Tancredi's perception and prompting of conscience as having spiritual significance.

For as Tancredi sees the apparition of Clorinda, he is vividly reminded of the abjection that had already purged him of evil – the very evil he senses he is about to repeat in destroying the tree. The description recalls depictions of Tancredi's emotional state in canto 12:

> E, dentro, il cor gli è in modo tal conquiso
> Da vari affetti che s'agghiaccia e trema,
> E nel moto potente ed improviso
> Gli cade il ferro, e 'l manco è in lui la tema.
> Va fuor di sé: presente aver gli è aviso

> L'offesa donna sua che plori e gema,
> Né può soffrir di rimirar quel sangue,
> Né quei gemiti udir d'egro che langue.   (13.45)

[And within, his heart is so conquered by a variety of emotions that he trembles and turns to ice, and in a powerful and sudden movement he drops his sword, and fear is absent in him. He is transported outside himself: appearing before him is his wounded lady pleading and moaning; he cannot bear to gaze on that blood again, or to hear those troubled groans languishing.]

With this response to the image of Clorinda, Tancredi not only renews the same strong passion he had shown previously – he is "conquiso / da vari affetti [conquered by various emotions] – but he is also transported "fuor di sé [outside himself]" once again. And with the images of Clorinda's death, he returns to the very horrors he had experienced in canto 12, reminded of his great guilt for the ruthlessness of which he had already repented.

In Tancredi's perception, to finish destroying the tree would be to repeat that same ruthlessness, thereby invalidating his act of repentance and jeopardizing the transformation he had begun. He cannot destroy her image without invalidating the passionate love for Clorinda that ties him to heaven, thereby severing that tie. For Tancredi to destroy those enchantments even in service to the community would be to risk destroying his soul, and in heeding the attack of conscience, he performs an honourable refusal to fall back into a desperate spiritual condition.

For Tasso, Tancredi's "weakness in love" is not so much a fault as a heroic strength, marking the importance of the individual pursuit of spirituality. Creating space for individual perception and conscience, Tasso allows Tancredi's failed arboricide to stand without criticism to counterbalance the civic and communal pursuits celebrated elsewhere – thus reiterating that the proper end of heroic poetry is the passionate pursuit of divine transcendence, which must never be subordinated even to civic virtue. Yet, as he falls short of the demands of civic authority, Tancredi's failure to destroy the forest also signals the limits of risk. For Tasso, risk undertaken to life, limb, and even moral standing is warranted if in service to a divine aim, but *not* risk perceived to jeopardize the channel to the divine.

Rinaldo

Compared to Tancredi, Rinaldo is more obviously "heroic" in the traditional sense. In his rejection of Armida and destruction of the enchanted wood, Tasso evokes a neo-Virgilian mode of heroism oriented towards acts of civic virtue, *pietas*, and community over individual pleasures, a mode that thereby surpasses the incomplete heroism seen in Tancredi. Or so it seems. Although Rinaldo may "succeed" where Tancredi "fails," Tasso offers an alternative way to read the knight's heroic endeavours, whereby the two knights' actions complement each other and work towards the same ends of sublime transcendence. In doing so, they form an implicit, alternative spiritual community based on individual conscience rather than authoritative rule of law, a community that Tasso consistently disguises for its obviously subversive implications.

Rinaldo may not perfectly fit the heroic narrative of the romantic hero, for his obsession with Armida is clearly not a direct source to the divine. Nonetheless, his basic heroic narrative – his transformation from pleasure-seeking lover to valiant, divinely oriented warrior – demonstrates the same orientation towards material sublime beauty, leading him to transcendence. He is first captivated by the sight of Armida (16.19). On separating from her, he falls into a very brief phase of abjection, marked by intense grief and shame over his own sin (18.9). He then receives a renewed vision of sublimity during his solitary vigil – the sight of natural earthly beauty (18.12) – which inspires him to break out of his grief and undergo spiritual transformation, becoming purged of the "vecchio Adam" (18.14.8). This, in turn, leads to divine union: "ventillar nel petto e ne la fronte / sentia gli spirti di piacevol òra [in that delightful hour, he feels spiritual breath on his chest and face]" (18.15), and as the "rugiada del ciel [dew of heaven]" falls upon his clothes, it "induce in esse un lucido candore [endows them with an immaculate luster]" (18.16). The poet thus compares Rinaldo's transformation to the rejuvenation of a dying flower, describing the transformation as an infusion of divine power that revitalizes him from spiritual death to spiritual life (18.16); this sublime transformation gives Rinaldo the "secura baldanza [firm boldness]" (18.17) to pursue his civic duty. In this sense, Rinaldo's heroic ethos is not so different from Tancredi's, for his transcendence becomes possible through both romance and the image of sublimity, each playing a critical role in his repentance and reconciliation with God. And in Rinaldo's pursuit of the sublime, Tasso features a heroic ethos that is first oriented towards sublimity and divine transcendence; only then can civic virtue and communal duty follow.

I would also suggest, however, that Rinaldo's unique ability to destroy the enchanted wood has less to do with a decision to put public duty over private duty, and more to do with his increased responsiveness to sublimity. While Tancredi continues in the pattern of the romantic hero throughout the epic, aspiring for the divine through the sublime image of his beloved, Rinaldo leaves behind his dependence on Armida, reorienting himself towards the beauty found in nature. Rinaldo breaks free of his dependence on her by two sights: the painful sight of his own degraded appearance during his stay on Armida's island, which correspondingly reveals Armida's lack of sublimity (as she is still an ignoble deceiver); and the sublime sight of the heavens, "bellezze incorrottibili e divine" (18.12.8), which leads him to identify a higher order of sublimity and object of desire, a different channel to the divine. Thus, Rinaldo recognizes that Armida herself is merely a false image of an original, a "torbida luce e bruna / ch'un girar d'occhi, un balenar di riso, / … in breve confin di fragil viso [vague and shadowy light, like a glance of the eyes, a flash of a smile … in the slight limits of a mortal face]" (18.13), of little relevance to his pursuit of heaven. And because he responds to the image of the heavens rather than the face of Armida, he is in a position to identify the enchantments of the forest as "vane sembianze" (18.38.7), as vague copies of images of divine beauty, which hold no potential spiritual value for him. In effect, it is not that Rinaldo transforms into an Aeneas figure accepting public duty over private desire, but that in being oriented towards a higher form of sublimity, he has no need of the depiction of temporal beauty that inspires Tancredi.

Rinaldo's destruction of the tree, then, need not inherently bring Tancredi's heroism into question, as if the one knight's performance of civic virtue makes the other's failure ignoble by comparison. Rather, these episodes represent different kinds of knowledge, perceptions, and promptings of consciences, which are implicitly allowed to coexist. Tancredi remains more dependent on a remembered vision of human beauty, and Rinaldo on a vision of natural beauty; and their corresponding differences create different moral allowances: a civic duty possible for one may be problematic for another. Yet they share an orientation towards an aesthetic of the sublime, and a passion for divine transcendence. Tasso imagines them existing in spiritual community despite their differences. As Sergio Zatti indicates, Tasso can be quite sympathetic to the pagans, questioning the poet's traditionally assumed celebration of Counter-Reformation authority structures.[50] I would agree that Tasso identifies nobility outside the narrow boundaries of religious sects, though his use of the sublime seems to point towards a largely Christian concept of transcendence. Ultimately, Tasso appears to imagine a spiritual community of limited pluralism, one in which individuals together pursue a passion for the sacred sublime, even where they differ in perception and promptings of conscience.

Furthermore, Tasso uses the respective enchanted wood episodes to once again challenge the authoritarianism of Counter-Reformation aesthetic requirements, which demand strict adherence to particular codes of morality and specific belief systems over the pursuit of the passions. As Rinaldo and Tancredi become "readers" of art in the enchanted wood, interpreting the writing on the cypress tree and the apparition created by the demonic art of Ismeno, they represent different modes of interpretation – one that sees primarily deception and falsity in art, and another that can see reflections of divine truth in that same work. One reader may be concerned about the immortality of a work, and another awed by its reflection of divine beauty. In this depiction, Tasso recognizes reflections of divinity infiltrating many areas of nature and art, suggesting that even immoral works can have redemptive potential, depending on the particular passions and conscience of the viewer. Through the knights' respective responses, Tasso shares the moral responsibilities of art with his readers, suggesting that they may take it upon themselves to determine what constitutes too great a moral risk, and what might just open a sublime channel to the divine.

Armida

As a final figure of romantic heroism, Armida undergoes the same basic heroic narrative as Tancredi: she becomes captivated by the sublime image of her beloved, Rinaldo, subsequently undergoes transformation, and ultimately experiences divine transcendence as the impetus to Christian conversion. Like Clorinda, moreover, Armida undergoes conversion entirely outside "official" channels of religious authority – in this case, through an illicit romance. As she responds to the image of Rinaldo, we see her begin a transformation from pagan murderess to noble lover, demonstrating many of the same heroic traits that Tasso associates with the pursuit of divine transcendence: noble passion, intuitive pursuit of beauty, and willingness to take great risks in her pursuit of the desired sublime object. Armida's pursuit of the sublime image of Rinaldo, I suggest, helps to explain the suddenness of her conversion – which has long troubled critics as lacking an "intermediate stage between intransigence and submission."[51] And Tasso portrays both Armida's romance and her transformation occurring through a similarly passionate pursuit of sublimity, which orients her towards spiritual ascent. As an indirect channel to the divine, too, Armida's love for Rinaldo suggests that even the immoral pleasures of her affair represent a worthwhile risk, justified for their role in enabling spiritual transformation.

Armida's first sight of Rinaldo not only delights her but places her in the condition of the sublime, and her response to it marks the first of several major changes in her character. After luring Rinaldo to her island, she comes upon him, "di vendetta vaga [eager for vengeance]" (14.65.8), but stops in her tracks at the sight of his face:

> Ma quando in lui fissò lo sguardo e vide
> come placido in vista egli respire,
> e ne' begli occhi un dolce atto che ride,
> benché sian chiusi (or che fia s'ei li gira?)
> pria s'arresta sospesa, e gli s'asside
> poscia vicina, e placar sente ogn'ira
> mentre il risguarda.   (14.66.1–7)

[But when she fixed her eyes on him and saw how peacefully he breathes, and in his handsome eyes a sign of sweet delight, even though they are closed (what if he turns them [towards her]?) first she stops, hesitating, then sat next to him, and feels all her wrath subside while she looks at him.]

Tasso represents the moment in which Armida "reads" Rinaldo's face as an instance of *ekstatic* psychological transport. As Rinaldo's "handsome eyes" strike and overwhelm Armida, they are closed and at less than full potency, as Tasso suggests that this is something different from the Dantean or Petrarchan convention in which the eyes serve as the passageway for *eros* from beloved to lover. Rather, what Armida observes is the still stronger force of the sublime, a mysterious force powerful enough to melt her wrath and instil in her a hitherto unknown passion for a sublime object. For the primary agent of change in Armida's affections is the "dolce atto che ride" of Rinaldo's closed eyes, an enigmatic expression involving delight that Esolen translates as "a kind of joy." This enigmatic force not only implies an experience of general pleasure, but more specifically recalls the elusive force of "un non so che" that so often in Tasso marks interactions with the sublime. On feeling this force, Armida accordingly becomes "sospesa" – meaning "doubtful," "hesitant," or more literally "suspended" – suggesting an interruption of emotional or intellectual certainty.[52] Like Clorinda and Tancredi on encountering "un non so che," Armida hesitates but instinctively follows its promptings, exchanging hatred for love. She also demonstrates the same romantic heroism as Tancredi when she actively "fixes" her eyes on Rinaldo, "pauses" in suspended thought, and "sits" beside him, giving way to the intuitive promptings of the sublime. In the process, she undergoes a radical transport from one condition to another: "[c]osí (chi 'l crederia?) sopiti ardori / d'occhi nascosi distempràr quel gelo / che s'indurava al cor piú che diamante, / e di nemica ella divenne amante [Thus (Who would believe it?) the sleeping fervor of concealed eyes melts the ice around her heart that has become harder than diamond, and she turns from enemy to lover" (14.67.5–8). With Armida's diamond-hard animosity suddenly giving away to love, Tasso depicts the sort of dramatic change that we might expect to see in a miraculous conversion experience, a change prompted not simply by pleasure but by sublimity. Tasso thus defines Armida's response to Rinaldo as a transformative act of romantic heroism – an intermediate step towards conversion.

As Rinaldo leaves Armida behind, she is brought a second time into a sublime condition, an experience that coincides with her growing passion for him and prompts a second stage of transformation. This time, however, rather than being transformed through the pleasures of romance, Armida transforms through the terrors of abjection, in which she psychologically splits into two selves that struggle against each another. In this painful psychological split, devoid of the pleasures of romance, Tasso implicitly paves the way for Armida to leave behind her evil self, choosing to love once and for all not only Rinaldo but also God, making the horror of losing Rinaldo the only force powerful enough to transform and reorient her love towards the divine, as we saw with Tancredi. When Armida sees Rinaldo leaving, she cries: "'l vide (ahi fera vista!) ... / frettoloso, fuggitivo il tergo [the sight (oh brutal sight!) ... of his back fleeing, hurrying]" (16.35). The tone and emotions differ from her first sight of Rinaldo, but the sense of delayed astonishment is similar: first, she "suspects"; then she is paralysed, unable to speak for shock; finally, she experiences total cognitive and emotional disruption. As she regains her ability to speak, her words reveal the psychological fracture of abjection: "'O tu che porte / Parte teco di me, parte ne lassi, / O prendi l'una o rendi l'altra [O you who take part of me with you, don't leave the other part, Oh take the one or return the other]'" (16.40). As we saw in Tancredi, Armida identifies two separate parts of herself: one is with Rinaldo, representing her new self, and the other remains with her, representing her old, murderess self. The cause of this fracture becomes apparent as she concludes her extended plea to Rinaldo, falling into the self-loathing and self-debasement characteristic of abjection: "Misera! Ancor presuma? Ancor mi vanto / Di schernita beltà che nulla impetra? [Wretch! Still think so? Am I still boasting of scorned beauty that no one wants?]" (16.51.1–2). In effect, Armida rejects her own sense of pride in her beauty – her most prized possession and the source of her narcissism. Fearing that her beauty is not as powerful and compelling as she once believed, she interprets Rinaldo's departure as a condemnation of her appearance, as if it were somehow an isolated part of her that had performed faulty service (12.65). Although this is obviously an improper reason for spiritual guilt, showing little meaningful sense of moral culpability or contrition, Armida performs a kind of proto-repentance when she turns against herself in abjection, recognizing that her own beauty is no object of worship after all. As she debases herself, she begins to turn against her former self, implicitly preparing to reject her self-idolizing nature, and to identify with a "new" self capable of loving divine beauty as well as earthly beauty.

As Armida goes to battle against Rinaldo in canto 20, her abjection deepens, widening the gap between the old, hateful self and the new, nobler self, preparing her for the ultimate rejection of the old. We see her growing confusion of identity in four specific descriptions that show her competing selves: first, she gazes upon Rinaldo on the battlefield "con occhi d'ira e di desio tremanti [with eyes of wrath and trembling desire]" (20.61.6); second, as she attempts to shoot Rinaldo in battle, "Sorse amor contra l'ira, e fe' palese / che vive il foco suo ch'ascoso tenne. / ... con lo strale un voto / súbito uscí, che vada il colpo a vòto [Love rose up against wrath, and revealed her flame that she kept hidden ... with the arrow (that she shoots at Rinaldo) there came a prayer that the shot would come to nothing]" (20.63); third, "mentre ella saetta, Amor lei piaga [while she shoots, she wounds Love]" (20.65); and fourth, as she flees the battlefield in defeat, "van seco pur anco / Sdegno ed Amor quasi due veltri al fianco [with her, too, come Scorn and Love, like two greyhounds at her side]" (20.117.7–8). These lines reveal the progression of Armida's two selves in combat, represented respectively by Desire/Love, and Wrath/Scorn. Crucially, while "desire" strengthens and grows into "love" in the final example, "wrath" becomes replaced with the comparatively weaker "scorn," suggesting that her love slowly comes to dominate her hatred, even before Armida reencounters Rinaldo. Implicitly, Armida is driven by her own abjection – provoked by the sublime sight of Rinaldo – to isolate and put away her once-dominant self, paving the way for her dramatic transformation.

In Armida's final reconciliation with Rinaldo, Tasso portrays her passion for the sublime sight of her beloved culminating in its proper divine end. Throughout the passage, Tasso emphasizes that it is again the sight of Rinaldo that brings her to reject her former self once and for all, allowing her finally to pursue divine love as an extension of human love. Not only does the sudden appearance of Rinaldo stop her from stabbing herself (20.128), but Tasso specifies that it is Rinaldo's tears falling on her *face* that prompt her dramatic transformation; the passage depicts an implicit baptism, with reviving effects of the "pioggia d'argento e matutina [silver morning dew]" (20.129.3). As she finds herself in awe at the sight of Rinaldo, unable to avoid gazing at ("rimirar") him, she then lifts up her eyes three times ("tre volte alzò le luci"), reorienting her attention to heaven (129.7–8). Her expression of conversion itself, "Ecco l'ancilla tua," follows Rinaldo's highly telling request that she "mirar ne gli occhi miei [gaze into my eyes]" (135.1) to confirm that he speaks the truth in promising to be her knight.[53] His statement points back to Armida's initial sight of Rinaldo's face when his eyes were closed, at which Tasso had asked provocatively, "or che fia s'ei li gira? [What if he opens them?]" (14.66.4). The answer, Tasso suggests, is a spiritual transformation even more dramatic than her initial transformation from murderess to lover, a transformation that prompts her heroic choice to pursue God.

In her conversion through the sublime sight of Rinaldo, Tasso establishes Armida, like Tancredi and Rinaldo, as a "reader" of the sublime, producing his final statement on the respective roles of sublimity, morality, and delight in heroic poetry. Where Tasso's contemporaries opposed alluring representations of immorality in literature, Tasso boldly connects the otherwise immoral romance episode of Rinaldo and Armida to spiritual transformation. Through the redeeming power of their romance, Tasso demonstrates that even immoral pleasure – the delights of Armida's Bower – can be a worthwhile risk, when its sublimity has the potential to lead the viewer towards its divine source. Even when it enters questionable moral terrain and turns away from civic duty, sublime poetry can be an agent in this journey, Tasso suggests, capable of evoking the kind of awe, passion, and desire ultimately satisfied by the Christian God. At the same time, Tasso qualifies the role of poetic pleasure in suggesting that, since pleasure cannot reform the sinful heart and tainted passions, it must sometimes be interrupted and sacrificed to strengthen the desire for the greater sublimity of divine transcendence. Both virtue and pleasure share space in the heroic pursuit of the divine, but neither may be allowed to interfere with spiritual transformation and divine rapture.

Yet in Tasso's representation, much of the burden rests with the reader, as the poet portrays the audience sharing with the author the responsibilities and pleasures of the same sublime task: pursuing God through poetry. As Armida becomes a heroic reader of the sublime, using her passion for Rinaldo to finally give up everything she knows out of love for him, Tasso not only celebrates the heroism of her extraordinarily risky choice, but extends an invitation to the poem's readers to enter the same sublime space and heroic community, a community passionately devoted to pursuing divine truth through the medium of sublime art.

The Heroism of Sublime Art: Tasso and His Readers

As we have seen, much of the heroic ethos of the *Liberata* is characterized by risk, undertaken by both charismatic and romantic figures: Tasso locates heroism in the wilful choice to hazard even civic duty in the passionate embrace of the sublime, culminating in divine transcendence. Inasmuch as Tasso associates sublime heroism with risk, he also represents his own authorship as a kind of charismatic heroism, taking risks to attract readers to a state of transcendence through expressions of *meraviglia*, even where they go against traditional authority. He demonstrates himself to be quite willing to question political regulation and social norms – to celebrate morally ambiguous poetry, to place individuality before civic duty where warranted – out of a desire to attract readers to God through the medium of poetic beauty, despite the hazards of doing so.

In a rare reference to his authorship within the *Liberata* itself, Tasso expresses his poetic endeavour as one great risk. After asking the Muse to "spira al petto mio celesti ardori [breathe heavenly passion into my heart]," the poet gains no assurance from this request, simply asking "perdona" if he departs from divine truth (1.2.5–6). Although the lines may reflect a standard modesty *topos*, they are only too indicative of the lack of assurance underlying Tasso's pursuit of sublime poetry, likely reflecting insecurity about the subversive nature of the *Liberata*. By contrast, Spenser uses the sublime to support theological positions that are generally more in line with his religious and political environment, potentially allowing a stronger sense of confidence. But throughout the *Liberata*, Tasso portrays the art of epic poetry as requiring the poet to hazard a variety of criticisms and consequences for a divine purpose.

The hazard underlying the *Liberata*, as a work of poetic beauty, has proven overwhelmingly worthwhile; the most "risky" aspects of the poem are those that have most captivated readers over the centuries. But while the poet of the *Liberata* was a younger man not yet weighed down by excessive fear – a heroic poet willing to risk disapproval for a divine purpose – that young poet evidently gave way to a more circumspect individual, as seen in the removal of any controversial or romance episodes in the revised *Gerusalemme conquistata* (1593). And with that removal, sublimity evaporates.

While the reasons for this removal are complex, a significant one was surely Tasso's growing frustration with the mutual author-reader relationship. As Tasso revised and subjected the poem to external criticism, he may have sensed in his own contemporary readership a lack of noble passion, an unwillingness to be captivated by artistic beauty and to see it as a reflection of divine glory: a wholly *unheroic* readership unable to fulfil its share of the responsibility. Without an audience to respond to the charismatic aspects of his work, Tasso lacked motivation to take the risks associated with producing sublime art, and the flat and colourless *Conquistata* reflects the cautious, calculated readership that Tasso feared. But this revision could take nothing from what the *Liberata* accomplishes with abundant passion, heroism, and sublimity.

3 Divine Mystery and the Inscrutable Sublime in Du Bartas's *Les Semaines*

As Tasso's contemporary, Guillaume de Salluste Du Bartas (1544–90) would bring the sublime into French epic poetry. To my knowledge, Du Bartas, unlike Tasso, has never been connected to the Longinian sublime. Yet, like the *Liberata*, and to a much greater extent than Ronsard's 1572 *Franciade* (a rather flat imitation of Virgil's *Aeneid*), Du Bartas's narrative poetry known as *Les Semaines* develops a Longinian heroic model that would play a significant role in shaping later Renaissance epic, especially *Paradise Lost*.

Les Semaines is an expansive, unfinished three-part collection of poetry that begins with *La Sepmaine* (1578), an imaginative account of the seven days of creation; following this is *La Seconde Semaine* (1584), an extended narrative of the Fall and its aftermath in Genesis; the final segment is *Les Suittes de la Seconde Semaines* (published posthumously in 1603), which retells biblical history from Noah through the kings of Israel and Judah. In current scholarship, this poetic sequence tends to be excluded from studies on the epic tradition. Today, Du Bartas is less often studied as a poet in his own right than as an influence on English poetry, especially in the popular translation/adaptation by Joshua Sylvester (1603–4).[1] Yet Anne Lake Prescott notes that Du Bartas was compared in his own time to major epic poets such as Homer, Dante, Ariosto, and Ronsard, and had a longstanding interest in classical literature and epic poetry; more recent work by Katherine S. Maynard argues for his inclusion in the Renaissance epic tradition.[2] Despite differences in form and reputation, *Les Semaines* presents its own claims to epic, grounded in a consistent heroic model that aligns with the values and aims of his early modern epic contemporaries – of inspiring in readers a desire for heroic awe.

In the resulting heroic model, Du Bartas uses descriptions of Longinian *ekplexis* – astonishment and terror – to develop an especially *sceptical* form of the sublime.[3] Impacted by the sceptical sublimity of Montaigne, as discussed below, Du Bartas makes Christian heroism a practice of embracing divine mysteriousness, in an effort to challenge the effects of religious dogmatism. As an advisor to Henri de Navarre, later Henry IV, during the French

Wars of Religion, Du Bartas saw the fabric of the entire nation threatened by the religious radicalism plaguing France. The nation was majority and officially Catholic, with many leaders eager to go to great lengths to preserve political supremacy and suppress the growth of Protestantism;[4] even moderate Catholics sought to limit freedoms officially available to Protestants and ensure France remained Catholic.[5] Meanwhile, some Protestants sought not only freedoms but ways to impose their own beliefs, carrying out widespread iconoclastic attacks on religious imagery. While Du Bartas was Protestant himself, he deeply resisted the constant vying for power on both sides – and the accompanying belief that one's own religious practices needed to be codified for all to follow. As stated explicitly in the introduction to "Triomphe de la Foi," Du Bartas was politically and personally invested in deescalating religious tensions to promote political and spiritual unity.[6] In *Les Semaines*, he takes his response to these tensions further by undermining certain knowledge, using a version of scepticism to promote toleration of different religious perspectives. Throughout this poetry, ultimately, Du Bartas reminds readers of the mysteriousness of God's ways and works, urging them to rest in the sublimity of the divine presence, and thereby cultivate humility in their intellectual and spiritual practice. And by using the sublime to celebrate true religion as a practice of personal reverence for God, Du Bartas shows his resentment towards the religious authorities who encouraged their subjects to martial their religious devotion in quests for political dominance.

While Du Bartas has not been connected to the Longinian sublime, several scholars have emphasized his interest in related concepts of transcendence, primarily through his depiction of Neoplatonic *furor* in *l'Uranie*. Prescott, for instance, suggests that Du Bartas's poetry establishes an "aesthetics of levitation," a fascination with flight; she notes as well that Gabriel Harvey refers to Du Bartas as a "right inspired and enravished Poet," for the "highnesse of his subject and the majesty of his verse."[7] Bruno Braunrot, meanwhile, observes the presence of something "sublime" (used uncritically) in his poetry. Braunrot suggests that in the poem's descriptions of supernatural occurrences, Du Bartas develops a tension between the concrete and the intangible, between the abstract and the tangible, using detailed descriptions of objects to evoke a sense of transcendence.[8] Moreover, *Les Semaines* often enters territory that feels distinctively Longinian, where characters experience the characteristically negative emotions of the sublime – not only elevation and ecstasy, but terror and horror as well.

In one example from the second day of creation, in *La Sepmaine*, Du Bartas addresses his post-Fall contemporaries through descriptions that highlight proper and improper human responses to aspects of the world that defy comprehension. The poet notes that, instinctively, "Le peuple est étonné [the people are astonished]" to look on such wonders as the appearance of multiple moons in the sky (I.2.713–14).[9] In response, some may resist these strong emotions, trying to "compassi[r] / Du compass de [leur] sens les fets du Tout-puissant [bring the deeds of the Almighty within the reach of (their) senses]" (I.1.717–18), but these are mere fools, he explains. Far better than trying to resolve this doubt is to simply "vanter sans fin les dois / Qui les mettent en ouvre" [praise endlessly the fingers that put them into being]" (I.1.26–7). For himself, the poet writes "sur tout je m'esmeu quand le courrous des Cieux / De prodiges armés, se presente à nos yeux [I am especially transported when the wrath of heaven, in prodigious hosts, appear to us]" (I.1.745–6). Sylvester's poetic translation renders the opening phrase (and difficult-to-translate verb "esmouvoir") as "my pierced soule inclines" – a Longinian expression of being awestruck.[10] Calling readers to fend off the temptation to seek explanations for heavenly mysteries, which he links elsewhere to pride, Du Bartas illustrates the elevating potential of embracing the unknown in humility and reverent fear, emphasizing that this is a heroic choice.

Throughout his poetry, such narratives, celebrating a properly awestruck ("pierced"), submissive ("inclining") posture before divine power, anticipate Kant's mathematical sublime, or the awe we feel when facing something so immeasurably great that it surpasses human abilities of comprehension; for Kant, these forms of sublimity overwhelm by "bring[ing] with them the idea of [their] infinity."[11] In a similar way, Du Bartas imagines the ways of God as unknowable and infinite in appearance to the human mind, and therefore having the potential to glorify and elevate. But while Kant's concept of the sublime is famously subjective – elevation itself a property of the *mind* encountering the apparently immeasurable object – Du Bartas insists that divine infinity is an ontological reality that itself overwhelms viewers.[12] In doing so, he heightens the stakes and the heroic potential of responding appropriately to divine mystery. As the passage above suggests, readers have a choice: they can pursue scientific explanations in an effort to dissolve the discomfort of the unknown, or they can welcome the feeling of being overwhelmed as a mechanism of transport into divine relationship. Across the poem, Du Bartas recurrently insists that divine inscrutability will be an ever-present stumbling block, or opportunity for heroic exaltation in the presence of God.

In "Eden," the poem offers an idyllic, preheroic snapshot of Du Bartas's portrait of the exalting potential of divine mystery in prelapsarian Eden, when Adam awakens in paradise "ravy [ravished]," not knowing "si c'est ou terre ou ciel [if it were earth or heaven]" (324, 326). The ambiguity of locale is an important detail; Adam neither knows nor feels the need to know where he is, because he has the greater awareness of being in God's hands. Since Adam is physically on earth while enjoying constant communication with God, his situation resembles Longinus's characterization of sublimity as the "gap between earth and heaven," suggesting, as in *Peri Hypsous*, a condition of otherworldly transport that is both indeterminate and exhilarating.[13] Because of Adam's willingness *not* to know, the poem suggests, his entire experience is saturated with divine ecstasy, as he soon afterward finds himself in a state of psychological, emotional, and spiritual transport:

> D'un ecstase plus sainct cela se fait encore,
> Lors que l'oeil voit à-clair ce que l'esprit adore
> [...]
> O doux ravissement, sainct vol, amour extréme
> Qui fais que nous baisons les lévres d'Amour mesme
> Hymen, qui …
> Maries pour un temps la terre avec le ciel:
> Feu qui dans l'alambic des pensees divines
> Sublime nos desirs, nostre terre r'affines.

[This, then, is the most holy ecstasy, when the eye sees clearly what the mind loves … O sweet ravishment, holy flight, extreme love that makes us kiss the lips of Love itself…. Hymen, who … for a time weds heaven and earth: Fire that in the alembic of divine thoughts sublimates our desires, refines our earth.] ("Eden," 373–4, 81–6)

In this early (and very Neoplatonic) depiction of Adam's close connection to God, major elements of Longinian sublimity are present as well – ravishment, flight, indistinctness of physical space, divine thoughts, even the root of the word "sublime" – and in their midst are an embrace of the unknown. As Adam accedes to the mysterious "pensees divines" [divine thoughts], his desires are "sublimated," or transformed in an inexpressible experience of rapture. Describing a world before original sin, the poem offers a vision of eternal glory, in which the capacity to be overwhelmed is not finally a marker of weakness, but a channel to exaltation and fulfilment.

The passage above foreshadows the concept of heroism that will emerge later in postlapsarian characters such as Adam and Abraham, as well as inversely in Satan's temptation and Eve's fall. For Du Bartas, to be heroic is to look upward to heaven rather than outward for political gain, to be hopeful of divine grace and glory rather than certain of one's correctness in matters of dogma. Moreover, for Du Bartas, to embrace divine mystery requires cultivating the *right* community. As shown in the fall of Eve, embracing divine mystery involves resisting those who would equate spirituality with worldly power – institutional authorities who would manipulate religious practice for material ends. In a short account of postlapsarian Adam, he undermines institutional authority further, suggesting that true community is found in those who share humbly in the hope of heavenly glory.

In his extended narrative of Abraham's call to sacrifice Isaac (a passage that was dramatized and held particular interest to early modern Europe), meanwhile, Du

Bartas emphasizes that this form of spiritual heroism is far from easy. Its challenge lies in withstanding not only discomfort, but even feelings of terror at the unknown. As Tasso does in the *Liberata*, Du Bartas shows emotional astonishment crossing the line from *ekplexis* into abjection, a violent, devastating condition of extended withdrawal representing moments of spiritual darkness. Through abjection, theorized as a "negative" version of the sublime, Du Bartas explores a natural but terrorizing condition of inwardness that results from a felt separation from God.[14] According to Du Bartas, this terror resolves only by embracing divine mystery, which in especially dark times demands communal support. But once again, for Du Bartas, this community is rooted not in affiliation with a particular institution or mutual assent to particularities of doctrine, but in a shared hope of heaven.

After first looking further at the major influences on Du Bartas's version of the sublime, I will examine the poem's portrayal of heroism, beginning with the inverse, negative model seen in Satan's temptation of Eve, followed by the positive model enacted by Adam and Abraham.[15]

Montaigne, Uncertainty, and the Early French Sceptical Sublime

While there may be no formal evidence that Du Bartas was knowledgeable of the sublime as a philosophy, there is plenty of reason to suspect that he was interested in the concepts that were circulating throughout Europe, appearing in some of Du Bartas's most pertinent theoretical models for heroic epic. He had numerous connections to scholars suspected or known to have a formal interest in the sublime – including Du Bellay, Philip Sidney, and the French scholar Marc-Antoine de Muret, with the latter producing a new edition of *Peri Hypsous* between 1550 and 1555.[16] In particular, Ronsard was a likely influence on Du Bartas's poetic theory, as his *Franciade* may well have helped inspire Du Bartas's attempt at the genre. As shown in chapter 1, Ronsard invokes Longinian principles of native genius, heightened emotion, and spiritual aims in his poetic theory, though not prominently in his actual epic.

But alongside the impact of Ronsard's model of sublime authorship, Montaigne's *Essais* (1580) model sublimity in a manner that may have been even more influential on the concept of intellectual humility developed in *Les Semaines*, despite differences in subject and form. Published just after Du Bartas's *La Sepmaine*, the *Essais* were available well in time to influence the latter two segments of *Les Semaines*.[17] As David Sedley shows, Montaigne's *Essais*, and particularly his *Apology for Raymond Seybond*, consistently affirm the value of scepticism as a mode of sublimity. As Sedley theorizes, the practice of scepticism – suspending judgment about an issue – increases a person's tolerance for uncertainty, thus enabling a fuller experience of the sublime. Meanwhile, the sublime lies beyond human comprehension and thus "plunges the mind into confusion" (and into scepticism). In essays on the ruins of Rome, Sedley argues, Montaigne brings sublimity and scepticism together by celebrating an indeterminacy that leads to awe, and that leads readers to cultivate an appreciation for "infinite grandeur."[18]

Du Bartas shares with Montaigne a marked distrust of the human intellect that shapes his pairing of sublimity and doubt in *Les Semaines*. For his part, Montaigne developed a reputation as a *sceptical fideist*, concluding that nothing could be known with certainty and that religious belief therefore depended on a blind faith.[19] Reflecting a similar view, Du Bartas repeatedly suggests that the primary methods of gaining knowledge – both reasoning and empiricism – are woefully limited and often untrustworthy; he insists that we must always hold back judgment, writing early in *La Seconde Semaine* that God himself, "pour nostre profit," may "desmentir et nos mains, et nos yeux [for our benefit, may deceive both our hands and our eyes]" ("Eden," 623).[20] In explaining the difficulties of knowing, the poem suggests that before the Fall, knowledge was never meant to be gained by effort, for in the original state, it was "non acquis, mais infus [not acquired, but infused]," or imparted directly by God ("Eden," 252). Du Bartas thus seems to imply that this automatic transmission of knowledge was one of the means of sustaining the human-divine relationship. With the original channel obstructed after the Fall, humanity would inevitably have difficulty attaining knowledge through any means, including rational or empirical methods. In the postlapsarian world, without entirely rejecting all forms of knowledge, Du Bartas identifies the fear of the unknown as a common barrier to restoring the full enjoyment of the relationship to God.

While both Montaigne and Du Bartas unite scepticism and sublimity, they do so for different reasons. Montaigne uses sceptical sublimity to celebrate the grandeur of an elusive Rome and the Renaissance response to it, but Du Bartas combines sublimity and doubt as a means of creating unity in a deeply divided culture. Maynard notes that Du Bartas works to build regional and national community in a divided France – and I agree that he does, though I would maintain that his final vision of community is more firmly centred on spiritual identity than civic and national identity.[21] As Peter Auger notes, Du Bartas developed one of his closest literary friendships with a foreign leader, King James of Scotland, honouring James openly in the fragment "La Magnificence" as "du ciel esleu [chosen by heaven]" and sharing early and unique versions of poetry with him (1278). Instead of an instrument to exalt France, Du Bartas's poetry was, as Auger puts it, "an instrument for developing foreign relations with Protestant nations across Europe," especially England and Scotland.[22] When Du Bartas does invoke France in *Les Semaines*, he celebrates not the glory of the nation but the "heureuse Paix [blessed Peace]" that prompts him to praise God ("J'espande … ton nom par l'Univers [I magnify … your name throughout the Universe]" ("Artifices," 36, 6). Du Bartas appears to have been interested in how poetry can create solidary among Christians not only of multiple religious persuasions, but also of other civic identities.

Like Tasso, Du Bartas celebrates experiences of the sublime to emphasize a particular hope that believers share – a hope of transcendence more secure and lasting than their hopes for strong nationhood. Yet his concept of transcendence differs from Tasso's in its emphasis on the unknown. While Tasso represents the sublime as an encounter with knowledge emerging through divine intuition, for Du Bartas, *ekplexis* comes by cultivating a disposition of unquestioning belief in God's supremacy, and by a constant, humble readiness to reject claims of certain knowledge, particularly when used for political ends. For Du Bartas, caught between vicious debates of warring French Catholics and Huguenots, the quest for rational certainty represented a constant temptation to wield power over others, a threat to society and to the individual soul.

Beginning with an account of the Fall early in *La Seconde Semaine*, and extending into *Les Suittes*, Du Bartas portrays numerous agents who are confronted with a crisis of divine inscrutability and either fail (like Satan, Eve, and, initially, Adam) or succeed (like Adam and Abraham) in being elevated and transported by their humble embrace of that mystery. Even after sin enters the world, Du Bartas celebrates the possibility that fallen humans can actively choose whether to view the unknown as a threat or a blessing, while insisting for his readers that they can best attain the ends of sublimity and divine glory not by seeking or selling out to institutional power, but by developing a vibrant spiritual life. In repeatedly invoking the heroic potential of the sublime, Du Bartas insists that humanity's highest, most glorious ends lay not in having one's own views given public or political authority, but in sharing heavenly bliss with a community of spiritual equals. Thus, while Du Bartas's theological explanations can at times seem incoherent or unsatisfying, his depiction of the heroic nonetheless offers an important vision of spiritual humility and cooperation of pressing concern for early modern Europe. His concepts of divine mystery and sublimity, moreover, would prove especially significant to Milton.

The Fall, Materialism, and a False Rapture

In the segment of *La Seconde Semaine* entitled "Imposture" (Deceit), which recounts the Fall of Genesis 3, Du Bartas emphasizes the natural human desire for sublimity, while analysing the major barriers to embracing the divine mystery that underlies sublime experience. Where the Genesis account of the temptation is very short, with the serpent appealing to Eve's ambition to become "like God, knowing good and evil," Du Bartas significantly expands the episode. In keeping with tradition, he associates the serpent with Satan, who entices Eve to invert the poem's final model of heroism – with Du Bartas's additions, the poem makes Eve's disobedience not only a matter of intellectual pride and ambition, but a preference for the material over the immaterial. Even in her failure, however, Du Bartas is less critical of a particular evil that Eve commits and more ready to condemn the way that earthly powers can tempt and deceive people to pursue material gain as an illusion of spiritual gain, especially those who lack genuine support.

In his rhetorical posturing, Satan urges Eve on towards glory and rapture, yet he ultimately deceives her by problematizing the mysteriousness of the divine order:

> Non, n'en croy rien, dit-il: ô belle, ce n'est pas
> Le desir de sauver les humains du trespas,
> Qui fait, que ce tien Dieu, non moins malin que sage,
> D'un fruict si bon et beau vous interdit l'usage.
> Un despit, une envie, une jalouse peur
> Sans relasche, cruels, luy bequetent le cueur,
> Voyant que de ce fruict la suspecte puissance
> Dissipera soudain la nuë d'ignorance
> Qui vous presse les yeux: voire fera que vous
> Serez Dieux ave luy: serez Dieux dessus nous.
> O gloire de ce Tout, avance donc, avance
> Ta bien-heureuse main. Que tarde-tu? Commance,
> Commance ton bon heur. Ne crain point le courrous
> De je ne sçay quel Dieu, qui n'est plus grand que vous,
> Si non tant qu'il te plaist. Pren la brillante robbe
> De l'immortalité; fay tost, et ne desrobbe,
> Envieuse marastre, à ta posterité
> Le souverain honneur de la divinité.   ("Imposture," 303–20)

[No, don't believe any of that, he said: O beautiful one, it is not the desire to save humans from the fall that makes a fruit so good and appealing forbidden to you – as God, no less clever than wise, would have it. But spite, envy, a jealous, cruel, unrelenting fear, batter the heart, seeing that the suspect power of this fruit will suddenly dissipate the cloud of ignorance that presses your eyes. Indeed, so you will become like gods with him: you will be like gods above us. O glory of it all, reach, then, reach your happy hand. What are you waiting for? Begin, begin your happy state. Do not fear the threat of I-know-not-what God, who is no greater than you, if you don't wish him to be. Put on the gleaming robe of immortality; do it now, and don't, like a jealous stepmother, divest from your posterity the sovereign honour of divinity.]

For all his emphasis on aspiring for divinity, Satan's main strategy is to contrast the liability of the abstract and the distant – the inscrutable divine command that Eve may die for an apparently harmless act – and the material substance of the fruit, described as "bon" et "beau." The goodness of the material fruit he presents as undoubtable, while the unknown intent of God's command he depicts as suspect: "Non, n'en croy rien [Don't *believe* (that the command is meant for your good)]." In effect, Satan convinces Eve that heavenly mysteries themselves are a monstrosity rather than a delight, and that a God who gives such a command must be corrupted by horrific sins of envy and cruelty. According to Satan, mystery itself is merely a cloak for evil and something easily demystified, to be dismissed as inhibiting the good the earthly domain has to offer.

In effect, Du Bartas warns that the origin of sin – and the great threat to humanity – is not a failure to appreciate the value of divine glory, but a belief that ecstasy and glory can be best attained by asserting control over earthly realms in a manner humanity was never intended to do. Satan himself assumes that glory is the greatest good and what Eve desires ("O gloire de ce Tout"; "Pren … l'immortalité"), but urges her to reject divine mystery as the route to achieving it. Holding the unknown in contempt, he argues that she can aspire to heavenly glory by seizing a forbidden material object.

As if Du Bartas is flaunting the deceptiveness of this strategy, Satan's approach then shifts from seeking to demystify God's mysteriousness to dismissing him because of that mysteriousness. After characterizing God as spiteful, jealous, and cruel, Satan then refers to him as "je ne sçay quel Dieu [I know not what God]" in an effort to highlight the abstractness of his character. Satan clearly intends the line negatively, scorning inscrutability as untrustworthy, but the phrase is not inherently pejorative. Rather, "je ne sçay quel" is a loose translation of the Italian "un non so che," which Tasso frequently uses to depict the rise of a divine (and sublime) intuition; as described in chapter 2, "un non so che" would be a precursor to Boileau's "je ne sais quoi." When Satan criticizes "je ne sçay quel Dieu," he pushes Eve to reject the very sublimity of God.

While both Tasso and Du Bartas refer in their respective expressions of sublimity to an intangible force, they represent this force operating in different ways.[23] In the *Liberata*, "un non so che" represents a channel of divine knowledge, a spiritual knowledge alternative to the knowledge claims set forth by Counter-Reformation religious authorities; in *Les Semaines*, "je ne sçay quel" refers to a sublime mysteriousness that overpowers the intellect entirely, pulling its subjects away from divisive religious controversy. In effect, when Eve follows Satan's deceptive logic, instead of seeing God's mysteriousness as a source of glory and exaltation, she pursues a form of certainty that will produce great division. Seeking "divinité" in her own physical and mental ability, Eve rejects the heavenly power she would need to transcend her earthly condition (as Adam transcends his before the Fall), embracing a material "good" as a substitute for divinity.

It is significant, however, that throughout this scene, Du Bartas directs his primary criticism at Satan rather than Eve, associating his instigation with that of religious leaders urging followers to acquire worldly power. After all, his urge that she "avance donc, avance" sounds like a commander instructing foot soldiers to continue an invasion. Eve, then, becomes victim to the deception that spiritual pursuits need political support. In depicting Eve passively acquiescing, Du Bartas places the blame for this implied imperialism chiefly on the head of her tempter, suggesting that Eve's faults include the lesser mistake of losing sight of the value of mysteriousness itself.

In his critique of Satan's anti-sublime rhetoric, moreover, Du Bartas offers a neglected source for Milton's portrayal of the sublime in *Paradise Lost*, which further develops the idea that sublimity can be a counter to institutional deception.[24] (I will consider additional connections between both poems' uses of the sublime in chapter 5, but will comment briefly here on how Du Bartas anticipates specific, previously acknowledged aspects of the Miltonic sublime.) As Sedley notes, Milton's Satan fails to achieve his aims because he does not appreciate mystery: he rejects "the sublime potential of doubting" and finds this doubt degrading, "an index of ruin."[25] Du Bartas never indicates what his own representation of Satan believes, but the character's rhetoric reflects the same resistance to uncertainty: he urges Eve to disparage God's command by attacking its inscrutability. Du Bartas's temptation scene thus offers a precedent that Milton apparently extends, as Milton's Satan even adopts a version of the earlier Satan's "je ne sçay quel Dieu" when he asks Eve "And what are Gods that Man may not become / As they?" (9.716–7). With his "and what are Gods," Milton's Satan represents divine mystery even more dismissively than his French prototype had done. Suggesting that the very concept of godhood is so enigmatic that there may be more than one deity, Milton's Satan makes the sense of enigma not only negative, but self-multiplying, such that knowledge even of aspects that were actually knowable breaks down.

In this, both Milton and Du Bartas promote the embrace of divine mystery as foundational to healthy spirituality, and, counterintuitively, as means of protecting truth itself. In their versions of the sublime, both poets follow Longinus in opposing sublimity to what they see as a lesser form of communication – rhetorical persuasion, which is at least on the surface concerned with gaining and promoting knowledge.[26] While Longinus dismisses persuasion merely as a lower, less meaningful form of experience than sublimity, for Du Bartas and Milton, persuasion can all too often be a tool for deceit, something far more dangerous than a mere absence of certainty. Milton's critique of rhetorical eloquence is well known – he was greatly concerned about its use as a tool for political deception – and as scholars have noted, this concern is fully apparent in Satan's eloquent deception of Eve in Book 9.[27] In the earlier version of this very scene, Du Bartas develops a critique of rhetorical persuasion that Milton may have noticed: using "propos affetez [affected discourse]" ("Imposture," 292), Du Bartas's Satan rejoices that Eve "prend goust à ses flateurs propos / … [il] poursuit sa poincte [finds his flattering remarks to her taste … (and he) pursues his point]" ("Imposture," 299–300). Du Bartas's description falls short of the complexity and nuance of Milton's, but may well have served as a baseline for Milton's representation of how Eve's longing for spiritual elevation can be so easily abused and manipulated to create division – first between Eve and Adam, then between humanity and God.

Milton and Du Bartas ultimately held different views of reason and knowledge. But both revealed in their depictions of the sublime a great concern about those who might exploit people's natural interest in knowledge and spirituality for worldly gain, as both Satans do in furthering a political rebellion against God. For both poets, if to different degrees, the love of divine mystery forms a direct link to the individual relationship to God, serving as a sublime blessing in itself. It also offers a protective shield against those who would seek to exploit religious devotion and create division.

Adam and the Inscrutable Sublime

Du Bartas shows little of Adam's fall, or of his or Eve's immediate response to it beyond what Genesis records, but after an extended description of the destruction that follows (including Cain's murder of Abel), he continues Adam's narrative in the segment "Les Artifices" with an invented account in which Adam begins to fulfil the poem's heroic model. In this passage, Du Bartas imagines Adam showing his third son, Seth, a vision of the future, by looking to God as the sole source of knowledge and transport.[28] Here, Du Bartas features Adam being brought back into the condition of the sublime after the Fall, by demonstrating the requisite willingness to be overwhelmed by the unknown. Unlike Eve, in this instance Adam is not alone. Making spiritual heroism a communal endeavour, Du Bartas insists that it is most importantly a quest of individuals *who are equals in the sight of God*, pursuing the goal of heavenly glory of their own will, simply supporting one another in the effort.

One especially noteworthy feature of the exchange between Adam and Seth is Adam's quiet refusal to lord any authority over his son as the first created man. When Seth asks his father to foretell future events, the first patriarch confesses that human eyes see only "la chose presente" and "la passée" [things present and past], with future events beyond the scope of human reach unless one is "rendu plus qu'humain / … lit au front du Trois-fois-Souverain [made more than human … (and) reads (it) on the face of the Triune God]" ("Artifices," 554–6). Confessing a lack of knowledge and power, Adam offers no patronizing words to Seth, as a figure asserting spiritual seniority might, but prays fervently for the opportunity to see God's face:

> Toi donq qui seul cognois toutes choses futures
> […]
>   … d'une prescience et certaine, et parfait
> […]

> Retire moy du corps, à fin qu'heureux je vive
> Au ciel avant ma mort. O ma vie, r'avive
> Pour un temps mon esprit: et fay qu'à ceste fois
> Je soy comme L'Echo de ta celeste vois.   ("Artifices," 557, 561, 569–72)

[Therefore, you who know all things to come … through a foreknowledge both certain and perfect … Transport me from my body, that I might live happily in heaven before my death. Oh my life, revive my spirit for a time, and make it so that I might be like the Echo of your voice.][29]

The lines are at once humble and bold, as Adam makes no effort to disguise his dependence, while asking for the privilege of echoing God himself. And in one of several occasions in the poem, Du Bartas affirms the connection between the embrace of uncertainty and the sublime, as Adam's request is granted instantly in a heroic rapture recalling that of prelapsarian Eden.

In one of the most sublime passages of the poem, Du Bartas continues:

> Il est soudain poussé d'une fureur secrete,
> [...]
> Ains comme l'Aigle perd sa branche accoustumee,
> Et ramant par les airs d'une gasche emplumée,
> Voit sous ses pieds la nue …
> De mesme Adam guindé sur les ardentes ailes
> Du Seraphique amour, perd les choses mortelles:
> Se paist du doux aether: fend les ronds estoillez:
> Et tient dessus le front de Dieu ses yeux collez.
> Il semble qu'un Soleil luy flambe sur la face,
> Et que son corps purgé s'éleve d'une brasse.   ("Artifices," 573, 581–90)

[He is suddenly possessed by a secret *furor* … like the eagle leaving behind its customary branch and soaring through the air on his majestic wing, sees the clouds beneath its feet … Likewise Adam mounting up on blazing wings of angelic love, leaves behind mortal things, feeds on soft ether: weaves through the starry skies: And beholds above the face of God, fixing his eyes. It seems that the Sun alights his face, that his purified body rises up a notch.]

When Adam confesses God's ultimately authority over spiritual knowledge, he soars into the heavens in ecstasy in a passage that unites Longinian (and Neoplatonic) concepts of transport with Christian imagery of apocalypse and sanctification. As he "mounts up" on "blazing wings," his divine flight recalls images of

Longinian flight, along with biblical accounts of prophets such as Ezekiel and Isaiah who are selected to experience God's presence in unique ways. Like Ezekiel, Adam is granted a miraculous vision of the glory of God; he is also "purified" like Isaiah, whose tongue is cleansed with burning coals as a symbol of his refinement from sin.[30] And as Du Bartas grants Adam, despite bearing responsibility for sin, the honour of being the only human character in *Les Semaines* to see God after the Fall in his mortal condition, he celebrates the reconciliation and glory available to those who place their hope in God, rather than power or status.

In the subsequent content of his vision, Du Bartas adds that while sublime glory demands intellectual and spiritual humility, it has an equalizing function, whose end is not to humble or weaken but to fully restore the value of the self. In a somewhat perplexing sequence of travel through time and space, Adam instructs his son and grandson, Seth and Enos, to look ahead to the example of Henoc, a later descendant, who following Genesis and Hebrews, is renowned for walking with God by faith, then being permanently raptured on that account years before his expected death.[31] As Adam describes it, Henoc,

> Qui mourant tout à soy, vit à Dieu seulement.
> Voy, voy come il s'exerce à souffrir la lumiere,
> Qui foudroyante luit en l'essence premiere:
> Comme libre du joug des corporelles lois,
> Et sequestré des sens, il vole quelquefois
> [...]
> Ayant la Foy, le Jeusne, et l'Oraison pour ailes
> [...]
> Comme pour quelque temps montant de forme en forme,
> En la forme de Dieu, heureux, il se transforme.
>
> ("Artifices," 652–6, 658, 661–2)

[Who dying completely to himself, lives for God alone. See, see how he exerts himself to endure the light, which shines violently in the First Being: As one free from the bonds of bodily laws and raptured from the senses, he flies for a space ... Having Faith, Fasting, and Prayer as wings ... For some time ascending from form to form, he transforms, blissfully, into the very image of God.]

The description of Henoc ascending to heaven recalls the "most holy flight" and "holy ecstasy" that Adam enjoys before sin corrupts his relationship to God. Yet Henoc's glorification ultimately progresses beyond what we see in Adam's example, revealing an even more radical version of Longinian *ekstasis*. Transforming "en forme de Dieu," Henoc seems to lose his sense of self completely, in a description resembling the Hindu concept of *nirvana* or *moksha* more than the biblical conception of resurrection.[32] The image is one of complete *ekstasis* – an absolute and final transport out of the self. This transport, however, does not emphasize a complete loss of individuality, but a compelling contrast between the degrading condition of sin and brokenness that had weighed Adam down since the Fall, and complete freedom from these constraints. In describing it out loud, Adam is not fearful, but admiring, ecstatic, and hopeful. After the traumas and trappings of the Fall, he gains a vision of the world's evils being lifted away and the soul being returned to its original design – a reminder that his ultimate hope lies in heavenly glory shared with a community of saints.

Further, that Adam observes and admires the heroic ascent of his own great-great-great-great-grandson represents an even more drastic disruption of hierarchy. Once again, Du Bartas reiterates that the pursuit of sublime glory has an equalizing function that humbles the powerful and elevates the weak, negating power traditionally ascribed to authority figures. Through a vision of spiritual heroism that inverts normal orders, he maintains that the best community is one where members mutually exhort one another towards a shared hope of eternal glory. In emphasizing what humanity cannot do or know, Du Bartas's vision maintains that true glorification brings equality rather than power.

Abraham and Isaac: Abjection and Ecstasy

In exploring the heroic challenge of sublimity, Du Bartas pays even more attention to the figure of Abraham, especially in the fragment, "Pères," where the patriarch responds to God's unfathomable command to sacrifice Isaac. While continuing to develop the link between intellectual humility, exaltation, and community, "Pères" more fully explores the psychological and affective dimensions of the pursuit of divine mystery.

Du Bartas's own version of this narrative obviously borrows from Genesis, but it also likely responds to Thomas Beza's dramatization of the episode, *Abraham sacrifiant* (1550). Beza, as Calvin's successor in Geneva, presents a more emotional Abraham than seen in Genesis, but still a more compliant, ultimately Calvinistic version in his explicit recognition of divine sovereignty. Part of the drama from Beza's narrative comes from the entrance of Satan, who tempts Abraham to disobey. In *Les Semaines*, however, Du Bartas's Abraham needs no incitement to confusion – he is completely overwhelmed by grief, horror, and doubt over God's purpose for the command. In a reaction much more vulnerable and relatable than recorded in Genesis, the patriarch is

> saisi de douleur, d'effroy, d'estonnement:
> L'Image de la mort dans ses yeux desjà nouë,
> Un rigoureux hiver tous ses members secouë,
> Et sur le champ herbu, tout de son long tombé,

> Devient en un moment palle, rouge, plombé:
> Une froide sueur de tout son corps degoutte,
> La parolle luy manque, il n'oit, il ne voit quotte.   ("Pères," 82–7)

[seized with pain, fright, and astonishment: The image of death is already whirling in his eyes. A harsh chill overtakes his limbs, and on the grassy field, fallen headlong, he turns pale, then flushed, overwhelmed. A cold sweat seeps from his whole body. Words fail him; he does not see or hear at all.]

The passage paints Abraham's grief in terms that epitomize the negative dimension of the sublime – his physical reaction closely echoes a poem of Sappho's quoted by Longinus:

> I see nothing with my eyes, and my ears thunder.
> The sweat pours down: shivers grip me all over. I am grown
>   paler than grass, and seem to myself to be
>   very near to death.[33]

That Abraham is alternately flushed and pale, blinded, deafened, and death-like recalls with remarkable similarity the features of Sappho's suffering, including the "contradictory sensations" and "most striking and intense ... congeries of emotions" that Longinus cites in his description.

In experiencing this form of terrorizing transport, Abraham also enters abjection, his condition characterized by a horrified crisis of identity, violent internal struggle, and even breakdown of the self. As we have seen, abjection entails a loss or breakdown of the boundaries of self, reflecting a body and mind caught between life and death, which Abraham experiences in this passage. Through Abraham's affective condition, Du Bartas does not emphasize a process of acknowledging and repenting of sin, as Tasso does in using abjection, but illustrates the threat that trust in God poses to one's most fundamental sense of identity. Affirming this loss of identity himself, Abraham claims that to kill Isaac would cost him his life, "que l'arrest escrit au firmament / A collée à la sienne [which the law of heaven has tied to his]" ("Pères," 110–11). He has identified so completely with Isaac as both his beloved child, and the hoped-for seed of the nation of Israel, that the command represents a complete division from his very being.

Invoking a set of affects more negative than anything seen thus far in *Les Semaines*, Du Bartas uses the severe intrusion on Abraham's sense of coherent selfhood to indicate the emotional and intellectual costs of the spiritual heroism he advocates, and the corresponding strength it demands. Du Bartas is not exhorting readers to prepare to take extreme action – Abraham's test was widely acknowledged to be of a unique kind – but to show readers how trust in divine mystery can persist even in the midst of the most terrifying powerlessness. And the use of abjection is especially fitting, since Abraham is so troubled by the command that he wonders if obeying it may cause him to become identified with evil itself: "Cela ne m'est pas moins à le penser horrible, / Cruel à le vouloir, qu'à le faire impossible [It's nothing less than horrible even to think of, cruel to desire, impossible to do]" ("Pères," 127–8). Abraham's test has troubled numerous philosophers and theologians, who have sought to explain how a good God can issue a command that appears to defy both a moral order (that people should not murder one another) and God's covenant with Abraham (that his nation would be realized through Isaac).[34] Can those who claim allegiance to God maintain trust in divine goodness, when every fibre of their reason urges otherwise, and when everything is on the line? As Abraham describes the irreconcilable contradictions the dilemma presents to him, he asks,

> Dieu fera guerre à Dieu? sa voix sera traitresse?
> Et son commandement combatra sa promesse?
> Ma foy renversera la baze de ma foy,
> M'estant tout un de croire, ou descroire sa loy?   ("Pères," 147–50)

[Will God make war with God? Will his voice betray itself? And will his commandment counter his promise? Will my faith undercut the basis of my faith, making it all the same to me – whether I trust or distrust his law?]

The passage reveals two related conflicts: God's faithfulness appears to be in conflict with itself, and Abraham in turn finds his faith to threaten itself. If he trusts in God's goodness to keep his promises, then he must kill Isaac; but in doing so, he fears he will undercut God's promise and render God's faithfulness null, along with his own ability to trust. And as he senses the threat to his faith, he likewise feels a threat to his very self.

The poem is clearly sympathetic rather than judgmental of Abraham's plight, but suggests nonetheless how impossible it is to show spiritual heroism by relying too heavily on one's own ability to know. The lines above, referencing two related but separate questions, offer the beginning of a solution. Abraham already knows the answers to the first set of questions – that God will not make war with God, or betray himself or his promises; Abraham just does not know the answer to the second question – how his faith can function in uncertain circumstances. As long as his focus remains on the character of God, he has the answers he seeks. It is when he considers whether *his* faith will make *his* beliefs void that the greater confusion sets in.

This passage and the following stanzas direct Abraham, and implicitly the poem's readers, to see that such a psychomachia creates an unnecessary burden. His abjection, his fear of losing himself, exposes a relatable yet problematic focus on himself and his desire for understanding that can be cleared up by a heroic forgetfulness of self, by a determination to marvel at divine greatness. A few lines down, Abraham counsels himself to do just that:

> Ne sonde point les abysmes profonds
> Des jugemens de Dieu, ils n'ont rive ni fonds,
> Contien toy dans les bords d'une sobre sagesse,
> Admire seulent ce qu'encor la foiblesse
> De la loy ne comprend
> [...]
> Tout ce qu'il fait est bon. Non point que l'Immortel
> Doive faire le bien à cause qu'il est tel:
> Ainçois le bien est bien à cause qu'il procede
> De la haute bonté, de celui qui possede
> Les tresors de Justice.   ("Pères," 169–73, 177–80)

[Do not try to sound the great abyss of divine judgments, where there is neither shore nor bottom. Confine yourself to a sober wisdom. And what the law, in its weakness, does not make clear, admire. All that he does is good. Not that the Immortal One must do good because it is good: goodness is good because it proceeds from the height of goodness, from the one who possesses all the riches of Justice.]

Unlike his earlier questioning, this passage avoids all use of first person; he shows a new readiness to embrace God's mysteriousness. In doing so, Abraham himself affirms a controversial truth claim about the nature of God's goodness: God is not good because he achieves an external standard of righteousness, but because he is the origin of that standard of righteousness.[35] Given God's inherent goodness, Abraham believes, he can identify fully with the divine will and leave his own unrest behind. In an exhortation that re-emerges in *Paradise Lost*, Abraham thereby frees himself to "admire" what he cannot understand by surrendering to mystery as a positive force. In admiring, Abraham finally prepares himself for heroic rapture, prefigured when he continues: "Je sens de son Esprit les mouvements secretz. / Il entretient mon coeur de ses discours sacrez [I can feel the secret movements of his spirit. He enters my heart with his holy speech]" ("Pères," 225–26). The "mouvements secretz" echo Longinus's concept of *ekstasis*, being drawn outside the self, here used to convey the process of being filled with the power of the Holy Spirit.

But Du Bartas acknowledges that unity with God is not yet complete – not to highlight any particular fault, but to reiterate the vital importance of communal support to pursuing heroic rapture. Just before the attempted sacrifice, Abraham reassures Isaac that he is not murdering him in wrath, as his son suspects. He expresses what appears to be (but is not) a complete embrace of divine inscrutability: "Il a mille moyens / Pour tirer, prevoyant, de la presse les siens. / Le Monde a pour timon sa sagesse admirable, / Il est egallement puissant et veritable. [Foreseeing, he has a thousand ways of saving his own. The world has his marvellous wisdom as its guide; he is as powerful as he is good]" ("Pères," 341–44). In a stunning expression of belief, Abraham acknowledges that what is unknown about God is even greater than the hope he once had in Isaac before his life was threatened – that God can recreate him as even better than before, and use any one of a thousand ways to do so.[36] Yet despite the display of faith, he falters and nearly changes his mind: in the next lines he recalls his "esmoy" and "perte" [agitation and loss] and hesitates to follow through ("Pères," 346, 347).

In this passage, Du Bartas conveys that intellectual recognition of divine greatness is just part of the equation when facing the more tragic mysteries of human events – Abraham needs encouragement, which comes from an individual with the least to gain from providing it. In response to his father's anguish, Isaac not only encourages his father to obey, but he begins with an image to move him to cultivate an appetite for sublime awe. He states: "Je voy les Cieux ouvers, Dieu me tend jà les bras [I see the Heavens open, God reaches out his arms to me]" ("Pères," 354). In effect, Isaac visualizes the magnificence of his own rapture – instead of argumentation, he uses the *enargeia* or *phantasia* that Tasso and Longinus had both emphasized in their discourses on the sublime. The image – of loss bringing greater joy – is designed to speak to Abraham's imagination rather than his intellect. That Abraham, after hundreds of lines of agonizing, finally prepares to obey the command at this moment again endorses the Longinian idea that sublimity is more powerful and more meaningful than argumentation and rationalization. The poem firmly emphasizes that imagination is superior to sight, and that it is only by emphasizing possibilities, rather than certainties, that a person can truly see mysteriousness as great.

Fulfilling the poem's heroic model, Abraham finally enters a state of rapture just after he prepares to sacrifice Isaac, when he is interrupted by "la tonnante voix, la voix du Souverain / Arrest son esprit, son oreille et sa main [the thundering voice of the Sovereign arrests his mind, ear, and hand]" ("Pères," 393–4). The phrase indicates that Abraham is paralysed, stunned in mind and body – left in a state of sublimity. As Abraham succeeds in passing the test, Du Bartas once again makes rapture a function of humility, action, and responsiveness to community, but shows in Abraham how connection to God can deepen in degrees. Unlike the rapture of Adam, Du Bartas features an extended series of steps that lead to divine *ekplexis* – beginning with abjection, where Abraham is internally withdrawn in focussing on his own (lack of intellectual) power, to the infusion of the Holy Spirit as he begins to forget himself, to the direct intervention of God's mercy in sublimity. But through Abraham's struggle and Isaac's encouragement, Du Bartas features the absolute responsiveness of God to those who seek him – even in the unexpected form of his own son's voice.

By including Isaac's encouragement, Du Bartas takes a significant departure from Genesis that solidifies the importance of community to his heroic model. In making this addition, moreover, Du Bartas offers a fascinating complement to Tasso's concept of heroism that speaks to the religious warfare threatening France. Both poets acknowledge the importance of human support to heavenly union, but while Tassoan heroes do so through the sight of human beauty pointing them heavenward, Du Bartas's heroes do so by helping one another imagine such sights for themselves. Perhaps Du Bartas is giving voice to his own personal Protestant beliefs, as he implicitly affirms the use of imagination over visual icons; but I believe the passage can also be interpreted as a broad message to warn a nation of sparring Protestant and Catholics about the importance of spiritual unity. If Isaac can support the obedience of his father at such great personal cost, Du Bartas implies, then his own readers can put aside their desire for political authorization of their beliefs. At issue, for Du Bartas, is a tendency among institutional leaders, especially within France but across all of Europe, to insist on ideological uniformity at the expense of mutual support and love.

In this vein, Du Bartas's emphasis on selflessness is striking. Even Milton, who will also incorporate self-subordination into the centre of his model of sublime heroism, does not describe the kind of complete obliteration of self we see in such figures as Abraham and Henoc from *Les Semaines*. Yet in such a doctrinally divided nation, it seems fitting that Du Bartas would emphasize this message of humility for audiences whose struggles for power threatened religious unity and the practice of genuine spirituality.

Although English readers did not always interpret and translate him as a tolerant and open-minded thinker, Du Bartas makes discernible efforts to sidestep doctrinal concerns through his heroic model.[37] As if featuring this desire for religious unity, moreover, Du Bartas's narrative of Abraham concludes with a distinctive avoidance of an opportunity to promote a Protestant concern for faith. In Hebrews, Abraham is specifically noted among many other biblical heroes for exemplifying great heroic faith, but Du Bartas celebrates Abraham for his *works*: when the voice of God at last addresses Abraham, the voice insists that the acts of other literary heroes are "moindre que tes faicts" [less than your deeds], and that he will be celebrated for his "merveilleux gestes" [marvellous actions] ("Pères," 404, 406).[38] The emphasis on virtuous action does not detract from Du Bartas's emphasis on interior transformation, for the fragment spends several hundred lines indicating the emotional, intellectual, and spiritual transformation that must takes place before Abraham can act. But in the context of religious warfare, the very mention of deeds is significant, because it contributes to a doctrinally non-committal depiction of a central Reformation controversy. Where many Catholics emphasized works, and many Protestants emphasized faith over action, Du Bartas portrays both feeding the other, bringing faith and works to a point of perfection. Towards the conclusion of his struggles, Abraham prays that God would "fay qu'une foy parfait / Accompagne ma main [make it so that a perfect faith should accompany my hand]" ("Pères," 387–8). As the episode concludes, Du Bartas clarifies what this "perfect faith" looks like: Abraham fixating on the goodness of God's character, with the imaginative support of his own son, which in turn draws him out of his fears and enables a work of active obedience. Faith and action work together to enable a heroic awe for divine mystery. And in emphasizing mystery, Du Bartas suggests that true spirituality is not about how well spiritual seekers reason their beliefs – or to which confessional camp they belong – but to whom they direct those beliefs. With a focus firmly on God, Du Bartas indicates, those seeking eternal glory can have assurance of the good coming to them, gaining tastes of immortality as they seek in humility to be overwhelmed by God's presence.

In deemphasizing matters of doctrine, Du Bartas moves to unite his French readers – yet his concept of unity is not only civic and national, but eternal. As Abraham and Isaac join together in heroic trust and obedience, they inspire one another towards rapture, Isaac imagining his final union with God, and Abraham being stunned by the thundering ("tonnante") voice of God interfering to make all things right. While both figures lessen themselves in service to God, they do so in the hope of permanent joy.

Although Du Bartas's heroic model is more anti-rational than any other in this study, his interest in divine mystery and inscrutability is far from unique to *Les Semaines*. As suggested, it had a particular appeal to Milton, who, despite a very different approach to learning, knowledge, and doctrine, also valued the ability to be amazed by divine infinity. Both authors share in their portraits of heroism an effort to unite intellectual humility, communal support, and transformative rapture in a form of sceptical sublimity not quite like anything seen in Greek, Roman, or Italian models of epic heroism. And despite great differences, Du Bartas's interest in mysteriousness also bears on Spenser's version of the Protestant sublime in *The Faerie Queene*.

4 Spenser's Protestant Sublime in the Legend of Holiness

Compared to *Les Semaines*, Spenser's *The Faerie Queene* uses the sublime to develop a particularly subtle challenge to English nationalism. In general, Spenser is ready to celebrate Protestant England and the authority of Queen Elizabeth in his epic, depicting both as forces resisting the Catholicism of France, Spain, and Ireland. On the surface of the poem, after all, the epic appears to fully endorse English national identity by making its title character, the Faery Queen, an embodiment of an idealized Elizabeth and emblem of national greatness. Yet, while Stephen Greenblatt maintains that Spenser "loved" power and "passionate[ly] worship[ed] … imperialism," I would argue that Spenser both held and expressed significant concerns about the scope of English authority and the demands it placed on the English people.[1] In *The Faerie Queene*, Spenser incorporates depictions of sublimity in ways that subordinate and problematize the significance of the English nation itself, urging particular wariness about England's exercise of authority over individual spirituality. In its subtext, the epic poem advises the English to resist pressures to conflate national and spiritual identity.

Particularly in the Legend of Holiness, understood by M.H. Abrams as a prototype for the entire epic, Spenser develops a spiritual allegory of irresistible salvation that reveals a markedly Calvinist model of the sublime.[2] Rather than endorsing theological dogmatism, however, this model works to elevate the importance of the personal connection to God over the connection to political entities. Throughout Book I, Spenser depicts the Redcrosse Knight encountering numerous expressions of divine holiness while in the overwhelmed condition of the sublime, echoing the Longinian principle that the sublime is irresistible – that it "gets the better of every listener."[3] In focussing on divine holiness as a sublime force that Redcrosse cannot withstand, Spenser makes the knight's politically authorized pursuit of the *virtue* of holiness secondary to his experience of salvation, allowing the spiritual allegory to overwhelm the political allegory. By distinguishing devotion to nation from relationship to God, Spenser subordinates the call to dedicate oneself to England beneath an appeal to recognize salvation by grace as the most fundamental source of Christian selfhood. In effect, compared to Tasso or Du Bartas, who emphasize the *choice* of embracing the sublime, Spenser creates a particularly complicated model of sublimity and heroism, a model that begins with receiving unmerited divine favour and ends with participating in a spiritual community based outside political affiliation. For Spenser, no institutional force on earth can create an attraction as irresistible (or make as compelling a claim to loyalty) as divine holiness, and it is only by acknowledging this principle that Redcrosse can discern the proper dedication that he does owe to worldly authority. Only then, according to Spenser, can he perform services of lasting value to society and nation.

Spenser – recently recognized by Patrick Cheney as Renaissance England's first truly sublime author – probably did not have access to Longinus.[4] But as Cheney notes, critics from William Hazlitt to Michael Murrin and James Nohrnberg have frequently, if nominally, linked *The Faerie Queene* to the sublime.[5] And while Spenser never developed an explicit theoretical framework for the sublime comparable to Tasso's theory of *meraviglia*, he took interest in Protestant discourses on theology, hermeneutics, and stylistics that, as we saw in chapter 1, have much in common with Longinian theory. In fact, *The Faerie Queene* showcases a number of characteristics that Reformers associated with the Bible, and that classical and early modern literary theorists correlated with sublime poetry: the capacity for the emotional vigour (*energeia*) that Sidney identifies at the heart of great poetry, and the grandeur and potency of imagination (*enargeia* or *phantasia*) that Puttenham and Tasso held as essential to great works of literature.[6] And like other epic poets before him, Spenser frequently represents characters who experience sublimity as part of their heroic narrative.

For Cheney, the Spenserian sublime is first and foremost a principle of authorship, a feature of art in which the poem recurrently dwells on the artistic significance of sublime images to present a "self-advertisement for England's laureate poet." In this view, Spenser promotes a concept of sublime authorship based on a specific heroic model, featuring "service to the nation in the context of eternity."[7] While acknowledging Spenser's sublime authorship and endorsement of service to nation, I would qualify the poem's approach to nationhood, emphasizing how Spenser uses the sublime to complicate the ethical purposes of his own poetry. Drawing on Reformed concepts of divine holiness, Spenser grounds Redcrosse's quest on recurrent (and sublime) encounters with various forms of the divine presence, encounters that establish the definitive priority of the individual relationship to God.[8]

Throughout Book I, Redcrosse consistently reacts to representations of divine holiness with strong forms of Longinian *ekplexis*. When he faces various "dreadfull" or "wondrous" representations of divine judgment or grace, he becomes "amazed," "astonied," or otherwise terrified at this overpowering presence before him. We see such a reaction particularly in his paralysed response to the threat of divine judgment, embodied in Fradubio and Orgoglio, his stricken response to the convicting words of Fidelia, and his "merveiling" at the work of divine grace during his battle with the Dragon. While these scenarios all make distinctive contributions to Spenser's model, each one represents the individual believer's overwhelmed response to an aspect of divine holiness, depicted as the most compelling and fundamental of all powers a human being might encounter.

For Spenser, holiness is an inherently sublime quality of divine magnificence – first and foremost a characteristic of God, whose expressions of both judgment and mercy demand full surrender. In emphasizing these moments of divine sublimity in Redcrosse's quest, Spenser subordinates the place of English politics and the devotion due to its authority figures. In the Legend of Holiness, national purposes come a distant second behind the greater aim of eternal relationship to God, depicted in terms consistent with Calvinist theology.

Both Reformers and their predecessors regularly characterized divine holiness as not only overwhelmingly powerful, but terrifying in its immanence, even to devout followers. Augustine, widely recognized as a forefather of the Reformation, expressed sublime bewilderment at the mystery of God's transcendence and indwelling presence:

> Do heaven and hell therefore contain you, since you fill them? … The vessels that are filled by you do not restrict you, for even if they are shattered, you are not poured forth … Since all things cannot contain you in your entirety, do they then contain a part of you, and do all things simultaneously contain the same part?[9]

While Augustine articulates his confusion at the incomprehensible nature of God, Calvin highlights more specifically the sublime terror that comes (even to the faithful) at being in the presence of divine judgment. He notes that Job, who "has a good conscience … is stricken dumb with astonishment [muet en son effroy], for he sees that not even the holiness of angels can please God" in his "incomprehensible" righteousness.[10] For those resistant to God, holiness was still more terrifying. As described in the accounts of several prominent biblical characters, the demand for perfection could completely overwhelm those aware of their failures. In an especially tragic example, Saul, the first king of Israel, having been informed of God's impending judgment for his visit to a medium, "fel streyght way all along on the earth, and was sore afrayed because of the wordes of Samuel, so that there was no strength in him" – transformed instantly from overconfident, complacent king into broken soul.[11] Reminiscent of Longinus's concept of the sublime's irresistibility, the Holy Otherness of God prompts an involuntary experience of sublime transport in everyone who senses its presence, whether a transport of spiritual elevation or of shattering ruin.

Moreover, in biblical and Reformed tradition, humanity must experience sublime transport – an overpowering encounter with God's presence – in order to begin the process of sanctification, or being made holy. Just as Longinus held that poets could produce sublimity only after having been inspired by a sublime reading experience, Christians, in a parallel manner, had to experience God's holiness with a sense of awe in order to be radically transformed by it.[12] Reformers could find a prime example in the conversion of the apostle Paul, who is stunned by the appearance of God on his journey to Damascus. "Trembling" and "astonied," the apostle is psychologically and emotionally transformed from self-righteous persecutor of Christians into humbled believer and follower; the experience anticipates Luther's point that true desire for goodness must be "put into the heart by the Holy Spirit" in a moment of radical, instantaneous change that could only originate from the outside.[13] Calvin, meanwhile, figures this process of miraculous transformation as rebirth: "the man dies to himself that he may begin to live unto God," and acquire a "desire of pious and holy living."[14] In this context, human holiness derives from the sublimity of divine holiness, a concept Spenser incorporates into the heroic development of Redcrosse.

The link between sublimity and Reformed concepts of holiness is important to Spenserian poetics for several reasons. In particular, it helps to reaffirm *The Faerie Queene*'s Protestantism against efforts to emphasize the poem's theological instability.[15] The efforts of Spenserian scholarship to broaden the scope of theological perspectives in the poem are important, but have perhaps gone too far. While Spenser may, as Claire McEachern suggests, depict a "richly dramatic … landscape of Elizabethan religious identities," his use of the sublime depicts salvation itself in staunchly Protestant terms.[16] Across the Legend of Holiness, Redcrosse's reactions to expressions of holiness consistently reflect Calvinist views of salvation – he is stupefied and transported out of himself in processes he cannot initially control; like the Longinian sublime, Spenserian salvation is entirely irresistible. Even in the latter cantos where Spenser seems most sympathetic to Catholic doctrine, he leaves little ambiguity or contradiction in his portrayal of the route to faith. By making divine grace both sublime and irresistible, he emphasizes that genuine heroic virtue comes from a divine process of transformation and preparation that begins outside the individual's control, a heavenly process whose purposes are distinct from and supersede worldly affairs. This is not to argue that Spenser depicts spirituality as entirely determined, but that he complicates the notion of heroic agency to a much greater degree than Tasso, Du Bartas, or Milton.[17] In Spenser's representation, as in Calvin's, autonomy itself is a fraught and mysterious concept, with dependence on divine sovereignty depicted in unreservedly positive terms.

Spenser's Reformed version of sublime heroism is also important to recognizing the role of the affections in Redcrosse's pursuit of divine holiness. The significant portion of scholarship that focusses on the Reformed aspects of the knight's heroic quest generally downplays the role of his profound psychological and emotional experiences (and, consequently, the role of affective experience in Calvinism and Puritanism).[18] In most cases, scholarship links the Reformed tradition to sobriety, with heightened passion tied to Catholic mysticism.[19] Yet Puritans have always shown a particularly strong interest in the passions – from Luther and Calvin onward, Reformers emphasized that the affections underlie transformation. As Abram van Engen argues, early Reformers endorsed even the "extreme affections" as one of the principal differences between their own approach to the spiritual life and those of the Catholic or Anglican Churches, where "ostentation in ceremonies" reigned.[20] Joseph Campana, a scholar who does emphasize the affective dynamics of Redcrosse's Reformed pursuit of holiness, characterizes the knight's quest as a "lived experience" involving vulnerability and empathy in imitation of Christ.[21] I would add that Redcrosse's encounters with the sublime work to centre Christian experience on a condition of awe, admiration, and astonishment at the divinity, and the divinity alone.[22] In representing Redcrosse's quest for holiness in terms of the sublime, Spenser makes holiness an aspect of God's presence that must violently disrupt the sinner from inside out – in a complex, emotionally devastating, and miraculously transformative experience. In this depiction of holiness, heaven becomes the ultimate source of fear, hope, and heroic purpose.

In Book I, Spenser develops a three-part model of Protestant sublimity underlying his portrayal of divine holiness, each part characterizing Redcrosse's response to one of three distinct expressions of holiness: 1) manifestations of divine judgment, 2) manifestations of divine grace, and 3) a mediated form of grace, or charisma, which is channeled through Christian community and transforms him into a heroic agent. Each of these parts of Spenser's model incorporates or anticipates major theological and philosophical ideas that are in conversation with the Longinian sublime.

First, when Redcrosse experiences dismay and terror at the presence of Fradubio, Orgoglio, and Despaire, Spenser characterizes these events as encounters with God's "dreadfull" judgment – isolating events that imprison the person within the inner self. In this stage, Spenser anticipates principles of Kristevan abjection that we have seen earlier and that intersect directly with the sublime. A psychological principle of identity crisis, abjection provides an especially useful lens into the Spenserian hero's horrified powerlessness at the prospect of divine judgment. Second, as Arthur defeats an "astownd[ed]" Orgoglio, Spenser adopts a framework supplied by Luther, Calvin, and other Reformers to describe the work of divine grace – envisioning an astonishing, ultimately irresistible force that transports the person outside the self and miraculously separates him from his old sinful nature. And third, with Redcrosse's transforming reaction to the grace demonstrated by characters such as Una and Fidelia, Spenser anticipates modern theories of charisma and charismatic authority, to show grace being transferred across the spiritual community. As introduced previously, charisma is a subset of the sublime – a powerful force of personality that binds individuals together. Unlike Tassoan charisma, however, which initiates a private process of divine *ekstasis*, Spenserian charisma is based on a Reformed concept of spiritual gifting within community, a mechanism by which Redcrosse becomes anchored in divine grace and begins to undergo sanctification. In his depiction of charisma, Spenser carefully distinguishes "true" from "false" forms, differentiating genuine spiritual community from authority figures whose ends are not really divine, but deceptive and destructive.

Sharing a sublime core, these three parts of Spenser's representation of holiness – judgment, grace, charisma – operate on Redcrosse in a manner that reformulates the nature of Christian heroism and identity. Ultimately, Spenser represents holiness originating in the perception of God and being transfused among Christians in a mysterious process that occludes borders between God and humanity, tying the believer firmly to an eternal spiritual community.

The Terror of Judgment: Abjection and the Counter-Sublime

As early as canto ii, Redcrosse discovers with horror the knight Fradubio imprisoned within a tree – a horror reflecting the psychological terror of sinners as they initially become aware of deserving divine judgment. By viewing Redcrosse's psychological and emotional condition in terms of abjection, we can see, more fully than has been previously recognized, the violently transformative nature of terror featured in recurrent depth throughout Book I.[23] In a thoroughly Calvinist depiction, Spenser makes terror central to the heroic knight's spiritual development, a terror rooted not in the fear of losing of political power, but in being found outside the will of God.

As seen in previous chapters, Kristevan abjection might be considered a dark sublime or counter-sublime, as both abjection and sublimity involve a subject's alienation from self and violent transformation – the latter entailing rapture and union, and the former entailing withdrawal and (fruitlessly attempted) separation and avoidance.[24] In particular, Spenser describes in comparatively Kristevan terms a complex erosion of identity beyond the subject's ability to control. For Kristeva, the individual senses fluid, ambiguous borders between the self and an encroaching "Other" and withdraws in horror, a process similar to that described by Spenser to map an elaborate breakdown of the concept of self.[25] In the *Gerusalemme liberata*, as heroes undergo abjection following the loss of the sublime sight of the beloved, the condition is a relatively brief intermediary stage of self-denial and contrition between desiring God and experiencing transport. *Les Semaines* depicts abjection as an intense but even more short-lived phase of humbling, where the hero is reminded of the supremacy of God and still must choose to follow him. But for Spenser, abjection represents a much lengthier phase characterized by fruitless efforts to avoid God and the knowledge of failing to meet his standards, along with the deepening, terrorizing realization of that impossibility. Spenser depicts a process of abjection as an inevitable precedent to Christian repentance and salvation, a phase of violent psychological transport making the individual increasingly and profoundly cognizant of the need for grace. For Spenser, reconciliation to God thus involves a horror more terrible and extended than anything shown by Tasso or Du Bartas, as it depicts the intense self-abasement and reconception of self that a sinner must undergo to enter relationship with God, along with the severe consequences of refusing salvation.

In this extended portrayal of abjection, Spenser's approach corresponds particularly with Reformed thinking about the human's relationship to God, especially the way a person, created in God's image and designed for an intimate relationship with God, might seek ill-desired, unattainable independence from him, before being traumatized by his holy presence. As Calvin writes, without Christ mediating between God and man, the only possible affect for the human sinner is horror at the Otherness of God, precipitating an attempt to flee his presence: "For as soon as God's dread majesty [l'horrible majesté] comes to mind, we cannot but tremble and be *driven far away* [le sentiment … nous effarouche et déchasse bien loing] by the recognition of our own unworthiness."[26] For Calvin, the mere idea of God's holiness creates in everyone a strong desire for separation, an inescapable terror at the recognition of one's inferiority, and ultimately, not only psychological destruction, but transformation:

> We see men who in his absence normally remained firm and constant, but who, when he manifests his glory, are so shaken [esbranlez] and struck dumb [effarouchez] as to be laid low by the dread of death – are in fact overwhelmed [opprimez] by it and almost annihilated [s'esvanouissent]. As a consequence, we must infer that man is never sufficiently touched and affected by the awareness of his lowly state until he has compared himself with God's majesty.[27]

For Calvin, an experience of abjection is not only universal to the human perception of God, but an integral component of divine reconciliation, as it produces the necessary spiritual self-knowledge to enable divine relationship – a concept central to the experience of Redcrosse.

Of the features of Kristevan abjection evident in Redcrosse's experiences with the prospect of judgment, the most persistent is an instability or dissociation from the sense of self. As Kristeva describes it, abjection involves recognizing the "loss" or "want" of the "foundations of its own being." First attempting to protect the self against the intrusions of the abject (the feared "Other"), the subject later acknowledges the loss of self and even participates in its own destruction.[28] A characteristic part of this process entails what Kristeva calls *negation* or *exclusion*, a condition of perpetual isolation or captivity when a subject is driven continually inside the self, horrified at the prospect of contact with the unwanted Other.[29] At the conclusion of the process of abjection comes a condition of ambiguousness, or a perpetually unstable sense of identity. In Kristevan terms, the subject at last comes to recognize, though with persistent horror, that its very existence depends on the outside object.[30] In Spenserian terms, the hero must experience a complete breakdown of the sinful self to be rebuilt in the likeness of Christ – not as a destruction of identity, but as the fulfilment of a being created in the image of God.

In the Legend of Holiness, Spenser uses these principles to depict the horrific erosion of identity a person feels upon recognizing the failure to live up to the holy standard of divine law. Featuring Redcrosse's terror of judgment in the Fradubio and the Orgoglio episodes, and depicting the hypothetical culmination of judgment in the Despaire episode, Spenser vividly represents how the knight of holiness must be confronted with the power of judgment before developing qualities of holiness himself, undergoing a complete breakdown of the former sense of self (as virtuous and morally independent). Redcrosse's abjection thus suggests another variation from Tassoan abjection: while Tassoan heroes retain some degree of choice in entering abjection, Redcrosse is more like Du Bartas's Abraham on being commanded to sacrifice Isaac – overwhelmed and compelled into the condition. But compared to Abraham's, Redcrosse's condition proves more long-lasting, not subject to dissolution soon after assenting to God's sovereignty, as Abraham does in *Les Semaines*. Spenser thus depicts a more intensive transformation: not until Redcrosse has been thoroughly horrified by the prospect of judgment, acknowledging his own inadequacy before divine perfection, can he be capable of pursuing holiness.

Fradubio: Judgment Predicted

Redcrosse's abjection first begins in canto ii, when warned by Fradubio of the duplicity of his current consort, Duessa. Having strayed from his spiritual purpose and community (represented in Una), Redcrosse falls into sin and becomes subjected to judgment, depicting the horror that drives the growing awareness of a false self, and the inescapability of the divine presence.

During Redcrosse's conversation with Fradubio in canto ii, the passage repeatedly emphasizes the knight's terror at everything from the sound of Fradubio's voice emerging from the branch to the conclusion of his tale. As Spenser writes of Redcrosse:

> Astond he stood, and vp his heare did houe,
> And with that suddein horror could no member moue.
>
> At last whenas the dreadfull passion
>   Was ouerpast, and manhood well awake,
>   Yet musing at the straunge occasion,
>   And doubting much his sence, he thus bespake.   (I.ii.31.8–32.4)[31]

The language of these lines is characteristic of the dark sublimity associated with abjection. Redcrosse is "astond" – shocked or dazed, bewildered, and terrified, according to the *OED* – a standard feature of Longinian transport: the knight's hair stands on end; he is immobilized by the "suddein horror"; and he is overwhelmed by a "dreadfull passion."[32] Douglas Biow maintains that what Redcrosse fears is ultimately the loss of his *virtuous* identity through the bewitchments of Duessa.[33] I would add that the knight also fears something more directly in line with abjection: the loss of his *autonomous* identity. The final line cited above, "doubting much his sence," suggests that Redcrosse distrusts the reliability of his usual mode of perception, via his five senses; this "doubt," in turn, is accompanied by transport, in a manner comparable to what we have seen previously in Tasso's Armida or Du Bartas's Abraham.[34] But where Armida and Abraham experience doubt as a means of rapture, Redcrosse experiences doubt in a manner that is definitively abject; he becomes aware of an unseen metaphysical presence that seems to threaten his desired concept of self, morally virtuous and independent.

Following Fradubio's first words to Redcrosse, Spenser indeed suggests that the knight's instinctive fear follows from the intrusion of an unknown supernatural force. As the knight wonders who is speaking to him – "what voice of damned Ghost from Limbo lake" (ii.32.5) – he intuitively acknowledges the unseen presence of hellish punishment and, by implication, divine judgment. As A.C. Hamilton notes, Fradubio does enter the punishment of the damned, and thus Redcrosse's words are even more accurate than he may realize.[35] In acknowledging something hellish, Redcrosse's encounter with Fradubio again recalls an episode from Tasso, when Tancredi encounters the demonic apparition of Clorinda emerging from a tree. Yet Tancredi's terror, despite its demonic source, was fully sublime – a reminder of the rightness of submitting to a noble desire for his beloved – while Redcrosse's fear is abject, offering a dire warning that his concept of reality is badly twisted. In finding Fradubio, Redcrosse demonstrates startled apprehension (not comprehension) of his own sinful condition and an omnipotent divine presence, which threatens the autonomy of his identity in ways he cannot yet grasp.

As Redcrosse hears Fradubio relate his own story, Spenser represents the destabilization that occurs at the mere prospect of judgment, which the knight sees in the abjected physical form of Fradubio. Partially human and partially plant, Fradubio exemplifies an obscured identity – a metaphysical ambiguousness and loss of humanity – related to what Kristeva describes in subjects of advanced abjection. As Fradubio tells Redcrosse, he has been "'enclosd in wooden wals full faste, / Banisht from living wights'" (ii.42.8–9) – effectively isolated within a tree that separates him not only from others but from his own human identity. Like those imprisoned in Dante's wood of the suicides in canto 13 of the *Inferno*, Fradubio is confined to plant form for having misused his intellect, and lost the mobility and social connection that would give him fully human status.[36] Compared to Dante's, Spenser's portrayal is equally uncanny, depicting a horrific intrusion on human identity that Redcrosse acknowledges, full of "ghastly dreriment" (ii.44.4), as he fears a similar outcome. In depicting this state of ambiguity, Spenser depicts the process of facing judgment as an erosion of the entire concept of self – in Fradubio, Redcrosse sees a projection of his own spiritual misshapenness and weakness that contrasts with the "righteous" and, therefore, "free" self he wants to believe himself to be.

In representing Redcrosse's fear lingering even after Fradubio's explanation, Spenser portrays abjection as necessary and productive, however counterintuitively, for receiving grace. At the conclusion to Fradubio's story, Redcrosse thrusts "[t]he bleeding bough … into the ground" (ii.44.6), an act demonstrating his horrified awareness of having violated the divine law. Spenser thus suggests that with such horror comes not only attempted concealment but a fruitful instability of self. As Redcrosse returns to Duessa "with trembling cheare" (ii.45.6), he clearly continues to be terrorized by the unseen power of judgment and its threat to his independent status, even after the bough is out of sight. In sensing this instability – including a moral distinction between himself and divine holiness – Redcrosse, Spenser implies, has already taken the first step towards transformation and dependence on God.

Orgoglio: Judgment Confronted

In the knight's confrontation with the giant Orgoglio in canto vii, Spenser depicts in abject terms the process by which a sinner undergoes complete separation from his "moral" and "independent" sense of self, overwhelmed by knowledge of judgment that threatens to make even the "valiant knight become a caytiue thrall" (vii.19.3). As Gless and other scholars have noted, one of Orgoglio's most important functions is "minister of divine judgment" – an emblem of apocalypse.[37] Supporting the external reading of Orgoglio, biblical apocalyptic passages were often read typologically during the Reformation, as applicable to the individual sinner's spiritual struggles.[38] In my view, Orgoglio might be seen as embodying something exterior and interior to the individual at once: the terrorizing threat of divine destruction that exists at the promised end, and a metaphysical terror of conscience that intrudes, abjectly, on the individual psyche, rupturing the sinner's self-concept.

In canto viii, Spenser compares the giant to

> almightie Joue in wrathfull mood, [who]
> To wreake the guilt of mortall sins is bent,
> hurl[ing] forth his thundring dart with deadly food,
> Enrold in flames, and smouldring dreriment,
> Through riuen cloudes and molten firmament.   (viii.9.1–5)

Scholars from John Upton to Cheney have seen Orgoglio's descent on Redcrosse as quintessentially sublime, as it certainly is; the thunderstorm reference in particular resembles several of Longinus's most core examples of sublimity.[39] As an agent of judgment, Orgoglio also represents the abject terror that violently shatters human identity, yet proves absolutely necessary to the process of spiritual renewal. As Orgoglio confounds and captures Redcrosse, Spenser figures the terror of "thundring" judgment overpowering the abject individual who can no longer preserve himself from the knowledge that he must face divine holiness and, moreover, cannot stand whole before it. Indeed, Redcrosse only narrowly escapes an eternal form of the destruction fated to sinners: the subsequent line, "were not heuenly grace, that him did blesse, / He had beene pouldred all" (vii.12.3–4), echoes the description of divine judgment found in 1 Peter 4:18 and throughout Calvinist writings and sermons: "And if the righteous scarcely be saued, where shal the vngodlie and the sinner appeare?" In this same Reformed tradition, Spenser uses the principle of abjection to depict the horrors of eternal judgment from which Christians can make only the narrowest, most harrowing escape.

The Orgoglio scene also features the need to acknowledge inadequacy before divine righteousness, to develop an altogether transformed self-perception, figured as an abject dissociation from self – from "moral" and "free" to "imprisoned by sin." Spenser describes the giant's attack as follows: "so exceeding was the villeins power / That with the winde it did him ouerthrow, / And all his sences stoond, that still he lay full low" (vii.12.7–9). The language is characteristic of the sublime, though it is an interesting detail that Redcrosse lays "low," as abject, instead of taking the characteristic flight of the sublime. Even more directly suggesting the internal transport of abjection, Redcrosse is left "disarmd, disgraste, and inwardly dismayde" (vii.11.6). Cut off from his arms, the very grace that ought to sustain him, and the courage proper to a knight, Redcrosse faces the prospect of being separated from every meaningful part of his former identity, as a power not yet fully understood to him threatens him to the core. Redcrosse's unstable self, in this passage especially, is part of an implicitly constructive transformation in self-perception. Calvin, we saw earlier, maintains that "man is never sufficiently touched and affected by the awareness of his lowly state until he has compared himself with God's majesty." In the same way, Redcrosse is confronted with a stunning image of divine holiness that forces him to count as lost his prior concept of self – as righteous and liberated – and to recognize instead the gaping difference between his own moral condition and God's immanent holiness drawing close to him. As he recognizes how his own utter sinfulness makes him inadequate to stand before that holiness, Redcrosse's stunning by Orgoglio suggests that the recognition of divine power is an experience as earthshattering as looking in a mirror and not seeing oneself at all.

This transformed self-perception continues after Redcrosse becomes Orgoglio's "caytive thrall," when Spenser figures the sinner's recognition of sinfulness as an abject destruction of identity rooted in self-loathing. Redcrosse now participates in his own physical self-destruction, but as emblematic of the process of killing off his sinful self, the Pauline "old man." He becomes nearly unrecognizable through the wasting away of human flesh: a "ruefull spectacle of death and ghastly drere," with "feeble thighs, vnhable to vphold / His pined corse" (viii.40.7–9). In this transformation, Spenser shows the knight participating in a process of self-hatred that is simultaneously destructive and restorative:

> His sad dull eies deepe sunck in hollow pits,
>   Could not endure th'vnwonted sunne to view;
>   His bare thin cheekes for want of better bits,
>   And empty sides deceiued of their dew,
>   Could make a stony hart his hap to rew;
>   His rawbone armes, whose mighty brawned bowrs
>   Were wont to riue steele plates, and helmets hew,
>   Were clene consum'd and all his vitall powers
> Decayd, and al his flesh shronk vp like withered flowres.   (viii.41)

In this description of Redcrosse's wasting away, Spenser presents many details of the knight's physical decay as a dynamic process, akin to the act of dissociation that a subject of abjection carries out in seeking to preserve itself. In the line describing Redcrosse's "thin cheeks" and "empty sides" as "deceiued," Spenser implies that an agent actually contributed to their deterioration, rather than suggesting that they simply wasted away on their own. This recalls Calvin's parallel description of mortification – the "sorrow of soul and dread" at the "awareness of divine judgment" that leaves the sinner "heartily displeased with himself … stricken and overthrown [espovanté et abatu]; humbled and cast down he trembles [se desconforte]; he becomes discouraged and despairs."[40] Thus, as Spenser describes Redcrosse's once "brawned" arms as actively "consum'd" (as opposed to atrophied), he speaks to the sinner's enslavement to false religion, as Hume notes, but also to the productive self-loathing that accompanies conviction.[41] For Redcrosse's starved condition anticipates that of Contemplation in canto x, whose protruding bones are visible: "For nought he car'd his carcas long vnfed" (x.48.7). The hermit's condition is emblematic of his ecstatic focus on heavenly matters; and although the knight's condition seems extremely negative – suggestive of pride's destructiveness – the resemblance suggests that there may also be an element of nobility to Redcrosse's self-mortification, even seeds of desire for heavenly righteousness.

By characterizing Redcrosse's condition as a grisly portrait of self-consumption, Spenser depicts the sinner finally confronting the standard of divine law in a state of radical interiority, dissociating from and turning *against* the self, in cooperation with the powers of judgment. Redcrosse's inability to escape the overwhelming awareness of divine perfection creates the desperation needed for contrition, repentance, and, eventually, transcendence, even while that very awareness places him in a necessarily extreme condition, leaving him, characteristic of Calvin's sinner, precariously poised between salvation and disaster.

Despaire: Judgment Imagined

Following Redcrosse's release from Orgoglio's dungeon, Spenser concludes the theme of divine judgment in the Cave of Despaire with an even more gruesome depiction of a final form of abjection that *might* have been, had grace not intervened. Spenser links the Despaire episode to the captivity of Redcrosse and Fradubio – each containing parallel forms of isolation and unstable identity – but in this case, to give a detailed portrait of the horrifying consequence of divine condemnation that the sinner, saved by grace, narrowly misses. Scholars tend to see this episode, like the first Orgoglio passage, as exposing Redcrosse's "spiritual privation," thereby reminding readers of the destruction that results from spiritual pride and the neglect of the doctrine of grace.[42] But the Despaire episode, I believe, has a major psychological purpose for readers in addition to an ethical and theological one. As Spenser imagines the hypothetical culmination of Redcrosse's and Fradubio's respective abjections, he uses the death-like condition of the ghastly recluse to represent a horrific perversion of *ekstasis*, a process in which, instead of being transformed into the likeness of Christ, condemnation takes over and even *becomes* the person's identity. And through this final, extensively detailed portrayal of abjection, Spenser points Redcrosse – and the Protestant reader – to embrace all the more joyfully the marvellous divine mercy that saves them from such fate.

While Spenser draws several connections between the earlier abjection of Redcrosse and that of Despaire, he particularly links the two figures' tendencies to isolate themselves, featuring the effects of divine judgment on the psyche as a complete reversal of the external transport that characterizes *ekstasis*. Sitting "astownd" just as Redcrosse had been in canto ii, and withdrawn "full sadly in his sullein mind" (ix.35.3), Despaire dwells far away from human society, "low in an hollow caue": the entire area is "dark, dolefull, dreary, like a greedy graue" – an appropriate image of lifelessness (ix.33.4, 2). The outside area is conspicuously absent of any "chearefull fowle"; its trees are without leaf or fruit, with carcasses scattered around, and the only signs of life are "wandring ghostes" and a "ghastly Owle" (ix.33.9, 6). Redcrosse had earlier sought to separate himself from the intrusion of divine law and its threat to his independence by frantically burying Fradubio's bloody bough, but without shunning other personal interactions. Despaire's isolation, however, suggests a radical exaggeration of Redcrosse's own condition, for Despaire hides *himself* away from all other forms of life – except for those who, like him, seek death. Through the geographical setting, Spenser figures Despaire's heightened seclusion as the inevitable consequence of the abject avoidance of judgment. The sinner begins by avoiding God, but, as condemnation becomes inevitable, he retreats from all forms of life into an internal, death-like prison of self-condemnation.

Spenser likewise represents Despaire undergoing an intensified version of Redcrosse's destructive dissociation from self. He vividly depicts the sinner who comes face-to-face with his own culpability and, turning against himself in horror, would (without grace) begin a process of transformation that inverts and distorts the transport of divine union. Recalling Redcrosse's emaciation upon his release from Orgoglio's prison, Despaire has "hollow eyne" and "raw-bone cheekes" (ix.35.8), matching Redcrosse's "rawbone" arms (viii.41.6), emblematic of a dramatic retreat within the self. While Redcrosse, his sides "deceiued" and arms "consum'd," suffers from inadequate sustenance – "for want of better bits" – Despaire appears as if "he did *neuer* dyne" (ix.35.9; my emphasis). Where Redcrosse seems dangerously close to death, Despaire has far passed this condition, as if frozen in a state of self-starvation.

Yet Spenser amplifies Despaire's agency in his own destruction, resisting the idea that spirituality is finally determined, as the recurrence of the sublime might suggest.[43] Where Redcrosse was imprisoned in abjection as a step towards being reconciled with God, Despaire participates in his abjection; in one of the most authentically tragic scenes in the entire *Faerie Queene*, he

> *chose* an halter from among the rest,
>   And hong with it him selfe, vnbid vnblest.
>   But death he could not worke himselfe thereby;
>   For thousand times he so him selfe had drest
>   Yet nathelesse it could not doe him die,
> Till he should die his last, that is eternally.   (ix.54.4–9; my emphasis)

By showing Despaire choosing a halter, and "dressing" himself for death, Spenser demonstrates the absurdity of a subject of abjection actively participating in his own desperate state. Thus, Despaire, in a condition of abjection far beyond that of Redcrosse, enters an experience very similar to Kristevan "jouissance" – a perverse *ekstasis* in the face of horror; he delights in the inescapability of death, yet finds a deviant pleasure in causing and experiencing misery.[44] In this, Despaire anticipates

Spenser's representation of Malbecco of Book III, whose "painefull pleasure turns to pleasing paine" – another victim/subject of abjection (III.x.60.4).[45] Thriving on suffering like Malbecco, Despaire ravenously urges Redcrosse towards suicide, eagerly provoking in the knight "a trembling horror" and "hellish anguish" (I.ix.49-3-4), as the recluse reminds the knight of his faults and the condemnation his sin deserves. At the first sign of weakness, Despaire "gan … him to ouercraw" – to exalt or rejoice at his growing despondency (I.x.50.5). These details underscore the great contradiction underlying Despaire: he appears to be passively accepting what he believes has been fated to him, yet at each step he exults in the destructive destiny he produces.

For Spenser, Despaire's choice signifies the abject reaction to the final judgment of the *un*saved, not the perception of judgment that precedes repentance. Much like Malbecco transforming into the spirit of *Gealousie*, Despaire seems to embody not only despondency but the very spirit of condemnation that, Spenser suggests, a person will choose without the intercession of grace. The result is self-annihilation from the outside in, as opposed to sublimity, which transports sinners outside themselves.

In a final parody of sublime transport, Spenser represents Despaire in a state of metaphysical ambiguity, a permanent extension of the ambiguity seen in Fradubio and Redcrosse; in this, Spenser shows the individual's confrontation with divine judgment as a horror so extreme that it resembles eternal death, a perversion of eternal rapture. Like Fradubio, Despaire lives only a half-life, neither entirely human nor entirely inhuman, and, like Redcrosse in Orgoglio's dungeon, is neither completely alive nor completely dead. Yet Spenser implicitly ties the length of Redcrosse's captivity to the typical gestation period – he is imprisoned for "three Moones … thrice" (I.viii.38.6) – a period that suggests birth, renewal, and thus the hope of a second chance, contrasting it with Despaire's self-captivity, which has only morbid undertones. Through continual attempts at suicide (I.ix.54), Despaire remains in an ongoing *process* of dying, just as Malbecco is "transfix[d] … with deathes eternall dart" (III.x.59.9). In effect, both figures achieve statuses weirdly beyond death, living in a kind of perverse resurrection and rapture comparable to damnation. Unlike Fradubio and Redcrosse, who await grace, Despaire represents the horror of what it means for an eternal human soul, facing condemnation, to retreat eternally into the self without the relief of mortality.

In depicting the many perversions of *ekstasis*, Spenser leads the reader even deeper into the horrors of judgment, anticipating the sublime as Edmund Burke describes it in his 1757 *Philosophical Enquiry into the Origin of Our Ideas of the Sublime and Beautiful*; in Redcrosse's perception of Despaire, Spenser portrays the terror of being on the brink of damnation and narrowly saved. Burke himself would not likely call the initial terror of Redcrosse before Despaire "sublime," for Burke confines sublimity to a distant threat from which the observer faces no real danger.[46] Redcrosse, who very nearly commits suicide, perceives a threat of judgment too close to reality to produce such elevation: "trembling horror did his conscience daunt, / And hellish anguish did his soule assaile" (ix.49.3–4). Yet from the perspective of Spenser's Protestant readers, and from that of Redcrosse *after* his escape, the episode may well look forward to Burkean sublimity, leaving those considering the scene confounded at the awfulness of the judgment and condemnation – aware of the damnation they deserve, and overwhelmed at their undeserved deliverance. Once Una reminds Redcrosse of his predestined salvation (ix.53), after all, the knight too begins to perceive the threat of judgment as hypothetical. With grace bridging the gap between the sinner and justice, Spenser uses the scene to raise the Protestant reader's mind in awed reverence at having escaped such terrors.

In featuring abject horror in such detail across all three passages, Spenser reinforces the reality of divine judgment, as it psychologically and metaphysically overwhelms all alike with awareness of the consequences of sin. Whether the confrontation with divine judgment leads to eternal death, as for Despaire, or prepares to heighten the individual's subsequent encounter with grace, as for Redcrosse, divine holiness, Spenser suggests, will inevitably transform human identity.

Ultimately, by including such an extended element of abjection to Redcrosse's heroic journey, Spenser's Protestant sublime develops an element of spiritual and moral humility present in Du Bartas's model of sublimity, though lacking in Longinus's depiction and relatively undeveloped by Tasso. While Longinus emphasizes the process of raising a subject into a god-like state, Spenser's Protestant sublime involves a more explicit confession of relative nothingness before the divine, going beyond even Du Bartas in its emphasis on deserved separation, as implied in portrayals of abjection. In Spenser's Protestant sublime, the presence of God's grace promises to exalt the sinner to heavenly heights, though ongoing awareness of justice and law humble the believer into a profoundly prostrate state of awe at divine power.

Arthur and the Sublime Violence of Grace

While Spenser uses a principle of abjection to convey the inception of spiritual transformation at the sight of divine judgment, he incorporates depictions more characteristic of *ekplexis* to track the similarly overwhelming force of divine grace, in the next stage of Redcrosse's quest for holiness. Yet Spenser creates great continuity between these two parts of the Protestant sublime, associating both grace and judgment with expressions of terror. In fact, portrayals of grace and *ekplexis* begin before the Despaire episode, in Arthur's stunning entrance (so often linked with grace) to Orgoglio's castle, so that Redcrosse's encounters with judgment and with grace overlap.[47] In highlighting the intersection between these two forms of holiness, Spenser stresses the unity of the divine character – indicating that God should be the ultimate object of fear and respect, and not only in his powers of judgment, but in his administration of mercy as well.

Spenser is far from the first to connect judgment and grace through the language of the sublime. Biblical and Reformed sources regularly portray the effects of grace as very similar to those of judgment. In Revelation, as well as the prophetic writings of the Old Testament, writers warn of the terrorizing threat of human armies or national disasters divinely authorized to destroy the rebellious Israelites, only to be countered by an even more terrifying divine intervention coming to save the chosen remnant. When the prophet Joel, for instance, describes the imminent attack of locusts on the Israelites as divine judgment for their rebellion, he writes:

> The earth shal tremble before him, the heauens shall shake, the sunne and the moone shalbe darke, and the starres shal withdrawe their shining. And the Lord shal vtter his voyce before his hoste: for his hoste is verie great: for *he is* strong that doeth his worke: for the daie of the Lord is great and very terrible, and who can abyde it![48]

Shifting to a promise of salvation for those who seek God, Joel concludes the passage in terms of natural disasters that parallel the intervention of judgment:

> And also upon the servants, and upon the maids in those days will I pour my Spirit. And I wil shewe wonders in the heauens and in the earth: blood and fyre, and pillers of smoke. The sunne shalbe turned into darkenes, and the moone into blood, before the great and terrible daie of the Lord come. But whosoeuer shal call on the Name of the Lord, shal be saued.[49]

Though the passage emphasizes the offer of salvation, the prophet includes details of natural wonders that seem to threaten rather than to excite with joy. Repeatedly describing the day as "great and [very] terrible," he offers a potent reminder that the offer of grace comes from the same source as the threat of destruction – and that the offer of grace must never be taken for granted.

Drawing from biblical references and Reformed theology, the depiction of Orgoglio's defeat emphasizes that divine mercy is so terrifying because it is so fundamentally irresistible. Here again, Spenser particularly echoes Longinus's point that it is "difficult, nay impossible, to resist" sublimity's effects.[50] Reformed writers emphasize that grace, like judgment, is as potent and threatening to the individual's sense of self as judgment, though in this case, because it draws the individual *out* of the former sense of self, freeing the person from the sin nature. Calvin writes that the work of grace is, in the words of Perry Miller, "a forcible seizure," an overriding of the "surprised will" that draws the recipient away from his/her basic nature, a form of *ekstasis*.[51] Speaking in similar terms of the irresistibility and power of grace to draw *out*, William Perkins notes that (only) grace can liberate and radically alter the corrupted human will:

> the will of man in it selfe is a natural thing: and therefore it is neither fit nor able to effect any supernaturall action (as all actions of godlines are) vnles it be first of all … eleuated aboue his condition by the impression of a supernaturall habit.[52]

While "impression" might suggest copying or imprinting, the word had a stronger and more active connotation in Perkins's time, referring to an impact, shock, or even attack.[53] According to Perkins, grace involves not only change but a forceful alteration to the mind and soul.

In the depiction of Orgoglio's defeat, Spenser's sublimity resonates with these Reformed discourses, a resonance that challenges allegations such as those of Virgil K. Whitaker that Spenser never represents "Calvinism's sense of the overwhelming majesty of God."[54] Divine holiness is on display in Arthur's stunning of Orgoglio with his magic horn, and in the unveiling of his shield, depicting an individual's first perception of grace as an experience just as emotionally powerful, transformative, and irresistible as an encounter with judgment.

The Magic Horn: Auditory Grace

The first step in Orgoglio's defeat occurs when Arthur's squire Timias opens the castle gates with the blast of a magic horn, an emblem borrowed from Italian romance, but here given a salvific meaning. As Hamilton notes, the horn has been linked to the preaching of the gospel of grace, whose "sounde went out through all the earth," just as the "shrilling sound" of Timias's horn reaches for miles around.[55] The horn has received somewhat less critical attention than the magic shield, but its sublime effects are just as significant: with the horn, Spenser highlights a different operation of grace – the way it initially stuns and gradually captivates.

In particular, it is fitting that Spenser chooses an auditory source of sublimity to describe the startling effects of grace. In descriptions of apocalypse, biblical writers tended to represent the impending threat of divine power with auditory phenomena – particularly trumpets and thunder.[56] In *Peri Hypsous*, too, Longinus often refers to "roaring" and "thunder" when describing the more terrorizing effects of the sublime.[57] As both Longinus and biblical prophets seem to suggest, the medium of sound presents an inherently greater sense of threat than that of sight, and Spenser adopts it to portray the work of grace in an initial phase, forecasting the stunning collapse of the powers of condemnation.

Spenser features these threatening effects of grace in the early stanzas of canto viii:

> Was neuer wight, that heard that shrilling sownd,
>> But trembling feare did feel in euery vaine;
>> Three miles it might be easy heard arownd,
>> And Ecchoes three aunswerd it selfe againe:
>> No false enchauntment, nor deceiptfull traine
>> Might once abide the terror of that blast,
>> But presently was void and wholly vaine:
>> No gate so strong, no locke so firme and fast,
> But with that percing noise flew open quite, or brast.
>
> The same before the Geaunts gate he blew,
>> That all the castle quaked from the grownd,
>> And euery dore of freewill open flew;
>> The Gyaunt selfe dismaied with that sownd,
>> Where he with his *Duessa* dalliance fownd,
>> In hast came rushing forth from inner bowre,
>> With staring countenance sterne, as one astownd,
>> And staggering steps, to weet, what suddein stowre
> Had wrought that horror strange, and dar'd his dreaded powre.   (viii.4–5)

With the stunning blast of the horn, Spenser portrays a remarkable continuity between Orgoglio's sublime terrorizing of Redcrosse and the giant's own experience of terror: he is left "astownd" and "dismaied," with "staggering" steps indicative of his great astonishment, while his castle, as an extension of himself, "quaked from the grownd." Meanwhile, Orgoglio, understood here as a psychological projection of Redcrosse, is caught off guard at the "horror strange," just as he had earlier caught the knight himself: he is bewildered at what could possibly have "dar'd his dreaded powre." With these descriptions, Spenser links the instinctive terror of Orgoglio with the instinctive dread Redcrosse had felt on hearing Fradubio's voice. The connection between the passages of sublimity and abjection signals the heightened intensity of grace, and the counterintuitive strangeness of the sinner's initial perception of it – at first sight, grace may appear so foreign and incomprehensible that it initially appears as frightening as judgment itself. At the same time, though the emotional effects are similar, the direction of the movement is reversed – the castle's enchanted defences are shattered, and each "dore" flies "open" – clearly foreshadowing the process of drawing Redcrosse out of his imprisonment and into a transport of divine union.

Spenser's portrayal of the horn also signifies the way that grace, for all its unstoppable power and even violence, may operate in less immediate ways, an underexamined aspect of Longinian theory as well as a particular emphasis of Reformed thinking. As we saw, Spenser demonstrates the horn's absolute irresistibility, like Reformed grace: its blast produces "terror" and "trembling feare" in *all* who hear it, corresponding to Longinus's point that the sublime "pleases all people at all times."[58] Yet Orgoglio is only initially astonished, not finally defeated by the horn. His gradual defeat by Arthur reflects the kind of sublime power that Longinus uses to describe the "diffuseness" and "widespread conflagration" of Ciceronian rhetoric, a form of sublimity he carefully distinguishes from the sudden "flash of lightning" of Demosthenes's sublimity.[59] Both early and modern Reformed thinkers have identified a similar distinction, maintaining that grace may be completely irresistible and immediate in its impact, but that its work is not limited to one single moment of astonishment. Herman Bavinck, an early twentieth-century Dutch theologian, argues that it is a particular characteristic of Reformed thought to recognize that "God does not always work faith and repentance in the human heart suddenly but often – indeed as a rule – causes them to proceed and develop from the implanted life gradually, by a psychological and pedagogical process."[60] Demonstrating this principle, Luther states that *because* the doctrine of grace is bewildering to the human mind, as it goes against the basic human inclination to earn favour by performance, it "must always be taught and continually exercised."[61]

Spenser incorporates these ideas from Reformed theology and sublime philosophy into the battle between Arthur and Orgoglio to demonstrate the psychological process by which grace operates, first stunning the individual, before taking hold of the sinner's mind and defeating the powers of condemnation that imprison it, though completing this task gradually, and with some violence. After producing an initial shock, the horn sets up a series of actions that weaken Orgoglio and lead to his downfall. At first, the giant appears to regain his former power: he swings his "dreadfull club" with a blow that Spenser compares to "thunderbolts" (viii.7.9) that strike the earth and leaves the ground "trembling with such feare ... like an erthquake" (viii.8.9). Yet this very blow incapacitates Orgoglio enough to create an occasion for Arthur to slice off Orgoglio's arm, leaving the giant "Dismayed" (viii.11.1), or "overwhelmed with fear" – a sublime condition suggesting his growing powerlessness.[62] Spenser also portrays the weakening of Orgoglio's main supporter in battle, the seven-headed beast, from whom Arthur must rescue his squire Timias. In striking "one of those deformed heads so sore" (viii.16.2), Arthur deals the beast a blow that leaves it roaring in "exceeding paine" (viii.17.1; my emphasis), provoking Orgoglio in turn to deal the blow that nearly proves fatal to Arthur, but instead proves to be Orgoglio's last. In Orgoglio's defeat, Spenser reveals the latent, mysterious, surprising operations of grace whose powerful inertia is not always evident to sight, yet whose potency and inevitability cannot be denied.

The Magic Shield: Visual Grace

Following Orgolio's stunned response to the magic horn, Spenser represents Arthur's magic shield – a second borrowing from Italian romance adapted to a salvific end – operating as an even stronger form of divine grace, clashing with and finally defeating the giant and the power of judgment he represents.[63] Unlike the horn, the unveiled shield renders the giant immediately impotent, as the shield produces *ekplexis* visually, a significant distinction that makes its sublimity even more powerful. Where the horn represented the initial work of grace terrifying the unsuspecting listener and gradually beginning the infusion process, the shield represents the definitive power of divine grace to complete the job – to draw the sinner completely out of the decaying sinful self and out of the range of divine judgment.

As indicated, Longinus himself tends to reserve visual descriptions – *phantasia* – for the more positive "enthralling" and "amazing" effects of the sublime, suggesting that, while the medium of sound may seem more threatening, the medium of sight produces effects that are more complete in their captivation.[64] Calvin likewise uses visual metaphors of sublimity to describe humans being fully and finally overwhelmed at the stark contrast between the sinner and God:

> [W]hen we look up to the sun and gaze straight at it, that power of sight which was particularly strong on earth is at once blunted [esblouye] and confused by a great brilliance, and thus we are compelled to admit that our keenness [vigueur] in looking upon things earthly is sheer dullness [eslourdissement] when it comes to the sun.[65]

Although Calvin does not refer specifically to grace in this passage, his description of the overwhelming (literally, "dazzling") effects of holiness compares closely with the way Spenser describes the shield's sublimity defeating Orgoglio:

> And in [Arthur's] fall his shield, that couered was,
>   Did loose his vele by chaunce, and open flew:
>   The light whereof, that heuens light did pas,
>   Such blazing brightnesse though the ayer threw,
>   That eye mote not the same endure to vew.
>   Which when the Gyaunt spyde with staring eye,
>   He downe let fall his arme, and soft withdrew
>   His weapon huge, that heaued was on hye,
> For to haue slain the man, that on the ground did lye.
>
>   … for he has redd his end
>   In that bright shield, and all their forces spend

> Them selues in vaine: for since that glauncing sight,
> He hath no poure to hurt, nor to defend;
> As where th'Almighties lightning brond does light,
> It dimmes the dazed eyen, and daunts the sences quight.   (viii.19, 21.4–9)

In effect, both Calvin's sun and Arthur's shield, when unveiled, leave viewers "blunted/dazzled," and "confused"/with "no poure to hurt," respectively – their senses utterly overpowered.

In echoing Calvin's claim that the perception of divine power vehemently overwhelms those it is revealed to, the passage recalls Redcrosse's earlier encounters with Fradubio and Orgoglio, when the knight's "sences" were confounded. Spenser maintains that in overwhelming Orgoglio, in "daunt[ing] his sences quight," the grace embodied in this passage not only transforms the status of the sinner, but produces a condition of speechless astonishment, similar to the effects of judgment described by Calvin.[66] Thus, Spenser indicates that grace is just as foreign and astounding to the human mind as the fact of deserving judgment. According to Spenser, believers, ever conditioned to seek their own justification, will sense the great difference between their own ways and God's when confronted with the power of grace, increasing their awe at his presence, even in the process of being drawn into divine fellowship. And in highlighting the sense of disparity between the self and God, Spenser in effect preserves an element of abjection in his depiction of grace, though he suggests that the aim of grace is not self-loathing (as in abjection), but self-forgetfulness: by beholding and being overwhelmed by the magnificence of God.

In this passage, Spenser begins to follow Tasso in depicting the sublime being transmitted visually, linking grace with the greater power of visual sources of the sublime, yet he ultimately tracks at least as closely with Du Bartas in associating sublimity with mystery and confusion, with the *un*known. The fact that Redcrosse remains imprisoned by Ignaro throughout Orgoglio's defeat suggests the sinner's continued ignorance of biblical doctrine after the first sight of grace. In the stunning of Orgoglio, Spenser portrays the initial encounter with judgment and the receipt of grace as experiences that are every bit as emotional as rational, for they must powerfully destroy prior patterns of belief – especially the tendency to see the self as basically good (a belief threatened by the presence of judgment), and the tendency to see real sin as something that cannot be forgiven (a belief threatened by grace).

While Redcrosse will gain some enlightenment in the later cantos, that enlightenment will continue to heighten the role of divine mystery. Cheney notes the importance of the unknown and the mysterious to Spenser's concept of the sublime, which he characterizes as a "force beyond reason."[67] I would add that in linking sublime grace with divine mystery, Spenser seems to echo Du Bartas for a distinctive end. As we saw previously, Du Bartas depicts divine inscrutability as a heroic test – a chance for the poem's heroes to show the humility to embrace the unknown, against their natural (fallen) inclination. For Spenser, however, divine mystery is itself irresistible, an aspect of the divine being that overwhelms the emotions and leaves the person no alternative but to acknowledge one's moral, intellectual, and spiritual inferiority, and begin to be transformed. Thus, Spenser is more doctrinally polemical than Du Bartas, but not primarily to foster political controversy; Spenser's aim, like Du Bartas', is to endorse spiritual humility. Thus, following Calvin and Luther, Spenser's concept of divine grace emphasizes the absolute dependence of the believer on God alone, re-establishing the priority of this concept of spiritual over political identity. For Redcrosse, this spiritual identity must be solidified before he can demonstrate heroism at all, and it must be his primary motivation as he becomes genuinely heroic.

From Despair to Holiness: Charismatic Transformation and Sublime Heroism

Redcrosse becomes a heroic agent of holiness only in the final part of Book I, as he enters the House of Holiness and conquers the Dragon; there, he enters the process of sanctification and becomes capable of acts of will. Since Spenser emphasizes Redcrosse's acts of virtue, the concluding cantos of Book I are among those most likely to encourage non-Reformed, even pro-Catholic readings of Book I, as endorsing works righteousness. Yet Spenser's depiction of the sublime creates important continuity with the Calvinist theology of earlier passages, retaining emphasis on Reformed concepts of divine sovereignty over sanctification. Particularly in this final part of Spenser's Protestant sublime, transformation occurs through the mediating role of a charismatic community, emphasized in Reformed theology – a mode of sublimity channelled among believers to support sanctification and acts of service. Throughout the final cantos of Book I, Redcrosse's transformation takes place within this interdependent spiritual community, in encounters punctuated by the kind of heightened affection that regularly recalls his earlier terror and astonishment at representations of divine judgment and grace. In a particularly cautious depiction of charisma, Spenser endorses a model of spiritual community that, as we will see, is distinct from political community, and whose allegiance to political figures is strictly limited.

Compared to forms of charisma seen earlier, Spenser's is distinctively Reformed. Where charismatic individuals are one of Tasso's means of *initially* pointing heroes towards heavenly purposes, for Spenser, charismatic community is a means of sanctification available to those who have already expressed faith. In Protestant discussions of sanctification, early theologians contended that, however instantaneous and divine the work of grace, the long-term process of transformation involved the distribution and use of the *charismata*, the spiritual gifts. The *charismata* originally appear in Acts, with the miraculous descent of the Holy Spirit on Pentecost; and as Calvin notes, the spiritual gifts exemplify the united group identity of Christians: "saints are gathered into the society of Christ on the principle that whatever benefits God confers upon them, they should in turn share with one another"; he describes these benefits as "graces" and "gifts of the Spirit."[68] Raphael Falco theorizes that the entire modern theory of charismatic authority is based on this biblical system. And although Falco does not discuss the connection to the sublime, he emphasizes the sense of marvel that underlies a charismatic community – the amazing, inspirational actions that bind participants together in a field of forces. In Falco's model of charisma, Christians believe that they each receive their own particular *charism* (gift of grace) that they in turn transmit to one another; this creates a strong sense of group identity that empowers them to mutual service and spiritual growth.[69] While typical social systems are regulated by formal codes and official authority figures, a charismatic system is ordered, as we have seen, by an experience of passionate possession by a divine power. In the Reformed sense as well, the *charismata* could be understood to secure believers in divine relationship by bringing them to a sustained emotional condition of sublime astonishment.[70]

In using charisma to emphasize the heightened emotions underlying sanctification, Spenser again emphasizes the role of the affections – even very strong affections – in faith, and in public, communal displays of faith as well as private devotion. As van Engen notes, in settings of Christian fellowship, the ability to feel not only sympathy and empathy, but even bliss and overwhelming joy in another believer's presence, was viewed as evidence of grace and divine transformation of the will. These emotions, in turn, were understood to be the basis for all virtuous action. In a process that echoes the Longinian sublime, these heightened emotions were understood to efface boundaries between the individual self and Other, allowing transfer of divine power – and sublime emotions – among believers that supports their performance of good works.[71] This obscuring of boundaries, moreover, did not eliminate identity, but fulfilled it. In the case of Redcrosse, the magnetism of charisma secures him more firmly in the faith, and provides the final basis to complete his heroic calling. This creates a markedly interdependent model of identity, where Redcrosse is not merely acted upon, as in the episodes of judgment and grace, but aided in ways that make it difficult to discern which actions are his own. This model of interdependent charismatic community thus provides the foundation of Spenser's distinctive model of heroism.

In Redcrosse, Spenser represents a charismatic community emerging immediately after Arthur's battle with Orgoglio, as Una responds by expressing her amazement, awe, and submission at Arthur's victory: "Fayre braunch of noblesse, flowre of chevalrie, / That with your worth the world amazed make, / How shall I quite the paynes, ye suffer for my sake?" (viii.26.7–9). Una's astonished reaction to Arthur is not a response to divinity directly, but to the knight's use of divine *gifts*. He himself is merely a finite instrument of grace, while she acknowledges in him a charismatic power that demands her inspired service, exemplifying the communication of grace among Christians. Elsewhere, Una herself demonstrates considerable charisma, and particularly a gift of exhortation as she urges Redcrosse to remember his salvation by grace, and shocks him out of his horror at Despaire's compelling words. Although Redcrosse remains far from spiritually healthy after her intervention, Una prompts in him a drastic and miraculous change of heart, indicating her ability to captivate by channelling grace. And following Redcrosse's release from captivity, Spenser represents the knight becoming attracted to the *charismata* of an even larger fellowship in the House of Holiness, whose "exceptional powers" inspire him further in the sanctification process, preparing him to complete his heroic defeat of the Dragon.

Before Spenser presents his authentic model of charismatic community in the later cantos of Book I, however, he features a false mode originating in earthly sources, which competes with and threatens to distract from heavenly purposes by tempting believers to idealize civic roles or national glory. In juxtaposing true and false forms of charisma (and true and false forms of sublimity), Spenser emphasizes that zeal must *not* be oriented finally to nation or earthly authority, but to the flourishing of all who truly follow God.

True and False Charisma: Against Earthly Glory

In Book I, the purest form of charisma in the poem is found in Una, embodiment of the inclusive, international group of followers of the Christian faith, to whom Redcrosse is bound in service and eventually betrothed.[72] While Una's most obvious false counterpart is Duessa, emblem of the false church and of Roman Catholicism, Spenser also compares her discreetly to Queen Lucifera. Both are described as "mayden Queenes," one a representative of the complete body of Christian believers, the other a malevolent version of Queen Elizabeth I who embodies the dangers of idolizing national authority and power.[73]

Despite her satanic resonances, Lucifera, as Cheney notes, is clearly portrayed as a charismatic figure and source of sublimity: her "light doth all mens eies amaze" (iv.16.9).[74] Yet Spenser critiques this charisma as false, because it is not a renewable and shareable gift, like authentic Christian *charismata*, which cannot be "used up." In short, Lucifera's charisma is marred and restricted by her pride and envy, such that she primarily makes demands of others (to glorify her) rather than contributing to their welfare, like genuine charisma. Spenser writes, "to the highest … [she] did still aspyre, / Or if ought higher were then that, did it desire" (iv.11.8–9). Not only does she envy others, but she envies her very throne: she has such "bright blazing beautie [that] did assay / To dim the brightnesse of her glorious throne, / As enuying her selfe, that too exceeding shone" (iv.8.7–9). In Spenser's depiction, Lucifera's charisma fails because it is self-referential, in a form of endless competition designed to elevate herself in the eyes of others, instead of pointing outward and upward towards divine grace and towards God. Thus, Lucifera's palace is a source of decay and death, such that the charisma that first entices knights culminates in a "dreadfull spectacle" (v.53.9) portending the terror of divine judgment.

In Lucifera's dungeon, Spenser features the dangers of idolizing earthly authority and national purposes instead of pursuing the sublimity of heaven. Through her false charisma, he warns that the temptation to worship the sublimity of Queen Elizabeth and English national glory is real, and if followed as an idol, proves as destructive as the attraction of Duessa, emblem of Roman Catholicism. Given the relative lack of impact that Lucifera has on Redcrosse, compared to Duessa, Spenser may be suggesting that Lucifera – and English power – poses less of a temptation to follow in an idolatrous way. Nonetheless, he makes clear that English leadership is itself a real threat to destruction and no better an object of worship than Roman authority. For Spenser, sublimity and heroism must be linked to heavenly purposes to have authentic value.

Una's charisma is different in that it does point upward, as an emblem of "heauenly grace" (vi.18.6). Yet in Una, Spenser issues a different warning about charisma, illustrating how even faithful bearers of charisma can create a temptation to idolatry in the unsaved. In canto 6, Una too – though very much against her will – leads the woodland creatures in a condition of pseudo-sublimity. Spenser writes that "All stand astonied at her beautie bright" (vi.9.8) and "wonder of her beautie souerayne" (vi.12.6), so that soon they "Do worship her, as Queene, with oliue girlond cround" (vi.13.9). Una herself resists and "restrayne[s]" their efforts to worship her, but to little purpose, because they merely transfer their worship to the "Asse" instead (vi.19.6–9). He thus locates in the woodland creatures a natural impulse to worship that turns easily to idolatry when salvation has not yet been effected. Though Spenser endorses the role of charisma when it points to divine glory, he nonetheless indicates that, in being channelled through a mortal figure, charisma is primarily designed to aid believers in faith rather than to serve as an original source of salvation.

As we will see, Milton follows up on this caution in *Paradise Lost* by not only warning of the dangers of charismatic authority, but altogether rejecting this power as idolatrous when embodied in created beings. For his part, Spenser makes charisma essential to Christian community, but highlights the great responsibility that leaders have to bear their charisma well, and illustrates how easily it can go wrong, especially as seen in Lucifera as a figure of English national power. Less than halfway through Book I, Spenser signals the threat of nationhood and sets limits on Redcrosse's responsibility to nation, depicting the more essential responsibility to a local, devoted body of believers who can spur each other on in the quest for holiness.

Charismata in the House of Holiness: Transformation of the Affections

The clearest depiction of authentic Spenserian charisma arises in the House of Holiness, where Redcrosse encounters a variety of figures whose *charismata* seem to compel him under their power and miraculously inspire his spiritual growth towards virtue.[75] King notes that the House of Holiness "functions externally as a metaphor for the church," to which I would add that it functions more specifically as a fellowship of Christians like that described by Paul, bonded together by charisma.[76] Looking at Paul's passage to the Romans, we see seven specific *charismata* distributed variously among Christians: prophecy, service, teaching, exhortation (and encouragement), generosity (or "distribution"), leadership, and acts of mercy. Each of these, I suggest, Spenser correlates directly to at least one figure in the House of Holiness, who together prove instrumental in Redcrosse's transformation: Fidelia exemplifies teaching; Speranza, exhortation; Mercie, her namesake; the oldest Bead-man, leadership; the remaining Bead-men, generosity and service; and Contemplation, prophecy. While many of these figures have been read as representing the Catholic doctrine of justification by good works, in which Redcrosse is trained, they might instead be seen as representatives of Christian *charismata* contributing to the knight's miraculous transformation by grace.[77] Of these figures, Fidelia's teaching and Contemplation's prophecy are the most sublime and most significant: Redcrosse, responding to each with astonishment, undergoes a transformation of affection, will, and capacity for virtue through an emotionally heightened communal experience. Scholars like Hume and King who see Spenser as a conservative Protestant tend to stress his emphasis on the steady course of teaching and intellectual growth that accompanies Redcrosse's salvation. I would add that the emotional impact of grace is just as important to Spenser, underlying the defeat of the individual's sinful will – a trend that becomes especially important in these passages.

It is especially significant that Redcrosse's first major moment of regeneration in the House of Holiness – his achieving "perfection of all heuenly grace" (x.21.3) – occurs during his interaction with Fidelia, as she contributes most to his emotional as well as intellectual transformation. Fidelia, we learn, is uniquely gifted in explaining mysteries of the Bible, which "none could read, except she did them teach, / She vnto him disclosed euery whitt, / And heauenly documents thereout did preach" (x.19.2–4). She does so in a manner that is quintessentially charismatic, by "pour[ing] out her larger spright" (x.20.1), resembling the Holy Spirit's divine inspiration of the apostles on Pentecost. Just as in Acts 2 the Holy Spirit enables the apostles to perform miraculous acts of healing and to make speeches that "amazed" the crowds, "Almightie God" gives Fidelia "such powre, and puissaunce great" that she can move mountains, stun "great hostes of men," and even command the sun to stop (x.20.9, 4, 2).[78] Like a transformed apostle at Pentecost, she "agraste" Redcrosse with her teaching (x.18.7) – the verbal form of "grace" suggesting the miraculous communal transfer of spiritual blessings.

While Fidelia's role in intellectual development is apparent, the passage also emphasizes the intuitive and emotional channels through which biblical teaching occurs, working to cultivate a condition of sublimity in response to the Word of God.[79] Kaske does recognize Spenser's emphasis on emotion in Fidelia's teaching, which is "hable, with her wordes to kill, / And raise againe to life the hart, which she did thrill" (x.19.8–9); but Kaske sees this emotion as negative, supporting her argument that Spenser portrays the Bible as a "self-contestatory, agonistic text" reflecting no coherent theological perspective.[80]

In representing Fidelia as charismatic, Spenser seems in my view to represent something quite different from Kaske's proposed interpretation of theological incoherence: the apostolic capacity to cultivate transport and effectively astonish others into a miraculous awareness of divine truth. Fidelia conveys principles that "weaker witt of man could neuer reach" (x.19.5), as her words lead Redcrosse from life to death and back again. With her ability to use words to "thrill," to "kill," and to "rayse againe to life," Fidelia recalls Longinus's description of Demosthenes, whose words can be as terrifying as a thunderbolt in the face.[81] In particular, Fidelia's words contain *energeia*, an emotional power much like the "forcibleness" that Sidney emphasizes in his discourse on sublime poetry.[82] Here, Fidelia affords an intuitive, emotionally-driven understanding similar to what we saw in Tasso, as her ability to "thrill" Redcrosse – to pierce or enslave him – suggests the sort of stunning divine intuition that, Halliwell argues, is at the heart of Longinus's concept of the sublime.[83] Spenser's emphasis remains different from that of Tasso, though, whose sublimity channels a clear form of knowledge to Clorinda and other heroes of the *Liberata*. Fidelia's sublime words represent a mere taste of the divine mystery that remains enigmatic during the mortal lifespan – that lies beyond the "reach" of the "witt of man" – as Spenser conveys the idea that the ways of God will only ever be unravelled in eternity. Yet, both forms of intuition contain some degree of knowledge, infused with strong emotion. In describing the face of Fidelia, Spenser reiterates the same stunning, blinding capacity of Arthur's unveiled shield: "Like sunny beames threw from her Christall face, / That could haue dazd the rash beholders sight, / And round about her head did shine like heuens light" (x.12.7–9). Like the earlier appearance of divine grace, Fidelia represents the ability of godly instruction to cultivate in Redcrosse an incomplete knowledge implanted by the radical transformation of the affections.

Specifically, Fidelia's *charism* of teaching cultivates in Redcrosse a passionate hatred for his sin nature, furthering Spenser's emphasis on strong emotion in sanctification. Extending Redcrosse's earlier encounters with divine judgment, he enters a second, even more spiritually productive condition of abjection. On listening to Fidelia's thrilling words, Redcrosse seems at first to renew his former condition in Despaire's cave; his "sinfull horror" is so strong that he is tempted to repeat his earlier suicide attempt, now being "prickt with anguish of his sinnes so sore, / That he desirde, to end his wretched dayes: / So much the dart of sinfull guilt the soule dismayes" (x.21.7–9). Under Fidelia's care, however, Redcrosse's "horror" is more spiritually advanced than it had been; her words "thrill" the knight into a more specific sorrow and self-loathing at his "sinfull guilt," rather than at a general dread of punishment. Fidelia's words bring about contrition, which Calvin considers the first part of actual repentance: an experience like abjection, but more directly sublime, in which the sinner is not imprisoned, but overwhelmed ("abatu") and prepared to be transformed ("il se souhaite estre autre qu'il n'est"). He adds that penitence, the next step, also proceeds like abjection from the fear of God, but instead of sinners remaining withdrawn inside the self, they are drawn out of the self ("retirez de nous-mesmes") and turned towards God ("convertis a Dieu").[84] Redcrosse's experience with Fidelia represents a similar process of emotionally heightened divine transport, or *ekstasis*, though especially reflecting the aid of charismatic community – with her help, he finally learns to loathe his sin properly, and thus begins the transformation process.

Fidelia thus showcases Spenser's emphasis on the charismatic, communal work of grace. Though Redcrosse becomes just as horrified and fearful of the divine presence as earlier, in combining his renewed fear with a proper understanding of its basis, Fidelia prepares him to take hold of Speranza's "comfort sweet" (x.22.1) and benefit from the lessons of "loue, and righteousness" (x.33.4) taught by Charissa and the guidance in "gratious[ness]" and "liberall[ity]" of Mercie (x.34.5). After this instruction of the mind and heart, Spenser depicts Redcrosse finally prepared to enter Calvin's stage of "vivification," the second phase of repentance, where the believer "looks to the goodness of God – to his mercy, grace, salvation, which is through Christ – he raises himself up, he takes heart, he recovers courage, and as it were, returns from death to life."[85] That this stage is preceded by a believer "thrilling" another emphasizes the sublime potential of Christian community – Spenser describes an almost uncanny cooperation among members of Christian fellowship, their passions as contagious as the divine understanding they share.

While Fidelia uses charismatic teaching to help Redcrosse through his first step towards regeneration, Contemplation shares with him a stunning prophetic vision that completes the knight's preparations for his heroic quest for holiness. In this episode, scholars have tended to focus either on the hermit's evocation of Catholic mysticism, or, in Protestant readings, on the intellectual illumination that the encounter affords Redcrosse: how the knight learns of his changeling status, his identity as St. George, and the significance of his earthly mission.[86] Yet the significance of Contemplation's prophetic vision may be as emotional as it is intellectual and still reflect a Reformed concept of prophecy.[87] As one of the *charismata*, prophecy's purpose is far more than pedagogical; it extends directly from the Old Testament tradition, in which prophets transformed the will by bringing listeners into a terrified condition.[88] By overpowering the affections, prophecy would cultivate terror of judgment and deep longing for the good. And like any agent of grace working towards sanctification, charismatic prophecy transforms the will and desire in a context of Christian fellowship. Spenser's portrayal of Contemplation is consistent with this Reformed perspective, as the hermit does not merely show Redcrosse what he must do, but in bringing the knight yet again into a condition of awed astonishment, contributes to the cultivation of desire that will allow him to see his mission through. At the very centre of this episode is its communal sublimity – how the knight's ecstasy, cultivated by another, shocks in order to transform.

Contemplation himself is charismatic in the Reformed sense, as he "oftcn saw [God] from heauens height" (x.47.2), and in the Longinian sense of being "wondrous quick and persaunt [piercing]" in "spright" (x.47.5); as with Fidelia, his charisma is channelled through his gift, the sublime vision he shares with Redcrosse and Una. Spenser's sublimity is nowhere more evident than in the passage describing the effects of the vision Contemplation shows Redcrosse of *Hierusalem*: "dazed were his eyne, / Through passing brightnes, which did quite confound / His feeble sence, and too exceeding shyne" (x.67.6–8). The knight is blinded by the glorious vision, while his other senses and even intellect are "confound[ed]." The entire vision is reminiscent of Longinus's emphasis on speechless astonishment: the knight "stood gazing" and "wondred much" (x.56.1, 6) at the heavenly city whose greatness "earthly tong / Cannot describe, nor wit of man can tell" (x.55.5–6). The vision appears beyond the capacity of human intellect, though much like Fidelia's teaching, it recalls Tasso's understanding of the sublime in affording Redcrosse a momentary, enigmatic glimpse of the sort of transcendent condition he will one day experience. And importantly, Redcrosse's astonishing vision of divine glory comes not alone, but through the charismatic leadership of Contemplation and in the company of Una, in fellowship.

Through Contemplation's particular gift, moreover, Spenser uses the sublime not only to inspire Redcrosse to continue his quest, but to create a major distinction between the value of his earthly and heavenly purposes. In a somewhat surprising manner for England's aspiring laureate poet, the passage creates a striking contrast between the splendour of Cleopolis (London) and Hierusalem, so that Redcrosse not only "wondred much" at the sight of the "vnknowen nation" (x.56.6, 9), but explicitly remarks, with great amazement, that the earthly city and tower he once thought were the "fairest … that might be seene" (x.58.4) now pale in comparison to the heavenly one, "that does far surpas" and "quite dims that towre of glas" (x.58.8–9). While Cheney argues that the Contemplation passage shows the poem's commitment to "human conduct in-formed by the spirit of the divine," I would suggest that the episode not only equips Redcrosse to perform heroic action in the world, but in the contrast between realms, has the equally important effect of *de*-sublimitizing the value of Cleopolis and the earthly mission itself.[89] The sublimity of the New Jerusalem gives Redcrosse such a compelling taste of heavenly glory that he begs the hermit to be allowed to remain above instead of returning to a world of "ioyes … fruitlesse" (x.63.2). Since the vision is implicitly perfect, the fact that Redcrosse must be urged to return to perform his earthly duty, dull and vague by comparison, suggests that its chief value lies not in inspiring (in some ways it manages to depress), but in magnifying the surpassing value of his heavenly destination. Afterward, the knight is too blinded even to see the earth, "So darke are earthly things compard to things diuine" (x.67.9).

In impressing on him the relative weakness of the glory of the "fairest Citty" of Cleopolis, the vision underscores that the divine orientation of his quest is what makes it heroic; the experience is designed to caution even while it inspires. Recalling cantos 4 and 5, the episode offers a reminder that the value of Redcrosse's earthly mission holds only when its leaders remain fixed on heavenly purposes, with earthly purposes firmly subordinated to them; to lose this focus is to idolize worldly leaders and authorities, as other knights idolized Lucifera to their own destruction. To that end, the vision itself takes place a great distance from Cleopolis, in the company of Una and Contemplation, who ensure that the knight's identity remain anchored first in a community that is not fundamentally national or political, but spiritual and divine.

Redcrosse and the Dragon: Sublime Heroism

Even in canto 11, when Redcrosse completes his quest and slays the Dragon, Spenser continues to emphasize the role of a Reformed charismatic community in sanctification, where Una channels a sublime energy to support the knight's acts of spiritual heroism. As with the House of Holiness passages, scholars have noted that the Dragon episode seems to support a Catholic theology, here because it appears to emphasize justification by good works.[90] But the role played by sublime community in Redcrosse's success, in channelling divine grace, helps to clarify the role of Calvinist views of sanctification and assurance in this episode as well. During the battle, Redcrosse benefits from his renewed faith and sense of vocation gained earlier in the House of Holiness, as well as the *charism* of Una, whose intercession during the battle channels divine power to sustain the knight's transformation of will and emotions. In effect, Spenser represents the magnetic force of Christian fellowship miraculously preserving Redcrosse's transcendent condition and passion for heavenly glory. Thus, Spenser credits divine power for Redcrosse's heroic victory even while giving meaning to the knight's actions, showing spiritual heroism to be an interdependent phenomenon, in a manner consistent with Calvinist doctrine.

To sustain heroic action, Redcrosse relies first and foremost on the divinely inspired, sublime words of Una to encourage perseverance in his heroic quest.

Preparing Redcrosse to face the Dragon, Una first exhorts her knight to greatness, implying his need to transcend his earthly nature throughout the battle:

> The sparke of noble corage now awake,
> And striue your excellent selfe to excell;
> That shall ye euermore renowmed make,
> Aboue all knights on earth, that batteill vndertake.   (xi.2.6–9)

Una's words, calling Redcrosse to rise above ("to excell") his "excellent selfe," evoke the language of the sublime. He must not only be great, but he must outdo the best version of his natural self by tapping into his "noble corage" (a property reminiscent of Longinus's *megalophués*) – he must act in his elevated, *ekstatic* condition, which he can do only by cooperating with divine grace. Una's words of encouragement to Redcrosse, as Hume notes, need not reflect the Pelagian belief that the human will is free to do good works without divine aid; Reformers such as Perkins held that after the moment of salvation, which is irresistible, the will would be transformed so that sinners could cooperate meaningfully with divine grace.[91] To this, I would add that Una's words refer to the transformation not only of the intellect, but of the passions corresponding to it. Invoking the *energeia* seen of Fidelia, Una reminds Redcrosse that to defeat the Dragon he must "awake[n]" and "excel," not simply persuading him to act differently, but powerfully *stirring* and inspiring him to cling to saving grace.

As the battle continues, the knight reaches several low points – even desiring death (xi.28.4) – that have led some scholars to find Spenser developing a Pelagian concept of backsliding, of near-mortal despair, again suggesting an emphasis on works righteousness in Redcrosse's actions.[92] But such readings do not recognize that Perkins and other Puritans readily acknowledged spiritual desperation and melancholy as part of the Christian life, even part of the workings of grace.[93] They also overlook the way Redcrosse remains in a state of *ekplexis* through the strength of his spiritual community helping to sustain his transformation. As the Dragon emerges, the monster produces a "roaring hideous sownd, / That all the ayre with terror filled wyd, / An seemed vneath to shake the stedfast ground" (xi.4.1–3), much like the effects of Orgoglio's entrance in canto vii. But while the Orgoglio encounter immediately brings the knight into an (initially) destructive abjection, this time Redcrosse himself does not even react to the thundering and quaking. Later, when the monster approaches him to fight, and the "clowds before him fledd for terror great, / And all the heuens stood still amazed with his threat," the knight shows no such evidence of being terrorized (xi.10.8–9). In fact, only twice does Spenser describe Redcrosse showing any signs of fear at all: at most he "*nigh* quake[s] for feare" as the Dragon approaches him for attack, and is "all amazd, and *almost* made afeared" as the monster blasts fire in his face (xi.15.8; 26.5; my emphasis). Redcrosse may indeed face temptation to lose faith and give way to despair, but the grace that has already begun to transform him now sustains his courage at a miraculously high level for much of the battle, while restoring him during momentary lapses – as when it "fortuned" him to fall into the well of life after a blow that left him for dead (xi.29.1). As the well restores and reinstates him, the passage indicates that Redcrosse's spirituality, like the Reformed understanding of any sinner's condition, is not to be defined by individual moments of weaknesses, but by the marvel of grace that redeems those moments and brings the person's efforts to victory regardless. Reinforcing Spenser's Reformed model of heroism, even great weakness becomes a strength, for only in weakness does the miracle of divine favour become fully apparent and restore Redcrosse to a sublime condition.

In the culminating passage of this scene, Spenser offers a particularly fascinating reference to Redcrosse's reliance on grace following his emergence from the well of life, epitomizing the role of the sublime, and charismatic community, in the poem's heroic model. As Redcrosse rises up miraculously from the well (one of two key moments of grace intervening directly during the battle), the narrator compares him to a young hawk that "merueiles at him selfe" as it soars through the air (xi.34.8). The comparison suggests a significant blurring of the boundaries of the self, as it implies that Redcrosse must have somehow been transported outside himself in order to look *at* himself, reflecting a sinner's awareness of divine grace giving him a new identity. The comparison suggests the major source of Redcrosse's heroism – his openness to miraculous aid beyond his own power. As Redcrosse, marvelling at his newfound strength, strikes the Dragon so as to leave his "dulled sences all dismaid" (xi.35.9), even the narrator declares his bewilderment at what "secret vertue" the knight has suddenly applied (xi.36.5). Pondering whether his sword was "hardned with that holy water," or his "baptized hands now greater grew," the narrator points to the great enigma of grace, whose channels cannot be fully traced, but whose source is divine, originating well outside Redcrosse's natural self – encompassing the water of life, as well as the strengthening of Fidelia, the vision of Contemplation, and the prayers and exhortations of Una throughout the passage. As Redcrosse shows a readiness to *delight* ("merveil") in such outside aid, in the breakdown of internal boundaries that allows him to "excell" him "selfe," Spenser depicts one of the most miraculous operations of grace, with language and imagery recalling Longinian *ekstasis*: its ability to open even a withdrawn, abjected sinner to the glories of divine mercy. For time and again in the battle, Redcrosse gains supernatural aid. After falling into the well of life, he later falls under the balm of the tree of life that gives him the element of surprise needed to finally defeat the Dragon. And the text scarcely distinguishes these forms of aid from the power of Redcrosse himself – Una herself rejoices at its conclusion that "her faithfull knight" had "atchieude so great a conquest by his might" (xi.55.9).

The knight's heroic achievement has many contributing factors, but at its centre is a miraculous openness, a readiness to take in outside support that, in turn, lends him confidence and a powerful emotional commitment to his task. Critically, however, instead of taking advantage of obscured boundaries to obliterate the sense of individuality, the presence of charisma fulfils Redcrosse's identity and distinctive purpose. This openness, this blurring of boundaries to sustain communal transfers of grace, in a condition of high ecstasy, exemplifies Spenser's concept of the heroic. And in emphasizing this openness to grace, Spenser emphasizes yet again the way identity (and community) must be rooted foremost in the spiritual realm.

In the final cantos of Book I, Spenser's emphasis on charisma and community provides a final commentary on the nature of faith and grace that extends the work of his predecessors. While Tasso portrays divine rapture as the experience of one individual astonishing another, and Du Bartas portrays it as two or three individuals looking towards God together, Spenser portrays rapture as something prompted and aided by an entire community of inspired believers. For Spenser, heroic faith is a function not only of heightened affections and a transformed heart, but of an active participation in a group identity – in the body of a church both sufficiently genuine and united to provide support in teaching, service, and encouragement. Thus, in *The Faerie Queene*, we see, alongside warnings about the trappings of Catholic pomp and a misguided dedication to religious and political institutions, warnings about the dangers of religious individualism. Without the support of an active religious community, Holiness is present only in the form of judgment – Fradubio and Orgoglio merely terrify, while Fidelia, Arthur, and Una promote the work of grace taking hold of the abject sinner. For Spenser, a charismatic community of believers – a spiritual community of people sharing a genuine faith – transports the sinner to a far greater extent than in any other heroic model in this study, this community actively sustaining the heightened affections that support faith and action.

Spenserian Holiness: Mysterious, Boundless, Sublime

As we have seen, Spenser offers a complex representation of Protestant holiness that draws together three forms of sublimity: the dreadfulness of judgment, the irresistibility of divine grace, and the collective magnetism of that grace, all three of which Redcrosse experiences en route to his defeat of the Dragon. Yet his experience is not linear and sequential: while the final canto contains hints that the quest for holiness has been completed and all that remains are "ease and euerlasting rest" (xii.17.9), the sublimity does not simply evaporate, leaving peace in its wake. Instead, Spenser layers all three kinds of sublimity into the final canto in surprising ways that reiterate Calvin's concept of the sublime mystery of the divine.

In particular, abject fear lingers in the Edenic community, with many people terrified of contact with the Dragon's corpse:

> [T]he sight with ydle feare did them dismay,
> Ne durst approch him nigh, to touch, or once assay.
>
> Some feard, and fledd; some feard and well it faynd;
>   One that would wiser seeme, then all the rest,
>   Warnd him not touch for yet perhaps remaynd
>   Some lingring life within his hollow brest.   (xii.9.8–10.4)

Despite the implicit comedy of the description, Spenser uses it to underscore the ongoing anxiety Christians might retain about the power of judgment, sin, and death. For Christians, a remnant fear of judgment may continue to haunt life on earth – a fear of condemnation of which sinners may never be finally rid before the expected return of Christ – as a reminder of the cost of grace and the humble reverence due to God. Moreover, Spenser uses this depiction of haunting fear to heighten the sense of divine inscrutability, for even the one who "would wiser seeme" finds it difficult to comprehend the interplay between judgment and grace. As Spenser portrays it, heroic participation in the sublimity of holiness is an ongoing process, requiring continual reminders of the reality of God's terrifying judgment, the promise of irresistible grace, and the miraculous strength afforded through Christian fellowship.

Spenser does represent a way of dismissing fear temporarily, however, as the betrothal ceremony of Redcrosse and Una features a "song of loue and iollity" (xii.38.9) suddenly being interrupted by "an heauenly noise / ... / Like as it had bene many an Angels voice, / Singing before th'eternall maiesty / In their trinall triplicities on hye"; everyone hearing this noise "felt secretly / Himselfe thereby refte of his sences meet, / And rauished with rare impression in his sprite" (xii.39.1, 3–4, 7–9). This baffling song at last wipes away all evil thoughts and anxieties and leaves "young and old" in a state of "exceeding merth" (xii.40.1, 3). Cheney notes that these creatures "become unwitting humans experiencing a baffling godhead," whereby Spenser looks ahead to Kant's idea of the sublime as a "mental state of dizzying consciousness ... when the mind comes up against the limits of human knowledge."[94] I would add that the "rauished" condition of the listeners at this "heauenly noise" also represents the culmination of the knight's experiences throughout his quest for holiness. In his search for virtue, Redcrosse becomes repeatedly stunned by the divine presence and, with the crowd at his betrothal feast, is stunned yet again into a condition of awed reverence. With sublime rapture closing out the Book, Spenser highlights that ecstasy is not merely a catalyst to spiritual transformation, but the final end of the Legend of Holiness – the emotions of euphoric divine worship.

After all, in pairing holiness and sublimity in Book I, Spenser anticipates his epic successor, John Milton, who will later theorize that the proper subject for poetry is "whatsoever in religion is holy and sublime." According to Milton, the poet's most important objectives should be to "celebrate in glorious and lofty hymns the throne and equipage of God's almightiness."[95] Looking at Spenser's overall poetics within and even beyond the Legend of Holiness, we might say that for Spenser as well, the final aim of poetry is not civic duty or "vertue," as claimed in the Letter to Raleigh, but worship, which is divine.

Throughout the remainder of *The Faerie Queene*, too, Spenser's poetics points towards an objective other than virtue, which the poem continually defers. Not only does Redcrosse's mission for Gloriana remain incomplete at the conclusion to Book I (the most teleological of the six), but in later Books Spenser features the deferral of Britomart and Artegall's quest for marital chastity and Calidore's failure to keep in check the Blatant Beast. And Spenser himself, of course, never finishes *The Faerie Queene*. Yet none of the quests would register as a failure by the standards of Book I, for Spenser shows little intention to resolve the complex sublimity of holiness in the opening Legend. Ultimately, each of these quests aims for divine praise, which is by definition eternal – and with each deferral, Spenser gestures yet again towards an infinite divinity.

5 Milton's Sacrificial Sublime: Idolatry and Relationship in *Paradise Lost*

Milton is the one Renaissance epic poet whose knowledge of Longinus is certain – and as suggested in chapter 1, he is intentional about incorporating Longinian poetic ideals into his writing. In his literary theory, as we saw earlier, Milton emphasizes that entering the sublime requires the decision to subordinate the self, recognizing one's weakness and dependence on divine mercy. In *Paradise Lost*, he develops a similar model of sublime epic heroism in his human heroes, Adam and Eve, that is unequivocally based on strong interpersonal relationships. As the pair pursues a condition of divine ecstasy in various ways, Milton demands that his heroes be capable of compelling acts of self-sacrifice to enter a condition of *ekplexis*.

In featuring sublimity as the final aim of epic heroism, Milton integrates central threads from the *Gerusalemme Liberata, Les Semaines,* and *The Faerie Queene* to develop a particularly intricate model of the sublime. Drawing from Du Bartas's emphasis on spiritual humility and Tasso's emphasis on heroic choice, Milton celebrates Adam and Eve's conscious decision to *choose* weakness, by subordinating the will and sacrificing the interests of the self in order to be exalted in relationship with God. By emphasizing the agency of Adam and Eve, Milton correspondingly rejects Spenser's Calvinist emphasis on the irresistibility of the sublime, reflecting an Arminian belief that salvation is not limited to those God has predestined but open to all who freely choose it.[1] But while pushing back against Spenser's Calvinism, Milton simultaneously incorporates *The Faerie Queene*'s critique of charismatic leadership into his depiction of Satan. Throughout the poem, Milton develops an extensive critique of the fallen angel's attempt to be recognized as a charismatic leader of his infernal empire, an effort that cuts him off from heavenly sublimity. In renouncing Satan's charismatic leadership as idolatrous, Milton issues a subtle critique of the desire for Virgilian nationalism and civic identity – an end that Adam and Eve, at the conclusion, heroically reject.[2]

Thus far, scholarship on the sublime in *Paradise Lost* has not emphasized the ways that Milton associates the sublime with heroism itself – overlooking the way that his protagonists demonstrate their heroism by pursuing sublimity, nor how Milton borrows from his predecessors in his representations of sublime epic heroism.[3] To date, scholarship has tended to associate the Miltonic sublime with the grand rebellion of Satan and the apocalyptic image of the Son during the War in Heaven (a model of sublime terror);[4] the portrayal of space in the Creation narrative (a model of sublime *admiratio*);[5] and the appearance of Eve (a model of sublime beauty).[6] But scholars have not considered Milton's portrayal of a *heroic* sublime in Adam and Eve, the principal protagonists and heroes of *Paradise Lost*.

As we have seen with previous epic heroes of *Les Semaines*, the *Gerusalemme Liberata*, and *The Faerie Queene*, Milton establishes divine transcendence as the core objective and the standard of heroism – but in *Paradise Lost*, this is a form of transcendent ecstasy distinctive to Milton, with his monistic view of the universe. In Book 5, the angel Raphael holds out to Adam and Eve an opportunity for material transformation, where they might be "turn[ed] all to Spirit, / Improv'd by tract of time, and winged ascend / Ethereal" (5.497–9).[7] Consistent with Milton's monism, this process is not an instant conversion from corporeal to incorporeal substance, or an immediate removal from Eden to heaven, but a gradual process where the human, material bodies of Adam and Eve may become angelic bodies – more fluid, though still material.[8] With this transmutation, the angel explains, they will have the opportunity to dwell "at choice / Here or in Heav'nly Paradise" (499–500), but in any case, to "ascend to God" (512). This experience, implicitly, offers unquantifiable bliss: Adam, noting how the angel's "excellence … / Transcend[s] his own so farr" (456–7), responds with fascination to the opportunity to surpass their current condition. And as Raphael explains, the opportunity to be transformed into the likeness of angels and granted access to heaven itself is not a given, but would demand "persever[ance]" (525) – and, in this respect, would represent a heroic achievement.

In *Paradise Lost*, Milton follows a line of predecessors in associating heroic exaltation with acts of humble self-sacrifice. Raphael establishes that Adam and Eve may be elevated and exalted by remaining in "obedience" to God through "voluntarie service" and "will / To love" (5.522, 529, 539–40). As an act of trust and devotion, they must identify totally with the divine will and subordinate their own to God's – recalling the self-doubting dependence shown by Du Bartas's heroes – but expressly out of *love* for God, out of a choice to subordinate their will to his. When the Fall prevents this idyllic model of sublime heroism from being realized, Milton continues to portray rapture as available to fallen humanity, but, extending Tasso's emphasis on risk and choice, makes it a function of sacrificial choices made in interpersonal relationships. By the epic's conclusion, Adam and Eve are thus reconciled and united to God by pursuing the sublime together in self-denying acts of love. In contrast, Satan merely pretends to sacrifice himself for the aim of gaining glory, thus representing a form of heroism that distorts Milton's central model and ends in a disastrous, warped form of sublimity.

In focussing on the experiences of Satan, Adam, and Eve, this chapter excludes the subject of most studies of the Miltonic sublime – its meta-sublimity, or its aesthetic effects on readers. That Milton produced the sublime in *Paradise Lost* is certainly evident, but by exploring the complex psychology of individual characters who are themselves caught up in the pursuit of *ekstasis*, this chapter furthers a point made by David Sedley – that Milton was deeply self-conscious in his use of the sublime.[9]

Heroic Transcendence and Sacrificial Toleration

Despite some differences from his predecessors, Milton appears to have shared their fascination with divine transcendence from the earliest stages of his career – he was intrigued, as they were, with the heroic dimensions of divine ascent, but especially by the social nature of that transcendence. Among Milton's descriptions of sublime ascent to the heavenly heights, the most powerful appears in *An Apology Against a Pamphlet* (1642), an antiprelatical tract and defence of his moral character against an attack made by Bishop John Hall. Requesting that he "may have leave to soare awhile," Milton imagines himself as a heroic figure undergoing sublime transport as he works to defend divine truth. He fights passionately for those who would be harmed by false teaching, identifying himself with the "invincible warrior Zeale":

> whose substance is ethereal, arming in compleat diamond ascends his fiery Chariot drawn with two blazing Meteors figur'd like beasts, but of a higher breed then any the Zodiack yields, resembling two of those four which Ezechiel and S. John saw, the one visag'd like a Lion to expresse power, high authority and indignation, the other of count'nance like a man to cast derision and scorne upon perverse and fraudulent seducers; with these the invincible warriour Zeale shaking loosely the slack reins drives over the heads of Scarlet Prelats, and such as are insolent to maintaine traditions, brusing their stiffe necks under his flaming wheels. Thus did the true Prophets of old combat with the false; thus Christ himselfe the fountaine of meekeness found acrimony anough to be still galling and vexing the Prelaticall Pharisees.[10]

Milton borrows his imagery from Ezekiel and Revelation, in which the prophets Ezekiel and St. John convey their respective visions of marvellous beasts in the heavens. They too represent the glory of the Lord in the very terminology of the sublime – Ezekiel describes the beasts as "fearful," the vision leaving him overwhelmed and prostrate, while John describes himself as "ravished."[11] Milton, however, participating more actively than either prophet in the ascent, describes himself experiencing transport out of his earthly self as a representation of his own elevated mental state. Imagining himself as the chariot-driver "Zeale" making noble ascent, Milton locates sublimity in his own zealous cooperation with divine purposes: in this case, the purpose of defending divine truth from the "heresies" and "corruptions" of Church leadership.[12]

In his passionate pursuit of truth, Milton develops a concept of sublimity that has a particularly communal slant, implying that the entire endeavour is motivated by concern for people threatened by false teaching. In the *Apology* he compares himself to "true Prophets of old [who] combat with the false," to "Christ himselfe" confronting the "Prelaticall Pharisees," and to Luther facing the "chiefe defenders of old untruths in the Romish Church."[13] In each case, he imagines himself joining the biblical prophets, Christ, and Luther in opposition to false leaders, in an effort to identify with and defend oppressed masses. In citing these figures, Milton envisions his own heroic efforts both drawing him nearer to God and providing religious freedom for faithful believers, enabling them, likewise, to participate in the pursuit of divine truth and eventual union with God. In Milton's vision of heroic ascent, there is no reference to achieving solipsistic glory.

While the *Apology* suggests a largely militant model of sublimity, elsewhere Milton imagines transcendence as something less violent, more personal and relational – based on acts of sacrificial toleration intended to build widespread unity in the wake of religious sectarianism. In arguing against censorship laws in *Areopagitica* (1644), Milton suggests that transcendence begins with the pursuit of divine truth. To gain true understanding, he writes, a given community must prepare for sublime ascent: to become like an "Eagle muing her mighty youth, and kindling her undazl'd eyes at the full midday beam; purging and unscaling her long abused sight at the fountain it self of heav'nly radiance."[14] In preparing to gaze on "heav'nly radiance" itself, Milton's imagined participants enter a condition of emotional rapture, a "glorious" state of being caught up in the divine realm. For Milton, this ascent demands the free exchange of written ideas to recover truth's "thousand [scattered] pieces." To embrace this freedom would require citizens to subordinate their desire for legal endorsement of their own system of belief out of concern for the interest of others, to allow wider toleration of diverse religious and political viewpoints.[15] In effect, he imagines the gathering of knowledge as a sublime work of cooperation and even love. As Milton writes, "How many other things might be tolerated in peace, and left to conscience, had we but charity," for doctrinal differences, "though they may be many yet need not interrupt the unity of Spirit."[16] For Milton, sublimity requires spiritual unity, which requires transcendence of self – the ability to identify with the interests of others, especially when they differ from one's own. Miltonic transcendence is not simply metaphorical, but deeply affective. Through the transcendence of self, an ecstatic encounter with the "heav'nly radiance" of divine knowledge becomes possible.

In *Paradise Lost*, Milton portrays the experience of the sublime as dependent on a similar willingness to be drawn outside the self in identification with others' needs. This is true of Raphael's promise to Adam and Eve before the Fall – in a process parallel to how food itself is "by gradual scale sublim'd" from fruit to human spirit (5.483). In this promise, Raphael suggests that the figurative transcendence of self, through subordination of the will to another's, leads to physical transcendence of self and divine ecstasy. And it is also true after the Fall, as Milton juxtaposes two contrasting attempts at divine transcendence (and heroism) – Satan's, versus Adam and Eve's.

First, in the already-fallen Satan, Milton represents a self-absorbed mode of sublimity, in which the archangel demonstrates charisma – he seeks to become sublime to others, and in doing so, remains too detached to enter the sublime himself. Sedley, one of few scholars to consider Satan's *deliberate* "attempt to be sublime" within the poem (as opposed to his unconscious aesthetic effects on readers), argues that the attempt fails because of the devil's resistance to doubting.[17] While I agree that Satan's concept of sublimity is hampered by his resistance to doubt, I suggest that he does produce a significant, if fleeting form of sublimity in the other devils, which Milton uses to present the hazards of the devil's appeal. In effect, despite his admiration for Tasso, Milton uses Satan to expose the fraudulent nature of charisma even more fully than Spenser, depicting it as idolatrous, conducive to corrupt institutional power structures rather than real relationships, and inadequate to Christian heroism. In effect, he ties charisma to a Virgilian pursuit of national glory, a devotion he finds destructive. For in elevating himself above the devils, Satan isolates himself, entering a condition of permanent abjection comparable to what we saw in Spenser's Despaire – a distorted form of *ekstasis* that signals, for Milton, the distortedness of Satan's charisma as a heroic model.

In the human protagonists, Milton portrays a more complex mode of heroism that comes to fruition after the Fall, as their concept of relationship evolves. In prelapsarian Eden, both Adam and Eve show signs of untrained emotional and relational capacities that still show unreadiness to fulfil the paradigm outlined by Raphael. While Eve tends to seek sublimity in herself, rather than in God's glory, Adam is at first limited in his ability to sustain strong emotion – particularly amazement at the revelation of divine glory; though sinless, he shows room to grow in his appreciation of divine mystery, as depicted in Raphael's account in Books 5–8. But through the suffering of the Fall (and in Adam's case, an experience of abjection that resembles Satan's), both characters progress rapidly as they choose to identify fully with each other in sacrificial love, and thus prepare to enter unity with God. In this model of sublime heroism, Milton ultimately preserves the basic economy of prelapsarian Eden, emphasizing the choice to subordinate the self. And in making transcendence a function of self-sacrifice, he offers a model to a divided nation in a time just as wracked by the aftermath of the Reformation as that of Tasso, Du Bartas, and Spenser.

In depicting Adam and Eve's post-Fall growth, I am not suggesting that Milton represents their prelapsarian condition as flawed, inferior to their postlapsarian condition, or even void of any vestiges of sublimity, but that Milton uses their state of innocence to celebrate the original potential invested in humanity for relational and emotional growth, a potential that is part of what makes their prelapsarian state so excellent. And by showing this growth in his model of the sublime, he creates an especially elaborate depiction of the psychological and spiritual dimensions of heroism. Throughout *Paradise Lost*, Milton draws from his epic predecessors to emphasize the intricacy of the emotions involved in aspiring to divine rapture, along with the various forms of courage and humility that facilitate relationships that are godly, heroic, and sublime.

The following sections look at Milton's competing representations of heroism, first at Satan's idolatrous endeavours to seek his own sublimity, then at Adam and Eve's self-sacrificing efforts to experience sublimity in unity with God, thereby achieving Milton's heroic ideal.

Satan: Charisma and the Idolatrous Sublime

Like King Aladino in the *Liberata*, Satan fights the experience of sublimity himself (in two key examples I will examine below); he much prefers to be the one to produce sublimity in his fellow devils. In this, he also resembles Tassoan charismatic heroes, using his charisma to captivate through speech, action, and appearance.[18] While Satan recalls Tassoan charisma in several ways, he does so most significantly through his offer to fight for and sacrifice himself for the banished devils: through his offer to "accept / *Alone* the dreadful voyage" to Eden (2.425–6; my emphasis), which alludes to comparable actions by Goffredo and Sofronia to support and protect the Christians.[19] Through their offers of sacrifice, all three figures earn the awe and reverence of their respective viewers, generating a sublime condition that, in the case of Goffredo and Sofronia, mediates the divine glory that pervades them and creates a direct channel to God.

Following Spenser, Milton critiques Tassoan charisma as a potential bridge to idolatry, though he extends Spenser's critique to not only "false" forms of charisma (like Lucifera's), but sublimity channelled through any created being. At the opening of Book 2, Satan very much recalls Lucifera, who "to the hyghest … did still aspyre" and "amazes" all who see her, just as Satan "aspires / Beyond thus high" and arises "High on a Throne of Royal State" (2.7–8, 1). But Satan also takes risks and offers sacrifices that she does not, allowing Milton to offer a more direct critique of Tassoan heroism than Spenser had done. Through comparisons to Tassoan heroes, Milton depicts Satan's charismatic "virtue" as a mere cover for self-aggrandizement and the accumulation of power, rather than a property of authentic relationship that enables transport outside the self.

Through Satan's decision to explore the New World on behalf of the fallen angels, Milton interrogates the decision of Goffredo to risk his own life fighting as an infantryman in the opening battle, when in Book 2 Satan accepts responsibility to take on the perilous journey on the pretence of fulfilling his duty. He tells the devils:

> I should ill become this Throne, O Peers,
> And this Imperial Sov'ranty, adorn'd
> With splendor, arm'd with power, if aught propos'd
> And judg'd of public moment, in the shape
> Of difficulty or danger could deterr
> Mee from attempting.   (2.445–50)

In proposing to take a "hazard huge" (473) to preserve his reputation as "matchless Chief" (487), Satan recalls Goffredo's efforts to fight as an infantryman in the *Liberata*, risking his life as an act of humble duty, but consequently bringing his troops into a condition of awe and astonishment. In the very process of lowering himself, Goffredo performs an action so unexpected and exceptional for a captain – adding feats of front-line combat to his already lengthy résumé of leadership exploits – that he proves himself all the more superior to his troops, reinforcing the gap between his status and theirs. By Goffredo's final appearance before the army at the conclusion of the poem, he has achieved a condition of total otherness: "Novo favor del Cielo in lui riluce / e 'l fa grande ed augusto oltra il costume" (new grace from Heaven shines in him and makes him great and majestic beyond the norm [altro che mortal cosa egli rassembra (He resembles something beyond mortal)]" (20.7.3–4, 8). As an illusory crown appears to descend onto his head (20.20), Goffredo's detachment from his troops becomes complete.

Although Tasso himself celebrates Goffredo's noble independence and seems to avoid implicating him for false motives or excessive pride, the captain's entry into battle retains some ethical ambiguity. Even the wise (and typically trustworthy) Raimondo accuses Goffredo of self-aggrandizement, of taking an unnecessary "rischio" in an effort to win for himself the "privata palma" (personal prize, the coveted Mural Prize of being the first to scale the wall) (11.22.1–2). His accusations may be answerable, but remain difficult to dismiss completely.

In *Paradise Lost*, Milton extends a version of Raimondo's accusation to Satan: how can a leader perform an act of truly worthwhile heroic risk, when that action makes the hero seem so much less accessible and relatable to others? As Satan confirms his offer, the devils "bend / With awful reverence prone; and as a God / Extoll him equal to the highest in Heav'n" (2.477–9) – in praising Satan, they entire a "Firm concord" (2.497) with each other, but certainly not with him. Instead, Satan himself perceives them as possible "Rivals" who might threaten to steal his glory (2.472). While Spenser had warned of a form of charisma that is self-referential and idolatrous, instead of pointing to heaven, Milton strengthens the sense of threat by depicting Satan, in the model of Tassoan figures, as even more dangerous for his efforts to manipulate viewers into subordinating themselves to him, deceived by the illusion of a noble spirit.

Milton takes this concern even further in comparing Satan to Sofronia, questioning not only Goffredo's charismatic leadership, but Sofronia's charismatic martyrdom. Like Satan, Sofronia offers herself sacrificially to save the Christian community from King Aladino, an offer that leaves her viewers astonished at her bold defiance of the Saracen king. In her response to the king's interrogation, where she takes sole responsibility for removing the Virgin Mary statue, Sofronia claims that she "non volsi far de la mia gloria altrui / né pur minima parte [did not want to share the smallest part of (her) glory with others]," that she wished to be "sola a l'onor, sola a le pene [alone in honor and punishment]" (2.23.1–2, 8). This claim seems to anticipate Satan's assertion that he must "accept as great a share / Of hazard as of honour ... / ... this enterprize / None shall partake with me" (2.454–66). With Satan's emphatic declaration of independence ("None shall partake") echoing Sofronia's ("not ... share the slightest part"), Milton implicates her, too, in a dangerous detachment motivated by "glory," despite her apparently noble orientation towards the divine. Sofronia's claim may be part of her noble lie to the tyrannical king, but her words are consistent with her overall charismatic persona. Her "lofty spirit" ("alta mente") (2.22.2), "proud head" ("capo altero") (2.25.5), and detachment from Olindo, who joins her at the stake despite her protests, gesture to a tendency to set herself apart from others by her willingness to suffer. And Sofronia's self-sacrifice indeed turns her into a public spectacle that awes the crowds, Clorinda, and King Aladino himself, anticipating the way Satan's "sacrifice" affirms his transcendent position above the other devils and draws their adoration. Like Sofronia, Satan attracts others because he seems so autonomous and unattainable, because he inspires reverence more than he inspires relationship – which Milton portrays as an inherent danger in the charismatic mode of heroism and the aesthetic of martyrdom that can accompany it.

In looking back to the *Liberata*, Milton portrays Satan's sacrifice as a form of self-reliance that extends naturally from his charisma but interferes with the mutuality necessary for divine union. Charismatic heroism itself recalls narratives of classical martyrdom, long associated with self-aggrandizing motives as well as with a problematic self-sufficiency. As J. Warren Smith argues, many early martyrdom narratives "employ the same adjectives – noble, manly, courageous – to describe the martyrs as classical pagan authors used to describe their heroes."[20] According to Smith, these narratives recall Aristotle's description of the "Noble Soul" (*megalopsychos*), who shows his or her high-mindedness by pursuing greatness and taking on sacrificial actions, but who is ultimately motivated by a desire for honour and nobility. Such narratives emphasize the virtue of the hero and "the glorious reward that awaits the martyr," as opposed to the characteristics of "true martyrdom," where "emphasis is placed on God's election and empowerment of the martyr for the completion of the work placed before her."[21] By emphasizing their self-sufficiency, such martyrs isolate themselves in the pursuit of solitary praise and glory as they highlight their own power. As Satan maintains, "None shall partake with me" (2.466), he also insists that he undertake each step of his quest entirely on his own strength and for his own glory, and in doing so, avoids forming connections. Through Satan's pretence of self-sacrifice and deliberate isolation, Milton implicitly critiques Sofronia's comparable detachment from others, which may appear commendably saint-like and may well bring viewers into a sublime condition, but which, in his view, makes both Satan and Sofronia into public spectacles, even idols.

In exposing the idolatrous implications of Satan's charisma, Milton thus goes beyond Spenser in implicating even apparently noble acts of charismatic leadership – he suggests that charisma is inherently too corrupted by pride to have heroic potential, with a mere appearance of virtue that is manipulative and destructive. It is hardly surprising that Milton would offer a more sweeping critique of charisma than the English laureate poet (who more often celebrated Queen Elizabeth I than not), though Milton's consistent critique of manipulative virtue is intriguing. For Satan was certainly not Milton's first critique of how "virtuous" martyrdom can disguise idolatry. In 1649, he invoked charisma and sublimity to challenge the social threat of the idealized image of Charles I in *Eikonoklastes*. The text is an iconoclastic effort to shatter the spectacle of kingship presented in the propagandist defence of the king, *Eikon Basilika*, but Milton not only sets out to expose and destroy the false sublimity of Charles; he also underscores the terror latent in the king's charisma.[22] The text regularly describes the king's image in the language of the sublime: his ability to present himself as a "Saint" or "Martyr" has the potential to leave the English people "fatally stupifi'd and bewitch'd," even to lead them to "ravishment," just as Goffredo and Sofronia leave their viewers variously "attonito," "conquiso" (8.81.7), and "stupefatto" (2.20.3).[23] And with its implications of divinity, the charismatic portrayal of Charles overwhelms viewers in a manner similar to Goffredo's appearance of overpowering his troops – when he "resembles something beyond mortal" (20.7.8). As Milton documents the king's unworthy attempts to "have the people come and worship," he exposes the dangerous power of an image, when a mere mortal represents himself in divine terms.[24] Milton himself is certainly not affected by Charles's charisma, but he does not need to be in order to recognize the king's charismatic capacity, however ephemeral a shadow that form of sublimity might be. For the uninitiated, he recognizes, the king's charisma may appear to reflect that divine glory very powerfully – a frightening prospect. For Milton, charisma itself is a transient yet treacherous sublimity that not only enthrals undiscerning viewers but terrifies more discerning ones, who ought to be horrified at the implications for their liberty.

Thus, while Tasso portrays charisma as inherently divine, its compelling force often supplying an important source of truth to check corrupt human authority structures, Milton represents charisma as definitively *not* divine, having a deceptively potent ability to perpetuate corrupt forms of authority – a power much

more universal and dangerous than that depicted by Spenser. Milton's appreciation for Tasso and his use of the *Liberata* as a poetic model is undeniable, and
he accordingly celebrates Tasso's depiction of sublime heroism in his portrayal
of Adam, as we will see; but his portrayal of Satan's charismatic heroism demonstrates the limits of his admiration. For Milton, Tasso's heroic model features a
level of awe and admiration that ought to be reserved for the relationship to God.
In Satan, Milton holds that no entity aside from God may have sacred significance,
and certainly not on the basis of earthly power.

In his critique of Satan's charismatic monarchy, Milton goes further, representing charisma as a false form of the sublime that is directly antithetical to the true
aim of humankind, rapture. He thus depicts Satan, in his efforts to cultivate cha
risma, necessarily losing out on sublimity and multiple goods bound up with it –
including social connections and even a coherent concept of self. In Satan, Milton
depicts charisma as not only unheroic but a great tragedy of human experience, as
he features the violence that charisma enacts against those who force themselves
into such an unnatural and antisocial role.

In Satan's progressive decline after Book 2, Milton portrays the overall trajectory of charisma as a collapse into abjection and total loss, in which the archangel, intent on furthering his own greatness before others, commits himself to a
tragic, warped version of *ekstasis*.[25] As discussed in previous chapters, Kristevan
abjection is akin to a dark counter-sublimity – characterized by a strong emotional reaction to a crisis of self, and prompting transport *within* the self, rather
than out of the self, as in the true Longinian sublime. While Satan's abjection
resembles aspects of what we have seen of Tancredi, Abraham, and the Redcrosse Knight, who all experience abjection as a part of the process of gaining
spiritual awareness, Satan's abjection most closely resembles the intensive erosion
of self we saw in Spenser's Despaire. Like Spenser, Milton adopts principles of
abjection to figure the simultaneously isolating, self-destructive, and counter-
sublime effects of trying to maintain independence from God. For Satan, instead
of charisma building relationships, it cuts him off from others; instead of experiencing liberation from the self, he realizes the loss of his once most central
attributes. Through the crisis of abjection, Milton represents the distortedness
of charisma as a heroic model.

As Satan falls into despair following his arrival in Eden, Milton portrays his
breakdown as an experience of transport that, with shocking abruptness, col-
lapses him back into himself, preserving a sense of horrified isolation like that
theorized by Kristeva. Describing Satan's preparation for his attack against Adam
and Eve, Milton writes:

> his dire attempt, which nigh the birth
> Now rowling, boiles in his tumultuous brest,
> And like a devillish Engine back recoiles

> Upon himself; horror and doubt distract
> His troubl'd thoughts, and from the bottom stirr
> The Hell within him, for within him Hell
> He brings, and round about him, nor from Hell
> One step no more then from himself can fly
> By change of place: Now conscience wakes despair
> That slumberd, wakes the bitter memorie
> Of what he was, what is, and what must be.   (4.15–25)

Exemplifying the internal transport of abjection, the "devillish Engine" that recoils within Satan looks ahead to Kristeva's description of a subject's sudden, "violent" crisis of identity.[26] It is not that Satan's condition changes at the moment of abjection, but that he develops a sudden awareness of the instability of his innermost self, of the "Hell within him," as when Redcrosse hears "aston'd" the voice of Fradubio and senses nearby the threat of punishment from "Limbo lake." Satan, however, recognizes explicitly that Hell (like an unwanted "Other" in Kristevan terms) has intruded and begun to take over his sense of self, creating a gap between his current self and the "memorie / Of what he was": a great being with nobility, purpose, and volition. He thus resembles more closely the figure of Despaire, as he experiences abjection as part of his damnation, and participates actively in his own self-destruction.

As part of Satan's abject crisis of identity, Milton features a direct connection between his attempt to preserve his charisma and the surrender of relationship, illustrating how charisma operates inversely to the unifying function of the sublime. As Satan despairs over his future, he lingers over a choice he must make between two potential, very different identities available to him: a public, charismatic, but unnaturally constrained self, and a hidden, submissive self with relational potential. His charismatic self is ambitious and intractable, publicly claiming he "could subdue / th'Omnipotent," and thus earn adoration "on the Throne of Hell, / With Diadem and Sceptre high advanc'd" (4.85–6; 4.89–90). This identity is compelling to his followers and Satan himself, though constructed and false. The submissive self, by contrast, is genuine and vulnerable, but concealed from others on account of its weaknesses: this part of Satan groans in "torments," "onely Supream / in miserie" (4.88, 91–2). As Satan considers whether there is "place / Left for Repentance" (4.79–80), he suspects that grace could be available to him "by submission" (4.81) – by choosing to identify with the vulnerable self. But, as he recognizes, repentance would require him to portray his flawed, authentic self in the public view, thus forcing him to discard the charismatic, spectacular image of grandeur he has already constructed. In rejecting this possibility, he maintains:

> *Disdain* forbids me, and my dread of shame
> Among the spirits beneath, whom I seduc'd

> With other promises and other vaunts
> Then to submit, boasting I could subdue
> Th'Omnipotent. Ay me, they little know
> How dearly I abide that boast so vaine.   (4.82–7)

In one of the most tragic lines of the poem, Satan acknowledges that his selection of the charismatic self cuts him off not only from God but from a fellowship he seems to long for: "Ay me! They little know…."

In the process of losing that fellowship, moreover, he begins to lose core components of his identity, dissociating from the agency he was known for. By giving in, Satan perceives that his fear of vulnerability – his "dread of shame," his fear of identifying with his private self – "forbids" him from deciding for himself. As he asserts his need to live up to the "promises and vaunts" that he could "subdue / Th'Omnipotent," or in other words, retain his charisma before the other devils, Satan allows his fear of vulnerability to decide his fate for him, despite a conscious awareness of how much he suffers and how little he gains for doing so. And by refusing to open himself to any form of authentic relational connection, he gives up even his former dynamic energy, making the decision to be enslaved to his own charisma.[27]

In effect, as Satan decides to elevate himself instead of seeking connection, Milton depicts the loss of self – a distortion of sublime *ekstasis* – as the natural consequences of such self-serving attempts to be sublime. As Satan chooses to be confined by his own charismatic image, Milton echoes Spenser's Despaire, who participates actively in his own powerlessness; as we saw, Despaire "chose an halter" for his own recurrent suicides that "could not doe him die" (I.ix.54.8). Yet while Despaire finds a perverse pleasure in this state, Milton depicts no joy in Satan's solipsism. In linking Satan's sense of powerlessness to his charisma, Milton creates a paradoxical connection between the exultant independence typically associated with charisma and the miserable restraint it actually creates. Satan's conscious despair in lacking choice is especially apparent following the initial moment of abjection, as he asks himself a string of rhetorical questions: "Me miserable! Which way shall I flie …? / Which way I flie is Hell; my self am Hell" (4.73, 75); and "is there no place / Left for Repentance, none for Pardon left? / None" (4.79–81); he concludes "[a]ll Hope excluded thus … / … all Good to me is lost" (4.105, 109). As he responds firmly to each question, the sense of certainty and denial of possibility is startling, for Satan denies his own much-vaunted freedom and heroic spirit, exposing the extent to which he is alienated from himself in the process of alienating himself from others, by the demands of his own false heroism. In a perversion of the sublimity he cannot attain, Satan, instead of experiencing transcendence and liberation from self (*ekstasis*), experiences a devastating loss of agency and will. And through this crisis of abjection, Milton depicts just how inherently destructive and distorted his charisma is – how poorly it imitates the sublimity it aspires to.

In exposing Satan's abject loss of self, furthermore, Milton links his charisma to a destructive Virgilian devotion to national glory, a devotion he directly opposes to the joy of the sublime. In Book 4, after his first sight of Adam and Eve, Satan himself enters briefly into a state of sublimity – after recovering his "faild speech," he maintains that his "thoughts pursue [them] / With wonder, and could love, so lively shines / In them Divine resemblance" (4.357, 362–4). Satan can feel sublimity being channelled through the pair and is momentarily tempted by it, in a passage that may remind readers of King Aladino's temptation to heed his sublime perception of Sofronia rather than stand by his own authority, as well as Aeneas's temptation to choose his desire for Dido over his mission to Rome. But like Aladino and Aeneas, Satan puts his duty to his own mission (his own infernal glory) above all else.[28] At the end of the passage, he maintains that though he "Melt[s]" (4.389) at the pair's innocence, "Honour and Empire with revenge enlarg'd, / By conquering this new World *compels* me now / To do what else though damnd I should abhorre" (4.390–2; my emphasis).[29] Even more than Aeneas, who is guided by the gods to pursue the honour and empire of Rome, Satan reveals that his planned conquest of Adam and Eve feels like a forced obligation. Milton, differing from Virgil (as well as Kant, who links duty and sublimity), thus draws a stark contrast between the blissful delights of the sublime and the enslaving Virgilian duty to "Empire" that Satan will pursue, in the process critiquing Satan's Tassoan commitment to his own charisma (his "Honour").[30] For Milton, charismatic leadership is dangerous not only when centred in a monarch, but when existing in any created being, as it promotes destructive commitments to institutional powers in all forms.

In a similar passage in Book 9, Milton extends the opposition between a sublime orientation towards divine love and a burdensome duty to nation, beginning just as Satan takes sight of Eve:

> her every Aire
> Of gesture or lest action overawd
> His Malice, and with rapine sweet bereav'd
> His fierceness of the fierce intent in brought:
> That space the Evil one abstracted stood
> From his own evil, and for the time remaind
> Stupidly good, of enmitie disarm'd,
> Of guile, of hate, of envie, of revenge;

> But the hot Hell that alwayes in him burnes,
> Though in mid Heav'n, soon ended his delight,
> And tortures him now more, the more he sees
> Of pleasure not for him ordain'd.   (9.460–70)

For a brief moment, Satan is psychologically "transported" with "sweet / Compulsion" (9.473–4) – "abstracted" from "his own evil," and "disarm'd" of his characteristic vices. In fact, because Satan is so inferior to Adam and Eve, as unfallen creatures in God's own image, his reaction to Eve is noticeably stronger even than Adam's (whose reaction I will consider below), and more fully characteristic of the sublime.[31] But once again, Satan forces himself to reject the sublime in favour of his deadly mission. Like Aeneas, who is finally pulled away from Dido because Mercury's words leave him "burn[ing]" to leave Carthage, Satan is torn away from Eve by the "hot Hell … that burnes" within him (4.375).[32] In Satan, Milton again separates sublimity and duty much more than his source; where Aeneas is momentarily "stunned" and "struck dumb" ("obmutuit amens") by the vision that directs him towards Rome (4.373), as Virgil associates Roman empire with sublimity, Satan experiences "burning" as an agonizing sense of obligation that is antithetical to the sublime. He has so fully enslaved himself to the "hot Hell" within him that he *makes* himself steer clear of sublimity – he "recollects" his hatred and "excites" his "thoughts of mischief" (9.471–2) in a doubly torturous act, because he cuts himself off from ecstasy with the sense that his hand is tied in doing so. The overwhelming desire to "reign in Hell" simply cuts off any possibility of experiencing the sublime, while deepening his awareness of his own powerless state – revealing how twisted, perverse, and crushing Milton finds the charismatic heroism that has brought him to this place.

In Satan's final appearance in Book 10, Milton features the absolute inadequacy of charismatic heroism as a path to sublimity or relationship, as Satan and his cohort fall far short of the relational harmony Milton prizes, entering a counterfeit unity of mutual discord. When Satan returns to the other devils, Milton creates a dramatic reversal of expectation; just as the devils are

> Sublime with expectation when to see
> In Triumph issuing forth thir glorious Chief;
> They saw, but other sight instead, a crowd
> Of ugly Serpents horror on them fell,
> And horrid sympathie; for what they saw,
> They felt themselves now changing …
> […]
> And the dire hiss renew'd, and the dire form
> Catcht by Contagion.   (10.536–44)

David Quint notes that this moment marks a cyclical aspect of the epic, as the devils revert to the prone position in which they appeared in Book 1.[33] I would add that in being transformed into serpents, the devils come into a perverse unity beyond anything they have yet experienced. Once separated from one another as they lay in dark silence, the devils now enter a "horrid sympathie," transferred among themselves by "Contagion" – a horrific perversion of the kind of authentic sympathy that Raphael idealizes, as well as the unity that Tasso's heroic model aims for. They are left with an imploded Underworld empire instead of the "triumph[ant]" rapture they were expecting, for Milton will have nothing to do with celebrating the kind of unity that Satan's charisma produces. Instead, with the explosion of the "dire hiss.... / Cast on themselves from thir own mouths" (10.537, 543, 547), they are caught in the same state of abjection that has ensnared Satan, united only in mutual scorn and shame rather than empathy, and together driven out of the "sublime" condition they once experienced in their worship of his charismatic persona.

In cultivating a charismatic image to gain worship, Satan loses the honour, infernal empire, and final threads of worth he once clung to, as the image he sacrificed so much to produce evaporates before his viewers' eyes. And in portraying the utterly dysfunctional relationship between Satan and his cohort, Milton features the sterility of charisma, the fallaciousness of a human-channelled form of divine power. For Milton, Christian epic heroism demands a different mode of sublimity that accounts more completely for the humility that Du Bartas, Spenser, and Tasso (in his romantic heroes) incorporate into their poems, a relational model that directs awe and astonishment finally to God.

Adam and Eve: Glory, Pleasure, and the Sacrificial Sublime

Against Satan's solipsistic and glory-seeking model of heroism, Adam and Eve represent a heroic model oriented towards *experiencing* the sublime, like their predecessors in Renaissance epic, rather than producing it. Yet, though Adam's heroic model begins at a completely different entry point from Satan's, Eve's heroic model does intersect with Satan's in prelapsarian Eden before joining Adam's by the poem's end. From her first emergence into the world, she is entranced, though innocently, by the possibility of her own sublimity, showing less inherent contentment in her circumstances than Adam. In her entrancement with her own image (4.449–80), she also shows less natural interest than Adam in relationships, and falls partly because she desires to be like God herself. In Eve's fall, Milton offers a second exploration of Tassoan charisma, though drawing from Du Bartas's depiction of her fall as well, to consider how the desire for charisma can be redeemed. Later, in her reconciliation to Adam, Eve demonstrates a fuller personal and spiritual humility than she had before facing the suffering brought on by the Fall, learning to value relationships in a way she had not; and after demonstrating the sacrificial love Milton associates with authentic heroism, she experiences sublimity in union with Adam.

In Adam, meanwhile, Milton offers a recuperation of Tassoan heroism, uniting elements of his model of romantic heroism with a measure of Du Bartas's celebration of divine mystery.[34] From the beginning, Adam needs no encouragement to be closely devoted to Eve, but he does show room to deepen his emotional experience of God. As we will see, Adam tends to perceive the world in a manner characteristic with the aesthetic mode known as the "picturesque," a weak version of sublimity that prompts an emotional condition of comfort and pleasure. With his pronounced orientation towards "happyness" and "delight," he does not yet embrace divine mystery in ways Raphael – and the poem – encourage, still unprepared to sustain the more profound emotions of Longinian *ekstasis*. While this inclination contributes to his fall, Adam overcomes the consequent separation from God and Eve by an experience of abjection that especially resembles the experience of Tassoan heroes (and Spenser's Redcrosse). Like Tancredi in particular, Adam undergoes abasement that humbles him intellectually and spiritually and deepens his emotional range, leading him towards a productive form of self-denial. With the support and love of Eve, he too chooses to identify with Eve and to make an offer of genuine sacrifice that shows his readiness to be reunited with God in ecstasy; and in so doing, he responds to divine glory with new depth. The result is a complex model of sublimity that departs more widely from Satan's than does Eve's, whose connection to the sublime has been considered more frequently than Adam's; thus, Adam's experience will be given slightly more focus.

After the Fall, the trajectories of Eve and Adam unite, as Milton emphasizes two central components of personal and spiritual development that must be present for a person to enter divine rapture: a Longinian spirit that embraces the experience of the sublime (which Eve alone possesses and Adam must develop), and a humble orientation towards the other above the needs of the self (which Adam possesses and Eve must develop). Equipped with both, Adam and Eve are better prepared – emotionally, psychologically, and spiritually – to enter a state of ecstasy and rich communication with God.

The Quest for Divine Sublimity and the Fall of Eve

N.K. Sugimura emphasizes Eve's yearning for sublimity in her earliest moments, beginning when she gazes longingly at her own reflection (4.465–6); Sugimura argues that Eve's wonder, however ennobling, creates desire for an artificially prolonged experience of sublimity, a desire that in turn leaves her vulnerable to Satan.[35] To this, I would add that Eve's weakness lies as well in her desire to pursue her own sublimity independently, not unlike Tasso's Sofronia. In being captivated by her reflection, Eve's weakness lies not in her fascination with her beauty, but in her instinctive lack of interest in Adam, as she turns away at first sight

(4.480). After acknowledging this minor fault, and before the Fall, Eve subconsciously battles temptation to be swept away by her own self-actualization – to reach "high exaltation" and be counted a "Goddess" (5.90, 78) – a version of Satan's desire to be viewed as sublime, though still innocent, as a planted dream. By the poem's conclusion, Eve's longing transforms into a desire for a cooperative pursuit of sublimity in the context of a devoted relationship, and to see her own glory emanating from God's, rather than standing on its own accord. For Milton, authentic sublimity and divine unity are a function of the ability to pursue properly directed worship in community over one's own honour.

In Book 9, then, Milton presents Eve's original sin as a fault of charismatic ambition that responds to both Tasso and Du Bartas. In a previous chapter, I suggested that Milton follows Du Bartas in making intolerance to divine mystery a mark of resistance to the sublimity of God; Milton's Satan imitates Du Bartas's Satan, who had tempted Eve by criticizing his unknowability (referring to him as "Je ne sçay quel Dieu" [I-know-not-what God]).[36] Through his expansion of the Genesis passage, Milton depicts Eve herself making a speech just before eating of the fruit, where she openly disrespects what she does not know about God as an implicit imperfection on *his* part: "For good unknown, sure is not had, or had / And yet unknown, is as not had at all" (756–67). But in addition to rejecting divine mystery like Du Bartas's Eve, Milton's Eve eats with "God-head [in] her thought" (9.790). Her fall shows a strong desire for her own exaltation that mimics the pursuit of individual glory seen in Tassoan figures, which Milton criticizes through Satan. In particular, Eve follows Satan's instructions to take a heroic risk with the potential to elevate herself: to "vent[ure] higher then [her] Lot" and eat, thus gaining "praise" for her "dauntless vertue" in "denounce[ing]" the "pain / Of death" (9.690, 693–5). In putting everything on the line to secure her own "praise," she resembles Goffredo, who also has the courage to take a major risk to win the Mural Prize, to elevate himself above others. Even though Eve does not explicitly aim to put herself ahead of anyone (at least until after she eats), like Satan and Goffredo had done, her failure to consider or refer to Adam at all – what he would think, or how he would or would not benefit – throughout the passage is noteworthy. She deliberates and acts without any thought to her primary companion, like a Tassoan figure who aspires independently; and in her fall Milton reiterates his critique of those who try to pass off such quests for praise and glory as heroic.

Milton's responsiveness to both *Les Semaines* and the *Liberata* creates some of the complexity of the Fall, which is difficult to reduce to a single characteristic or error. Where Du Bartas warned of the dangers of needing to know, Milton adds to this an emphatic warning about the desire to glorify and exalt the self alone, so celebrated in classical epic and even in Renaissance forms, such as the *Liberata*. In Milton's portrayal, neither Eve's desire for knowledge nor her desire for glory or independence is inherently evil, but in the form they take, these longings prove fatal. Eve's fall represents a double failure of sublimity – the failure to see divine mystery as sublime, and the failure to seek sublimity properly, by seeking first the sublime glory of God.

Additionally, through Eve's fall Milton shows how the failure to properly pursue the sublime starts to weaken the ability to sustain sublime emotions, driving the person not closer to God but further away. Far from becoming raptured after eating, Eve becomes "delight[ed]" and merry ("jocund and boone" [787, 793]), resembling Adam's typical condition *before* the Fall, as we will soon see. As this happens, her very desire for the glory and the heightened emotion of sublimity becomes corrupted to the emotion of envy, as she ponders whether to keep the fruit to herself, in an effort to be "Superior" to Adam (9.825); that envy in turn is quickly overruled by her envy of "another Eve" (9.828). Milton thus shows how antithetical the improper pursuit of the sublime is to relationships – as Eve seeks sublimity alone, she not only fails, but becomes even less inclined to subordinate her interests and show true humility, and even less capable of experiencing the sublime. Eve's fall stresses yet again that the sublime is only possible by desiring the greatness and honour of another, not the self. For Milton, without this attitude, the capacity for the sublime itself fades and evaporates.

The Fall of Adam: Delight, Mystery, and the Picturesque

In his own fall, Adam reveals a different and more subtle version of Eve's failure to be impressed by the sublime mysteriousness of God, stemming from his earliest experiences in prelapsarian Eden. From the beginning, Adam is almost constantly associated with delight and "happyness": Adam asserts that God has "plac't us here / In all this happiness" (4.416–17), while Raphael remarks, "That thou art happie, owe to God; / That thou continu'st such, owe to thy self" (5.520–1). Raphael urges the pair to hold firmly to their "happie state" (5.536), and even reports that God himself claims to have created them "Thrice happie men" (7.625). But beyond "happyness" and "delight" – certainly not condemned in the poem – is the more intense passion of ecstasy, which Milton portrays as the more appropriate response to God's presence, and a passion Adam does not yet readily sustain.

The distinction between happy delight and the transcendent experience of divine union corresponds closely to the distinction that would be made in eighteenth-century aesthetic theory between the picturesque and the sublime.[37] In essence, both the picturesque and the sublime involve certain sensory experiences (visual, auditory, and otherwise) that produce challenging emotional effects, but those associated with the picturesque are not as strong, not rising to the same deep astonishment and ecstasy of the sublime. In a comparison of the terms, Angus Fletcher writes that the sublime generally aims for "size and grandeur" as well as austerity, while the picturesque is like a "microscopic sublimity" that aims for variety, intricacy, and irregularity. Because the picturesque does not have the sense of perfect order and symmetry that characterizes beauty, it may stretch or challenge the senses of the viewer, but without posing the same sense of overwhelming threat. In this regard, the most important difference lies in their respective effects: Fletcher writes that "where the sublime produces 'terror,' or rather, awed anxiety, the picturesque produces an almost excessive feeling of comfort."[38] The picturesque delights, without creating pain or significant distress. While ecstasy astonishes and paralyses, the picturesque heightens interest and curiosity.

The distinction between the picturesque and the sublime is an important one for Milton even early in his career, roughly corresponding to the distinction between his early poems "L'Allegro" and "Il Penseroso." "L'Allegro" is filled with references to "pleasures" (40; 69), "mirth" (13, 152), and "delight" (91), all edged with the weak sublimity of the picturesque. Milton writes that the singing of the Lark "startle[s] the dull night" (42), creating a slight disturbance for the listener. But the overall aesthetic, with its variety of sights, sounds, and experiences, aims to please and meet the desires of the senses.[39] Quite differently, "Il Penseroso" is characterized not by happiness but by a latent condition of "Peace," "Quiet," and "Contemplation" that leads to ecstasy.[40] According to the poem, only by stilling the heart and soul can the soul finally be "rapt" in "holy passion" (40–1) and experience the music of heavenly choirs that "dissolve … into exstasies, / And bring all Heav'n before [the viewer's] eyes" (165–6). Sublimity is a "holy" experience with "Heav'n" – and for Milton, a degree of sobriety and even self-denial foreign to the picturesque mode are prerequisites for experiencing such "exstasies"; a person must be able to set aside the immediate desires in order to transcend his/her natural state. These poems demonstrate a major distinction in Milton's early thinking between picturesque delight as the fulfilment of desires, and sober sublimity as the transcendence of those desires for something greater. And while these early poems do not promote relationships explicitly, they strongly associate sublimity with connection to God.

Uvedale Price, the original theorist of the picturesque, notes that Milton uses the picturesque mode in *Paradise Lost* to describe Adam's initial reaction upon awakening in prelapsarian Eden. Recalling the moment to Raphael, Adam remembers his own assessment in such terms: "[I] feel that I am happier than I know" (8.282).[41] This response is generally consistent with Adam's experiences before the Fall. Both in describing his connection to Eve, and in reacting to the displayed power of God, Adam regularly responds with delight, happiness, and curiosity rather than astonishment, suggesting that he is not yet capable of experiencing the full weight of the sublime.

In particular, Adam takes great pleasure in learning about the creation of the world and events preceding it. This quest appears strikingly innocent compared to Eve's pursuit of knowledge during the Fall, though I would argue, as Regina Schwartz suggests, that Milton problematizes Adam's pursuit as well. As Schwartz notes, Milton develops a distinction between knowledge as presumption, sought with the aim of dominating (the "secret gaze" seen in Satan and the other devils), and knowledge that aims to further divine praise ("open admiration").[42] In his extended discourse with Raphael, Adam often pursues knowledge in a manner that, according to Schwartz's framework, is not sinfully presumptuous, but does not seek praise as its aim either. Consequently, in his quest for concrete information, he bypasses opportunities to experience the sublimity of God as Raphael portrays it.

At one point, Raphael describes God's victory in the war in heaven, spanning the end of Book 5 and all of 6, apparently expecting a major reaction from Adam to the representation of divine glory. The familiar passage concludes with the Son routing the rebellious angels from Heaven:

> in his right hand
> Grasping ten thousand Thunders, which he sent
> Before him, such as in thir Soules infix'd
> Plagues; they astonisht all resistance lost.
> [...]
> [The Son] half his strength ... put not forth, but check'd
> His Thunder in mid Volie, for he meant
> Not to destroy, but root them out of Heav'n:
> The overthrown he rais'd, and ...
> [...]
> Drove them before him Thunder-struck, pursu'd
> With terrors and with furies to the bounds
> And Chrystal wall of Heav'n, which op'ning wide,
> Rowld inward, and a spacious Gap disclos'd
> Into the wastful Deep.   (6.835–8, 853–62)

As Leslie Moore notes, early Milton scholars found the War in Heaven to be the most "sublime" passage of the poem, prompting considerable praise in their commentaries. Both John Dennis and the Earl of Roscommon defined the passage as sublime, while Samuel Barrow's "In Paradisum Amissam" bases its well-known praise of the sublimity of *Paradise Lost* on Milton's portrayal of the Son's intervention and the fall of the rebel angels.[43] Joseph Addison's commentary notes specifically the triumph of the Son coming forth "in the fulness of Majesty and Terrour" as the chief of the "very sublime images" in the poem; here, he suggests, Milton's astounding poetic imagination is on full display: his condition "so inflamed with this great Scene of Action, that where-ever he speaks of it, he rises, if possible, above himself … The Pomp of his Appearance, amidst the Roarings of his Thunders, the Flashes of his Lightnings, and the Noise of his Chariot Wheels, is described with the utmost Flights of Human Imagination."[44] For Addison, the episode is not simply grand, but edged with "Terrour" – among the most overpowering Milton ever develops.

In contrast to these overwhelmed reactions, Adam does not express or sustain the kind of emotion Raphael seems to expect. He initially responds with "admiration" and "deep Muse to heare / Of things so high and strange" (7.52–3), but quickly, Milton writes, the narrative is "driv'n back" from his mind, unable to mix with "Blessedness. Whence Adam soon repeal'd / The doubts that in his heart arose" (7.57, 59–60). Adam experiences nothing like the terror identified by early Milton scholars, and even his "admiration" is short-lived, as he soon changes the subject to the creation of the world. Milton makes clear that Adam has done nothing wrong – it is his "blessedness" that prevents him from responding more profoundly to the exercise of divine force against an evil that is foreign to him. Yet, the passage registers Milton's general agreement with Du Bartas about the ability to value mystery. After all, his pushing aside "doubts" represents a telltale rejection of the sublime – one of the key failures of Milton's Satan, as Sedley argues, and an impulse evident in the temptation of Du Bartas's Satan, too.[45] While the narrative is full of opportunities to embrace heavenly mystery as sublime, as did the Adam, Noah, and Abraham of *Les Semaines*, Adam does not yet demonstrate an inclination to register, with astonishment, the gravity of divine holiness that Milton depicts elsewhere, as he naturally seeks the pleasures of learning more about the physical universe. Thus, where Du Bartas's Abraham tells himself to "admire" what he cannot understand, Milton's Adam must eventually be cautioned by Raphael that heavenly "secrets" are not intended "to be scanned" but "admire[d]" (8.74–5). The angel suggests that God intentionally "plac'd Heav'n from Earth so farr, that earthly sight, / If it presume, might erre in things too high, / And no advantage gaine" (120–2). He continues: "Heav'n is for thee too high / To know what passes there; be lowlie wise" (172–3). In Raphael's insistence that Adam embrace uncertainty, Milton not only hints at the problem of pride, but suggests that his protagonist's continual "desire to know" (7.61) serves as a barrier to his capacity for sublimity – and to his readiness to fully enjoy God's presence.

Before the Fall, then, Adam's natural preference for the delights of knowing over the sublimity of "admir[ing]" suggests that he does not demonstrate – yet – a fully mature Longinian *megalophués*, the greatness of soul necessary to entertain great thoughts and passions.[46] Consequently, he is unable to bask in awe at divine glory and the holy presence of God, to worship and relate to God as deeply as he might. In prayer, Adam does express theoretical awareness of the profound sublimity of divine glory, as he refers to the "Unspeakable" God, whose goodness is "beyond thought" (5.156, 59), but he does not seem prepared to put this principle into practice by dwelling on divine mysteries with the awed amazement that Raphael's narrative might have prompted. And in preferring variety and delight to sublimity, he shows the relative immaturity of his emotional capacity and unconscious resistance to the overwhelming power of God's character – a vulnerability that will contribute to the events of Book 9.

Adam's overall perception of Eve, meanwhile, is also characteristic of the picturesque – he responds to her with intense interest and delight. And while this characterization is not necessarily problematic in itself, in combination with Adam's natural resistance to God's sublimity, it too contributes to his vulnerability to temptation, though, I would suggest, in a manner a bit different than scholars have sometimes maintained.

While early Milton critics tended to associate Eve with the beautiful for her "sweet attractive grace," and critics such as Moore and Sugimura associate her with the sublime, the description of Eve when she is with Adam in fact brings out images of "wildness" and "unevenness" emphasized by Price:[47]

> Shee as a vail down to the slender waste
> Her unadorned golden tresses wore
> Disheveld, but in wanton ringlets wav'd
> As the Vine curles her tendrils, which impli'd
> Subjection, but requir'd with gentle sway.   (4.304–8)

Here and elsewhere, Eve appears to Adam in the picturesque mode, prompting a response of disorderliness and what Price calls "excessive comfort." With her infamous "wanton ringlets" and "disheveld" hair, as well as her "submissive Charms" (4.498), and "peculiar Graces" (5.15), Eve's appearance has a certain irregularity that falls in between the symmetry and finish that characterize "beauty" and the more overwhelming effect of "transport."[48] Adam himself uses both terms – "beauty" and "transport" – when describing their physical relationship to Raphael: "Commotion strange, in all enjoyments else / Superiour and unmov'd, here onely weake / Against the charm of Beauties powerful glance" (8.531–3). But he seems to mean something in between the Burkean concept of beauty and Longinian transport, as he speaks of a wild and raw power forceful enough to weaken him more than mere beauty might, though not to paralyse or overwhelm him in the full manner of sublime ecstasy. He insists that he is not "foild" by Eve (8.608), still "free / to choose the best" (8.610–11). Eve does more than simply delight Adam's senses – put more accurately, she "challenges" them – but she is not meant to create in him the stronger "awed anxiety" characteristic of the sublime, which is reserved for God.[49]

That Eve brings *Satan* into a condition of the sublime, as we saw, is a function of his inferiority to her. As an unfallen creature in God's own image, she is morally spotless and thereby has a stunning effect over the degraded angel, representing a significant exception to Milton's views of charisma. But Adam is not Eve's inferior, and therefore he is not designed to feel for Eve the same kind of awed astonishment that Satan does. And he does not do so in prelapsarian Eden. Unlike Tasso, whose heroes are readily transported by a sublime beloved, Milton makes authentic Longinian ecstasy a property of the relationship to God, not to other human beings, their equals, who are to pursue sublimity in the presence of God in unity with each other, not through the charisma of the other.

In distinguishing between the picturesque and the sublime, I believe, Milton does not problematize Adam's response to Eve as such, a possibility that has often been suggested as a reason for the Fall.[50] Instead, I suggest that he problematizes Adam's inability to sustain the stronger passion of ecstasy that his relationship to God should prompt and that the gravity of the situation demands. In this passage, then, Adam falls not because of excess passion for Eve, but because he is not sufficiently captivated by representations of divine power. When he first sees Eve after her transgression, he does sense in her fallenness the terror of divine justice for the first time: he is "amaz'd" and "Astonied … and Blank, while horror chill / Ran through his veins, and all his joynts relax'd" (9.889–91), as he intuits Eve's sin. But in seeing this, he fails to follow through on the awe of God's presence that should overcome all other emotions, even the unsettling delight of Eve, and in doing so, he fails to fulfil all three models of sublime heroism outlined by Spenser, Tasso, and Du Bartas. With the use of the word "Astonied," Milton's description recalls Spenser's portrayal of the Redcrosse Knight during his encounter with Fradubio, when the knight enters the sublime upon realizing that divine judgment is imminent. Compared to Redcrosse, however, Adam chooses more consciously not to let this terror take sufficient hold of him. He is in fact more like Tasso's King Aladino, resisting "un non so che" at the sublimity of Sofronia's divine empowerment; he allows himself to distrust the value of the intuition and fails to choose the sublime option (9.928–43). And in doing this, like Du Bartas's Eve, Adam declines to imagine that God might have other blessings in reserve – that his mysteriousness could contain possibilities unimaginable to him. Adam's decision may appear to anticipate the sacrificial love that finally characterizes Milton's model of sublimity – seen perfectly in the Son, and later in Adam and Eve themselves – but he enacts only a perversion of it. Though he might seem to act nobly, his desire is not to save Eve by love, but rather to salvage a source of delight ("Femal charm" [9.999]) instead of responding to the sublimity of God.[51]

Abjection, Growth, and Unity

After Adam and Eve fall, Milton represents their reconciliation and recovery from despair as a process of accelerating development of qualities they had not yet cultivated, and that support a stronger orientation towards God – most of all, a Longinian disposition prepared to encounter God's presence as sublime, and a humble spirit prepared to sacrifice its own interests to others. As they do so, Adam and Eve restore communication to God while arriving at Milton's concept of heroism.

While their process of heroic recovery draws from both Du Bartas's and Spenser's models of sublime heroism, Adam's despair, which resembles a state of abjection, especially recalls Tasso's portrayal of abject suffering as a catalyst for the sublime, allowing Milton to further redeem Tasso's heroic model after critiquing his glorification of charisma. In Adam specifically, abjection causes humility, and shifts his previous orientation toward pleasure, which deepens his emotional range, while leading him to appreciate divine mysterious as he had not done before. (Adam's despair will be discussed at greater length than Eve's, simply because Milton portrays it at far greater length.)

Adam's despair has been compared to Satan's, but to my knowledge has not, like Satan's, been identified with abjection.[52] Beginning with the speech "O miserable of happie!" (10.720), Adam turns against himself in hatred, undergoing a violent internal struggle where he too imagines with horrified helplessness the encroachment of divine judgment. At the culmination of his speech, he cites a "fear / [That] comes thundering back with dreadful revolution / On my defensless head; / both Death and I / Am found Eternal" (10.813–16). But despite similarities between Adam's experience and Satan's, Adam's abjection departs from Satan's in essential ways, as Satan's more closely resembles the eternal self-imprisonment of Spenser's Despaire, while Adam's resembles Tancredi's in reorienting his emotions away from pleasure-seeking and towards divine reverence.

As with Tancredi, Adam's abjection represents the process of developing the proper contrition for sin that enhances emotional depth. Just as Tancredi turns on himself after realizing the evil of his ruthless slaughter of Clorinda, Adam recognizes and dwells on his own corruption in self-loathing: "from mee what can proceed / But all corrupt, both Mind and Will deprav'd / Not to do onely, but to will the same" (10.824–6); the sentiment is similar to Tancredi's fear of his very self: "Temerò me medesmo; e da me stesso / sempre fuggendo, avrò me sempre appresso [I will fear myself; and always fleeing from myself, will always have myself nearby]" (12.77.7–8). Much like a subject of abjection remains haunted by an unwanted "other," Adam shows a disturbed awareness of the total depravity of soul that he can never escape, and with that realization, he gains an awareness of the terrors of divine power he had lacked earlier. With this comes also a greater capacity to *feel*, as he is driven "into what Abyss of fears / And horrors ... out of which / [he finds] no way, from deep to deeper plung'd!" (10.842–4). Once resistant to "terror," as we saw, Adam is now forced to dwell in a state of horror, and thus develop an emotional response consistent with the reality of evil. Though his response is riddled with misogyny and expressions of hopelessness, Adam displays at the same time a productive readiness to see sin as it is and hate its effects. For Milton, this intense, rightful hatred of sin is the first step (in a fallen context) towards preparing the heart to sustain and fully experience the ecstasy of unity with God.

As Adam's emotional capacity strengthens through suffering, Milton also depicts his suffering as the mechanism that pushes him to appreciate what lies beyond himself and his own intellectual limits – in short, he develops the humility that underlies the ability to experience the sublimity of God's presence. Satan, as we have seen, is determined to seek his own glory. As part of this independence, he asks only closed, rhetorical questions that reveal an arrogant preference for certain destruction over the possibility of salvation: "is there no place / Left for Repentance, none for Pardon left? / None" (4.79–81); and "[a]ll Hope excluded thus … / … all Good to me … lost" (4.105, 109). While Satan resists the unknown, Adam offers a series of open-ended queries that demonstrate a significant shift in intellectual attitude – he no longer looks for specific answers as he had earlier, but acknowledges what remains unknown of God's will. He thus asks questions he cannot answer: "is this the end / Of this new glorious World[?]" (10.720–1), and "Why comes not Death, / … To end me? Shall Truth fail to keep her word, / Justice Divine not hast'n to be just?" (10.854–7). Where Satan answers his questions with a resounding negative, Adam shows uncertainty about his present and future. Though Adam imitates Satan when he cries, "O Conscience, into what Abyss of fears / And horrors hast thou driv'n me; out of which / I find no way" (10.842–4), his conclusion, "out of which I find no way," is much less conclusive than Satan's comparable "Hope excluded thus." Rather than confirming that no outlet or alternative exists, Adam simply acknowledges his own helplessness. As we saw in the *Liberata*, Tancredi, after recognizing the depths of his sin, turns for help to the newly ascended Clorinda in an all-night vigil of prayer. It will take Adam a few hundred additional lines to turn to God directly, but in the questions above, he too demonstrates a total dependence on the powers of heaven, a spiritual humility that unites with recognition of his lack of understanding. In demonstrating both spiritual and intellectual humility, he thus combines the heroic qualities of Tancredi and of Abraham, who in *Les Semaines* looks directly to God to put his lingering incertitude into perspective. And as we saw, Abraham's humble openness to the mysteries of God's ways prefigures the external transport of the sublime. In *Paradise Lost*, Adam's ability to embrace divine mystery does not come until later, relative to Abraham's, but already Milton uses the similarities between Adam, Tancredi, and Abraham, and the contrast between Satan and Adam, to illustrate the type of intellectual and spiritual dependence that precede deep unity with God.

In a final step, Milton illustrates how these forms of humility underlie a proper feeling towards other created beings, and how both precede the ability to transcend the self. Unlike Satan, who limits his lament of the effects of sin to those on himself, Adam looks outward, addressing the descendants who will be most harmed by his fault, just as Tancredi addresses the fallen Clorinda with remorse. When Adam thinks of his "Posteritie," and how it now "stands curst: Fair Patrimonie / That I must leave ye, Sons" (10.818–19), he demonstrates an empathy that is completely foreign to Satan, as he offers to protect them from the consequences of his actions. The imploring offer of sacrifice may seem wishful, but the desire appears heartfelt: "On mee, mee onely, as the sourse and spring / Of all corruption, all the blame lights due / So might the wrauth" (10.832–4). In this statement, Adam unknowingly lays the final piece of the foundation for his own transformation. In his willingness to sacrifice himself for another's benefit, he expresses the greatest possible form of identification with another individual, a willingness to sacrifice himself. In transcending self-interest, he prepares for a spiritual alteration as well – a metaphorical *ekstasis*, being drawn out of the self. His statement represents a capacity for self-denial recalling that seen in "Il Penseroso," and signals accordingly his ability to experience sublimity as Milton portrays it – with an aim of unity with God, and with other created beings.

In a parallel experience, Eve returns to the same heroic trajectory as Adam through her own despair, as she demonstrates a desire for relationship that had been limited in earlier passages – a desire that further illustrates the link between sacrifice and divine reconciliation. Milton does not directly portray her thought processes as he does Adam's, but he suggests that she transforms by interiorizing the suffering Adam verbalizes while she observes from nearby, thus affirming the importance of their domestic companionship to the pursuit of divine unity. As Eve recognizes the consequences of her own sin on Adam and all of humanity, she demonstrates an even fuller version of the empathy, humility, and dependence that Adam had just expressed over many more lines, and makes a genuine offer of martyrdom that "corrects" the charismatic model of Tasso. She thus responds to Adam's misogynistic outburst with her urgent plea, "Forsake me not thus, Adam," and insists on her ability to identify with his interests sacrificially:

> What love sincere, and reverence in my heart
> I beare thee …
>   … thy suppliant
> I beg, and clasp thy knees; bereave me not,
> Whereon I live, thy gentle looks, thy aid,
> Thy counsel in this uttermost distress,
> My onely strength and stay: forlorn of thee,
> Whither shall I betake me, where subsist?
> [...]
> Between us two let there be peace, both joyning,
> As joyn'd in injuries …
> [...]
>   … both have sin'd, but thou
> Against God onely, I against God and thee,

> And to the place of judgment will return,
> There with my cries importune Heaven, that all
> The sentence from thy head remov'd may light
> On me, sole cause to thee of all this woe,
> Mee mee onely just object of his ire.   (10.915–22, 924–5, 930–6)

Instead of withdrawing inwardly like Satan, or running from Adam as she had after her first creation, she looks outward and insists that *Adam* not run from her, declaring her dependence on his "looks," "aid," and "counsel." While Eve's forfeiture of self-confidence and sense of individuality after the Fall represents a significant loss, Milton does portray a productive aspect to her newfound dependence, as it causes her to declare her need for companionship in a way she had not yet done.[53] Unlike Tassoan heroes – the isolated, exalted Goffredo, or Sofronia, characterized by a "capo alto" and marked reluctance to acknowledge or marry Olindo after her release – Eve seeks to be "joyn'd" with Adam with all her heart. In doing so, she shows the depths of her humility towards Adam by taking the position of a suppliant. With her plea, "On me, sole cause to thee of all this woe, / Mee mee onely just object of his ire," she extends Adam's offer of sacrifice even further, showing that she is even more capable of empathy, since she makes her offer in earnest, to someone who has just personally offended her. And by depicting her offer of sacrifice as genuine, Milton thus supplants the (perceived) self-aggrandizing heroic model of Goffredo and Sofronia with one that acts without reference to the exaltation of the self – a relational model that looks to others for strength and understanding, and seeks first to serve the interests of the other.

In this dialogue, Milton furthers the mutuality of this model by showing Eve and Adam together demonstrating the "will / to Love" that Raphael had set forth as a heroic condition to being "turn[ed] all to Spirit" and experiencing the poem's version of transcendence. Eve's self-subordinating offer is clearly depicted as heroic, as it leaves Adam "disarm'd" (10.945); the act prompts him to return with his own comparable offer to "speed before thee, and be louder heard, / That on my head all might be visited" (10.954–5), deeply affected by her act of charity.[54] Although they have already disobeyed God and can no longer prove their humility in that way, Milton endorses their demonstration of love for each other instead as a substitute form of self-subordination, showing how seriously he still takes his own assertion in *Areopagitica* that "charity" is the key to preventing differences from interrupting "the unity of Spirit" – and the key to the ecstasy the poem holds out, if belatedly.

Consequently, Milton uses his own concept of sublimity to represent Adam and Eve's reconciliation with each other coinciding with their reconciliation with God. As if explicitly affirming Milton's claim from *Areopagitica*, Adam and Eve move swiftly from their mutual offers of self-sacrifice to a reconnection with God, a union with sublime undercurrents that grow stronger in the final books.[55]

Reversing the experience of Satan, who sacrifices relationship and sublimity together, Adam and Eve embody a heroic model where interpersonal connection facilitates direct communication with God.

Having demonstrated the relational and emotional capacities that had been lacking earlier, Adam and Eve undergo "Commiseration" (10.940), a state of mutual empathy and unity that inverts the "Contagion" and collective "horror" experienced by the devils upon being transformed into serpents. They agree to repent and submit to God's will together, to "prostrate fall / Before [God] reverent, and there confess / Humbly our faults, and pardon beg … / … from hearts contrite, in sign / Of sorrow unfeign'd and humiliation meek" (10.1087–9, 1091–2). And as Adam and Eve humble themselves in this way, turning to God in prayer, they enter an explicitly divine union at the start of Book 11, and with it, the sublime itself:

> Thus they in lowliest plight repentant stood
> Praying, for from the Mercie-seat above
> Prevenient Grace descending had remov'd
> The stonie from thir hearts, and made new flesh
> Regenerate grow instead, that sighs now breath'd
> Unutterable, which the Spirit of prayer
> Inspir'd, and wing'd for Heav'n with speedier flight.   (11.1–7)

Recalling Raphael's promise, Adam and Eve are "sublim'd" in a different way: though they are not transformed from a physical to a spiritual state, their hearts are transformed from "stonie" to "flesh," made miraculously capable of transcending their sinful natures. This transformation, in turn, enables inspired communication with God himself, figured in terms of a psychological transport. In place of the physical "ascent" mentioned earlier by Raphael, they are "inspired" by the divine "Spirit of Prayer"; their words take "speedier flight" so that they communicate directly with both God and the Son. In theological terms, their prayer directly recalls Paul's description of the intercession of the Holy Spirit.[56] By breathing "sighs … / Unutterable," Adam and Eve pray in a manner that is beyond words – the definition of the sublime itself – where human language is insufficient to express thought and experience, in the realm of the infinite.[57]

Through contrite readiness to subordinate themselves, Adam and Eve thus prepare for "prevenient Grace" to enter their softened hearts, heralding the deeper ecstasy of the final books, as we will soon see. The simultaneous events of heaven look ahead to this sublimity as well. During their prayer, we see that the Son is serving as "Advocate," "interpret[ing]" and observing that their "contrition" helps ready them to be "Made one with me as I with thee am one," to "dwell in joy and bliss" (11.33, 27, 44, 43). While the Son is looking forward in time, the passage suggests that this unity is already in progress – and hints of the sublime are already palpable. In the reconciliation of Books 10–11, Milton thus makes the suffering of abjection itself not an impediment to divine union as it could have been, but a means of developing the proper empathy and emotional depth that he portrays as essential to the experience of God's presence.[58]

In uniting abjection and spiritual transformation in this way, Milton follows earlier depictions of sublime epic heroism, including Spenser's, in making both abjection *and* community major mechanisms of divine transcendence. But the scene of Adam's abjection highlights the critical difference in Milton's model: divine reconciliation, for Milton, is not a function of an irresistible sublime, as when Redcrosse is captivated by the words of Fidelia. Adam and Eve must instead make a conscious decision to move towards divine unity without any evident form of sublime inspiration, a move towards unity that is even more wilful than that made by Tassoan heroes, who have some prompting. Adam and Eve submit themselves to God and each other in the midst of great despair. They also reveal fuller and more personal form of humility than we saw of *Les Semaines*. In addition to submitting intellectually to the supremacy of God, as Du Bartas's Abraham does, Adam and Eve choose the more difficult path of submitting mutually to each another even as they offend each other deeply and directly. For Milton, the resulting unity is all the more astounding for the way it occurs between a pair that is profoundly aware of the tendency to sin. Tasso, Du Bartas, and Spenser never imply that their heroes' companions are perfect, but perhaps nowhere does Renaissance epic emphasize the importance of cooperating with people who are flawed and degenerate as strongly as in Book 10 of *Paradise Lost*. For Milton, redeeming, heroic love has its most sublime potential when it is deliberately enacted and directed towards peers, or even inferiors – especially towards those who do not seem to deserve it.

In effect, despite Milton's considerable overlap with Spenser, as both poets emphasize the dangers of charisma and the importance of communal support in salvation, the two major authors of Protestant English epic fall on different ends of a spectrum left open by Longinus. Where Spenser emphasizes the irresistibility of the sublime, and how, in Longinus's words, it "gets the better of every listener,"[59] Milton highlights a different dimension of *Peri Hypsous* – its call for readers of the sublime to actively cultivate aesthetic taste. Towards the end of the treatise, Longinus argues that the capacity for sublimity itself must be cultivated intentionally over and above the natural tendency to idleness: "what wastes the talents of the present generation is the idleness which all but a few of us pass our lives, only exerting ourselves or showing any enterprise for the sake of getting praise or pleasure"; this requires a person to exert the will against its inclination for ill, to develop the "immortal part."[60] In keeping with his Arminian view of salvation, Milton represents Adam and Eve initiating the process of divine union themselves, beginning with their reconciliation, and pointing towards divine ecstasy.

Even in their differences, however, the two English epics use Longinus for purposes that support rather than compete with one another: one poet emphasizes God's omnipotence as a feature of his sublime glory, and the other admonishes readers to use their God-given agency to their greatest ability – to develop the Longinian spirit that enables them to experience deep joy. Both poets (along with Tasso and Du Bartas) incorporate the sublime as a depiction of what it means to honour God and fulfil the highest potential of the self.

Post-Fall Sublimity

In the final passages of the poem, Milton shows the fulfilment of this heroic model, as Adam in particular sustains the Longinian spirit and orientation towards God he had not fully demonstrated in earlier passages. In Book 12, in his conversation with Michael, Adam defines Christian heroism as follows:

> Henceforth I learne, that to obey is best,
> And love with feare the onely God, to walk
> As in his presence, ever to observe
> His providence, and on him sole depend,
> [...]
>
>   ... by small
> Accomplishing great things, by things deemd weak
> Subverting worldly strong, and worldly wise
> By simply meek; that suffering for Truths sake
> Is fortitude to highest victorie.　　　　　　　　(12.561–4, 566–70)

As the poem indicates across Book 12 and elsewhere, to "love with fear" suggests maintaining a proper psychological and emotional orientation towards God – a deep respect bordering on astonishment at his greatness. And as Adam indicates here (after learning by experience), "suffering for Truths sake" does more than abase the sufferer; it promises "highest victorie," which in the context of the passage refers not only to glory in the future, but also in the present, as the use of the present tense form "is" suggests. Thus, where Quint notes that Milton transfers heroism firmly from the realm of triumphant martial exploits to the realm of "apparent weakness," I would add that Milton values the virtues associated with weakness and humility not for themselves, but for how they foster in the hero a desire and capacity for sublimity.[61] In short, suffering is the primary means of the humbling that is not its own end, but that sustains the proper capacity for enjoying the experience of God's presence *as sublime*.

Just earlier in the same passage, Adam demonstrates the connection between humility and sublimity in his response to several divine prophecies. Where with

Raphael he had delighted in the accumulation of knowledge, with Michael he embraces divine mystery in joyful astonishment. Upon learning of the promise of the divine incarnation and the virgin birth of Christ, he is left with "joy / Surcharg'd," "without the vent of words" (12.373–5):

> O Prophet of glad tidings, finisher
> Of utmost hope! now clear I understand
> What oft my steddiest thoughts have searcht in vain,
> Why our great expectation should be call'd
> The seed of Woman: Virgin Mother, Haile,
> High in the love of Heav'n, yet from my Loynes
> Thou shalt proceed, and from thy Womb the Son
> Of God most High; So God with man unites.   (12.375–82)

Only with such a deep understanding of the consequences of sin and death – his own and as prophesied by Michael – is Adam able to appreciate the full sublimity of the promise. His response is far removed from his intellectual stance earlier, when he would have sought to know more about this great theological mystery of the virgin birth. Transformed by suffering, Adam no longer seeks to demystify the glorious – he is content to know that God has promised a new form of unity between himself and mankind that will make possible an eternal reconciliation. Beyond that, the mystery is the very basis of its sublime appeal – Adam finally demonstrates the proper "taste" that, as Sedley argues, Satan so disastrously lacks.[62]

In the same way, Adam demonstrates his newfound Longinian sensibility upon hearing of the defeat of Satan and exaltation of the Son, as he responds:

> O goodness infinite, goodness immense!
> That all this good of evil shall produce,
> And evil turn to good; more wonderful
> Then that which by creation first brought forth
> Light out of darkness! full of doubt I stand,
> Whether I should repent …
>
>   … or rejoyce
> Much more, that much more good thereof shall spring.   (12.469–76)

Most notable here is Adam's uncharacteristic contentment to remain in "doubt," revealing an ability to delight in divine mystery for its own sake. With Raphael, he had "repeal'd doubt," too curious to appreciate the sublimity of God; now he rejoices in the mere possibility of a *felix culpa* (fortunate fall), but without attempting to resolve the theological question. Like Du Bartas's

Abraham, Adam finds in doubt a bliss greater than knowledge – the bliss of being united to the source of "infinite" goodness, where he can cling to the assurance that he need not have the answers himself to rest in the understanding that they exist.

But perhaps the poem's clearest affirmation of sublimity triumphing over despair occurs even earlier, at the conclusion of Book 11, when Adam, despairing over the scenes of hardship and suffering to come in human history, sees the rainbow that follows the destruction of Noah. In an instant, "the heart of Adam erst so sad / Greatly rejoyc'd, and thus his joy broke forth" (11.868–9). Exhilarated by the scene, Adam notes that the vision "revive[s] him, that he now "Farr less … lament[s] for one whole World / Of wicked Sons destroyd, then I rejoyce / For one Man found so perfet and so just, / That God voutsafes to raise another World" (874–7). As Barbara Lewalski points out, Milton portrays Noah as a foreshadowing of Christ – and thus it is unsurprising that Adam would respond in a similar condition of sublimity that he would later show towards the revelation of the Messiah in Book 12.[63] But the passage suggests something further about the sublime: that it lies not only in such rare revelations of future glory as received by Adam, but in reflections of hope and grace that are afforded to believers daily, in occurrences as regular as the rainbow. The passage foreshadows a message of Book 12, when Adam is promised a bliss "happier farr" than paradise itself, the unity with the Holy Spirit, as a "paradise within" (12.587).

As these passages suggest, the condition most proper to Adam goes beyond obedience – it is the joy of sublimity. Even while he cannot expect to be in a constant state of the sublime, the final books point repeatedly to his entry into this heightened state. Eve, too, though we do not see an immediate emotional response to the content of her dream, expresses her own form of joy that she will be granted the "favour" of being the vessel by which the "Promis'd Seed shall all restore," despite her unworthiness (12.622–3); and in learning of the promised union with God, she expresses her eagerness to go on with Adam, to leave the garden together hand in hand. In the closing lines, Milton emphasizes the fulfilment of characteristics that had been incomplete. While Adam had once resisted mystery, and Eve had once looked for her own glorification and sublimity, she now submits before the sublimity of God, implied in her sense of an indefinite "great good / Presaging" (12.612–13). She also acknowledges that the means to this greater good lies in relationship: "now lead on; / In me is no delay; with thee to goe, / Is to stay here; without thee here to stay / Is to go hence unwilling" (12.614–17). For all the tragedy of the final books, the poem ends with a deep sense of hope and joy, as humility, companionship, and sublimity coincide.

That Adam and Eve enter this higher-order experience after the Fall is not to suggest that *Paradise Lost* supports the theological position of *felix culpa*.

Adam and Eve might have achieved their condition of sustained sublimity –
beyond the "happie" condition of prelapsarian Eden – by being obedient in
the first place.[64] With the option of perfect obedience closed off, Adam and
Eve achieve it prematurely and with great suffering; the poem as is remains
deeply tragic. Yet Milton uses the heightened emotions of the conclusion to
illustrate a generous portion of grace available to those fallen beings who
would choose to suffer for it and seize it: he affirms that the most profound
experiences and greatest possibility of individual fulfilment result not from
pleasure or self-glorification, but from the decision to subordinate the self to
God in reverence.

Milton and the Eternal City

As suggested, more than any poet studied here, Milton makes Adam and Eve's
pursuit of the sublime dependent on *actively choosing* to move towards others in
sacrificial love; and in doing so, he furthers the critique of the Virgilian orientation
towards empire that earlier poets had hinted at and that we saw embodied in Satan.
When Eve insists on her readiness to follow Adam ("without thee here to stay, /
Is to go hence unwilling"), she insists that loyalty is first and foremost to a person,
not to a place. Having lost Eden, she no longer cares where she goes, for she is
merely a wanderer in a world that was never meant to be her home and must never
be served as if it were a source of eternal joy. With Adam, she shares an immortal
soul and immortal hope, and it is this shared recognition of immortality – and the
hope of an eternal homeland – that drives her to follow him. And in joining him,
Eve insists that she is not merely doing her duty, but following her desires – that
"in [her] is no delay" (12.615). Thus, where Satan had identified his pursuit of
empire as a duty that trumps his pursuit of delight, Milton opposes this burdensome pursuit with Adam and Eve's (painful) yet also joyful quest towards eternal
glory. The conclusion thus creates another stark contrast between the pursuit of
nation and the pursuit of heaven – the former an obligation and isolating burden,
and the latter a relational joy.

Milton's concept of sublime heroism issues a restrained though urgent message to readers still longing for the glory of England (or France, or Spain, or
Rome) – that to place hope in the glory of nations is a mistake, promising
suffering and loss. Showing his cynicism towards the English nationalism he
had celebrated earlier in his career, Milton contends in *Paradise Lost* that it is
far better to give up these divisive (and enslaving) desires and seek instead a
spiritual community with eternal value, a community sustained by love and
personal sacrifice.[65] And this warning taps into a sentiment that had been
present much earlier in Renaissance epic poetry. As Adam and Eve leave Eden
together in this shared understanding of their pursuit of heaven, they recall
the implied divine community of Tancredi, Clorinda, Rinaldo, Armida, and

Goffredo in the *Liberata*; Adam, Seth, Enos, and Henoc in *Les Semaines*; and Redcrosse, Una, and Arthur in *The Faerie Queene*, who also find divine pursuits as superior, and acknowledge that their civic duties have value only to the degree that they further heavenly values. In these preceding epic heroes, Adam and Eve find good company as they live out Milton's principle that the captivating potential of earthly institutions is strictly limited, and never worthy of becoming a god.

Conclusion:
Virgil, Empire, and Sublimity in *Paradise Regained*

Over the last four chapters, I have argued that Tasso, Du Bartas, Spenser, and Milton all use the Longinian sublime to reimagine epic heroism, celebrating the cultivation of a heightened emotional and psychological condition of awed reverence for the divine. While each of these poets develops distinctive individual concepts of sublimity and heroism, their poetry represents a collective transformation of classical models, an effort to explore the internal and vertical rather than the external and horizontal components of heroism: to be heroic is to allow oneself to be overwhelmed by divine glory, instead of prioritizing dutiful service to the nation-state.

Under the influence of the sublime, though, Renaissance epic does not promote interiority to the point of isolation, but endorses a specific kind of community – a community focussed on spiritual bonds and ends, rather than national ones. The very condition of Longinian *ekstasis* – transport *out* of the self – suggests an occlusion of individual boundaries that, in epic, creates unity not only with God, but with other followers. Understood to be divine and heaven-based, sublimity draws believers out of themselves and away from their earthly roots and towards heavenly ends, transcending civic commitments. In endorsing this kind of community, poets show great interest in the doctrine of the "invisible church." Unlike the "visible" church, understood to include all who openly profess faith within a formal community (whether belief is authentic or not), the invisible church – important to early modern Protestants from Luther to Richard Hooker – consists of one body of believers including all past, present, and future followers of God.[1]

Though a doctrine traditionally associated with Reformation theology, the concept of the invisible church also helps to form Catholic depictions of epic heroism and Christian community, such as those developed by Tasso. For both Catholic and Protestant epic poets in this study, the concept of an "invisible" church predominates in many cases over formal ecclesiastical structures (being in many cases tantamount to political leadership). While Milton shows his disillusionment with national community more prominently in *Paradise Lost*, and privileges the personal companionship of Adam and Eve, Tasso, too, in the *Liberata*, subordinates duty to Counter-Reformation authority by privileging the sublimity channelled by unauthorized figures such as Clorinda and Armida. In *Les Semaines*, Du Bartas represents Adam, Seth, Enos, and Henoc being drawn together towards heroic transcendence in a mutually inspiring vision – despite existing at different historical moments and outside a specific national identity – as Adam urges the others to follow the example prefigured before them. Even Spenser, who largely affirms the authority of the Church of England in *The Faerie Queene*, emphasizes that the heavenly city of the New Jerusalem, not London, is Redcrosse's final objective. It is the heavenly city, revealed to him by Contemplation after a series of encounters in charismatic community, that leaves the knight overwhelmed with zealous desire and that gives meaning to his actions on earth. In effect, Tasso, Du Bartas, Spenser, and Milton all emphasize that the quest for transcendence, though individual, inevitably draws pursuers together in a pursuit that subordinates civic commitments to eternal, heavenly relationships.

With this emphasis on cultivating sublime spiritual community, Renaissance epic thus presents an important response to Virgil's *Aeneid*, and not only in the most evident sense of subordinating the values of civic virtue and service to nation. Renaissance epic also takes on the Virgilian concept of the sublime. As suggested in the previous chapter, Virgil portrays the sublime as a function of the glorious empire of Rome. Thus, Aeneas longs and "burns" to build the empire promised to his descendants (4.375), an empire meant to stun the world with its ideals of justice, mercy, and peace.[2] A chief aim of the *Aeneid* is to instil in readers a longing to be subsumed within the greater community of Rome, leaving them in awe of its deified leaders.

In Renaissance epic, the heroic drive for this glorious vision often re-emerges as a parody, where characters such as Lucifera and Satan place themselves at the centre of a glorious spectacle, but in doing so merely cultivate idols in themselves. But Milton denounces the sublimity of empire even more directly in the sequel to *Paradise Lost: Paradise Regained* (1671).[3] To conclude, I would like to explore Milton's attempt to expose empty promises of the Virgilian sublime, including his effort, building from key threads in earlier Renaissance epic, to further the opposition between epic and nationalism, and redefine the genre's relationship to the sublime.

Virgil and the Illusion of Virtuous Empire

In this epic of Satan's unsuccessful temptation of the Son, Milton depicts how the *Aeneid's* aims of national glory and empire – especially when depicted as sublime – fail to produce goodness or justice, serving instead as spiritual stumbling blocks. In Book 4, after laughable attempts to entice the Son with the material attractions of food and wealth in the early parts of the poem, and a more potent effort to persuade him to display his glory to the world in Book 3, Satan changes tactics. To open the final round of temptations, he makes the Son an alluring offer of imperial conquest to save the world from itself, a temptation based on an illusion of justice and mercy that Milton quickly takes apart.

Leading the Son to the top of a mountain, the devil opens with a fitting invocation of Rome, with a clear reference to Virgilian empire:

> The City which thou seest no other deem
> Then great and glorious Rome, Queen of the Earth
> So far renown'd, and with the spoils enricht
> Of Nations.   (4.44–7)

In his plea to trust the devil rather than God, Satan makes a considerable effort to present the intended conquest in both a sublime and virtuous light – he cites the opportunity to oust the tyrannical emperor, the "monster" Tiberius, from the throne and leave the people "free from servile yoke" (100, 102), in a spectacle of grandeur and glory. Along with a nod to Milton's own ideas of liberty, Satan effectively offers the Son the opportunity to live up to Virgilian ideals by restoring the intentions of the Roman empire itself: pursuing conquest and power, the Tempter says, would create an opportunity to promote virtue on the widest possible scale, the mission of Rome according to the *Aeneid*. Like a new Aeneas, the Son must therefore aim at "no less then all the world, / Aim at the highest, without the highest attain'd / Will be for thee no sitting, or not long / On David's Throne" (105–8). By warning that the Son's power will be threatened without his accession, Satan again hearkens back to the key concept of the *Aeneid* that worldly empire and spiritual glory are inextricably linked, that the promises of eternity are dependent on acquisition of worldly power.

As we might expect, Milton has the Son reject this Virgilian program in particularly harsh terms, suggesting that a powerful and just nation-state enacting spiritual purposes, such as that celebrated in the *Aeneid*, is a fantasy, a deception that only distracts followers of God from love of the eternal heavenly kingdom. As the Son rejects the proposition, he rejects the sublimity of empire as a particularly dangerous "good" because of the pretence to reflecting the glory of heaven and the righteousness promoted there. While empire might appear to bring about such goods as widespread peace and justice, the Son maintains that its people – themselves subjects in a realm that had carried out conquest with good intentions – have since become "vile and base," "ambitious," "cruel," "luxurious," and "greedier still" (132, 137, 139, 141). The effects of even well-intended conquest are, in effect, not justice or divine love, but vice. Thus, the Son maintains that empire is something merely "call'd magnificence" (111), and to be firmly rejected: "nor doth this grandeur and majestic show / … / More then of arms before, allure mine eye, / Much less my mind" (110–13). According to the Son, there is no inherent good to be found in imposing rule on a fallen world for spiritual purposes; it is far better to forget the impossible prospect of a godly world power and look instead to a heavenly kingdom, of which "there shall be no end" (4.151). In effect, Satan's proposition is particularly dangerous because of its false resemblance to real virtue and heroism, and, in this, because it makes a false promise of genuine community, where its people would merely encourage each other in their vice. As the epic emphasizes, only in heaven can there be a noble, virtuous spiritual government worthy of glorification.

Since the *Aeneid* was generally the most highly regarded classical model of epic in the early modern period, the poem's rejection of Virgilian values reflects a major trend of lasting significance to the genre's legacy – a trend of particular importance in the following century. As Joseph Crawford notes, by the late 1700s, epic underwent a sort of revival in Britain, giving rise to a group of aspiring British poets inspired by the French Revolution. For poets such as James Ogden, William Hildreth, Sarah Leigh Pike, and Samuel Hull Wilkocke, this Revolution supplied a new occasion for these poets to celebrate British nationalism against the ideals of the new French republic.[4] The movement in turn inspired a renewal of interest in epic, and particularly Virgilian epic. According to poet-critic William Hayley's 1782 *Essay on Epic Poetry*, Britain, at this time, was anxiously anticipating its own Virgil; he notes that no one had yet "embrace[d]" the "brighter cause" of "British freedom" to earn the "wreath" of British laureate poet.[5]

But in terms of creative production, this renewed interest would be largely in vain, because of the ways Renaissance epic had changed the genre and its relationship to Virgil. For these early modern poets, *Paradise Lost* was such a masterwork of epic that its model had to be followed closely – poets imitated scenes and even celestial characters, despite drastic differences in political aims.[6] For all their investment in Roman nationalistic epic, aspiring British poets felt keenly the need to live up to the standards of British epic, particularly as established by Milton. Crawford argues that this British epic movement failed because of overly slavish imitation, and because the purposes were too mismatched. With its republican ideals, *Paradise Lost* simply did not translate into compelling imperial epic.[7] I would also argue that, particularly with Milton's influence, the epic genre had become so firmly reoriented towards spiritual transcendence that it did not work to celebrate Christian heroism and promote nationalistic purposes simultaneously, as the 1790s poets attempted. For while Virgilian values certainly underscored much of early modern epic heroism, as epic heroism came to celebrate the aspiration for divine ecstasy and spiritual community, the values of nation and state became firmly subordinated in a way that would be difficult to reverse in Christian epic after Milton. Building from other Renaissance models, *Paradise Lost* and *Paradise Regained* had structured heroism according to a choice between sublime desire for unity with God, or duty to nation and empire – *when*, not if, the two came into conflict. And as much as Virgil had influenced the genre in the Renaissance, Hayley and other scholars identified this clear disparity of purpose between the epic of Virgil and the English Renaissance – they could not bring the two together in theory or practice. Ultimately, the eighteenth-century effort to make the two purposes inseparable would prove to be a failure.

This is not at all to argue that Renaissance epic had proven its absolute literary superiority over the epic of Virgil. Rather, what Renaissance epic poets – culminating with Milton – brought more fully to light was a message latent in the *Aeneid* itself, infiltrating the poem's explicit vision of absolute submission to nation and public good. This was the idea that the emphasis on earthly power could result in a perilous devaluing of the individual. Virgil himself seems to have been aware of this tragedy, in such passages as Aeneas's loss of Creusa, the suicide of Dido, and the deaths of Turnus and Queen Amata.[8] Even Aeneas, after a lifetime of pursuing his duty to Rome, is slated to die an ignoble death and "lie unburied in the sand" (4.856). Although the *Aeneid* promises him a share in the great destiny of the Roman Empire, that promise, too, is of limited scope: after gaining a hero's welcome in the Elysian Fields, Aeneas would either be reincarnated ("summoned" to "return" after drinking of the river Lethe) or transformed into "ether pure" (6.989–91, 986).[9] Either way, the final vision of the *Aeneid*, and the end of the hero's mission supporting it, is the evaporation of the individual self into the greater whole.

Renaissance epic, by contrast, makes efforts to reverse this vision, to preserve the value of individual identity. The poems' visions celebrate the heroic future, whether earthly or heavenly, of individuals – of Tancredi, Clorinda, Armida, Abraham, Isaac, Redcrosse, Adam, Eve, and others. In these epics' incorporation of the sublime, they imagine the possibility of psychological, emotional, and spiritual unity with God, in which each individual will be preserved, and his or her full value made complete in glory.

Heroic Awe and the Affirmation of the Self

In its depiction of the individual, Renaissance epic thus produces a significant and intriguing tension: that Christian heroism demands the humility to cultivate awed reverence for heavenly glory, seeking this condition above worldly power, yet with the aim to glorify rather than efface the individual self. This principle emerges again in *Paradise Regained*, when the Son offers a somewhat surprising defence of the significance of individual exaltation. Denying Satan's claim about the human investment in glory, the Son asks

> Why should man seek glory? who of his own
> Hath nothing, and to whom nothing belongs
> But condemnation, ignominy, and shame?
> [...]
> [S]acrilegious, to himself would take
> That which to God alone of right belongs;

> Yet so much bounty is in God, such grace,
> That who advance his glory, not thir own,
> Them he himself to glory will advance.   (3.134–6, 140–4)

While at first appearing to diminish the significance of the individual, the Son instead affirms the importance of honouring distinctive beings in the same way that God himself is elevated and honoured. Instead of vaporizing after death, the Christian hero will "himself to glory … advance." In its celebration of the individual, this model of Renaissance epic heroism brings up echoes of the Homeric practice of *aristeia* (greatness), where heroic warriors are filled with a divine energy to become unstoppable objects of awe and astonishment. While such moments of exaltation in the *Iliad* regularly affirm individual glory, Milton, in the *Paradise Regained* passage, affirms this principle in a less competitive sense, using the idea – both biblical and Longinian – that glory and sublimity are expandable properties. In this concept, glory is not a zero-sum quantity that one might take from another, as Iliadic heroes sought to do, but something that can be shared without limitation. Longinus writes that new sublime writers who enter the scene will "share the enthusiasm of … others' grandeur," suggesting that heightened emotions themselves proliferate and grow to the same level in the new writer as they once existed in the first, increasing the total amount of glory available to all; these words echo the biblical promises that those who follow God will "appear with him in glory" and be a "partaker of the glory."[10] For Milton, too, *all* who "advance [God's] glory" stand to be glorified. This vision stands in contrast to the objectives of nations and other earthly institutions, which regularly threaten to subsume the good of the individual through their need for preservation.

This is not to suggest that Milton or any other Renaissance epic poet denies the importance of earthly institutions, but that they are adamant about locating the fulfilment of humanity's deepest desires elsewhere. National and religious entities may offer visions of glory and a semblance of spiritual power to appeal to the natural human desire for significance and protection, but to this, Tasso, Du Bartas, Spenser, and Milton caution that an institution's claim to godliness is no guarantee of true spiritual authority or purpose. Instead, each poet offers an ostensibly Longinian recuperation of Homeric glory, consistent with Christian visions of the afterlife, where they maintain that God alone can supply the kind of meaningful exaltation that human beings earnestly desire.

In effect, while Renaissance epic as a genre (particularly *Paradise Lost* and *Paradise Regained*) may seem to turn towards "mild" virtues such as humility, obedience, love, and patience, this study suggests that these poems ultimately orient their concepts of heroism towards the heightened emotions of the sublime, celebrating the individual self within vibrant spiritual communities. Just as Longinus imagines that glory and exaltation, not selflessness, are the most fundamental conditions of the human, Renaissance epic poetry from multiple theological perspectives regularly suggests that the desire for elevation, to participate in something greater than the self, is innate – the only question is where a person will seek this experience. In the vision offered by Renaissance epic, those people seeking status via earthly institutions and their leaders will sooner or later be crushed, but those willing to be awed in reverence of the divine will gain a sense of value and belonging that surpasses earthly prestige by far. And in the end, Renaissance epic suggests that acknowledging greatness beyond the self need not mean the lessening of the self, even when there may be a temporary cost – rather, it proposes this readiness, when properly oriented, as the most promising path towards the glory that human beings so often seek.

Notes

Introduction: The Sublime in Renaissance Epic

1　Quotations from *Paradise Lost* are taken from Barbara Lewalski's edition: *John Milton: Paradise Lost* (Malden, MA: Blackwell, 2007).

2　My concept of sublimity is Longinian, though I follow Robert Doran in maintaining that major theorists of the sublime – Longinus, Kant, Burke, and others – understand the idea as a paradoxical experience of being both overwhelmed and exalted (Doran finds this "dual transcendence structure" latent in all major theories of the sublime): *The Theory of the Sublime from Longinus to Kant*, 4.

3　*OED*, "melt, v." *Peri Hypsous* uses *ekplexis* as a synonym for the sublime, especially when describing its more negative and unsettling effects: W.H. Fyfe and Donald Russell, trans., *On the Sublime*, in *Aristotle: The Poetics. "Longinus": On the Sublime. Demetrius: On Style*, edited by Jeffrey Henderson (Cambridge: Harvard University Press, 1995), sect. 15.2, 214–5. All Longinus quotations are taken from this edition.

4　Studies of the Miltonic sublime will be discussed in chapter 5.

5　Caroline van Eck, et al., ed., *Translations of the Sublime: The Early Modern Reception and Dissemination of Longinus' Peri hupsous in Rhetoric, the Visual Arts, Architecture, and the Theatre* (Boston: Brill, 2012).

6　Cheney, *English Authorship and the Early Modern Sublime: Spenser, Marlowe, Shakespeare, Jonson* (Cambridge: Cambridge University Press, 2018).

7　Richard Helgerson looks at several early modern efforts to forge national identity through literature, focussing on England, where Spenser wrote to Gabriel Harvey about the desire for a "kingdom of our own language": *Forms of Nationhood: Elizabethan Writing of England* (Chicago: University of Chicago Press, 1992), 1–18.

8　Philip Ford notes that Virgil's influence persisted into the Renaissance more than any other classical author: "Virgil versus Homer: Reception, Imitation, Identity in the French Renaissance," in *Virgilian Identities in the French Renaissance* (Suffolk: Boydell and Brewer, 2012), 141.

9   Gregory, *From Many Gods to One: Divine Action in Renaissance Epic* (Chicago: University of Chicago Press, 2006), 15.

10   *Horace: A Letter to Augustus*, trans. Michael Winterbottom, in *Classical Literary Criticism*, ed. Russell and Winterbottom, 124, 129.

11   A.C. Hamilton, ed., *Spenser: The Faerie Queene*, 2nd ed. (Harlow, England: Longman, 2007), l. 8, 33–4.

12   Andrew Fichter in particular emphasizes how Renaissance epic celebrated political dynasties in *Poets Historical: Dynastic Epic in the Renaissance* (New Haven: Yale University Press, 1982); and David Quint demonstrates how many Renaissance epic poems such as Tasso's *Liberata* supported those in power (unlike epic "losers" like Milton in *Paradise Lost*): *Epic and Empire: Politics and Generic Form from Virgil to Milton* (Princeton: Princeton University Press, 1993). More recently, Anthony Welch's impressive study of the oral tradition and its importance to epic poetry also considers the dynastic ambitions of several early modern epic poems: *Renaissance Epic and the Oral Past* (New Haven: Yale University Press, 2012).

13   In a representative definition of epic heroism, Gregory defines heroism as "deeds of exceptional valor that bear consequences for the community to which the hero belongs": *Many Gods to One*, 16.

14   Cheney notes that Longinus's idea of poetry is predicated on "greatness" rather than "ethical … goodness," like the theories of Aristotle and Horace; Longinus emphasizes the production of "terrifying exaltation": *English Authorship and the Early Modern Sublime: Spenser, Marlowe, Shakespeare, Jonson* (Cambridge: Cambridge University Press, 2018), 37, 50–1. Thus, for Cheney, the sublime can be an "emotional principle of *counter-national authorship*," though, as in his reading of Spenser, sublimity may also function "in service of the nation": *English Authorship*, 41, 21. On the distinction between Horatian-Aristotelian poetics and Longinus, see also Northrop Frye, *Anatomy of Criticism: Four Essays* (Princeton: Princeton University Press, 1957), 66–7, 93–4.

15   Elizabeth Jane Bellamy develops a related argument that the epic genre has dynastic and imperial aims, while individual epics show "repressed," but "observable traces" of an unconscious resistance to these nation-building purposes: *Translations of Power: Narcissism and the Unconscious in Epic History* (Ithaca, NY: Cornell University Press, 1994), 32. In the recovery of *Peri Hypsous* and the developments associated with the Reformation, I will argue, Renaissance epic poets found specific historical and theological reasons to resist nationalistic aims that are not repressed, but strategically understated.

16   Bond, *Spenser, Milton, and the Redemption of the Epic Hero* (Newark: University of Delaware Press, 2011); and Warner, *The Augustinian Epic: Petrarch to Milton* (University of Michigan Press, 2010).

17   *On the Sublime*, sect. 35.2–3, 274–5, echoing Ecclesiastes 3:11. Cheney describes Longinus' "commitment to the *capacity of the human for divinity*": *English Authorship*, 40.

18   *On the Sublime*, sect. 35.3, 274–5. The authorship of *Peri Hypsous*, or *On the Sublime*, is notoriously problematic, but following convention I will refer to the author as simply Longinus.

19 Based on subsequent questions and answers, Calvin clearly understands "knowledge" of God to mean personal understanding and connection to God, not just intellectual knowledge of him: *Rudimenta fidei christianae, sive catechismus. Huic adjunctus nunc est catechismus alius magis compendiarius* (Genève: Henri II Estienne, 1575). Post-Reformation Digital Library.

20 *On the Sublime*, sect 1.4, 162–3. This is not to deny that the sublime has an ethical component; but Longinus specifies that instead of being the proper *telos* of literature, innate virtue and nobility are prerequisite to great literature, freeing writers from the "love of pleasure" that enslaves: *On the Sublime*, sect. 44.6–12, 300–5.

21 *On the Sublime*, sect. 36.1, 276–7.

22 Halliwell, *Between Ecstasy and Truth: Interpretations of Greek Poetics from Homer to Longinus* (Oxford: Oxford University Press, 2011), 366.

23 *On the Sublime*, sect. 9.2, 184–5. While the concepts of the "noble mind" and "nobility" appear to have classist implications, Longinus seems to understand *megalophrosynê* as a concept of personal psychology independent of social status. Doran argues that Burke and Kant identify the *megalophrosynê* as "heroic," because it entails struggling productively *against* limitations of class. Nobility of mind, as a disposition associated with aristocracy, thus becomes a means of "exalt[ing] the bourgeois individual": *The Theory of the Sublime*, 20–2. Renaissance epic anticipates the link between sublimity and heroism found in later aesthetic theory, though primarily in a metaphysical and spiritual rather than a social sense. Epic heroes who cultivate a capacity for the sublime do not typically seek to assert their prestige in doing so, but to fulfil their identify as image bearers of God.

24 *On the Sublime*, sect. 36.1, 277, 44.8, 303.

25 Calvin himself acknowledges in the introduction to the Geneva Catechism that different churches may use catechisms that differ from his, and that this presents no problem as long as those creating them are intent on pointing others to God and building spiritual unity.

26 James Porter, in a discussion of the sublimity of Homeric heroism, notes that Longinus assumes that his readers will recognize Homer as the quintessential sublime poet: *The Sublime in Antiquity* (Cambridge: Cambridge University Press, 2016), 360–80.

27 Thomas Blackwell, *An Enquiry into the Life and Writings of Homer* (London, 1753), 26.

28 Greene, *Descent from Heaven: A Study in Epic Continuity* (New Haven: Yale University Press, 1963), 22–3.

29 *On the Sublime*, sect. 9.2, 185, citing the *Odyssey*, 11.543–67. As I will consider in chapter 1, Longinus also indicates that the *Odyssey* is less sublime, a claim that Renaissance scholars discuss and dispute.

30 *On the Sublime*, sect. 9.10–13, 191–5, citing the *Iliad*, 17.645–7.

31 Fry, "Longinus at Colonus: The Grounding of Sublimity," *The Reach of Criticism: Method and Perception in Literary Theory* (New Haven: Yale University Press, 1983), 78. In emphasizing the emotions associated with mortality and absence, the sublimity that pervades Homeric epic anticipates the kind of sublimity featured by later

scholars such as Jean-François Lyotard. Lyotard contends that the sublime evokes an impossible gap between reality and representation, emphasizing the ways sublime art reflects the inaccessibility of knowledge: "The Sublime and the Avant-Garde," *Paragraph: A Journal of Modern Critical Theory* 6 (1985): 1–18.

32 *On the Sublime*, sect. 9.9, citing Genesis 1:3–9.

33 Till, "The Sublime and the Bible," in *Translations of the Sublime*, 57–63. As Till demonstrates, Longinus emphasizes a combination of rhetorical simplicity and conceptual profundity (just as Ajax is a man of few words while producing weighty emotions) that appealed to Reformation theorists.

34 Boitani, *The Tragic and the Sublime in Medieval Literature* (Cambridge: Cambridge University Press, 1989), x. While Boitani acknowledges that the sublime itself has both negative and positive dimensions, he draws a sharp distinction between the metaphysics and emotions of spiritual tragedy (which involves negative emotions that may be theorized as "sublime") and blissful emotions of triumph, the "climax" of the sublime.

35 In a recent study, Katherine S. Maynard argues for the importance of French epic, including the work of Du Bartas, to the Renaissance epic genre, alongside the higher profile poems of Italy and England: *Reveries of Community: French Epic in the Age of Henri IV* (Evanston, IL: Northwestern University Press, 2017).

36 For instance, a few recent studies of the post-1674 sublime include Hélène Ibata's *The Challenge of the Sublime: From Burke's Philosophical Inquiry to British Romantic Art* (Manchester: Manchester University Press, 2018); Stephen Zepke's *Sublime Art: Toward an Aesthetics of the Future* (Edinburgh: Edinburgh University Press, 2017); Emily Brady's *The Sublime in Modern Philosophy: Aesthetics, Ethics, and Nature* (Cambridge: Cambridge University Press, 2013); Gene Ray's *Terror and the Sublime in Art and Critical Theory: From Auschwitz to Hiroshima to September 11*, 2nd ed. (New York: Palgrave MacMillan, 2011); and Alan Richardson's *The Neural Sublime: Cognitive Theories and Romantic Texts* (Baltimore: Johns Hopkins University Press, 2010).

37 Cheney, *English Authorship*. Sedley, *Sublimity and Skepticism in Montaigne and Milton* (Ann Arbor: University of Michigan Press, 2005). As noted, van Eck's edited collection, *Translations of the Sublime*, represents another major contribution, though the vast majority of essays are on the seventeenth century, and none focus on literature, the main subject of Longinus's treatise. Specific contributions from this volume, and other studies on the early modern sublime, will be discussed below.

38 *On the Sublime*, sect. 13.1, 210–11.

39 *On the Sublime*, sect. 13.2, 210–11.

40 *On the Sublime*, sect. 35.2, 274–5.

41 James Porter notes that the sublime need not be tied exclusively to Longinus, for a concept of sublimity could and did exist in contexts such as the medieval period, when Longinus was unknown: *The Sublime in Antiquity*, 18. While I acknowledge that the sublime was broader than Longinus, he and the writers influenced by him (directly and indirectly) will remain the central figures of this study, which focusses on a period when Longinus was becoming a major figure in rhetorical and literary theory.

42 As will be discussed in chapter 1, Till shows how *Peri Hypsous* was at the centre of a web of Hellenistic rhetoric that Protestant theologians used to commend biblical style: "The Sublime and the Bible," 56. Direct influence in these instances is difficult to demonstrate, but the resonances are especially compelling.

43 Longinus's concept of a natural sublime is especially apparent in his statement that the sublime is the "echo of the noble mind" (sect. 9.1, 182–5), suggesting the rise of a particular psychological effect in a poet who will in turn transmit this psychological condition to audiences – a passage discussed further in chapter 1. On the controversy throughout intellectual history over where sublimity has been understood to reside, see also William Slocombe, *Nihilism and the Sublime Postmodern: The (Hi)story of a Difficult Relationship from Romanticism to Postmodernism* (New York: Routledge, 2013), 26–9.

44 Doran, *The Theory of the Sublime from Longinus to Kant*, 82–94.

45 Furthermore, Platonic and Neoplatonic concepts of *furor* do not always overlap with the sublime. As Michael Heyd notes, Plato's *Phaedrus* distinguishes between a divine *furor* characteristic of prophecy and a state of *furor* that is simply pathological madness: *"Be Sober and Reasonable": The Critique of Enthusiasm in the Seventeenth and Early Eighteenth Centuries* (Leiden: Brill, 1995), 45. The former intersects with the sublime significantly, but the latter, being irrational, falls outside the theory of Longinus, who typically links emotion and intellect in his idea of sublimity, as Halliwell notes throughout *Between Ecstasy and Truth*.

46 Longinus associates *ekplexis* with terror and tragedy in *On the Sublime*, sect. 15.2, 214–17.

47 *On the Sublime*, sect. 35.2, 273–5. The emotional range of the sublime thus goes well beyond the concept of wonder – another important topic of Renaissance scholarship and certainly overlapping with the sublime; see Stephen Greenblatt's "Resonance and Wonder," in *Learning to Curse: Essays in Early Modern Culture* (New York: Routledge, 1990), 216–47; T.G. Bishop's *Shakespeare and the Theatre of Wonder* (Cambridge: Cambridge University Press, 1996); Douglas Biow's *Representations of the Marvelous in Medieval and Renaissance Epic* (Ann Arbor: University of Michigan Press, 1996); and James Biester's *Lyric Wonder: Rhetoric and Wit in Renaissance English Poetry* (Ithaca: Cornell University Press, 1997).

48 Kristeva, *Powers of Horror: An Essay on Abjection*, trans. Leon S. Roudiez (New York: Columbia University Press, 1982), 11. Bellamy also connects psychoanalytical theory to epic, though not to abjection specifically and not in terms of the Longinian sublime: *Translations of Power*.

49 Weber, *On Charisma and Institution Building*, trans. S.N. Eisenstadt (Chicago: University of Chicago Press, 1968). C. Stephen Jaeger links charisma to the sublime; in recent work on charisma in art, he theorizes charisma as a spirit of magnificence that invades artistic representations and gives them life and power: *Enchantment: On Charisma and the Sublime in the Arts of the West* (Philadelphia: University of Pennsylvania Press, 2012), 11.

50 See also Raphael Falco, *Charismatic Authority in Early Modern English Tragedy* (Baltimore: Johns Hopkins University Press, 2000), discussed further in chapter 3.

1. Longinus in Renaissance Theories of Heroic Poetry

1 *The Defense and Enrichment of the French Language,* in *The Regrets with The Antiquities of Rome, Three Latin Elegies, and The Defense and Enrichment of the French Language,* trans. Richard Helgerson (Philadelphia: University of Pennsylvania Press, 2006), 379. All quotations and translations of Du Bellay's poetry and prose are taken from Helgerson's bilingual edition, with a few minor alterations to the English translations.

2 C.M. Mazzucchi, "Tradizione Manoscritta del Περὶ Ὕψους," *Italian medioevale e umanistica* 32 (1989): 205–26. Mazzucchi notes that a manuscript dating from the tenth century travelled from Constantinople into Italy in the fifteenth century. The manuscript came into the hands of Cardinal Bessinario in 1468, and eventually into the possession of Catherine de Medici, becoming one of the founding manuscripts of Florence's *Biblioteca Centrale Nazionale* in the sixteenth century. Along the way, scholars made copies of the manuscript, which then came into the hands of Robortello and Manuzio. Only fragments of this manuscript remain.

3 As Mazzucchi notes, the Porto edition was based largely on Manuzio's edition but with a few variations. Surviving copies of the original Manuzio printing are now rare and available only in select repositories in Europe, but the Robortello and Porto editions have been digitized and are publically accessible. Bernard Weinberg offers a complete catalogue of early editions and translations of *Peri Hypsous* in "Translations and Commentaries of Longinus, 'On the Sublime,' to 1600: A Bibliography," *Modern Philology* 47 (1950): 145–51. Gustavo Costa has also done several important studies showing the reception and circulation of the *Peri Hypsous* among sixteenth-century Italian theorists: see "Paolo Manuzio e lo Pseudo-Longino," *Giornale storico della letteratura italiana* 161 (1984): 60–77; "Appunti sulla fortuna dello Pseudo-Longino nel Seicento: Alessandro Tassoni e Paganino Gaudenzio," *Studi secenteschi* 25 (1984): 123–43; "The Latin Translations of Longinus's *Peri Ypsous* in Renaissance Italy," in *Acta Conventus Neo-Latini Bononiensis. Proceedings of the Fourth International Congress of Neo-Latin Studies, Bologna, 26 August to 1 September 1979,* ed. R.J. Schoeck (Binghamton, NY: 1985), 224–38; "Pietro Vettori, Ugolino Martelli e lo Pseudo Longino," *Da Longino a Longino: i luoghi del Sublime,* ed. Luigi Russo (Palermo: Aesthetica, 1987), 65–79; and "Storia del Sublime e storia ecclesiastica," *Aevum Antiquum* (2003), 319–50. Other important studies will be discussed later.

4 In 1581, Porto also completed an eighty-page Latin commentary on *Peri Hypsous,* a rare manuscript available only in European repositories: Weinberg, "Translations," 149.

5 Eva Madeleine Martin discusses Muret's translation in "The 'Prehistory' of the Sublime in Early Modern France: An Interdisciplinary Perspective," in *The Sublime: From Antiquity to the Present,* ed. Timothy Costelloe (Cambridge: Cambridge

University Press, 2012), 78–9. According to Weinberg, the anonymously translated Latin manuscript was probably completed in the early sixteenth century, but is now missing: "Translations," 146.

6 Weinberg, "Translations," 147–51. See also Costa, "Latin Translations." This translation would serve as the basis of the edition published by Gerard Langbaine, discussed below.

7 Da Falgano, *Libro della Altezza del Dire* (Florence, 1575); Da Falgano's translation was finally published in 2011: *Libro della altezza del dire*, ed. Angelo Cardillo (Napoli: Liguori, 2011). The first French translation, "De la sublimité de discours," was published anonymously; see Martin, "The 'Prehistory' of the Sublime," 79. The first English translation, "On the Height of Eloquence," was completed by John Hall.

8 Marc Fumaroli notes this connection between Erasmus and Longinus, maintaining that Erasmus's text sparked a surge of interest among scholars such as Robortello and Manuzio in the poetic theory of Aristotle, Plato, and, ultimately, Longinus, leading to the publication of *Peri Hypsous*. "Rhétorique d'école et rhétorique adulte: remarques sur la réception européenne du traité 'Du Sublime' au XVIe et au XVIIe siècle," *Revue d'Histoire littéraire de la France* 1 (1986): 33–51, 43. On the "sermo humilis," or low style, and its connection to the Longinian sublime, see Erich Auerbach, *Mimesis: The Representation of Reality in Western Literature*, trans. Willard R. Task (1953; Princeton: Princeton University Press, 2003), 109–22.

9 Fumaroli notes in "Rhétorique d'école et rhétorique adulte" that the aim of such writing was "l'éblouissement" [dazzlement] rather than "l'élégance," 42.

10 *Commentarii in Primum Librum Aristotelis de Arte Poetarum* (1560; Munich: Wilhelm Fink Verlag 1967), 149; my translation.

11 Refini calls Patrizi's text the most Longinian of the Italian Renaissance: "Longinus and Poetic Imagination in Late Renaissance Literary Theory," in *Translation of the Early Modern Sublime*, ed. Caroline van Eck, et al. (Boston: Brill, 2012), 37.

12 Eugenio Refini, "Longinus and Poetic Imagination in Late Renaissance Literary Theory," 33–53, 40.

13 Fumaroli, *L'Age d'Eloquence. Rhétorique et «res literaria» de la Renaissance au seuil de l'époque classique* (Geneva: Droz, 1980): 176–8. In "Rhétorique d'école et rhétorique adulte," 33–51, Fumaroli suggests that Benci's lectures in Rome may also have disseminated *Peri Hypsous* to Corneille and Balzac.

14 Cheney, *Marlowe's Republican Authorship: Lucan, Liberty, and the Sublime* (Basingstoke: Palgrave, 2009); and *English Authorship and the Early Modern Sublime: Spenser, Marlowe, Shakespeare, Jonson* (Cambridge: Cambridge University Press, 2018).

15 According to Cheney, a Cambridge bookshop held copies of Porto's 1570 Greek edition of Longinus in 1578: "English Authorship and the Early Modern Sublime," in *Medieval and Early Modern Authorship*, ed. Guillemette Bolens and Lukas Erne (Tübingen, Germany: Narr Verlag, 2011), 143.

16 William Ringler, "An Early Reference to Longinus," *Modern Language Notes* 53.1 (1938): 23–4. Judith Anderson, *Reading the Allegorical Intertext: Chaucer, Spenser, Shakespeare, Milton* (New York: Fordham University Press, 2008), 438, n. 42.

17 Monk, *The Sublime: A Study of Critical Theories in XVIII-Century England* (New York: MLA, 1935; reprinted 1960). Monk also holds that Longinus himself understands the sublime as a rhetorical principle, unlike Kant and Burke, though that position has been more widely challenged. In distinguishing the sublime as a philosophical category from the sublime as a principle of style, I recognize that the Renaissance notion of style is itself problematic, though, with Doran, I would contend that there remains a meaningful distinction between the sublime as a heightened psychological and emotional condition, and the sublime as a principle of style, a feature of language and rhetoric. On Longinus's role in the development of the "sacred grand style" emerging from this tradition, see Debora Shuger, *Sacred Rhetoric: The Christian Grand Style in the English Renaissance* (Princeton: Princeton University Press, 1988), 154–92.

18 Mattioli, "Il Sublime e lo Stile: Suggestione Cinquecentesche," in *Da Longino a Longino: I Luoghi del Sublime*, ed. Russo, 55; Mattioli maintains that "sia inerente all'idea del sublime la tendenza ad andar oltre la dimensione puramente formale dello stile e … questo sia verificabile già nel Cinquecento [the tendency to go beyond the purely formal dimension of style is inherent to the idea of the sublime and this is already evident in the sixteenth century.]" Refini, "Longinus and Poetic Imagination," 37–8.

19 Baldine Saint Girons, "The Sublime from Longinus to Montesquieu," trans. Fred L. Rush, Jr., in *Oxford Encyclopedia of Aesthetics,* ed. Michael Kelly, *Oxford Art Online* (Oxford University Press, 2014); and Doran, *The Theory of the Sublime from Longinus to Kant* (Cambridge: Cambridge University Press, 2015), 103. In "Rhétorique d'école et rhétorique adulte," 47–8, Fumaroli argues that *Peri Hypsous* was strangled by the hyper-Aristotelianism of the Catholic Church, and it was not until the treatise reached France, and writers such as Montaigne and his Flemish acquaintance Justus Lipsius encountered the sublime, that the Renaissance saw a more authentic Longinian spirit on display – a focus on the nobility of soul required to produce great literature.

20 van Huss, "Anmerkungen zur Rezeption von Longins 'Erhabenem' im Cinquecento," *Romanistisches Jahrbuch* 62 (2011): 165–87. Along these lines, Weinberg notes that the overall emphasis on literary style in Renaissance rhetorical treatises led a number of early scholars to interpret the Longinian sublime as a function of ornament and style instead of as a philosophical and psychological concept: see *History of Literary Criticism in the Italian Renaissance*, 2 vols. (Chicago: University of Chicago Press, 1961), 805–6.

21 For instance, Doran notes that each of the early translators adds a reference to speech in his title, whether inserting "de orationes" or "dicendi," or "Of Eloquence" to the original's simple "*On the Sublime*": *The Theory of the Sublime*, 98. Pizzimienti titles his translation "*Liber de Grandi orationis genere,*" Pagano titles his "*De Sublimi dicendi genere,*" while Falgano titles his "*Della Altezza del Dire.*" In the seventeenth century, de Petra similarly titles his edition "*Liber de Grandi, sive Sublimi genere Orationi,*" Langbaine entitles his "De grandi loquentia sive Sublimi dicendi genere," and Hall titles his 1652 edition "*Of the Height of Eloquence.*"

22 *Libro della Altezza del Dire di Dionysio Longino Rhetore Tradotto dalla Greca nella Toscana Lingua da Giovanni di Niccolò da Falgano Fiorentino* (Florence, 1575), 73v, translating section 39.4 of *Perì Hýpsous*. Biblioteca Nazionale Centrale, MS Magl. VI.33.

23 Stated in Pizzimenti's dedicatory letter to Aldo Manuzio: *Dionysii Longini Rhetoris Praestantissimi liber de Grandi orationis genere, Domenico Pizimentio Vibonensi interprete* (Naples, 1566), 4r.

24 *On the Sublime*, trans. W.H. Fyfe and Donald Russell *Aristotle: The Poetics. "Longinus": On the Sublime*, ed. Jeffrey Henderson (Cambridge: Harvard University Press, 1995), sect. 8.1, 180–1. In this chapter, where I discuss commentaries and translations of *Peri Hypsous*, I will supply Greek quotations and English translations, both taken (with a few minor alterations) from the translation by Fyfe and Russell.

25 *On the Sublime*, sect. 9.1, 182–5.

26 Aphthonius, Hermogenes, and Dionysius Longinus, *Oi en tê rhêtorikê technê koryphaioi. Aphthonios, Hermogenês, D. Longinos*, ed. Franciscus Porto (Geneva, 1569), 12. Bibliothèque de Genève, Web.

27 *Dionysiu Longinu Rētoros Perì Hypsus Biblion*, ed. Francesco Robortello (Basel, 1554), 14–15. Bayerische Staats Bibliothek, *Münchener Digitalisierungszentrum*.

28 Pizzimenti, 10r, translating sect. 9.2, 184–5, of *Perì Hýpsous*.

29 *Dionysii Longini De Sublimi dicendi genere liber a Petro Pagano latinitate donatus* (Venice, 1572), 9r.

30 *On the Sublime*, sect. 9.4, 184–5.

31 Pagano, 7v, translating sect. 8.2, 180–1, of *On the Sublime*.

32 Da Falgano, 13v. In this passage, Falgano's "furore divino" references the concept of Platonic *furor*, a principle of divine inspiration in which the poet is in a condition of frenzy. *Furor* and sublimity do overlap substantially, but da Falgano emphasizes a "negative" dimension of violence and terror that is typically more characteristic of Longinian *ekplexis* than Platonic *furor*.

33 *On the Sublime*, sect. 15.9, 222–3.

34 Pagano, 20r; da Falgano, 36r; and Pizzimenti, 17v. Pagano seems to have made a typographical error in writing "auditorum" instead of "auditorium," the accusative singular form of "audience."

35 *On the Sublime*, sect. 1.4, 162–3.

36 This image, an identical reprint of de Petra's original, is reproduced from Langbaine's 1636 edition: *Dionysiou Longinou rhetoros Peri hypsous logou biblion*, ed. Gerard Langbaine (Oxonii, 1636), 21. Courtesy of Yale University Press. Image produced by ProQuest as part of Early English Books Online.

37 De Petra, *Dionysiou Longinou rhetoros Peri hypsous logou biblion*, 59, on sect. 15.1. Refini notes that de Petra is cross-referencing a passage from Quintillian that also emphasizes the role of emotion: "Longinus and Poetic Imagination," 45. Refini, Doran, and Cheney note the centrality of *phantasia* to Longinus's concept of the sublime: *The Theory of the Sublime*, 38–40; and *English Authorship*, 12. For detailed studies on classical conceptions of *phantasia*, see Alessandra Manieri, *L'immagine poetica nella teoria degli antichi. Phantasia ed enargeia* (Pisa: Istituti editoriali e poligrafici

internazionali, 1998); and Gerard Watson, *Phantasia in Classical Thought* (Galway: Galway University Press, 1988).

38 *On the Sublime*, sect. 9.4, 184–5.

39 For an additional reading of the mythological figures and their significance in this image, see Cheney, *English Authorship*, 26–8; and Lydia Hamlett, "The Longinian Sublime, Effect and Affect in 'Baroque' British Visual Culture," in *Translations of the Sublime*, 204–6.

40 Title page to Gerard Langbaine's 1638 edition of *Peri Hypsous: Dionysiou Longinou rhetoros Peri hypsous logou biblion*, ed. Gerard Langbaine (Oxonii, 1636), 21. Beinecke Rare Book and Manuscript Library, Yale University.

41 Martin suggests that Ronsard played a role in the early dissemination of Longinus's treatise: "The Prehistory of the Sublime," 78. Scholars who have discussed the early modern French sublime include Fumaroli, David Sedley (who focusses on Montaigne), and Emma Gilby, in a study of seventeenth-century French drama: *Sublime Worlds: Early Modern French Literature* (London: Routledge, 2006). To my knowledge, no one besides Martin has identified the significance of the sublime to the work of Ronsard or Du Bellay.

42 Philip Ford identifies a significant influence of Erasmus on Ronsard in "Erasmian Irenism in the Poetry of Pierre de Ronsard," in *The Reception of Erasmus on the Early Modern Period*, ed. Karl A.E. Enenkel (Leiden: Brill, 2013), 163–78.

43 *On the Sublime*, sect. 13.2–3, 210–11.

44 *Défence*, 371.

45 *Défence*, 377–9.

46 *Défence*, 379.

47 *Défence*, 403.

48 *Oeuvres Complètes de P. de Ronsard: Publiées sur les textes les plus anciens avec les variants et des notes par M. Prosper Blanchemain* (Paris: P. Jannet, 1858), 29; my translation.

49 Ronsard, *Oeuvres Complètes*, 9; compare to Longinus, *On the Sublime*, sect. 9.1, 182–5.

50 Ronsard, *Oeuvres Complètes*, 28.

51 Ronsard, *Oeuvres Complètes*, 20.

52 Ronsard, *Abrégé de l'art poëtique François* (London: Eragny Press, 1903), 3–6; my translation.

53 Sharon May Poliner identifies the Demon with the "darker depths of poetic inspiration" in "Du Bellay's Songes: Strategies of Deceit, Poetics of Vision," *Bibliothèque d'Humanisme et Renaissance* 43:3 (1981): 509–25, 522.

54 *Songes*, 1.11.

55 Fumaroli, "Rhétorique d'école et rhétorique adulte," and Sedley, *Sublimity and Skepticism in Montaigne and Milton* (Ann Arbor: University of Michigan Press, 2005).

56 Hassan Melehy notes that Du Bellay's choice of the word "divinité" in this passage is characteristically vague compared to Spenser's adaptation in his *Visions of Bellay*, though since Du Bellay also uses the more concrete "Dieu" in the line above, I believe that he too is thinking of a specific eternal hope in the Christian deity: *The Poetics of Literary Transfer* (Farnham, UK: Ashgate, 2013), 110.

57 Martin notes that Muret and de Petra, among others, are in this group: "The Prehistory of the Sublime," 79.

58 Melehy, *The Poetics of Literary Transfer in Early Modern France and England*, 92.

59 On the influence of Ronsard and/or Du Bellay in England, see especially Anne Lake Prescott, *French Poets and the English Renaissance: Studies in Fame and Transformation* (New Haven and London: Yale University Press, 1978); Melehy, *The Poetics of Literary Transfer*; and A.E.B. Coldiron, "How Spenser Excavates Du Bellay's 'Antiquitez'; or, The Role of the Poet, Lyric Historiography, and the English Sonnet," *The Journal of English and Germanic Philology* 101, no. 1 (2002): 41–67.

60 Costa, "Tasso e il Sublime," *Rivista di Estetica* 27 (1987): 49–63.

61 In an analysis still representative, Mariella Cavalchini and Irene Samuel note Tasso's contradictory poetics in their introduction to his edition, but conclude that at its core, Tasso's theory is basically Aristotelian and Horatian in its focus on building morality: *Discourses on the Heroic Poem*, trans. Cavalchini and Samuel (Oxford: Oxford University Press, 1973), xxii–xxxiv.

62 Paleotti, *Discourses on Sacred and Profane Images*, trans. William McCuaig (Getty: Los Angeles, 2012), 237. Another Catholic authority figure and writer of similar persuasion was Giovanni Andrea Gilio da Fabriano. Robert Gaston notes how, in his *Dialogo degli errori della pittura* (1564), da Fabriano demonstrated a "severity of judgment" that committed "unwarranted subjection of artistic freedom to Catholic ideology": "How Words Control Images: The Rhetoric of Decorum in Counter-Reformation Italy," in *The Sensuous in the Counter-Reformation Church*, ed. Marcia B. Hall and Tracy E. Cooper (Cambridge: Cambridge University Press, 2013), 87.

63 Segni, *Lezioni sopra le cose pertinenti alla poetica* (MS Ashb. 531), II, 83v, quoted in Bernard Weinberg, *History of Literary Criticism in the Italian Renaissance* (Chicago: University of Chicago Press, 1961), 303. Aristotle's concept of *catharsis* is notoriously difficult to define, but Segni extends the idea of eliminating emotion to a place of distortion.

64 Rhu, "From Aristotle to Allegory: Young Tasso's Evolving Vision of the *Gerusalemme Liberata*," *Italica* 65, no. 2 (1988): 116.

65 *Discorsi del poema eroico*, in *Discorsi dell'arte poetica e del poema eroico*, ed. Luigi Poga (Laterza: Bari, 1964), 68. All quotations from the *Discorsi* will be taken from this edition; the translations are my own. See also Annabel Patterson, "Tasso and Neoplatonism: The Growth of his Epic Theory," *Studies in the Renaissance* 18 (1971): 105–33, which considers the *Discorsi*'s departure from Aristotelianism and Neoplatonic emphasis on poetic beauty and delight.

66 Doran, *Theory of the Sublime*, 103–5; and Graziani, "Le Miracle de l'Art: Le Tasse e la Poétique de la Meraviglia," *Revue des Études Italiennes* 42 (1995): 117–39; see also Irene Montori, "Representing creation, experiencing the sublime: The Longinian tradition in Tasso and Milton," *SEDERI* 30 (2020): 69–89. Graziani notes Tasso's reading of Robortello, Pagano, and Vettori (122, n. 9). Mario Praz and Sergio Zatti briefly link Tasso to Longinus using examples from the *Gerusalemme liberata*, as I discuss in the second chapter.

67   Doran, *The Theory of the Sublime*, 104–5. Doran does not argue that Tasso's poetics were fully Longinian, but that his concept of *meraviglia* was a forerunner to Boileau's concept of sublimity.

68   In emphasizing the work's Longinian character, I acknowledge the possible impact of other Hellenistic rhetoricians such as Hermogenes and Demetrius, whose works were also being rediscovered and read in the sixteenth century, while suggesting that the Longinian echoes that inform Tasso's thoughts are an important part of a wider trend. On the influence of Hermogenes and Demetrius on Tasso's theory of style, see Hermann Grosser, *La Sottiglieza del Disputare: Teorie degli Stili e Teorie dei Generi in Età Rinascimentale e nel Tasso* (Florence: Nuova Italia Editrice, 1992); and Annabel Patterson, *Hermogenes and the Renaissance: Seven Ideas of Style* (Princeton: Princeton University Press, 1970), which also includes discussion of Sidney.

69   *Discorsi del poema eroico*, 74. Tasso's *Discorsi dell'arte poetica* (1587, composed in the 1560s) also discusses *meraviglia*, but this discourse seems more conventional and further removed from the Longinian sublime than that in the *Discorsi del poema eroico*; possibly, Tasso's thinking about the sublime developed between the composition of the *Arte* and the *Poema eroico* as he more fully absorbed Longinus (or Longinus's mediators) over the years. Yet even the early poetic treatise contains its own discourse on the sublime, including a noteworthy statement that the poet's aim is to "ravish" (rapiri) the audience; Tasso seems to have always been somewhat attuned to Longinus's unconventional idea of literature's purpose.

70   Bartholomaei Marantae Venusini, *Lucullianarum Quaestionum Libri Quinque* (Basel, 1564), 88, cited in Weinberg, *History of Literary Criticism*, 171–3. Aristotle argues for the importance of the marvellous [*thaumasion*] to tragedy – he writes that the unexpected is "marvelous" – but his definition of the term does not seem to contain the "negative" inflections suggested by Longinus and Tasso: *Poetics*, in *The Basic Works of Aristotle*, ed. Richard McKeon (New York: Random House, 1941). On the role of Aristotle's theory of the marvellous in sixteenth-century culture, see Joy Kenseth's edited collection, *The Age of the Marvelous* (Hanover, N.H.: Dartmouth, 1991).

71   Da Falgano, 32v, translating sect. 15.2, 214–15. Da Falgano also uses *meraviglia* to translate *ekplexis* when rendering the passage in sect. 1.4: "παντη δε γε συν εκπληξει του πιθανου και του προσ χαριν αει κρατει το θαυμασιον [indeed, the marvellous, with its ability to paralyse, always wins out over the persuasive and the pleasing]"; Falgano writes: "la meraviglia accoppiata insieme con lo stupore vince sempre mai e trapassa la fede [meraviglia, together with amazement, always prevails and surpasses conviction]."

72   Longinus, sect. 35.5, 274–5; and da Falgano, 68r.

73   Micaela Rinaldi documents Tasso's relationship with Patrizi (though not in terms of the sublime) in *Torquato Tasso e Francesco Patrizi: Tra Polemiche Letterarie e Incontri Intellettuali* (Ravenna: Longo, 2001).

74   Patrizi, *Della Poetica*, 3 vols., ed. Danilo Aguzzio Barbagli (Firenze, 1971), II., 259–60, and III.112, citing sect. 15.9 of Longinus. Apparently quoting from

memory, Patrizi remembers Longinus's words in a slightly incorrect order, but with insignificant effects on meaning.

75 Patrizi, *Della Poetica*, II.259.

76 *Discorsi del poema eroico*, 73.

77 *Discorsi del poema eroico*, 245–6.

78 *La Visione di M. Francesca Porta: Da Castel Nuovo della Garfagnana* (Fiorenza [*sic*]: Giorgio Marescotti, 1578), 14.

79 *Discorsi del poema eroico*, 72.

80 As Cavalchini and Samuel note in their edition, Tasso consistently mistakes *energeia* (emotional forcefulness) for its close relative *enargeia* (vivid visualization), but he is clearly referring to the latter: *Discourses on the Heroic Poem*, 189.

81 *Discorsi del poema eroico*, 243.

82 *Discorsi del poema eroico*, 246.

83 Vettori, *Commentarii in Primum Librum*, 149. Claudio Scarpati notes Tasso's familiarity with Vettori's work: *Studi sul Cinquecento Italiano* (Milan: Vita e pensiero, 1982), 165–79.

84 Graziani, "Le miracle de l'art," 130–1.

85 *Discorsi del poema eroico*, 140.

86 Baldine Saint Girons also identifies risk as inherent to the sublime, emphasizing how the sublime inevitably depreciates all else by contrast, leading to the "destitution" [deposition] of the individual who contemplates it: *Fiat lux. Une philosophie du sublime* (Paris, Quai Voltaire, 1993), 298, 299. Though Saint Girons recognizes the risks of creating and contemplating the sublime, she does not highlight the heroic potential of choosing to do so, which Tasso in particular depicts in his prose and poetry.

87 *Discorsi del poema eroico*, 245–6.

88 Praz, commenting on the *Liberata*, cites Longinus's comment that the greatest writers use "hyperbata o trasposizioni e spostamenti nell'ordine delle cose che han da dire, in modo da imitare la passione, il cui linguaggio mostra una certa dose di *disordine* [hyperbaton or transpositions or displacements in the order of things that they have to say, in a way that imitates passion, their language showing a certain dose of disorderliness]": *Il Giardino dei sensi: Studi sul manierismo e il barocco* (Torino: Arnoldo Mondadori Editore, 1975), 111. Goyet notes Longinus's preference for "interruptions, hyperbates, metabasis": "The Meaning of *Apostrophè* in Longinus's *On the Sublime*," in *Translations of the Sublime*, 13–32, 31.

89 *On the Sublime*, sect. 12.4, 208–9.

90 *Discorsi del poema eroico*, 204.

91 *Discorsi del poema eroico*, 204.

92 *Discorsi del poema eroico*, 202.

93 *Discorsi del poema eroico*, 121.

94 *Discorsi del poema eroico*, 202–3.

95 Pizzimenti also notes the technique of reordering sentence structures in his marginalia, 21v.

96 *On the Sublime*, sect. 22.4, 240–1.

97   *On the Sublime*, sect. 33.2, 266–7.

98   *Discorsi del poema eroico*, 187, 248.

99   *Discorsi del poema eroico*, 220, 217.

100   *Discorsi del poema eroico*, 117, 103.

101   This is not to suggest that Tasso has ties to the Protestantism of Porto and others, yet his struggles over his faith and his religious commitments were extreme, and the possibility that he was sympathetic to an aspect of Protestantism is intriguing. As discussed in chapter 2, on the impact of the sublime on the *Liberata*, Tasso also had interest in the mystical tradition – a tradition feared by the Counter-Reformation for its implied resistance to the official mediation of Church authorities in the relationship to God.

102   Bruno dedicated the *Eroici Furori* to Sidney, whose acquaintance he made after moving to England in 1583.

103   As noted earlier, *furor* can be Longinian or not depending on whether it is understood to characterize genuine divine inspiration; Michael Heyd observes Plato's distinction between the conditions of prophecy and pathological madness in the *Phaedrus*. *"Be Sober and Reasonable": The Critique of Enthusiasm in the Seventeenth and Early Eighteenth Centuries* (Leiden: Brill, 1995), 45.

104   Bruno, *De Gli Eroici Furori*, ed. Eugenio Canone (Toronto: University of Toronto Press, 2013), 40–2.

105   Bruno, *Eroici Furori*, 266–8.

106   *On the Sublime*, sect. 44.6–8, 301–3.

107   Though published after Sidney's death, the *Defence* is usually dated between 1580 and 1582: see A.C. Hamilton, *Sir Philip Sidney: A Study of his Life and Works* (Cambridge: Cambridge University Press, 1977), 17.

108   Till, "The Sublime and the Bible," in *Translations of the Sublime*, 61.

109   Till, "The Sublime and the Bible," 59, 61. *Calvin: Institutes of the Christian Religion*, 2 vols., trans. Ford Lewis Battles, ed. John T. McNeill (1536; Philadelphia: Westminster Press, 1967), I.8.1, 81. Where included, original language from the *Institutes* is taken from *Institution de la religion chrestienne*, 2 vols. (Paris: C. Meyrueis, 1859). Université de Genève, Web.

110   Till, "The Sublime and the Bible," 61. *On the Sublime*, sect 9.9, 190–1.

111   *The Defence of Poesy*, in *Sir Philip Sidney: The Major Works*, ed. Katherine Duncan-Jones (Oxford: Oxford University Press, 2008). All Sidney quotations are taken from this edition. My earlier comment that Tasso's Longinian echoes are part of a wider trend applies equally to Sidney and Puttenham.

112   *The Defence of Poesy*, 231.

113   *The Defence of Poesy*, 242.

114   *The Defence of Poesy*, 246.

115   *The Arte of English Poesie*, in *English Renaissance Literary Criticism*, ed. Brian Vickers (Oxford: Oxford University Press, 2007), 227. All Puttenham quotations are taken from this edition.

116 *The Defence of Poesy*, 217.

117 Shuger discusses the broad importance of *enargeia* to early modern Catholic and Protestant theologians alike, who used it to emphasize the role of the imagination and passions in faith: *Sacred Rhetoric*, 199–223. On Puttenham's use of *enargeia* (and *energeia*), though not in terms of the sublime, see Lynda Gaylon, "Puttenham's *Enargeia* and *Energeia*: New Twists for Old Terms," *Philological Quarterly* 60 (1981): 29–40.

118 *The Defence of Poesy*, 218–19.

119 *Arte of English Poesie*, 201.

120 *The Defence of Poesy*, 231, 222.

121 *The Defence of Poesy*, 214.

122 *The Defence of Poesy*, 219.

123 *The Defence of Poesy*, 249–50

124 *On the Sublime*, sect. 44.8, 302–3.

125 Philippians 3:19–20.

126 *The Defence of Poesy*, 249–50.

127 *Dedication to Mathew Royden*, in *English Renaissance Literary Criticism*, 393. Chapman adds: "[b]ut that poesy should be as perviall as oratory, and plainness her special ornament, were the plain way to barbarism, and to make the ass run proud of his ears; to take strength away from lions, and give camels horns" (393).

128 *On the Sublime*, sect. 9.13–14, 195.

129 Chapman, "On Translating and Defending Homer," in *English Renaissance Literary Criticism*, 522; *On the Sublime*, sect. 12.3, 206–7.

130 "On Translating and Defending Homer," 522.

131 "On Translating and Defending Homer," 523.

132 "On Translating and Defending Homer," 522.

133 *On the Sublime*, sect. 36.1, 276–7.

134 Galatians 5:24.

135 Annabel Patterson argues that Milton seems to have had Longinus in mind when developing the overarching design of *Paradise Lost*, for he models the structure and sequence on *Peri Hypsous*. Following Longinus, who juxtaposes the biblical *fiat lux* – "Let there be light" – with a discussion of Homeric war, Milton places the Creation narrative directly after the War in Heaven episode, thereby connecting the sublimity of divine glory with the sublimity of the heroic: *Reading between the Lines* (London: Routledge, 1993), 268.

136 *John Milton: Prose*, ed. David Loewenstein (Malden, MA: Wiley-Blackwell, 2013), 177–8. All citations of Milton's prose are taken from this edition.

137 *Reason of Church Government*, 90.

138 *Of Education*, 90–1.

139 Isaiah 6:5–7.

2. The Tassoan Sublime and the Counter-Reformation: Charisma and Romance in the *Gerusalemme liberata*

1 While Italian nationalism would not gain widespread support as a political movement until much later, Machiavelli was already invested in reviving Roman glory and sowing seeds of Italian unity and independence in the early sixteenth century: see Mikael Hörnqvist, *Machiavelli and Empire* (Cambridge: Cambridge University Press, 2004).

2 Quotations from the *Liberata* are taken from the edition by Giuseppe Lipparini (Milano: Carlo Signorelli, 1944).

3 As seen in the previous chapter, Counter-Reformation officials feared and opposed art that pursued delight for its own sake, a fact that greatly concerned Tasso later in his life. Jo Ann Cavallo and Matthew Treherne have documented the impact of Inquisition censorship by Silvio Antoniano and other leaders on Tasso's composition of the *Liberata*: see Cavallo, *Romance Epics of Boiardo, Ariosto, and Tasso: From Public Duty to Private Pleasure* (Toronto: University of Toronto Press, 2004), 220–6; and Treherne, "Pictorial Space and Sacred Time: Tasso's *Le Lagrime della Beata Vergine* and the Experience of Religious Art in the Counter-Reformation," *Italian Studies* 62 (2007): 5–25.

4 David Quint, *Epic and Empire: Politics and Generic Form from Virgil to Milton* (Princeton: Princeton University Press, 1993), 214, 252. In a more recent assessment, Anthony Welch maintains that Tasso may have "thrashed about inside the neo-Aristotelian critical regime, but he never threw it off," for "he was bent on vindicating himself by the fastidious standards of neoclassical [and Tridentine] poetics": *Renaissance Epic and the Oral Past* (Chicago: University of Chicago Press, 2012), 27, 35–6.

5 Cavallo, *Romance Epics of Boiardo, Ariosto, and Tasso*, 218–225. Anticipating this position is a wave of mid-twentieth-century criticism by Benedetto Croce, *Poesia Antica e Moderna* (Bari, Italy: Laterza, 1943); Eugenio Donadoni, *Torquato Tasso* (Florence: La Nuova Italian, 1967); and Giovanni Getto, *Malinconia di Torquato Tasso* (Naples: Liguori, 1979); followed up by the more recent work of Sergio Zatti, *The Quest for Epic: From Ariosto to Tasso*, trans. Sally Hill and Dennis Looney, ed. Looney (Toronto: University of Toronto Press, 2006), 135–60.

6 Patterson, "Tasso and Neoplatonism: The Growth of his Epic Theory," Studies in the Renaissance 18 (1971): 105. Thomas M. Greene also discusses Tasso's Neoplatonism in *The Descent from Heaven: A Study in Epic Continuity* (New Haven: Yale University Press, 1963), 207–19. Unlike Patterson, Greene sees Tasso's Neoplatonism as one element among many being merged into an eclectic poem rather than a means of reconciling competing objectives. He also finds in the poem at least one depiction of "sublimity" (a term he uses uncritically and without reference to Longinus), but sees this aesthetic mode as uncharacteristic for Tasso (207).

7 Mario Praz and Sergio Zatti, the only scholars to my knowledge to mention the Longinian sublime in Tasso's *Liberata*, briefly suggest that certain representations, such as the portrayal of Armida's bower, blend nature and art, thus recalling the principle of dissimulation discussed by Longinus in section 22.1: Praz, *Giardino dei Sensi: Studi sul Manierismo e il Barocco* (Torino: Arnoldo Mondadori Editore, 1975), 111;

and Zatti, *The Quest for Epic: From Ariosto to Tasso*, ed. Dennis Looney, trans. Sally Hill and Looney (Toronto: Toronto University Press, 2006), 211.

8 As I argued in the previous chapter, risk is at the heart of the Longinian sublime, as well as a hallmark of Tasso's own theory of *meraviglia* in epic. As Longinus maintains, those who "never run any risks and never aim at the heights" can never achieve the sublime, which therefore requires a certain heedlessness, a position reflected in the *Discorsi*, as well as *On the Sublime*, sect. 33.3, 266–7.

9 *Discourses on the Art of Poetry*, cited from the translation by Lawrence Rhu, *Genesis of Tasso's Narrative Theory: English Translations of the Early Poetics and a Comparative Study of their Significance* (Detroit: Wayne State, 1993), 104.

10 At the conclusion, Longinus critiques certain vices as antithetical to the sublime, including the "love of money" and "love of pleasure, that enslave us," even while elsewhere he recurrently (though not always) discusses the experience of the sublime as a delight: *On the Sublime*, trans. W.H. Fyfe and Donald Russell, in *Aristotle: The Poetics. "Longinus": On the Sublime. Demetrius: On Style*, ed. Jeffrey Henderson (Cambridge: Harvard University Press, 1995), sect. 44.6–12, 300–5.

11 The "charismatic" and "romantic" modes of action do overlap, as characters such as Rinaldo may switch between them, although for most characters, one or the other mode predominates.

12 This is not to argue that Tasso's poetry is always consistent, but to suggest that there is a coherence to the way he uses the sublime to critique Counter-Reformation authority while endorsing a life of faith.

13 Diana Robin, "Renata di Francia," in *Encyclopedia of Women in the Renaissance: Italy, France, and England*, ed. Robin, Anne R. Larsen, and Carole Levin (Oxford: ABC-CLIO, 2007), 322.

14 Mazzotta notes Tasso's particular interest in the work of fourth-century Christian mystic Pseudo-Dionysus, arguing that Pseudo-Dionysus's *Mystical Theology* offered Tasso a theological and poetic model for the use of images and symbols to represent divinity: "Italian Renaissance Epic," in *The Cambridge Companion to Epic*, ed. Catherine Bates (Cambridge Companions Online: Cambridge University Press, 2010), 114.

15 In a study of mysticism in sixteenth-century Spain, Pedro Santonja notes that the Inquisition compared the movement to Lutheranism and declared it heretical for deprioritizing the mediating role of the church: *La herejía de los alumbrados y la espiritualidad en la España del siglo 16: Inquisición y sociedad* (Valencia, Spain: Generalitat Valenciana, 2001). On the persecution of mystics in Italy, see Anne Jacobson Schutte, *Aspiring Saints: Pretense of Holiness, Inquisition, and Gender in the Republic of Venice, 1618–1750* (Baltimore: Johns Hopkins University Press, 2001); and Moshe Sluhovsky, *Believe Not Every Spirit: Possession, Mysticism, and Discernment in Early Modern Catholicism* (Chicago: University of Chicago Press, 2007).

16 The *OED* defines mysticism as "a belief in the possibility of union with or absorption into God by means of contemplation and self surrender; belief in or devotion to the spiritual apprehension of truths inaccessible to the intellect."

17 Barbieri, "'To Be in Heaven': St. Philip Neri between Aesthetic Emotion and Mystical Ecstasy," in *The Sensuous in the Counter-Reformation Church*, ed. Marcia B. Hall and Tracy E. Cooper (Cambridge: Cambridge University Press, 2013), 206–7. Barbieri does not discuss Longinus or the sublime. On the role of the passions in Catholic rhetoric, see also Debora Shuger, *Sacred Rhetoric: The Christian Grand Style in the English Renaissance* (Princeton: Princeton University Press, 1988), 76–80.

18 Marcia B. Hall, "Introduction," in *The Sensuous in the Counter-Reformation Church*, 6.

19 Costanza Barbieri, "'To Be in Heaven': St. Philip Neri between Aesthetic Emotion and Mystical Ecstasy," in *The Sensuous in the Counter-Reformation Church*, 206–7.

20 Halliwell, *Between Ecstasy and Truth: Interpretations of Greek Poetics from Homer to Longinus* (Oxford: Oxford University Press, 2011), 333–4. Halliwell's position aligns with what we see in the *Liberata*, though David Sedley takes a slightly different view of sublimity, arguing that rather than leading to knowledge, the sublime is inherently connected to scepticism: *Sublimity and Skepticism*. In my view, Longinus himself allows a productive flexibility about sublimity and knowledge. As we will see, Du Bartas departs from Tasso, connecting the ability to experience the sublime with the ability to tolerate uncertainty, while Spenser, as Patrick Cheney emphasizes, often portrays characters who are both bewildered and in a condition of the sublime: *English Authorship and the Early Modern Sublime* (Cambridge: Cambridge University Press, 2018).

21 Halliwell, *Between Ecstasy and Truth*, 337.

22 Talvacchia, "The Word Made Flesh: Spiritual Subjects and Carnal Depictions in Renaissance Art," in *The Sensuous in the Counter-Reformation Church*, 65, 71–2. In one of her chief examples, Talvacchia cites the Italian poet and playwright Anton Francesco Grazzini (1503–84).

23 As indicated in a previous chapter, Stephen Jaeger links charisma and sublimity in *Enchantment: On Charisma and the Sublime in the Arts of the West* (Philadelphia: University of Pennsylvania Press, 2012), 2.

24 Weber, *On Charisma and Institution Building*, ed. S.N. Eisenstadt (Chicago: University of Chicago Press, 1968), 48.

25 As Donald McIntosh states, "the charismatic object or person is experienced as possessed by and transmitting an uncanny and compelling force": "Weber and Freud: On the Nature and Sources of Authority," *American Sociological Review* 35 (1970): 901–11.

26 Eisenstadt, *Introduction*, xx.

27 Michael Murrin and Lawrence F. Rhu argue that Tasso's allegory was in fact central to his thinking about the *Liberata*. Murrin, *The Allegorical Epic: Essays in its Rise and Decline* (Chicago: University of Chicago Press, 1980), 87–127, 232–42; and Rhu, "From Aristotle to Allegory: Young Tasso's Evolving Vision of the *Gerusalemme Liberata*," *Italica* 65, no. 2 (1998): 111–30. I would contend with Cavallo and Walter Stephens that Tasso's allegory was an afterthought intended to appease his censors, and not an accurate reflection of the poem itself: Cavallo, *Romance Epics*, 199–200; and Stephens, "Saint Paul Among the Amazons: Gender and Authority in *Gerusalemme Liberata*,"

Discourses of Authority in Medieval and Renaissance Literature, ed. Kevin Brownlee and Stephens (Hanover, NH: University Press of New England, 1989), 200.

28 Translations of the *Liberata* are my own.

29 As the Israelites approach the Promised Land, the spies inform Joshua that the Canaanites are terrified, based on reports of the miracles associated with the exile from Egypt: "'Tradidit Dominus omnem terram hanc in manus nostras, et timore prostrati sunt cuncti habitatores ejus [The Lord has given all of this land into our hands, and all of its inhabitants are overcome with fear].'" Cited from *The Vulgate Bible*, 6 vols., ed. Swift Edgar (Cambridge, MA: Harvard University Press, 2010), vol. 1: *The Pentateuch* (2010): Joshua 2:24.

30 As argued further below, I would maintain that Tasso uses Goffredo's participation in the Crusade ironically, to critique the very authorities who incited the invasion in a particularly subtle way. I do not think he saw the Crusades themselves as divinely ordained, given his evident sympathy towards the Saracens, which Zatti has illustrated: *L'uniforme cristiano e il multiforme pagano saggio sulla Gerusalemme liberata* (Milan: Il Saggiatore, 1983). Ultimately, I believe that Tasso is exploring the heroic and spiritual potential in Goffredo's military courage and orientation towards the divine, while remaining aware of the problematic context. Even so, the effort to unite divine inspiration, spiritual heroism, and the military conquest of people of other faiths as he does remains troubling.

31 *Torquato Tasso: Jerusalem Delivered*, ed. Anthony M. Esolen (Baltimore: Johns Hopkins University Press, 2000), 463, n. 20.

32 Cavallo, *Romance Epics*, 193–204.

33 As we saw in the previous chapter, Longinus refers to this nobility of soul as *megalophués*, and Tasso, in the *Discorsi*, as *altezza*; both theorists establish this as a principal source of the sublime.

34 *Il Giardino des Sensi*, 104–5. As Praz notes, seventeenth-century sublime theorist Dominique Bouhours catalogues the French phrase (1671), citing the Italians as the originators and taking the majority of his examples from Tasso. Robert Doran argues that the French "je ne sais quoi" is not related to the sublime, noting that the phrase typically refers to a "social sentiment" or "aesthetic judgment for which no rational grounds can be found": *The Theory of the Sublime from Longinus to Kant* (Cambridge: Cambridge University Press, 2015), 106–7. This may be so in many seventeenth-century usages, though as Doran himself notes, Boileau does use the expression in his translation of Longinus; and in any case, Tasso uses the corresponding Italian phrase in a manner that is consistent with Longinus's idea of a divine impulse or intuition that Halliwell discusses: *Between Ecstasy and Truth*, 333–4.

35 Louis Marin, "1674: On the Sublime, Infinity, *Je Ne Sais Quoi*," in *A New History of French Literature*, ed. Denis Hollier (Cambridge, MA: Harvard University Press, 1994), 340.

36 Halliwell, *Between Ecstasy and Truth*, 334.

37 Praz, *Giardino dei Sensi*, 112. Dissimulation is also the core feature of Castiglione's implicitly charismatic courtier.

38 Longinus writes that the sublime affects all who hear or read it without exception; it is "difficult, no, impossible to resist its effect…. (It) pleases all people at all times": *On the Sublime*, sect. 7.3–4, 179–81.

39 van der Laan, "Tasso's Homeric Counter-Factuals," *MLN* 127, no. 1 (2012): 23–44, 32.

40 Kristeva herself notes that abjection and sublimity represent two different moments of the same journey, though she does not go into detail: Julia Kristeva, *Powers of Horror: An Essay on Abjection*, trans. Leon S. Roudiez (New York: Columbia University Press, 1982), 11. Both abjection and sublimity seem to involve different forms of extreme emotional experience in response to a crisis of self – whether being drawn outside the self, as in Longinian *ekstasis*, or undergoing violent struggle within the self, as in Kristevan abjection.

41 Kristeva, *Powers of Horror*, 2–4. Elizabeth Jane Bellamy links the *Liberata* to psychoanalytical theory, though not to abjection specifically: *Translations of Power: Narcissism and the Unconscious in Epic Theory* (Ithaca, NY: Cornell University Press, 1994), 133–88.

42 Analogous to how the Catholic sacrament of penance has an element of austerity – sincere remorse and satisfaction or restitution for sin – as prerequisite to divine reconciliation, Longinus implies that those aspiring to sublimity must actively temper their innate human tendencies towards vice. In the conclusion to *Peri Hypsous*, he notes that the primary obstacles to sublimity include greed, love of pleasure, insolence, boastfulness, and other faults that cause people to value their "mortal" side and "neglect the development of their immortal part" (sect. 44, 300–3). Thus, even though Longinus does not incorporate abjection into his theory of the sublime, his theory allows for the possibility of a significant reformation of self.

43 Esolen, 469, n. 41. Biow, *Mirabile Dictu: Representations of the Marvelous in Medieval and Renaissance Epic* (Ann Arbor: University of Michigan Press, 1996), 137–40.

44 Halliwell, *Between Ecstasy and Truth*, 348.

45 See, for instance, 1 Timothy 6:12: "certa bonum certamen fidei [fight the good fight of faith]"; and Ephesians 6:16: "sumentes scutum fidei in quo possitis omni tela nequissimi ignea extinguere [tak(e) up the shield of faith, with which you can extinguish all the flaming arrows of the most evil one]."

46 N.K. Sugimura links the related noun "vaghezza" to the sublime: "The Passion of Wonder in *Paradise Lost*," *Essays in Criticism* 64.1 (2014): 1–28.

47 Tancredi's desperation recalls Jesus's drastic command in Matthew 5:30: "Et si dextra manus tua scandalizat te, abscide eam, et projice abs te [And if your right hand disgraces you, cut it off, and throw it away.]"

48 This passage recalls Dante's response to the bleeding tree in the wood of the suicides (*Inferno*, canto xiii.44–5), as well as Orlando's reaction to seeing the names of Angelica and Medoro and the accompanying verses carved on trees in Ariosto's *Orlando Furioso* (23.102–11). The sublimity of Tancredi's response is Tasso's distinctive addition: Dante's primary reaction is one of pity ("tanta pietà m'accora," 13.84), while Orlando's, after the initial incredulity, is of jealousy and grief ("sí tutto in preda del dolor si lassa," 23.112.2); *Divina Commedia*, ed. C.H. Grandgent (New York: Heath, 1913).

49 Although Tancredi begins to cut down the tree after the murmuring begins – he gives two strokes as blood oozes from the tree – he seems even then to be pursuing rather than resisting the "non so che," out of curiosity about the tree's mysteries: "vederne ei si consiglia [he decides to investigate]" (13.41). My reading of this passage differs from the interpretation of Erminia Ardissino, who suggests that the episode represents the importance of distinguishing between true and false signs: *L'Aspra Tragedia: Poesia e Sacro in Torquato Tasso* (Firenze: Olschki, 1996). In this passage, I believe Tasso indicates the value of the individual conscience in the quest for transcendence, condoning Tancredi's decision.

50 Zatti, *L'uniforme cristiano.*

51 Rhu, *Genesis of Tasso's Narrative Theory*, 24.

52 Sedley argues that this kind of sceptical uncertainty goes hand-in-hand with sublimity, each condition frequently leading directly to the other: *Sublimity and Skepticism*, 15. In this case, though, I would argue that Armida's "sceptical" condition is less indicative of a deliberate suspension of certainty (as scepticism is typically defined) than of a moment of transformation. In other words, she is prompted to give up her knowledge of hatred and exchange it for an urge to love.

53 Armida's line "Ecco l'ancilla tua" alludes not only to Mary's words at the Annunciation, but also to the phrase repeated on the Terrace of Pride in Dante's *Purgatorio* (10.44) as sinners are trained in the virtue of humility – both intertextual references to spiritual submission and transformation.

3. Divine Mystery and the Inscrutable Sublime in Du Bartas's *Les Semaines*

1 On Du Bartas's reception in England, see especially Peter Auger, *Du Bartas's Legacy in England and Scotland* (Oxford: Oxford University Press, 2019).

2 Prescott, *French Poets and the English Renaissance: Studies in Fame and Transformation* (New Haven and London: Yale University Press, 1978), 183. Maynard, *Reveries of Community: French Epic in the Age of Henri IV* (Evanston, IL: Northwestern University Press, 2017), 39–58.

3 On Du Bartas's investment in scepticism, though not in terms of the sublime, see also Lehtonen, "Heroic Adaptations of Genesis 3: Knowledge and Skepticism in Renaissance Biblical Epic," in *The Bible and Western Christian Literature*, ed. Elisabeth Jay, vol. 2, *Renaissance and Reformation*, ed. Sophie Read (London: Bloomsbury, forthcoming). The essay identifies contrasts between Du Bartas', Milton's, and Lucy Hutchinson's investments in the philosophy of scepticism and concepts of intellectual virtue.

4 The Protestant Henri IV came to power just one year before Du Bartas's death in 1590, converting to Catholicism in 1593.

5 Maynard, *Reveries of Community*, 4.

6 In this poetic fragment, Du Bartas declares his disdain for religious tensions: "lesquelles je desire voir non seulement estcinte, ains mesme ensevelies sous un Eternel obli [which I would like to see not only extinct, but buried in eternal oblivion]": *La Muse Chrestiene*, Bordeaux, 1574, f(o) AB 2v.

7   Prescott, *French Poets*, 209, and 194, citing Harvey, *Pierces supererogation*, in *Elizabethan Critical Essays*, ed. G. Gregory Smith (London: Oxford University Press, 1904), II, 265–6.

8   Braunrot, *L'Imagination poétique chez du Bartas: Éléments de sensibilité baroque dans* la Création du monde (Chapel Hill, NC: University of North Carolina Press, 1973), 123–33.

9   *La Seconde Semaine*, ed. Yvonne Bellenger (1584; Paris: Société des Textes Français Modernes, 1991). All citations from *Les Semaines* are from the editions of Bellenger. Unless noted otherwise, all translations of Du Bartas are my own.

10   *The Complete Works of Joshuah Sylvester*, 2 vols., ed. Alexander B. Grosart (1880; Sagwan Press, 2015), I.2.818.

11   Kant, *Critique of the Power of Judgement*, ed. and trans. Paul Guyer and Eric Matthews (Cambridge: Cambridge University Press, 2000), 5:255.

12   As Doran notes, both Kant and Burke speak of the sublime as the subjective "appearance" of infinity: *The Theory of Longinus*, 228, citing Kant's *Critique of the Power of Judgement*, 5:255; and Burke's *Philosophical Enquiry into the Origin of Our Ideas of the Sublime and the Beautiful* (1757/1759), ed. Adam Phillips (Oxford: Oxford University Press, 1990), 67.

13   *On the Sublime*, trans. W.H. Fyfe and Donald Russell, in *Aristotle: The Poetics. "Longinus": On the Sublime. Demetrius: On Style*, ed. Jeffrey Henderson (Cambridge: Harvard University Press, 1995), sect. 9.4, 184–5.

14   Julia Kristeva, *Powers of Horror: An Essay on Abjection*, trans. Leon S. Roudiez (New York: Columbia University Press, 1982), 2–4, 11. As suggested previously, Kristeva theorizes that abjection and sublimity represent two different moments of the same journey.

15   Other characters in the expansive *Les Semaines* fit this model, but those of Adam and Abraham emphasize different aspects, including substantial material not included in Genesis.

16   On the connection to Sidney, see Alan Sinfield, "Sidney and Du Bartas," *Comparative Literature* 27 (1975): 8–20. Eva Madeleine Martin discusses Muret's role in the sublime, and his likely connection to scholars known to Du Bartas: "The 'Prehistory of the Sublime in Early Modern France," in *The Sublime: From Antiquity to the Present*, ed. Costelloe (Cambridge: Cambridge University Press, 2012), 78–9.

17   Jean Céard's introduction to *La Sepmaine* suggests that Du Bartas and Montaigne may have attended the same school, Le Collège de Guyenne: *La Sepmaine ou Creation du monde*, Tome I., ed. Jean Céard (Paris: Classiques Garnier, 2011), 10, n. 4.

18   Sedley, *Sublimity and Skepticism in Montaigne and Milton* (Ann Arbor: University of Michigan Press, 2005), 9–11.

19   Richard H. Popkin, *History of Scepticism from Erasmus to Spinoza* (Berkeley: University of California Press, 1979), 44–6.

20   On Du Bartas's distrust of empiricism, see Stephane Lamacz, "La Construction du savior et la réécriture du de rerum natura dans la Sepmaine de Du Bartas," *Bibliothèque d'Humanisme et Renaissance* 64, no. 3 (2002): 617–38.

21   Maynard, "Region, Nation, and Empire in the Long Poems of Guillaume Salluste Du Bartas," in *Reveries of Community*, 39–58.

22   Auger, *Du Bartas' Legacy*, 5–6, 49–50.

23 As indicated in a previous chapter, Longinus appears to leave the relationship between sublimity and knowledge ambiguous. While they can coincide (as Sedley argues, and as they do for Du Bartas), sublimity can in some cases be conducive to a higher form of knowledge, as Stephen Halliwell argues in *Between Ecstasy and Truth: Interpretations of Greek Poetics from Homer to Longinus* (Oxford: Oxford University Press, 2011).

24 There remains little specific analysis of how Du Bartas contributes to *Paradise Lost*. George Coffin Taylor cites a number of textual parallels in *Milton's Use of Du Bartas* (Harvard: Harvard University Press, 1934). Auger is more helpful but focusses mostly on how *Paradise Lost* critiques *Les Semaines*, rearranging content from *Les Semaines* to encourage readers to take a more critical approach to spiritual and worldly affairs: *Du Bartas' Legacy*, 201.

25 Sedley, *Sublimity and Skepticism*, 110, 118.

26 As we have seen, critical to Longinian theory is the idea that the aim of sublime poetry is not to "persuade, but to transport the audience out of themselves": *On the Sublime*, sect. I.4., 162–3.

27 For instance, Stanley Fish and Thomas Sloane both argue that Milton rejects the rhetorical tradition: Fish, *How Milton Works* (Cambridge, MA: Harvard University Press, 2001), 122–4; and Sloane, *Donne, Milton, and the End of Humanist Rhetoric* (Berkeley: University of California Press, 1985), 1, 249. Ryan J. Stark offers a similar but more nuanced argument in "Cold Styles: On Milton's Critiques of Frigid Rhetoric in *Paradise Lost*," *Milton Quarterly* 37:1 (2003): 21–30.

28 The vision Du Bartas's Adam describes to Seth also has interesting parallels to the vision Michael displays to Adam in Books 11–12 of *Paradise Lost*.

29 In another Longinian echo, as Adam begs to have his body taken away ("retirer"), Sylvester translates the term in this passage as "ravish": II.1.iv.624.

30 Ezekiel 1; Isaiah 6:7.

31 According to Genesis 5:23–4, Henoc, or Enoch, lives to be 365 against a contemporary norm in the 800's and 900's. See also Hebrews 11:5–6.

32 In Hinduism, *moksha* and *nirvana* are similar concepts, both resembling the sublime, with *nirvana* defined as "the extinguishing of worldly desires and attachments" to allow union with Brahman, or the Absolute: *The Concise Oxford Dictionary of World Religions* (Oxford: Oxford University Press, 2000); *moksha* is defined as the "liberation from the cycle of existence" and complete identification with the "ultimate, changeless ground of all things": *Oxford Dictionary of Philosophy*, 3rd ed. (Oxford: Oxford University Press, 2016).

33 *On the Sublime*, sect. 10.1–3, 198–9, citing Sappho, frag. 31.

34 Søren Kierkegaard's *Fear and Trembling* (1843) offers one of the most in-depth explorations of Abraham's test.

35 Du Bartas thus responds to the "Euthyphro dilemma," named for a debate between Socrates and a religious professional named Euthyphro about whether the gods themselves are subject to a higher moral code. John Hare provides an overview of this philosophical debate as it has continued through the millennia: "Religion and Morality," *The Stanford Encyclopedia of Philosophy*, ed. Edward N. Zalta (Winter 2014), Web.

36 This goes beyond what Abraham says earlier in the same passage, when he recognizes
that God may bring Isaac back to life – here, Isaac anticipates what is said about
Abraham's belief in his son's resurrection in Hebrews 11 ("Pères," 157–8).

37 Prescott notes how English translations emphasized Protestant views in ways that Du
Bartas's did not: *French Poets and the English Renaissance*, 187.

38 Hebrews 11 mentions a series of heroes who act "by faith," with verses 17–19 noting
that Abraham offered Isaac as a sacrifice by his faith.

4. Spenser's Protestant Sublime in the Legend of Holiness

1 Greenblatt, *Renaissance Self-Fashioning from More to Shakespeare* (Chicago: University
of Chicago Press, 1980), 174. Greenblatt of course is referring, among other
applications, to Spenser's attitude towards the Irish expressed in his *View of the Present
State of Ireland* (1596). Despicable as Spenser's treatment of the Irish was, I would
disagree that his actions were based simply on a desire for the expansion of English
power for its own sake, since he was motivated in part by concerns about the threat
an alliance between Catholic Ireland and Spain might pose to religious practice
in England. At the same time, in arguing for Spenser's concerns about English
nationalism and authority, this chapter is not meant to suggest that Spenser was
always consistent in his beliefs and practices, but that he does register concerns in *The
Faerie Queene* about how citizens relate to their earthly authorities.

2 Abrams, *The Fourth Dimension of a Poem: and Other Essays* (New York: Norton, 2012), 201.

3 Longinus writes in the same passage that the sublime "exercises an irresistible power
and mastery": *On the Sublime*, sect. 1.4, 163.

4 Cheney, *English Authorship and the Early Modern Sublime: Spenser, Marlowe, Shakespeare,
Jonson* (Cambridge: Cambridge University Press, 2018), 58.

5 Cheney, *English Authorship*, 64–75, citing *The Prince of Poets: Essays on Edmund Spenser*,
ed. John R. Elliott, Jr. (New York: New York University Press, 1968); Michael Murrin,
The Allegorical Epic: Essays in its Rise and Decline (Chicago: University of Chicago Press,
1980), 24–5; and James Nohrnberg, *The Analogy of "The Faerie Queene"* (Princeton:
Princeton University Press, 1976), xii. Kenneth Borris also recognizes the importance
of the Longinian sublime to Spenser, though Borris focusses predominantly on
the "positive" dimensions of the sublime emphasized in Platonism – "wonder,"
"ecstasis," and "supernatural awe" – rather than the paralysing terror of *ekplexis*,
which I argue is central to Spenser's Calvinist model of sublime heroism: *Visionary
Spenser and the Poetics of Early Modern Platonism* (Oxford: Oxford University Press,
2017). Irene Montori likewise identifies Spenser as an author of the early modern
sublime in *Milton, the Sublime and Dramas of Choice: Figures of Heroic and Literary Virtue*
(Rome: Edizioni Studium, 2020).

6 In a similar vein, Angus Fletcher explicitly calls *The Faerie Queene* a "sublime poem"
because it "challenges all our powers of imagination and speculation": *Allegory: The
Theory of a Symbolic Mode* (Ithaca: Cornell University Press, 1964), 269–70.

7 Cheney, *English Authorship*, 97, 90.

8 Cheney also considers the Reformed context of the Spenserian sublime, though he reads Spenser's Protestantism as supporting an investment in English nationhood.

9 *The Confessions of St. Augustine*, trans. John K. Ryan (Garden City, NY: Doubleday, 1960), 43–4.

10 *Calvin: Institutes of the Christian Religion*, 2 vols., trans. Ford Lewis Battles, ed. John T. McNeill (1536; Philadelphia: Westminster Press, 1967), III.12.1, 755–6. Original language from the *Institutes* is taken from *Institution de la religion chrestienne*, 2 vols. (Paris: C. Meyrueis, 1859). Université de Genève, Web.

11 1 Samuel 28:20. All remaining Biblical quotations are taken from *Geneva Bible: A Facsimile of the 1560 Edition*, ed. Lloyd E. Berry (Peabody, MA: Hendrickson, 2007).

12 *On the Sublime*, sect. 13.2, 211.

13 Acts 9:6; "Preface to the Epistle of St. Paul to the Romans," *Martin Luther's Basic Theological Writings*, 2nd ed., ed. Timothy F. Lull (Minneapolis: Augsburg, 2005), 100.

14 *Calvin: Institutes*, III.3.3, 480.

15 Among scholars emphasizing the poem's doctrinal instability or even resistance to Calvinism, see Darryl Gless, who argues that Spenser "invites a broader spectrum of particular realizations than scholars have been prepared to recognize": *Interpretation and Theology in Spenser* (Cambridge: Cambridge University Press, 1994), 9; Andrew Hadfield, who argues for Spenser's indebtedness to the medieval Catholic tradition in suggesting that the "impact of the Reformation ha[d] not yet been absorbed" by the time *The Faerie Queene* was published: "Spenser's Religion – Yet Again," *Studies in English Literature 1500–1900* 15, no. 1 (2001): 21–46; Carol Kaske, who argues for contradictions in Spenser's theology: *Spenser and Biblical Poetics* (Ithaca: Cornell University Press, 1999); and Virgil K. Whitaker and John N. Wall, Jr., who see Spenser as a moderate Anglican sympathetic to Catholic perspectives and resistant to Calvinism: *The Religious Basis of Spenser's Thought* (New York: Gordian Press, 1966); and "The English Reformation and the Recovery of Christian Community in *The Faerie Queene*," *Studies in Philology* 80.2 (1983): 142–62.

16 Claire McEachern, "Spenser and Religion," in *The Oxford Handbook of Edmund Spenser*, ed. Richard McCabe, *Oxford Handbooks Online* (2012), 1.

17 This chapter operates from the premise that divine sovereignty and free will can meaningfully exist, though not without substantial intellectual challenges, a view held by numerous philosophers and theologians (though strongly opposed by many as well). On the compatibility of the sovereignty of God with the freedom of the will, see Jason Turner, "Compatibilism and the Free Will Defense," *Faith and Philosophy* 30, no. 2 (2013): 125–37.

18 Hume, *Edmund Spenser: Protestant Poet* (Cambridge: Cambridge University Press, 1984), 91; and King, *Spenser's Poetry and the Reformation Tradition* (Princeton: Princeton University Press, 1990), 62–4. Other major studies on Spenser's Protestantism in Book I, especially the many examining his iconoclasm, also do not focus on Redcrosse's emotional condition: see, for instance, Ernest Gilman, *Iconoclasm and*

Poetry in the English Reformation: Down Went Dagon (Chicago: University of Chicago Press, 1986); and Kenneth Gross, *Spenserian Poetics: Idolatry, Iconoclasm, and Magic* (Ithaca, NY: Cornell University Press, 1986). Especially in the sixteenth century, Puritans were typically Calvinist in their theology, though Arminian Puritans like Milton did become more common afterward, as Christopher Hill notes: *Milton and the English Revolution* (London: Faber, 1977), 268.

19 Discussing the sobriety of the Reformed tradition, Whitaker, for instance, argues that Sans Joy represents Puritan gloom and uses this to challenge Spenser's Protestantism: *Religious Basis of Spenser's Thought*, 69. My argument also departs from the claim of Katherine Eggert that the tropes of rapture and ravishment in *The Faerie Queene* emerge from the "discards of Protestant theology," rather than Protestant theology itself. While Eggert does not discuss Longinus, she uses similar terminology to suggest that Spenser's depictions reflect an "alternative venue for sensualized delight," given the iconoclastic impulses of Protestantism: "Spenser's Ravishment: Rape and Rapture in The Faerie Queene," *Representations* 70 (2000): 1–26.

20 Van Engen, *Sympathetic Puritans: Calvinist Fellow Feeling in Early New England* (Oxford: Oxford University Press, 2015), 16. Similarly, Debora Shuger notes the strong role assigned to the passions by English Reformers William Perkins and Philip Melanchthon: *Sacred Rhetoric: The Christian Grand Style in the English Renaissance* (Princeton: Princeton University Press, 1988), 65–74.

21 Campana, *The Pain of Reformation: Spenser, Vulnerability, and the Ethics of Masculinity* (New York: Fordham University Press, 2012), 49. Scholars such as Michael Schoenfeldt also offer important studies on the passions in *The Faerie Queene*, though Schoenfeldt's and other studies tend to focus less on the Reformation context: *Bodies and Selves in Early Modern England: Physiology and Inwardness in Spenser, Shakespeare, Herbert, and Milton* (Ann Arbor: University of Michigan Press, 2000).

22 It is important to distinguish the Reformed emphasis on extreme affection in religious practice from the specific phenomenon of "enthusiasm" described by writers such as Michael Heyd and Ronald A. Knox. From the "Zwickau prophets" of 1521 Wittenberg (designated "Schwärmer," or "stirred-up bees," by Martin Luther), to the Anabaptists criticized by Henry Bullinger and others, enthusiasts were criticized for claiming divine inspiration outside the authority of Scripture. As Heyd shows, they were roundly condemned not only for extreme physical expressions of emotion – "physical ecstasies and convulsions" – but for "apocalyptic pronouncements" and immoral behaviour: *"Be Sober and Reasonable": The Critique of Enthusiasm in the Seventeenth and Early Eighteenth Century* (Leiden: Brill, 1995), 11–18. Knox describes the development of this phenomenon before and after the Reformation in *Enthusiasm: A Chapter in the History of Religion*.

23 Protestant readings of these passages generally focus little on Redcrosse's terror: King does not discuss it, while Hume's focus on the wickedness of Redcrosse's foes suggests that his terror is a destructive emotion hindering his quest, rather than contributing to his salvation: *Edmund Spenser*, 89–91. Gless interprets Redcrosse's

terror before Orgoglio as a representation of spiritual deadness, though not as part of the process of psychologically experiencing divine judgment: *Interpretation and Theology*, 123.

24 As indicated above, abjection is an internal process that cannot technically be considered Longinian *ekstasis* – which by definition is a transport *outside* the self – but Kristeva herself suggests that abjection and sublimity overlap significantly, as she refers to sublimity and sublimation multiple times: *Powers of Horror: An Essay on Abjection*, trans. Leon S. Roudiez (New York: Columbia University Press, 1982), 11–12.

25 Kristeva, *Powers of Horror*, 2–4. For an analysis of how Spenser anticipates Kristevan abjection in a different context (not in terms of religion, theology, or the sublime), see Lehtonen, "The Abjection of Malbecco: Forgotten Identity in Spenser's Legend of Chastity," *Spenser Studies* 29 (2014): 179–96.

26 *Institutes* III.20.17, 874–5; my emphasis.

27 *Institutes*, I.1.3, 39. Longinus hints at a similar phenomenon when describing the terrorizing potential of the sublime and the audience's instinct of separation from it. On Demosthenes's powerful rhetoric, he writes: "You could sooner open your eyes to the descent of a thunderbolt than face his repeated outbursts of emotion without blinking": *On the Sublime*, sect. 34.1, 273.

28 Kristeva, *Powers of Horror*, 5.

29 Kristeva, *Powers of Horror*, 6–7.

30 Kristeva, *Powers of Horror*, 9.

31 All Spenser quotations are taken from A.C. Hamilton, ed., *Spenser: The Faerie Queene*, 2nd ed. (Harlow, England: Longman, 2007).

32 See *OED*, "astoned."

33 Biow, *Mirabile Dictu: Representations of the Marvelous in Medieval and Renaissance Epic* (Ann Arbor: University of Michigan Press, 1996), 168.

34 Though Armida's "doubt" draws her towards knowledge, and Abraham's helps him accept ignorance, both nonetheless lead to productive ecstasy.

35 Hamilton, *Spenser: The Faerie Queene*, 50n32.

36 Although Spenser may not have known Dante or had the *Commedia* in mind when portraying Fradubio's imprisonment, he would surely have been thinking, in addition to Tancredi and Clorinda, of Ruggiero and Astolfo from canto viii of the *Orlando Furioso* (as well as Aeneas and Polydorus from the *Aeneid*, 3.22–68); Astolfo's imprisonment in particular seems Dantean, reflecting the English knight's rejection of his intellect as he gives in to Alcina's seduction.

37 Gless, *Interpretation and Theology*, 135; Hamilton, in a comment in *Spenser: The Faerie Queene*, also notes that Spenser couches the episode in apocalyptic terms by introducing Orgoglio's intrusion with the phrase "at the last" (93n7). On Orgoglio as a projection of Redcrosse's sinful pride or lust, or as a figure of Catholic tyranny, see especially Hume, in *Edmund Spenser*, 92–4; and King, who focusses on the iconoclastic implications of the episode: *Spenser's Poetry and the Reformation Tradition*, 89–99.

38 Gless notes that English Reformers like John Bale and Henry Bullinger insist that apocalyptic texts aim chiefly not "to depict the end of the world and the Last Judgment but to propagate central doctrines of Christianity": *Interpretation and Theology*, 119.

39 *The Works of Edmund Spenser: A Variorum Edition*, ed. Edwin Greenlaw et al., 11 vols. (Baltimore: Johns Hopkins Press, 1932–57), I: 257; Cheney, *English Authorship*, 124–5.

40 *Calvin: Institutes*, III.3.3, 595.

41 Hume, *Edmund Spenser*, 89.

42 Gless, *Interpretation and Theology*, 143; see also Hume, *Edmund Spenser*, 97–8.

43 In noting the paradoxical agency of Despaire, I would also argue that Spenser resists the concept of "double predestination," the idea that God not only elects the saved but determines the unsaved onto a path of evil and damnation. In the case of Despaire, Spenser seems to understand the concept of "reprobation" – or God's treatment of the unsaved – in line with the understanding of many Calvinists: that God chooses *not* to intervene in the decisions of those who turn away from him. Then and now, theologians have hotly debated this question of whether God makes salvation impossible for some; Tobias Gregory discusses this controversy in the Renaissance: *From Many Gods to One: Divine Action in Renaissance Epic* (Chicago: University of Chicago Press, 2006), 202–6.

44 As David B. Johnson notes, Kristeva's concept of abjection involves *jouissance*, a response of masochistic fascination at being utterly "without hope of transcendence"; see "The Postmodern Sublime," in *The Sublime: From Antiquity to the Present*, ed. Timothy Costelloe (Cambridge: Cambridge University Press, 2012), 127; and Kristeva, *Powers of Horror*, 9–10.

45 Lehtonen, "The Abjection of Malbecco," 189–91.

46 Burke, *A Philosophical Enquiry into the Origin of Our Ideas of the Sublime and Beautiful*, ed. Adam Phillips (Oxford: Oxford University Press, 1990), I.vii, 36–7. Although Burke does not cite the Despaire passage in particular, he does refer to the Mammon episode as an example of the sublimity of sound (II.xix, 77).

47 Cheney identifies Arthur's "magnificence" as sublime: *English Authorship*, 76–7.

48 Joel 2:10–12.

49 Joel 2:30–2.

50 *On the Sublime*, sect. 7.3, 179.

51 Miller, "'Preparation for Salvation' in Seventeenth-Century New England," *Journal of the History of Ideas* 4.3 (1943): 261.

52 Perkins, *A Treatise of God's Free Grace, and Man's Free Will*, 132.

53 *OED*, "impression."

54 Whitaker uses this claim to deny Spenser's Calvinism: *The Religious Basis of Spenser's Thought*, 57–8.

55 Hamilton, *Spenser: The Faerie Queene*, 103n4, citing Romans 10:18. The most significant allusion, from *Orlando Furioso*, has the knight Astolfo using the magic horn to send enemies fleeing in terror (xv.19–22, 54–5).

56 This is not absolute, but a common pattern. Much of the first half of Revelation, for instance, is organized according to the trumpet blasts of seven angels, with trumpet blasts or thundering voices preceding the miraculous visions.

57 As with many principles, Longinus is not perfectly systematic in characterizing oral and visual forms of sublimity, but there does seem to be a pattern to the distinction. For example, he mentions the terrifying effects of the thunderous blare of a trumpet (sect. 9.6, 187), and the "terrible roar" of a tempest (sect. 10.5, 203), but casts the visual splendour of *phantasia* more positively (sect. 15.1–2, 215).

58 *On the Sublime*, sect. 7.4, 181.

59 *On the Sublime*, sect. 12.4–5, 209.

60 Bavinck, *Reformed Dogmatics: Volume 4: Holy Spirit, Church, and New Creation*, trans. John Vried, ed. John Bolt (Grand Rapids, MI: Baker Publishing, 2008), 124–5.

61 Luther, "Lectures on Galatians," in *Luther's Works*, vol. 26, ed. Jaroslav Pelikan and Walter A. Hansen (1535; St. Louis: Concordia, 1963), 4–5.

62 *OED*, "dismayed."

63 Spenser borrows the image from Atlante's enchanted shield in *Orlando Furioso* (2.55–56, 8.11, 22.84–6), but according to John Harington, Ariosto represents something nearly opposite: "the great pompes of the world" that blind the vain: *Orlando Furioso: Translated into English Heroical Verse by Sir John Harington*, ed. Robert McNulty (1591; Oxford: Oxford University Press, 1972), 39.

64 *On the Sublime*, sect. 15.1–2, 215.

65 *Calvin: Institutes*, I.1.2, 38.

66 *Calvin: Institutes*, I.1.3, 39.

67 Cheney, *English Authorship*, 94.

68 *Calvin: Institutes*, IV.1.3, 1014. Paul describes these gifts as follows: "For as we haue many members in one bodie, and all members haue not one office, So we being many are one bodie in Christ, and euerie one, one anothers members. Seing then that we haue gifts that are diuers, according to the grace that is giuen unto vs, whether we haue prophecie, let us prophecie according to the proportion of faith. Or an office [or the gift of service], let vs waite on the office: or he that teacheth, on teaching: Or he that exhorteth, on exhortation: he that distributeth, let him do it with simplicitie: he that ruleth, with diligence: he that sheweth mercie, with cherefulnes" (Rom. 12:4–8).

69 Falco, *Charismatic Authority in Early Modern English Tragedy* (Baltimore: Johns Hopkins University Press, 2000), 3.

70 Despite the nominal similarity, the Reformed understanding of charisma bears little resemblance to charismatic movements such as Pentecostalism, which emphasize the presence of miraculous signs such as faith healing and speaking in tongues; for Reformers, the aim of charisma was psychological and spiritual transformation.

71 Van Engen, *Sympathetic Puritans*, 20–1.

72 Una does have ties to the Church of England, with scholars such as Nandra Perry and Roy Strong identifying links between Una's imagery and Queen Elizabeth: Perry, "Elizabeth I as Holy Church in Spenser's *Faerie Queene*," *Renaissance Press* (1977):

33–48; Strong, *Portaits of Elizabeth: Elizabethan Portrature and Pageantry* (London: Thames and Hudson, 1977), 71, 74. At the same time, her name and heritage, of "ancient Kinges and Queenes," whose "scepters stretcht from East to Westerne shore" (i.5.4–5), identifies her as the "catholic" church, the church understood as encompassing all true followers of the Christian faith. This would necessarily include the many who were not English, despite English imperial ambitions. Like all Spenserian figures, she may at times stand for different things; but when compared to Lucifera, another figure channelling the sublime, who more clearly reflects English political ambition, Una's association with the broader fellowship of Christians seems especially prominent.

73   For studies on Lucifera as a figure of Elizabeth, see Michael O'Connell, *Mirror and Veil: The Historical Dimension of Spenser's 'Faerie Queene'* (Chapel Hill, NC: University of North Carolina Press, 1978), 52–4; Robin Headlam Wells, *Spenser's 'Faerie Queene' and the Cult of Elizabeth* (London: Croom Helm, 1983), 32–3; Paul Suttie, "Edmund Spenser's Political Pragmatism," *Studies in Philology* 95 (1993): 64–5; and Sayre Greenfield, *The Ends of Allegory* (Newark, DE: University of Delaware Press, 1998), 41–2, 81.

74   Cheney notes that Lucifera's sublimity is real, maintaining that it is "in itself not a marker of evil" since it resembles that of Prince Arthur: *English Authorship*, 111.

75   As scholars have noted, it is not until the House of Holiness that Spenser associates the knight of holiness with his virtue (x.45.9).

76   King, *Spenser's Poetry and the Reformation Tradition*, 60–1, citing John Hankins, *Source and Meaning in Spenser's Allegory: A Study of "The Faerie Queene"* (Oxford: Clarendon Press, 1971), 55–6.

77   Whitaker, *Religious Basis of Spenser's Thought*, 46–7; and Paul Alpers, *The Poetry of The Faerie Queene* (Princeton: Princeton University Press, 1967), 348–9.

78   Acts 2:1–47. Moving mountains was attributed biblically to Fidelia's namesake of faith (Matthew 17:20).

79   King, for instance, sees her as a "wise tutor" and "religious advisor" consistent with the Protestant emphasis on instruction: *Spenser's Poetry and the Reformation Tradition*, 63.

80   Kaske, *Biblical Poetics*, 110.

81   *On the Sublime*, sect. 34, 273.

82   See chapter 1.

83   *OED*, "thrill."

84   *Calvin: Institutes*, III.3.3, 596; and III.3.5, 597.

85   *Calvin: Institutes*, III.3.3, 595.

86   In a representative Protestant reading, Hume focusses on what Redcrosse learns through the dialogue: *Edmund Spenser*, 101–2. Among those associating the heightened emotions of the episode with Catholic mysticism are Whitaker, *Religious Basis of Spenser's Thought*, 54–5; and John M. Steadman, "Felicity and End in Renaissance Epic and Ethics," *Journal of the History of Ideas* 23 (1962): 125–6. Gless offers an argument more similar to mine, as he reads the episode as a translation of

Catholic mysticism into a more rationalist Protestant depiction, though he differs in finding the emotions "subordinate to the analytical process of reason": *Interpretation and Theology*, 161.

87 Despite some overlap in the descriptions of ecstasy and rapture, Spenser's Reformed depiction of prophecy departs from the Enthusiastic tradition described by Heyd, which again was noted for extreme physical behaviour (such as convulsions) and claims of direct divine inspiration unmediated by Scripture. In *The Faerie Queene*, Spenser surrounds the figure of Contemplation with biblical imagery, as if insisting on the prophecy's ties to Scripture; as Hamilton notes, Contemplation has the eye of an eagle – attribute of St. John of Revelation – and his vision recalls both that of Jacob's ladder and Moses's ascent to Mount Sinai: *Spenser: The Faerie Queene*, 132n47; 134n54; 134n56.

88 For instance, in defending the divine origins of biblical prophecy, Calvin writes in the *Institutes* that John, one of the Bible's most important prophets, "thundering from the heights, must certainly impel to the obedience of faith … [these words] more capable than any thunderbolt to batter their obstinacy" (I.8.10, 91).

89 Cheney, *English Authorship*, 95. In commenting on this passage, Borris notes similarly that Spenser follows Plato and the *Republic*'s insistence that "a [bedazzled] man returning from divine contemplations … must then embrace the active life": *Visionary Spenser*, 164, citing Plato, *Collected Dialogues*, ed. Edith Hamilton and Huntington Cairns, trans. various (Princeton: Bollingen–Princeton University Press, 1961), 7.517d–18b, 519c–21a. I agree that Spenser insists on the link between heavenly inspiration and the embrace of the active life, though again I would contend that his use of the sublime in this passage noticeably stresses the gap that remains between earthly and heavenly goals – in ontology, in value, and in intended emotional force.

90 Kaske, "The Dragon's Spark and Sting and the Structure of Red Cross' Dragon Fight: *The Faerie Queene* I.xi-xii," *Studies in Philology* 66 (1969): 609–38; and Gless, *Interpretation and Theology*, 164; Gless argues that the battle can equally support Pelagian or Reformed perspectives.

91 Hume, *Edmund Spenser*, 68–9, citing Perkins, *The Workes* (Cambridge, 1608–9), 715. The fourth century theologian Pelagius argued for the importance of good works to attaining salvation, against the emphasis of Augustine (and the Reformers) on divine sovereignty.

92 Kaske, "The Dragon's Spark and Sting," 609–38; and Gless, *Interpretation and Theology*, 164. While Reformers emphasized the perseverance of the saints, the Pelagian and Arminian view held that sinners who profess genuine faith can go on to lose their salvation.

93 Perkins, *A treatise tending under a declaration, whether a man be in the estate of damnation, or in the estate of grace*, in *The Workes of William Perkins. The First Volume* (London, 1612), 378.

94 Cheney, *English Authorship*, 96.

95 Milton, *Prose: Major Writings on Liberty, Politics, Religion, and Education*, ed. David Loewenstein (Oxford: Wiley Blackwell, 2013), 177–8.

5. Milton's Sacrificial Sublime: Idolatry and Relationship in *Paradise Lost*

1   On Milton's Arminianism, see Tobias Gregory, "The Tragedy of Creaturely Error," in *From Many Gods to One: Divine Action in Renaissance Epic* (Chicago: University of Chicago Press, 2006), 178–216; and Sarah van der Laan, "Milton's Odyssean Ethics: Homeric Allusions and Arminian Thought in *Paradise Lost*," *Milton Studies* 49 (2009): 49–76.

2   Ryan Hackenbracht argues persuasively that Milton expresses grand hopes for the nation of England in the afterlife, particularly early in his career: *National Reckonings: The Last Judgment and Literature in Milton's England* (Cornell: Cornell University Press, 2019). My reading of the sublime in *Paradise Lost*, however, suggests that he becomes disillusioned in his later career with the idea of English nationalism.

3   Irene Montori looks at Miltonic connections between the sublime and heroic virtue, though she does not see a robust model of heroism in *Paradise Lost*; Montori suggests that the poem presents an incomplete concept of heroism, deferring answers to its questions until *Samson Agonistes: Milton, the Sublime and Dramas of Choice: Figures of Heroic and Literary Virtue* (Rome: Edizioni, 2020). Milton's imitation of these three poets has been well established in classic studies by F.T. Prince, *The Italian Element in Milton's Verse* (Oxford: Clarendon Press, 1954); and C.P. Brand, *Torquato Tasso: A Study of the Poet and of his Contribution to English Literature* (Cambridge: Cambridge University Press 1965). David Quint outlines numerous textual allusions to the *Liberata* in *Paradise Lost* in *Inside Paradise Lost: Reading the Designs of Milton's Epic* (Princeton: Princeton University Press, 2015). For Du Bartas's influence on Milton, see studies cited in chapter 3. While there are several shorter comparative studies of Spenser and Milton, the only book-length study to my knowledge is Maureen Quilligan's work: *Milton's Spenser: The Politics of Reading* (Ithaca, NY: Cornell University Press, 1983).

4   Studies of Satan and other subterranean figures include Arthur Barker, "'… And on His Crest Sat Horror': Eighteenth-Century Interpretations of Milton's Sublimity and of His Satan," *University of Toronto Quarterly* 11 (1941–2): 421–36; Kenneth Gross, "Satan and the Romantic Satan: A Notebook," in *Re-membering Milton: Essays on the Texts and Traditions*, ed. Mary Nyquist and Margaret W. Ferguson (New York: Methuen, 1987), 318–41; Steven Knapp, *Personification and the Sublime: Milton to Coleridge* (Cambridge: Harvard University Press, 1985); Victoria Kahn, "Allegory and the Sublime in *Paradise Lost*," in *John Milton*, ed. Annabel Patterson (London: Longman, 1992), 185–201; Leslie E. Moore, *Beautiful Sublime: The Making of "Paradise Lost," 1701–1734* (Stanford: Stanford University Press, 1990); and David Sedley, *Sublimity and Skepticism in Montaigne and Milton* (Ann Arbor: University of Michigan Press, 2005).

5   On the Son and the Creation narrative, see Moore, *Beautiful Sublime*, 17–56; David Norbrook, "The Sublime Object: Milton, Lucy Hutchinson, and the Lucretian Sublime," *Tate Papers* 13 (2010); Norbrook, *Writing the English Republic: Poetry, Rhetoric, and Politics, 1627–1660* (Cambridge: Cambridge University Press, 1999); and Montori, "Representing creation, experiencing the sublime: The Longinian tradition in Tasso

and Milton." *SEDERI* 30 (2020): 69–89. Older scholarship on this topic will be discussed below.

6 See especially Moore, *Beautiful Sublime*, 57–99.

7 While the word "sublime" was used chiefly in adjective form before Milton's time, Milton also uses the word as a verb, to suggest the alchemical process of transformation from one state to another. Sandy Feinstein discusses this usage in "Milton's Devilish Sublime," *Ben Jonson Journal* 5 (1998): 149–66. All quotations of *Paradise Lost* are taken from Barbara Lewalski's edition: *John Milton: Paradise Lost* (Malden, MA: Blackwell, 2007).

8 For a more detailed discussion on the nature of Milton's angels, see Stephen M. Fallon's *Milton among the Philosophers: Poetry and Materialism in Seventeenth-Century England*, 141–6.

9 Sedley argues that before the Longinian revival of 1674, following Nicolas Boileau's popular translation of *Peri Hypsous*, Milton's "self-conscious sublimity" was uncommon and deserves more exploration: *Sublimity and Skepticism*, 110.

10 *John Milton: Prose. Major Writings on Liberty, Politics, Religion, and Education*, ed. David Loewenstein, 100. In *Paradise Lost*, Milton also incorporates an image of heroic transport similar to the one in his *Apology*, when the Son rides the "Chariot of Paternal Deity" to rout Satan and the rebel angels on God's behalf during the War in Heaven (6.749–59).

11 Ezekiel 1:1–29, and Revelation 4:2.

12 *Apology*, Loewenstein, 100.

13 *Apology*, Loewenstein, 100–1.

14 *Areopagitica*, Loewenstein, 209. In this passage, Milton imagines the pursuit of truth in a manner that recalls Tasso's concept of the sublime – as the passionate aspiration for divine union that leads to intuitive knowledge; in *Paradise Lost*, Milton will be more explicit than Tasso about the importance of mystery to the proper glorification of God.

15 Milton famously writes that "truth" has been endangered after having been "hewed … into a thousand pieces, and scatter'd … to the four winds": *Areopagitica*, Loewenstein, 205. Milton is not committed to universal toleration, however, but extends it to a certain spectrum of Protestants in *Areopagitica*.

16 *Areopagitica*, Loewenstein, 211.

17 Sedley, *Sublimity and Skepticism*, 110.

18 Milton also incorporates into Satan aspects of charismatic heroes from classical epic such as Achilles, who likewise channels divine power and glory at various moments. But in Tasso's Christian epic, Milton finds a striking model for the spectacular, sacrificial, pseudo-Messianic charisma seen in Satan. An earlier version of this subsection first appeared in "The Satanic Sublime in *Paradise Lost*: Tasso, Charisma, Abjection," *Modern Philology* 116, no. 3 (2019): 211–34. © 2019 by the University of Chicago. All rights reserved. 0026-8232/2019/11603-0002.

19 Critics have noted parallels between Milton's Satan and Tassoan antagonists, including Tasso's own Satan, and the Egyptian Caliph: see Quint, *Inside Paradise Lost*, 4–5; and

Lewalski, *Paradise Lost*, 37n1. But as yet, scholars have given little attention to parallels between Satan and Tassoan protagonists. Edward Weismiller notes a connection between Satan's and Goffredo's respective garnering of followers and offers of self-sacrifice, but does not consider the possible significance: "Materials Dark and Crude: A Partial Genealogy for Milton's Satan," *Huntington Library Quarterly* 31:1 (1967): 75–93.

20 Smith, "Martyrdom: Self-denial or Self-exaltation? Motives for Self-Sacrifice from Homer to Polycarp; A Theological Reflection," *Modern Theology* 22:2 (2006): 179. Smith cites Aristotle, *Posterior Analytics* 2.13, 97b16–20.

21 Smith, "Martyrdom: Self-denial or Self-exaltation?," 179. Smith cites Aristotle, *Posterior Analytics* 2.13, 97b16–20.

22 On Milton's iconoclasm, major studies include Loewenstein, *Milton and the Drama of History: Historical Vision, Iconoclasm, and the Literary Imagination;* Laura Lunger Knoppers, *Historicizing Milton: Spectacle, Power, and Poetry in Restoration England* (Athens: University of Georgia Press, 1994); and Lewalski, "Milton and Idolatry," *Studies in English Literature, 1500–1900* 43:1 (2003): 213–32. See also Rhema Hokama's recent "Praying in Paradise: Recasting Milton's Iconoclasm in *Paradise Lost*," *Milton Studies* 54 (2013): 161–80.

23 *Eikonoklastes*, Loewenstein, 279, 281, 317.

24 *Eikonoklastes*, Loewenstein, 279.

25 Rebecca M. Rush also links Satan with Kristevan abjection: "Satan's Mural Breaches: Transgression and Self-Violation in *Paradise Lost*," *Milton Studies* 54 (2013): 107–35, 317–23.

26 Kristeva, *Powers of Horror: An Essay on Abjection*, trans. Leon S. Roudiez, 13–14.

27 Gregory notes that Milton features a significant tension in Satan's character between great agency and total confinement: *From Many Gods to One*, 195.

28 Katherine Calloway also argues that Satan is modelled on the character of Aeneas, though she sees Milton's view of Aeneas as generally more positive than I tend to: "Beyond Parody: Satan as Aeneas in *Paradise Lost*," *Milton Quarterly* 39, no. 2 (2005): 82–92.

29 In Book 9, Satan similarly maintains that he is "constraind / Into a Beast" (9.165).

30 As Doran notes, Kant associates acts done for the sake of duty with the sublime: "Duty! Sublime and mighty name that embraces nothing charming or insinuating but requires submission," in *Critique of Pure Reason*, trans. Paul Guyer and Allen Wood (Cambridge: Cambridge University, 1998), 5:86, cited in *The Theory of the Sublime*, 198. This is not to suggest that Milton believes duty to be fundamentally incompatible with the sublime, but that he sees it as a distinct and lower-order drive to be subordinated to the promptings of sublimity.

31 In a similar instance from Book 4, at the words and sight of Zephon, Satan is "abasht …, / And felt how awful goodness is" (4.847–8), despite having once been superior to Zephon in rank.

32 *Aeneid*, trans. Allen Mandelbaum.

33 Quint, *Inside Paradise Lost*, 209.

34 As indicated in chapter 3, I am not suggesting that Milton and Du Bartas take the same view of knowledge (as Milton is no *sceptical fideist* and does not share Du

Bartas's distrust of reason and empiricism), but I am proposing that both poets find considerable value in divine mystery that energizes their concepts of heroism and sublimity, and that this element of *Paradise Lost* may be due in part to *Les Semaines*. Milton's own approach to knowledge will be discussed further below.

35 Sugimura identifies this longing as "vaghezza" and traces the historical connection of vaghezza to the sublime: "The Passion of Wonder in *Paradise Lost*," *Essays in Criticism* 64.1 (2014): 1–28.

36 For further comparison of Milton's and Du Bartas' views of knowledge in this scene and a few others, but not in terms of the sublime, see also Lehtonen, "Heroic Adaptations of Genesis 3: Knowledge and Skepticism in Renaissance Biblical Epic," in *The Bible and Western Christian Literature*, ed. Elisabeth Jay, vol. 2, *Renaissance and Reformation*, ed. Sophie Read (London: Bloomsbury, forthcoming).

37 Although the picturesque was not formally theorized until Uvedale Price in 1794, Angus Fletcher notes that the theory has "perhaps existed for millennia," but originates from "seventeenth- and eighteenth-century fads of landscape 'improvement,' the cultivation of 'special effects' in gardening, and by extension the cultivation of these effects in the visual, literary, and even musical arts": *Allegory: The Theory of a Symbolic Mode* (Ithaca: Cornell University Press, 1964), 252–3.

38 Fletcher, *Allegory*, 253. Fletcher bases his argument on that of Price: *Sir Uvedale Price on the Picturesque: with an Essay on the Origin of Taste*, ed. Thomas Lauder (Edinburgh, 1842).

39 As Price notes, the picturesque is not limited to visual perception, even though the term "picturesque" suggests an association with images: "There is, indeed, a general harmony and correspondence in all our sensations when they arise from similar causes, though they affect us by means of different senses; and these causes, as Mr. Burke has admirably pointed out, can never be so clearly ascertained when we confine our observations to one sense only": *Sir Uvedale Price on the Picturesque*, 80.

40 All quotations from these poems are taken from *John Milton: Complete Shorter Poems*, ed. Stella P. Revard (Oxford: Wiley-Blackwell, 2009).

41 *Sir Uvedale Price on the Picturesque*, 141.

42 Schwartz, *Remembering and Repeating: Biblical Creation in Paradise Lost* (Cambridge: Cambridge University Press, 1988), 47, 57. See also Lehtonen, "Heroic Adaptations," which argues that Milton distinguishes between acquiring knowledge as a means of seeking power, and seeking knowledge of the ways and character of God. Sedley, in *Sublimity and Skepticism*, does not focus on Milton's positive views of knowledge, but his analysis of Satan through the lens of scepticism takes an approach that is largely compatible with these distinctions.

43 Moore, *Beautiful Sublime*, 109–23.

44 *The Works of Joseph Addison: The Spectator, no. 315–635*, 3 vols., vol. 2 (New York, 1837), 333: 32; 333: 31.

45 Sedley, *Sublimity and Skepticism*, 110.

46 *On the Sublime*, trans. W.H. Fyfe and Donald Russell, in *Aristotle: The Poetics. "Longinus": On the Sublime. Demetrius: On Style*, ed. Jeffrey Henderson (Cambridge: Harvard

University Press, 1995), sect. 8.1, 180–1. This concept and passage are discussed in the first chapter.

47 Comparably, Price describes the aesthetic of trees (in contrast to flowers, deemed "beautiful" for their "symmetry" and "regular and finished design") as picturesque, because "everything appears so loose and irregular, that symmetry seems out of the question": *Sir Uvedale Price on the Picturesque*, 93.

48 Burke describes beauty as "smooth" and "polished," whereas Eve's "disheveled" appearance suggests a more rugged aesthetic: *A Philosophical Enquiry into the Origin of Our Ideas of the Sublime and Beautiful*, ed. Adam Phillips (Oxford: Oxford University Press, 1990), III.xxvii, 113.

49 Fletcher distinguishes the picturesque from the sublime in these terms in *Theory of a Symbolic Mode*, 253.

50 Moore claims that Eve "exercise[s] a level of power and energy opposed to the aesthetic definition [of beauty]" – closer to that of the sublime – thereby precipitating Adam's decision to fall with her: *Beautiful Sublime*, 69. Other scholars have faulted Adam for allowing himself to become too vulnerable to the passions Eve produces in him: see, for instance, Norbrook, *Writing the English Republic*, 485–7; and Sharon Achinstein, *Milton and the Revolutionary Reader, Literature in History* (Princeton: Princeton University Press, 1994), 25.

51 By contrast, Quint argues that Adam does act nobly towards Eve in this scene: *Inside Paradise Lost*, 218.

52 Though she does not use the term, Rachel Trubowitz argues that Adam falls into a condition of despair similar to Satan's, remaining in a "near-paralytic state of self-created intellectual and emotional bondage" in which he can still be found "clinging to Nature": see "Sublime/Pauline: Denying Death in *Paradise Lost*," in *Imagining Death in Spenser and Milton*, ed. Elizabeth Jane Bellamy, Patrick Cheney, and Michael Schoenfelt (New York: Palgrave, 2003), 140–8.

53 Eve's dependence on Adam also marks the onset of the divine curse that her desire will be for her husband – but in this case, the curse brings with it a blessing as well.

54 Quint suggests that Adam is "ungallant" in abruptly dismissing Eve's offer, though Adam's response does seem to me to have a heroic element, reassuring her of his willingness to sacrifice himself for her: *Inside Paradise Lost*, 215. Joan S. Bennett also suggests that Eve is the hero of the poem based on this passage: *Reviving Liberty: Radical Christian Humanism in Milton's Great Poems* (Cambridge: Harvard University Press, 1989), 118.

55 By contrast, Colin Burrow maintains that Milton withholds a presentation of the union of humanity with God, focussing instead on Adam and Eve's reconciliation with each other: Burrow, *Epic Romance: Homer to Milton* (Oxford: Clarendon Press, 1993), 275.

56 Paul writes that the Holy Spirit intercedes for believers in prayer in "sighs, which cannot be expressed": Romans 8:27.

57 Citing multiple definitions, Philip Shaw describes the sublime as that which cannot be fully presented through language: *The Sublime* (London: Routledge, 2006), 1–4. Even

though Longinus describes language as the vehicle for sublimity, he, too, suggests that human ideas "often pass beyond the limits that confine us," indicating that the sublime is a function of ideas rather than language: Longinus, *On the Sublime*, sect. 35.3, 275.

58 By contrast, Trubowitz maintains that Adam does not recover fully from despair, a condition she finds less constructive than I do: "Sublime/Pauline," in *Imagining Death*, 142.

59 *On the Sublime*, sect. 1.4, 163.

60 *On the Sublime*, sect. 44.11, 305; sect. 44.8, 303.

61 Quint, *Inside Paradise Lost*, 62.

62 Sedley, *Sublimity and Skepticism*, 109.

63 Lewalski, *Paradise Lost*, 310n876–8.

64 While critics such as Earl Miner have defended Milton's assent to the concept of the *felix culpa*, more recent scholars such as Diana Benet tend to argue that Milton does not support the idea: see Miner, "Felix Culpa in the Redemptive Order of *Paradise Lost*," *Philological Quarterly* 47 (January 1968): 43–54; and Benet, "Satan, God's Glory and the Fortunate Fall," *Milton Quarterly* 19 (May 1985): 34–7. Offering a more nuanced perspective, John C. Ulreich argues that Milton presents the concept as a "spiritual paradox," in which "moral freedom is necessarily created by the loss of spontaneous innocence": see "Eve as the Hero of Paradise Lost," in *All in All: Unity, Diversity, and the Miltonic Perspective*, ed. Charles W. Durham and Kristin A. Pruitt (Selinsgrove: Susquehanna University Press, 1999), 82, n. 21. While Milton does represent Adam and Eve gaining moral freedom as a consequence of the Fall, I believe he may have imagined an alternative means of gaining moral freedom even if the pair had not eaten – a possibility that C.S. Lewis imagines at the conclusion to his imitation of *Paradise Lost*, *Perelandra* (1943), part of his space fiction trilogy, in which the corresponding Adam and Eve figures do not fall.

65 David Loewenstein also suggests that Milton becomes less nationalistic later in his career, though he does not discuss Milton's hopes for an alternative, spiritual community: "Late Milton: Early Modern Nationalist or Patriot?" *Milton Studies* 48 (2008): 53–71.

Conclusion: Virgil, Empire, and Sublimity in *Paradise Regained*

1 Peter Lake discusses early modern concepts of the invisible church in *Anglicans and Puritans? Presbyterianism and English Conformist Thought from Whitgift to Hooker* (London: Allen & Unwin, 1988); see also W. Bradford Littlejohn, *The Peril and Promise of Christian Liberty: Richard Hooker, the Puritans, and Protestant Political Theology* (Grand Rapids, MI: Eerdmans, 2017). Discussing the roughly equivalent concept of the *ecclesia universalis* (universal church), the eternal community of living and deceased believers, Ryan Hackenbracht argues that this dimension of identity was important to Protestant thought and religious practice in seventeenth-century England specifically: *National Reckonings: The Last Judgment and Literature in Milton's England* (Cornell: Cornell University Press, 2019), 4–6.

2 *Aeneid*, trans. Allen Mandelbaum.
3 Though its official publication date is three years before Milton's final edition of *Paradise Lost*, *Paradise Regained* followed the first edition by five years and was clearly written to follow the Genesis epic.
4 Joseph Crawford describes the boom of British nationalistic epic in "Milton's Heirs: Epic Poetry in the 1790s," *Studies in Romanticism* 49, no. 3 (2010): 427–43.
5 William Hayley, *An Essay on Epic Poetry in Five Epistles*, 110–11, cited in Crawford, "Milton's Heirs," 428–9.
6 Crawford, "Milton's Heirs," 481–3.
7 Crawford, 486–9.
8 On Virgil's hesitation towards nationalism, see C.M. Bowra, "Aeneas and the Stoic Ideal," *Greece & Rome* 3, no. 7 (1933): 8–21.
9 The nature and scope of Virgil's distinctive concept of *metempsychosis* (reincarnation) remains ambiguous and debated. While Ovid and others record Aeneas's transformation into a deity, Virgil does not.
10 *On the Sublime*, sect. 13.2–3, 210; Colossians 3:4; 1 Peter 5:1.

References

Abrams, M.H. *The Fourth Dimension of a Poem: and Other Essays.* New York: Norton, 2012.

Achinstein, Sharon. *Milton and the Revolutionary Reader, Literature in History.* Princeton: Princeton University Press, 1994.

Addison, Joseph. *The Works of Joseph Addison: The Spectator, no. 315–635.* Vol. 2. New York, 1837.

Alpers, Paul. *The Poetry of The Faerie Queene.* Princeton: Princeton University Press, 1967.

Anderson, Judith. *Reading the Allegorical Intertext: Chaucer, Spenser, Shakespeare, Milton.* New York: Fordham University Press, 2008.

Ardissino, Erminia. *L'Aspra Tragedia: Poesia e Sacro in Torquato Tasso.* Florence: Olschki, 1996.

Ariosto, Ludovico. *Orlando Furioso: Translated into English Heroical Verse by Sir John Harington.* 1591. Ed. Robert McNulty. Oxford: Oxford University Press, 1972.

Aristotle. *The Basic Works of Aristotle.* Ed. Richard McKeon. New York: Random House, 1941.

Auerbach, Erich. *Mimesis: The Representation of Reality in Western Literature.* Trans. Willard R. Task. 1953; Princeton: Princeton University Press, 2003.

Auger, Peter. *Du Bartas' Legacy in England and Scotland.* Oxford: Oxford University Press, 2019.

– "The Semaines' Dissemination in England and Scotland until 1641." *Renaissance Studies* 26, no. 5 (2011): 625–40.

Augustine of Hippo. *The Confessions of St. Augustine.* Translated by John Ryan. Garden City, NY: Doubleday, 1960.

Barbieri, Costanza. ""To Be in Heaven': St. Philip Neri between Aesthetic Emotion and Mystical Ecstasy." In *The Sensuous in the Counter-Reformation Church,* edited by Marcia B. Hall and Tracy E. Cooper, 206–29. Cambridge: Cambridge University Press, 2013.

Barker, Arthur. ""… And on His Crest Sat Horror': Eighteenth-Century Interpretations of Milton's Sublimity and of His Satan." *University of Toronto Quarterly* 11 (1941–2): 421–36.

Bavinck, Herman. *Reformed Dogmatics*. Vol. 4, *Holy Spirit, Church, and New Creation*. Translated by John Vried. Edited by John Bolt. Grand Rapids, MI: Baker Publishing, 2008.

Bellamy, Elizabeth Jane. *Translations of Power: Narcissism and the Unconscious in Epic History* Ithaca, NY: Cornell University Press, 1994.

Bellenger, Yvonne, ed. *La Seconde Semaine*. 1584. Paris: Société des Textes Français Modernes, 1991.

– *Les Suittes de la Seconde Semaine*. 1603. Paris: Société des Textes Français Modernes, 1994.

Benet, Diana. "Satan, God's Glory and the Fortunate Fall." *Milton Quarterly* 19 (May 1985): 34–7.

Bennett, Joan S. *Reviving Liberty: Radical Christian Humanism in Milton's Great Poems*. Cambridge: Harvard University Press, 1989.

Berry, Lloyd, ed. *Geneva Bible: A Facsimile of the 1560 Edition*. Peabody, MA: Hendrickson, 2007.

Biester, James. *Lyric Wonder: Rhetoric and Wit in Renaissance English Poetry*. Ithaca: Cornell University Press, 1997.

Biow, Douglas. *Mirabile Dictu: Representations of the Marvelous in Medieval and Renaissance Epic*. Ann Arbor: University of Michigan Press, 1996.

Bishop, T.G. *Shakespeare and the Theatre of Wonder*. Cambridge: Cambridge University Press, 1996.

Blackwell, Thomas. *An Enquiry into the Life and Writings of Homer*. London, 1753.

Boileau-Despréaux, Nicolas. *Oeuvres Complètes de Boileau*. 1674. Edited by Charles Antoine Gidel. 4 vols. Paris, 1870–3.

Boitani, Piero. *The Tragic and the Sublime in Medieval Literature*. Cambridge: Cambridge University Press, 1989.

Bond, Christopher. *Spenser, Milton, and the Redemption of the Epic Hero*. Newark: University of Delaware Press, 2012.

Borris, Kenneth. *Visionary Spenser and the Poetics of Early Modern Platonism*. Oxford: Oxford University Press, 2017.

Bouhours, Dominique. *Entretiens d'Ariste et d'Eugène* (1671). Edited by Bernard Beugnot and Gilles Declercq. Paris: Champion, 2003.

Bowker, John, ed. *The Concise Oxford Dictionary of World Religions*. Oxford: Oxford University Press, 2000.

Bowra, C.M. "Aeneas and the Stoic Ideal." *Greece & Rome* 3, no. 7 (1933): 8–21.

Brady, Emily. *The Sublime in Modern Philosophy: Aesthetics, Ethics, and Nature*. Cambridge: Cambridge University Press, 2013.

Brand, C.P. *Torquato Tasso: A Study of the Poet and of his Contribution to English Literature*. Cambridge: Cambridge University Press, 1965.

Braunrot, Bruno. *L'Imagination poétique chez du Bartas: Éléments de sensibilité baroque dans la Création du monde*. Chapel Hill, NC: University of North Carolina Press, 1973.

Bruno, Giordano. *On the Heroic Frenzies: A Translation of De gli eroici furori*. 1585. Ed. Eugenio Canone. Toronto: University of Toronto Press, 2013.

Burke, Edmund. *A Philosophical Enquiry into the Origin of Our Ideas of the Sublime and Beautiful.* 1757. Ed. Adam Phillips. Oxford: Oxford University Press, 1990.

Burrow, Colin. *Epic Romance: Homer to Milton.* Oxford: Clarendon Press, 1993.

Calloway, Katherine. "Beyond Parody: Satan as Aeneas in 'Paradise Lost.'" *Milton Quarterly* 39, no. 2 (2005): 82–92.

Calvin, Jean. *Calvin: Institutes of the Christian Religion.* 1536. 2 vols. Translated by Ford Lewis Battles. Edited by John T. McNeill. Philadelphia: Westminster Press, 1967.

– *Institution de la religion chrestienne.* 2 vols. Paris: C. Meyrueis, 1859. Université de Genève. Web.

– *Rudimenta fidei christianae, sive catechismus. Huic adjunctus nunc est catechismus alius magis compendiarius.* Genève: Henri II Estienne, 1575. Post-Reformation Digital Library.

Campana, Joseph. *The Pain of Reformation: Spenser, Vulnerability, and the Ethics of Masculinity.* New York: Fordham University Press, 2012.

Cavalchini, Mariella, and Irene Samuel. Introduction to *Discourses on the Heroic Poem*, by Torquato Tasso. Trans. Cavalchini and Samuel. Oxford: Oxford University Press, 1973. xi–xxxiv.

Cavallo, Jo Ann. *Romance Epics of Boiardo, Ariosto, and Tasso: From Public Duty to Private Pleasure.* Toronto: University of Toronto Press, 2004.

Céard, Jean. Introduction to *La Sepmaine ou Creation du monde.* Edited by John Céard. Tome I, no. 1, vol. 10. Paris: Classiques Garnier, 2011.

Chapman, George. *Dedication to Mathew Royden.* 1585. In *English Renaissance Literary Criticism*, edited by Brian Vickers, 392–4. Oxford: Oxford University Press, 2007.

— "On Translating and Defending Homer." 1611. In *English Renaissance Literary Criticism*, 512–25.

Cheney, Patrick. *English Authorship and the Early Modern Sublime: Spenser, Marlowe, Shakespeare, Jonson.* Cambridge: Cambridge University Press, 2018.

— "'The forms of things unknown': English Authorship and the Early Modern Sublime." *Medieval and Early Modern Authorship.* Edited by Guillemmette Bolens and Lukas Erne. Tübingen, Germany: Narr Verlag, 2011. 137–60.

– *Marlowe's Republican Authorship: Lucan, Liberty, and the Sublime.* Basingstoke: Palgrave, 2009.

Coldiron, A.E.B. "How Spenser Excavates Du Bellay's 'Antiquitez'; or, The Role of the Poet, Lyric Historiography, and the English Sonnet." *The Journal of English and Germanic Philology* 101, no. 1 (2002): 41–67.

Costa, Gustavo. "Appunti sulla fortuna dello Pseudo-Longino nel Seicento: Alessandro Tassoni e Paganino Gaudenzio." *Studi secenteschi* 25 (1984): 123–43.

— "The Latin Translations of Longinus' *Peri Ypsous* in Renaissance Italy." *Acta Conventus Neo-Latini Bononiensis. Proceedings of the Fourth International Congress of Neo-Latin Studies, Bologna, 26 August to 1 September 1979.* Edited by R.J. Schoeck. Binghamton, NY: Medieval and Renaissance Texts and Studies, 1985. 224–38.

— "Paolo Manuzio e lo Pseudo-Longino." *Giornale storico della letteratura italiana* 161 (1984): 60–77.

— "Pietro Vettori, Ugolino Martelli e lo Pseudo Longino." In *Da Longino a Longin*, edited by Luigi Russo, 65–79. Palermo: Aesthetica Edizioni, 1987.

– "Storia del Sublime e storia ecclesiastica." *Aevum Antiquum* 3 (2003): 319–50.

– "Tasso e il Sublime." *Rivista di Estetica* 27 (1987): 49–63.

Costelloe, Timothy, ed. *The Sublime: From Antiquity to the Present.* Cambridge: Cambridge University Press, 2012.

Crawford, Joseph. "Milton's Heirs: Epic Poetry in the 1790s." *Studies in Romanticism* 49, no. 3 (2010): 427–43.

Croce, Benedetto. *Poesia Antica e Moderna.* Bari, Italy: Laterza, 1943.

Da Falgano, Giovanni di Niccolò. *Libro della altezza del dire.* Ed. Angelo Cardillo. Trans. Giovanni di Niccolò Da Falgano. Napoli: Liguori, 2011.

– trans. *Libro della Altezza del Dire di Dionysio Longino Rhetore Tradotto dalla Greca nella Toscana Lingua da Giovanni di Niccolò da Falgano Fiorentino.* Florence, 1575. Biblioteca Nazionale Centrale, MS Magl. VI.33.

Dante Alighieri. *Divina Commedia.* Ed. C.H. Grandgent. New York: Heath, 1913.

De Petra, Gabriele. *Dionysii Longini Rhetori praestantissimi liber de Grandi, sive Sublimi genere Orationi, Latine reditus … a Gabriele de Petra.* Geneva: Johannes Tornaesius, 1612.

Donadoni, Eugenio. *Torquato Tasso.* Florence: La Nuova Italiana, 1967.

Doran, Robert. *The Theory of the Sublime from Longinus to Kant.* Cambridge: Cambridge University Press, 2015.

Du Bartas, Guillaume de Salluste. "Triomfe de la Foi." *La Muse Chrestiene.* Bordeaux, 1574. f(o) AB vol. 2.

Du Bellay, Joachim. *The Regrets with The Antiquities of Rome, Three Latin Elegies, and The Defense and Enrichment of the French Language.* Trans. Richard Helgerson. Philadelphia: University of Pennsylvania Press, 2006.

Edgar, Swift, ed. *The Vulgate Bible: Douay-Rheims Translation.* 6 vols. Cambridge, MA: Harvard University Press, 2010–13.

Eggert, Katherine. "Spenser's Ravishment: Rape and Rapture in *The Faerie Queene.*" *Representations* 70 (2000): 1–26.

Eisenstadt, S.N. Introduction to *On Charisma and Institution Building,* by Max Weber. Edited by Eisenstadt. Chicago: University of Chicago Press, 1968. ix–lvi.

Elliott, John R. Jr., ed. *The Prince of Poets: Essays on Edmund Spenser.* New York: New York University Press, 1968.

Falco, Raphael. *Charismatic Authority in Early Modern English Tragedy.* Baltimore: Johns Hopkins University Press, 2000.

Fallon, Stephen M. *Milton among the Philosophers: Poetry and Materialism in Seventeenth-Century England.* Cornell: Cornell University Press, 1991.

Feinstein, Sandy. "Milton's Devilish Sublime." *Ben Jonson Journal* 5 (1998): 149–66.

Fichter, Andrew. *Poets Historical: Dynastic Epic in the Renaissance.* New Haven: Yale University Press, 1982.

Fish, Stanley. *How Milton Works.* Cambridge, MA: Harvard University Press, 2001.

Fletcher, Angus. *Allegory: The Theory of a Symbolic Mode.* Ithaca, NY: Cornell University Press, 1964.

Ford, Philip. "Erasmian Irenism in the Poetry of Pierre de Ronsard." In *The Reception of Erasmus on the Early Modern Period*, edited by Karl A.E. Enenkel, 141–61. London: Brill, 2013.

– "Virgil versus Homer: Reception, Imitation, Identity in the French Renaissance." In *Virgilian Identities in the French Renaissance*, edited by Phillip John Usher and Isabelle Fernbach, 163–178. Suffolk: Boydell and Brewer, 2012.

Fry, Paul. *The Reach of Criticism: Method and Perception in Literary Theory*. New Haven: Yale University Press, 1983.

Fumaroli, Marc. *L'Age d'Eloquence: Rhétorique et «res literaria» de la Renaissance au seuil de l'époque classique*. Geneva: Droz, 1980.

– "Rhétorique d'école et rhétorique adulte: remarques sur la réception européenne du traité 'Du Sublime' au XVIe et au XVIIe siècle." *Revue d'Histoire littéraire de la France* 1 (1986): 33–51.

Gaston, Robert W. "How Words Control Images: The Rhetoric of Decorum in Counter-Reformation Italy." In Hall and Cooper, *The Sensuous in the Counter-Reformation Church*, 74–90.

Gaylon, Lynda. "Puttenham's *Enargeia* and *Energeia*: New Twists for Old Terms," *Philological Quarterly* 60 (1981): 29–40.

Getto, Giovanni. *Malinconia di Torquato Tasso*. Naples: Liguori, 1979.

Giacomini, Lorenzo. *Del furor poetico. Discorso fatto ne l'Academia degli Alterati ne l'anno MDLXXXVII, in idem, Orationi e discorsi*. Florence: Sermartelli, 1587.

Giamatti, A. Bartlett. *The Earthly Paradise and the Renaissance Epic*. Princeton: Princeton University Press, 1966.

Gilby, Emma. *Sublime Worlds: Early Modern French Literature*. London: Routledge, 2006.

Gill, Meredith J. "'Until Shadows Disperse': Augustine's Twilight." In Hall and Cooper, *The Sensuous in the Counter-Reformation Church*, 252–72.

Gilman, Ernest. *Iconoclasm and Poetry in the English Reformation: Down Went Dagon*. Chicago: University of Chicago Press, 1986.

Gless, Darryl. *Interpretation and Theology in Spenser*. Cambridge: Cambridge University Press, 1994.

Goyet, Francis. "The Meaning of *Apostrophè* in Longinus's *On the Sublime*." In *Translations of the Sublime: The Early Modern Reception and Dissemination of Longinus' Peri hupsous in Rhetoric, the Visual Arts, Architecture, and the Theatre*, edited by Caroline van Eck et al., 13–32. Boston: Brill, 2012.

Graziani, Françoise. "Le Miracle de l'Art: Le Tasse e la Poétique de la Meraviglia." *Revue des Études Italiennes* 42 (1995): 117–39.

Greenblatt, Stephen. "Resonance and Wonder," in *Learning to Curse: Essays in Early Modern Culture*. New York: Routledge, 1990. 216–47.

Greene, Thomas M. *The Descent from Heaven: A Study in Epic Continuity*. New Haven: Yale University Press, 1963.

Greenfield, Sayre. *The Ends of Allegory*. Newark, DE: University of Delaware Press, 1998.

Greenlaw, Edwin et al., ed. *The Works of Edmund Spenser: A Variorum Edition*. 11 vols. Baltimore: Johns Hopkins Press, 1932–57.

Gregory, Jr., E.R. "Du Bartas, Sidney, Spenser." *Comparative Literature Studies* 7, no. 4 (1970): 437–49.

Gregory, Tobias. *From Many Gods to One: Divine Action in Renaissance Epic*. Chicago: University of Chicago Press, 2006.

Gross, Kenneth. "Satan and the Romantic Satan: A Notebook." In *Re-membering Milton: Essays on the Texts and Traditions*, edited by Mary Nyquist and Margaret W. Ferguson, 318–41. New York: Methuen, 1987.

– *Spenserian Poetics: Idolatry, Iconoclasm, and Magic*. Ithaca, NY: Cornell University Press, 1986.

Grosser, Hermann. *La Sottiglieza del Disputare: Teorie degli Stili e Teorie dei Generi in Età Rinascimentale e nel Tasso*. Florence: Nuova Italia Editrice, 1992.

Hackenbracht, Ryan. *National Reckonings: The Last Judgment and Literature in Milton's England*. Cornell: Cornell University Press, 2019.

Hadfield, Andrew. "Spenser's Religion – Yet Again." *Studies in English Literature 1500–1900* 15, no. 1 (2001): 21–46.

Hall, John, trans. *"Longinus: Of the Height of Eloquence."* London, 1652.

Hall, Marcia B. Introduction to *The Sensuous in the Counter-Reformation Church*, edited by Maria B. Hall and Tracy E. Cooper. Cambridge: Cambridge University Press, 2013. 1–20.

Hall, Marcia B., and Tracy E. Cooper, eds. *The Sensuous in the Counter-Reformation Church*. Cambridge: Cambridge University Press, 2013.

Halliwell, Stephen. *Between Ecstasy and Truth: Interpretations of Greek Poetics from Homer to Longinus*. Oxford: Oxford University Press, 2011.

Hamilton, A.C., ed. *The Spenser Encyclopedia*. Toronto: University of Toronto Press, 1990.

– ed. *Spenser: The Faerie Queene*. 1596. 2nd ed. Harlow, England: Longman, 2007.

– *Sir Philip Sidney: A Study of his Life and Works*. Cambridge: Cambridge University Press, 1977.

Hamlett, Lydia. "The Longinian Sublime, Effect and Affect in 'Baroque' British Visual Culture." In *Translations of the Sublime*, 187–220.

Hankins, John. *Source and Meaning in Spenser's Allegory: A Study of "The Faerie Queene."* Oxford: Clarendon Press, 1971.

Hare, John. "Religion and Morality." In *The Stanford Encyclopedia of Philosophy*, edited by Edward N. Zalta (Winter 2014). Web.

Harvey, Gabriel. *Pierces Supererogation*. In *Elizabethan Critical Essays*. Edited by G. Gregory Smith. London: Oxford University Press, 1904.

Hayley, William. *An Essay on Epic Poetry in Five Epistles*. Edited by M. Celeste Williamson. 1782. Gainesville: Scholars' Facsimiles and Reprints, 1968.

Helgerson, Richard. *Forms of Nationhood: Elizabethan Writing of England*. University of Chicago Press, 1992.

– trans. *The Regrets with The Antiquities of Rome, Three Latin Elegies, and The Defense and Enrichment of the French Language*. Philadelphia: University of Pennsylvania Press, 2006.

Heyd, Michael. *"Be Sober and Reasonable": The Critique of Enthusiasm in the Seventeenth and Early Seventeenth Centuries.* Leiden: Brill, 1995.

Hill, Christopher. *Milton and the English Revolution.* London: Faber, 1977.

Hokama, Rhema. "Praying in Paradise: Recasting Milton's Iconoclasm in Paradise Lost." *Milton Studies* 54 (2013): 161–80.

Homer. *The Iliad.* Translated by Robert Fagles. New York: Penguin, 1990.

Horace. *The Art of Poetry.* Trans. D.A. Russell. In *Classical Literary Criticism,* edited by Russell and Michael Winterbottom, 98–110. Oxford: Oxford University Press, 1989.

– *A Letter to Augustus.* Translated by Michael Winterbottom. In *Classical Literary Criticism,* 91–7.

Hörnqvist, Mikael. *Machiavelli and Empire.* Cambridge: Cambridge University Press, 2004.

Hume, Anthea. *Edmund Spenser: Protestant Poet.* Cambridge: Cambridge University Press, 1984.

Ibata, Hélène. *The Challenge of the Sublime: From Burke's Philosophical Inquiry to British Romantic Art.* Manchester: Manchester University Press, 2018.

Jaeger, C. Stephen. *Enchantment: On Charisma and the Sublime in the Arts of the West.* Philadelphia: University of Pennsylvania Press, 2012.

Johnson, David B. "The Postmodern Sublime." In *The Sublime,* 118–34.

Kahn, Victoria. "Allegory and the Sublime in *Paradise Lost.*" In *John Milton: A Collection of Critical Essays,* edited by Annabel Patterson, 185–201. London: Longman, 1992.

Kant, Immanuel. *Critique of the Power of Judgement.* Ed. and trans. Paul Guyer and Eric Matthews. Vol. 5. Cambridge: Cambridge University Press, 2000.

– *Critique of Pure Reason.* Trans. Paul Guyer and Allen Wood. Vol. 5. Cambridge: Cambridge University Press, 1998.

Kaske, Carol. "The Dragon's Spark and Sting and the Structure of Red Cross' Dragon Fight: *The Faerie Queene* I.xi-xii." *Studies in Philology* 66 (1969): 609–38.

– *Spenser and Biblical Poetics.* Ithaca, NY: Cornell University Press, 1999.

Kenseth, Joy, ed. *The Age of the Marvelous.* Hanover, NH: Dartmouth, 1991.

King, John N. *Spenser's Poetry and the Reformation Tradition.* Princeton: Princeton University Press, 1990.

Knapp, Steven. *Personification and the Sublime: Milton to Coleridge.* Cambridge: Harvard University Press, 1985.

Knoppers, Laura Lunger. *Historicizing Milton: Spectacle, Power, and Poetry in Restoration England.* Athens: University of Georgia Press, 1994.

Knox, Ronald A. *Enthusiasm: A Chapter in the History of Religion.* Oxford: Oxford University Press, 1950.

Kristeva, Julia. *Powers of Horror: An Essay on Abjection.* Translated by Leon S. Roudiez. New York: Columba University Press, 1982.

Lake, Peter. *Anglicans and Puritans? Prebysterianism and English Conformist Thought from Whitgift to Hooker.* London: Allen & Unwin, 1988.

Lamacz, Stephane. "La Construction du savior et la réécriture du de rerum natura dans la Sepmaine de Du Bartas." *Bibliothèque d'Humanisme et Renaissance* 64, no. 3 (2002): 617–38.

Langbaine, Gerard, ed. *Dionsyii Longini Rhetoris Praestantissimi Liber de grandi loquentia sive Sublimi dicendi genere, Latine redditus.* Oxford: William Turner, 1638.

Lehtonen, Kelly. "The Abjection of Malbecco: Forgotten Identity in Spenser's Legend of Chastity." *Spenser Studies* 29 (2014): 179–96.

– "Heroic Adaptations of Genesis 3: Knowledge and Skepticism in Renaissance Biblical Epic." In *The Bible and Western Christian Literature.* Edited by Elisabeth Jay. Vol. 2, *Renaissance and Reformation*, edited by Sophie Read. London: Bloomsbury, forthcoming.

– "*Peri Hypsous* in Translation: The Sublime in Sixteenth-Century Epic Theory." *Philological Quarterly* 95, no. 3–4 (2016): 449–66.

– "The Satanic Sublime in 'Paradise Lost': Tasso, Charisma, Abjection." *Modern Philology* 116, no. 3 (2019): 211–34.

Lewalski, Barbara, ed. *John Milton: Paradise Lost.* 1674. Malden, MA: Blackwell, 2007.

– "Milton and Idolatry." *Studies in English Literature, 1500–1900* 43.1 (2003): 213–32.

Lewis, C.S. *Perelandra.* 1943. New York: Scribner, 2003.

Littlejohn, W. Bradford. *The Peril and Promise of Christian Liberty: Richard Hooker, the Puritans, and Protestant Political Theology.* Grand Rapids, MI: Eedermans, 2017.

Loewenstein, David, ed. *John Milton Prose: Major Writings on Liberty, Politics, Religion, and Education.* Oxford: Wiley Blackwell, 2013.

– "Late Milton: Early Modern Nationalist or Patriot?" *Milton Studies* 48 (2008): 53–71.

– *Milton and the Drama of History: Historical Vision, Iconoclasm, and the Literary Imagination.* Cambridge: Cambridge University Press, 1990.

Longinus. "On the Sublime." Translated by W.H. Fyfe and Donald Russell. In *Aristotle: The Poetics; Longinus: On the Sublime; Demetrius: On Style*, edited by Jeffrey Henderson, 159–306. Cambridge, MA: Harvard University Press, 1995.

Luther, Martin. "Lectures on Galatians." 1535. *Luther's Works.* 55 vols. Vol. 26. Edited by Jaroslav Pelikan and Walter A. Hansen. St. Louis: Concordia, 1963.

– "Preface to the Epistle of St. Paul to the Romans." In *Martin Luther's Basic Theological Writings.* 2nd ed., edited by Timothy F. Lull. Minneapolis: Augsburg, 2005.

Lyotard, Jean-Françoise. "The Sublime and the Avant-Garde." *Paragraph: A Journal of Modern Critical Theory* 6 (1985): 1–18.

Manieri, Alessandra. *L'immagine poetica nella teoria degli antichi. Phantasia ed enargeia.* Pisa: Instituti editoriali e poligrafici internazionali, 1998.

Manuzio, Paolo. *Dionysii Longini de sublimi genere dicendi.* Venice: Paolo Manuzio, 1555.

Maranta, Bartolomeo. *Lucullianarum Quaestionum Libri Quinque.* Basel: Anno Salutis Humanae, 1564.

Marin, Louis. "1674: On the Sublime, Infinity, *Je Ne Sais Quoi.*" In *A New History of French Literature*, edited by Denis Hollier, 340–6. Harvard: Harvard University Press, 1994.

Martin, Eva Madeleine. "The 'Prehistory' of the Sublime in Early Modern France: An Interdisciplinary Perspective." In Costelloe, *The Sublime*, 77–102.

Mattioli, Emilio. "Il Sublime e lo Stile: Suggestione Cinquecentesche." In Russo, *Da Longino a Longino*, 55–64.

Maynard, Katherine S. *Reveries of Community: French Epic in the Age of Henri IV*. Evanston, IL: Northwestern University Press, 2017.

Mazzotta, Giuseppe. "Italian Renaissance Epic." In *The Cambridge Companion to Epic*. Ed. Catherine Bates. Cambridge Collections Online: Cambridge University Press, 2010.

Mazzucchi, C.M. "Tradizione Manoscritta del Περι Υψους." *Italian medioevale e umanistica* 32 (1989): 205–26.

McEachern, Claire. "Spenser and Religion." *The Oxford Handbook of Edmund Spenser*. Ed. Richard McCabe. *Oxford Handbooks Online*. Oxford University Press, 2012. 1–22.

McIntosh, Donald. "Weber and Freud: On the Nature and Sources of Authority." *American Sociological Review* 35 (1970): 901–11.

Melehy, Hassan. *The Poetics of Literary Transfer in Early Modern France and England*. Farnham, UK: Ashgate, 2013.

Miller, Perry. "'Preparation for Salvation' in Seventeenth-Century New England," *Journal of the History of Ideas* 4, no. 3 (1943): 253–86.

Milton, John. *An Apology Against a Pamphlet*. In Loewenstein, *John Milton Prose*, 92–102.

– *Areopagitica*. In *John Milton Prose*, 181–213.

– *Eikonoklastes*. In *John Milton Prose*, 275–318.

– "Il Penseroso." In *John Milton: Complete Shorter Poems*, edited by Stella P. Revard, 53–8. Oxford: Wiley-Blackwell, 2009.

– "L'Allegro." In *John Milton: Complete Shorter Poems*, 48–52.

– *Of Education*. In *John Milton Prose*, 170–80.

– *Reason of Church Government*. In *John Milton Prose*, 61–91.

Miner, Earl. "Felix Culpa in the Redemptive Order of *Paradise Lost*." *Philological Quarterly* 47 (January 1968): 43–54.

Monk, Samuel H. *The Sublime: A Study of Critical Theories in XVIII-Century England*. New York: MLA, 1935.

Montaigne, Michel de. *An Apology for Raymond Sebond*. Translated by M.A. Screech. New York: Penguin, 1987.

Montori, Irene. *Milton, the Sublime and Dramas of Choice: Figures of Heroic and Literary Virtue*. Rome: Edizioni Studium, 2020.

– "Representing creation, experiencing the sublime: The Longinian tradition in Tasso and Milton." *SEDERI* 30 (2020): 69–89.

Moore, Leslie E. *Beautiful Sublime: The Making of "Paradise Lost," 1701–1734*. Stanford: Stanford University Press, 1990.

Murrin, Michael. *The Allegorical Epic: Essays in its Rise and Decline*. Chicago: University of Chicago Press, 1980.

Nohrnberg, James. *The Analogy of "The Faerie Queene."* Princeton: Princeton University Press, 1976.

Norbrook, David. "The Sublime Object: Milton, Lucy Hutchinson, and the Lucretian Sublime." *Tate Papers* 13 (2010). Web.

– *Writing the English Republic: Poetry, Rhetoric, and Politics, 1627–1660*. Cambridge: Cambridge University Press, 1999.

O'Connell, Michael. *Mirror and Veil: The Historical Dimension of Spenser's 'Faerie Queene.'* Chapel Hill, NC: University of North Carolina Press, 1978.

Oxford Dictionary of Philosophy, 3rd ed. Oxford: Oxford University Press, 2016.

Oxford English Dictionary Online. Oxford University Press, 2020.

Pagano, Petro, trans. *Dionysii Longini De Sublimi dicendi genere liber a Petro Pagano latinitate donatus.* Venice, 1572.

Paleotti, Gabriele. *Discourses on Sacred and Profane Images.* Translated by William McCuaig. Getty: Los Angeles, 2012.

Patrizi, Francesco. *Della Poetica.* 1586. 3 vols. Ed. Danilo Aguzzi Barbagli. Firenze: Istituto Nazionale di Studi sul Rinascimento, 1969–71.

Patterson, Annabel. *Hermogenes and the Renaissance: Seven Ideas of Style.* Princeton: Princeton University Press, 1970.

– *Reading between the Lines.* London: Routledge, 1993.

– "Tasso and Neoplatonism: The Growth of his Epic Theory." *Studies in the Renaissance* 18 (1971): 105–33.

Perkins, William. *A Treatise of God's Free Grace, and Man's Free Will.* Cambridge, 1602.

– *The Workes.* 3 vols. Cambridge, 1608–9.

Perry, Nandra. "Elizabeth I as Holy Church in Spenser's *Faerie Queene." Renaissance Press* (1977): 33–48.

Pizzimenti, Domenico. Dedicatory letter to Aldo Manuzio. *Dionysii Longini Rhetoris Praestantissimi liber de Grandi orationis genere, Domenico Pizimentio Vibonensi interprete.* Naples, 1566.

Plato. *Collected Dialogues.* Edited by Edith Hamilton and Huntington Cairns. Translated by Various. Princeton: Princeton University Press, 1961.

Poliner, Sharon May. "Du Bellay's Songes: Strategies of Deceit, Poetics of Vision." *Bibliothèque d'Humanisme et Renaissance* 43, no. 3 (1981): 509–25.

Popkin, Richard H. *History of Scepticism from Erasmus to Spinoza.* Berkeley: University of California Press, 1979.

Porta, Francesco. *La Visione di M. Francesca Porta: Da Castel Nuovo della Garfagnana.* Fiorenza [*sic*]: Giorgio Marescotti, 1578.

Porter, James. *The Sublime in Antiquity.* Cambridge: Cambridge University Press, 2016.

Porto, Francesco, ed. *Dionysii Longini Rhetoris Praestantissimi liber de Grandi orationis genere, Domenico Pizimentio Vibonensi interprete.* Naples: Johannes Maria Scotus, 1566.

– ed. *Oi en tē rhētorikē technē koryphaioi. Aphthonios, Hermogenês, D. Longinos.* Geneva, 1569.

Praz, Mario. *Il Giardino dei sensi: Studi sul manierismo e il barocco.* Torino: Arnoldo Mondadori Editore, 1975.

Prescott, Anne Lake. *French Poets and the English Renaissance: Studies in Fame and Transformation.* New Haven: Yale University Press, 1978.

– "The Reception of Du Bartas in England." *Studies in the Renaissance* XV (1968): 144–73.

Price, Uvedale. *Sir Uvedale Price on the Picturesque: with an Essay on the Origin of Taste.* Edited by Thomas Lauder. Edinburgh, 1842.

Prince, F.T. *The Italian Element in Milton's Verse.* Oxford: Clarendon Press, 1954.

Puttenham, George. *The Arte of English Poesie.* 1589. In Vickers, *English Renaissance Literary Criticism,* 190–296.

Quilligan, Maureen. *Milton's Spenser: The Politics of Reading.* Ithaca, NY: Cornell University Press, 1983.

Quint, David. *Epic and Empire: Politics and Generic Form from Virgil to Milton.* Princeton: Princeton University Press, 1993.

– *Inside Paradise Lost: Reading the Designs of Milton's Epic.* Princeton: Princeton University Press, 2015.

Ray, Gene. *Terror and the Sublime in Art and Critical Theory: From Auschwitz to Hiroshima to September 11.* 2nd ed. New York: Palgrave MacMillan, 2011.

Refini, Eugenio. "Longinus and Poetic Imagination in Late Renaissance Literary Theory." In *Translations of the Sublime,* 33–53.

Revard, Stella P., ed. *John Milton: Complete Shorter Poems.* Oxford: Wiley-Blackwell, 2009.

Rhu, Lawrence F. "From Aristotle to Allegory: Young Tasso's Evolving Vision of the *Gerusalemme Liberata*." *Italica* 65, no. 2 (1998): 111–30.

– *Genesis of Tasso's Narrative Theory: English Translations of the Early Poetics and a Comparative Study of their Significance.* Detroit: Wayne State University Press, 1993.

Richardson, Alan. *The Neural Sublime: Cognitive Theories and Romantic Texts.* Baltimore: Johns Hopkins University Press, 2010.

Rinaldi, Micaela. *Torquato Tasso e Francesco Patrizi: Tra Polemiche Letterarie e Incontri Intellettuali.* Ravenna: Longo, 2001.

Ringler, William. "An Early Reference to Longinus." *Modern Language Notes* 53, no. 1 (1938): 23–4.

Robin, Diana. "Renata di Francia." In *Encyclopedia of Women in the Renaissance: Italy, France, and England,* edited by Robin, Anne R. Larsen, and Carole Levin, 321–3. Oxford: ABC-CLIO, 2007.

Robortello, Francesco, ed. *Dionysiu Longinu Rētoros Perì Hypsus Biblion.* Basel, 1554. Bayerische Staats Bibliothek, *Münchener Digitalisierungszentrum.*

Ronsard, Pierre de. *Abregé de l'art poetique François.* London: Eragny Press, 1903.

– *Oeuvres Complètes de P. de Ronsard: Publiées sur les textes les plus anciens avec les variants et des notes par M. Prosper Blanchemain.* Paris: P. Jannet, 1858.

Rush, Rebecca M. "Satan's Mural Breaches: Transgression and Self-Violation in *Paradise Lost*." *Milton Studies* 54 (2013): 107–35.

Ruskin, John. *The Stones of Venice.* Vol. 3. New York: Alden, 1885.

Russo, Luigi, ed. *Da Longino a Longino: i luoghi del Sublime.* Palermo: Aesthetica Edizioni, 1987.

Saint Girons, Baldine. *Fiat lux. Une philosophie du sublime.* Paris: Quai Voltaire, 1993.

– "The Sublime from Longinus to Montesquieu." Translated by Fred L. Rush, Jr., *Oxford Encyclopedia of Aesthetics.* Edited by Michael Kelly. *Oxford Art Online.* Oxford: Oxford University Press, 2014.

Santonja, Pedro. *La herejía de los alumbrados y la espiritualidad en la España del siglo 16: Inquisición y sociedad.* Valencia, Spain: Generalitat Valenciana, 2001.

Scarpati, Claudio. *Studi sul Cinquecento Italiano*. Milan: Vita e pensiero, 1982.

Schoenfeldt, Michael. *Bodies and Selves in Early Modern England: Physiology and Inwardness in Spenser, Shakespeare, Herbert, and Milton*. Ann Arbor: University of Michigan Press, 2000.

Schutte, Anne Jacobson. *Aspiring Saints: Pretense of Holiness, Inquisition, and Gender in the Republic of Venice, 1618–1750*. Baltimore: Johns Hopkins University Press, 2001.

Schwartz, Regina. *Remembering and Repeating: Biblical Creation in Paradise Lost*. Cambridge: Cambridge University Press, 1988.

Sedley, David. *Sublimity and Skepticism in Montaigne and Milton*. Ann Arbor: University of Michigan Press, 2005.

Segni, Agnolo. *Lezioni sopra le cose pertinenti alla poetica*. Florence, 1581. Biblioteca Medicea Laurenziana, MS Laur. Ashb. 531. In Bernard Weinberg. *History of Literary Criticism in the Italian Renaissance*. Chicago: University of Chicago Press, 1961.

Shaw, Philip. *The Sublime*. London: Routledge, 2006.

Shuger, Debora. *Sacred Rhetoric: The Christian Grand Style in the English Renaissance*. Princeton: Princeton University Press, 1988.

Sidney, Sir Philip. *The Defence of Poesy*. 1595. *The Defence of Poesy, Sir Philip Sidney: The Major Works*. Ed. Katherine Duncan-Jones. Oxford: Oxford University Press, 2008.

Sinfield, Alan. "Sidney and Du Bartas." *Comparative Literature* 27 (1975): 8–20.

Sloane, Thomas. *Donne, Milton, and the End of Humanist Rhetoric*. Berkeley: University of California Press, 1985.

Slocombe, William. *Nihilism and the Sublime Postmodern: The (Hi)story of a Difficult Relationship from Romanticism to Postmodernism*. New York: Routledge, 2013.

Sluhovsky, Moshe. *Believe Not Every Spirit: Possession, Mysticism, and Discernment in Early Modern Catholicism*. Chicago: University of Chicago Press, 2007.

Smith, J. Warren. "Martyrdom: Self-denial or Self-exaltation? Motives for Self-sacrifice from Homer to Polycarp; A Theological Reflection." *Modern Theology* 22, no. 2 (2006): 169–96.

Stark, Ryan J. "Cold Styles: On Milton's Critiques of Frigid Rhetoric in *Paradise Lost*." *Milton Quarterly* 37, no. 1 (2003): 21–30.

Steadman, John M. "Felicity and End in Renaissance Epic and Ethics." *Journal of the History of Ideas* 23 (1962): 117–32.

Stephens, Walter. "Saint Paul Among the Amazons: Gender and Authority in *Gerusalemme Liberata*." *Discourses of Authority in Medieval and Renaissance Literature*. Ed. Kevin Brownlee and Stephens. Hanover, NH: University Press of New England, 1989.

Strong, Roy. *Portraits of Elizabeth: Elizabethan Portraiture and Pageantry*. London: Thames and Hudson, 1977.

Sugimura, N.K. "The Passion of Wonder in *Paradise Lost*." *Essays in Criticism* 64, no. 1 (2014): 1–28.

Suttie, Paul. "Edmund Spenser's Political Pragmatism," *Studies in Philology* 95 (1993): 56–76.

Sylvester, Joshuah. *The Complete Works of Joshuah Sylvester*, 2 vols. Edited by Alexander B. Grosart. 1880. Sagwan Press, 2015.

Talvacchia, Bette. "The Word Made Flesh: Spiritual Subjects and Carnal Depictions in Renaissance Art." In Hall and Cooper, *The Sensuous in the Counter-Reformation Church*, 65.

Tasso, Torquato. *Discorsi Dell'Arte Poetica e del Poema Eroico*. Edited by Luigi Poga. Laterza: Bari, 1964.

– *Gerusalemme Conquistata: MS. Vind. Lat. 72 della Biblioteca Nazionale di Napoli*. Edited by Claudio Gigante. Alessandria: Edizioni dell'Orso, 2010.

– *Gerusalemme Liberata*. Edited by Giuseppe Lipparini. Milano: Carlo Signorelli, 1944.

– *Jerusalem Delivered*. Translated by Anthony M. Esolen. Baltimore: Hopkins, 2000.

Taylor, George Coffin. *Milton's Use of Du Bartas*. Harvard: Harvard University Press, 1934.

Till, Dietmar. "The Sublime and the Bible: Longinus, Protestant Dogmatics, and the 'Sublime Style.'" In van Eck, et al., *Translations of the Sublime*, 55–64.

Treherne, Matthew. "Pictorial Space and Sacred Time: Tasso's *Le Lagrime della Beata Vergine* and the Experience of Religious Art in the Counter-Reformation." *Italian Studies* 62 (2007): 5–25.

Trubowitz, Rachel. "Sublime/Pauline: Denying Death in *Paradise Lost*." In *Imagining Death in Spenser and Milton*, edited by Elizabeth Jane Bellamy, Patrick Cheney, and Michael Schoenfelt, 131–50. New York: Palgrave, 2003.

Turner, Jason. "Compatibilism and the Free Will Defense." *Faith and Philosophy* 30, no. 2 (2013): 125–37.

Ulreich, John C. "Eve as the Hero of Paradise Lost." In *All in All: Unity, Diversity, and the Miltonic Perspective*, edited by Charles W. Durham and Kristin A. Pruitt, 67–82. Selinsgrove: Susquehanna University Press, 1999.

van der Laan, Sarah. "Milton's Odyssean Ethics: Homeric Allusions and Arminian Thought in *Paradise Lost*," *Milton Studies* 49 (2009): 49–76.

– "Tasso's Homeric Counter-Factuals." *MLN* 127, no. 1 (2012): 23–44.

van Eck, Caroline, et al., eds. *Translations of the Sublime: The Early Modern Reception and Dissemination of Longinus' Peri hupsous in Rhetoric, the Visual Arts, Architecture, and the Theatre*. Boston: Brill, 2012.

van Engen, Abram. *Sympathetic Puritans: Calvinist Fellow Feeling in Early New England*. Oxford: Oxford University Press, 2015.

van Huss, Bernard. "Anmerkungen zur Rezeption von Longins 'Erhabenem' im Cinquecento." *Romanistisches Jahrbuch* 62 (2011): 165–87.

Vettori, Pietro. *Commentarii in Primum Librum Aristotelis de Arte Poetarum*. 1560. Munich: Wilhelm Fink Verlag, 1967.

Vickers, Brian, ed. *English Renaissance Literary Criticism*. Oxford: Oxford University Press, 2007.

Virgil. *The Aeneid*. Trans. Allen Mandelbaum. New York: Bantam, 1971.

Wall, John N. Jr. "The English Reformation and the Recovery of Christian Community in *The Faerie Queene*." *Studies in Philology* 80.2 (1983): 142–62.

Warner, Christopher. *The Augustinian Epic: Petrarch to Milton*. University of Michigan Press, 2010.

Watson, Gerard. *Phantasia in Classical Thought*. Galway: Galway University Press, 1988.

Weber, Max. *On Charisma and Institution Building*. Edited by S.N. Eisenstadt. Chicago: University of Chicago Press, 1968.

Weinberg, Bernard. *History of Literary Criticism in the Italian Renaissance*. 2 vols. Chicago: University of Chicago Press, 1961.

– "Translations and Commentaries of Longinus, 'On the Sublime,' to 1600: A Bibliography." *Modern Philology* 47 (1950): 145–51.

Weismiller, Edward. "Materials Dark and Crude: A Partial Genealogy for Milton's Satan." *Huntington Library Quarterly* 31, no. 1 (1967): 75–93.

Welch, Anthony. *Renaissance Epic and the Oral Past*. New Haven, CT: Yale University Press, 2012.

Wells, Robin Headlam. *Spenser's 'Faerie Queene' and the Cult of Elizabeth*. London: Croom Helm, 1983.

Whitaker, Virgil K. *The Religious Basis of Spenser's Thought*. New York: Gordian Press, 1966.

Wofford, Susanne. *The Choice of Achilles: The Ideology of Figure in the Epic*. Stanford: Stanford University Press, 1994.

Zatti, Sergio. *L'uniforme Cristiano e il Multiforme Pagano Saggio sulla Gerusalemme Liberata*. Milan: Il Saggiatore, 1983.

– *The Quest for Epic: From Ariosto to Tasso*. Translated by Sally Hill and Dennis Looney. Edited by Dennis Looney. Toronto: Toronto University Press, 2006.

Zepke, Stephen. *Sublime Art: Toward an Aesthetics of the Future*. Edinburgh: Edinburgh University Press, 2017.

Index

grace, 199, 124; and heroic frenzy (Giordano Bruno), 43; and heroism, 9, 60; and knowledge, 90; and *meraviglia*, 34, 36, 53; and *perturbazione*, 39–40; and religious transformation (Philip Sidney), 46, 48

ekstasis (or ecstasy; *ekstatic*), 3, 4, 5, 7, 9, 25, 27, 46, 79, 86–7, 95, 96–7, 100, 108, 138, 155, 161, 165, 167; abject perversion of, 116–19, 144, 149, 151, 153; and charisma, 59, 132; and community, 174; and grace, 120, 135, 136; and knowledge, 57, 71; and *meraviglia*, 37; and Neoplatonism, 14. *See also* Longinus; transport

empire, 33, 140, 152–4, 172, 175–8. *See also* glory; nationalism

enargeia and *evidenza*, 38, 47–8, 100, 105. See also *phantasia*

energeia, 47, 105, 131, 135

Enthusiastic (religious tradition), 206n22

epic poetry, divine vs. civic purposes of, 4–5, 31–3, 38–9, 42, 48–9, 51–2; emotional vs. ethical purposes of, 34–5, 37–8, 47, 48–9

equality (spiritual), 94, 95–7

Erasmus, Desiderius, 20, 29

Este family, 56

Ezekiel, 96, 142

The Faerie Queene: abjection in, 109–19, 122, 125; and civic duty, 5, 104, 134, 139; critique of charismatic authority, 109, 128–9; divine judgment in, 109–20, 125, 129; grace in, 108, 119–26; heroism in, 105, 108, 126, 127, 129, 134–7; magic horn, 121–4; magic shield, 124–6; as sublime poem, 105; thunder, 123, 135; visual vs. auditory sublime, 121–3, 124–6. *See also* Protestantism

Falco, Raphael, 127

Fall of humanity: in *Paradise Lost*, 154–5, 155–7, 162; *Les Semaines*, 87, 90–2

felix culpa, 170, 171–2, 217n64

Ficino, Marsilio, 50, 85. See also *furor*; Neoplatonism

Flacius, Matthias, 45

Fletcher, Angus, 157–8, 215n37, 216n49

Fumaroli, Marc, 20, 187nn8–9, 188n19

furor, 14, 30, 42, 50, 85, 95, 185n45, 189n32, 194n103. *See also* Ficino; Neoplatonism; Plato

Gerusalemme Conquistata, 82

Gerusalemme Liberata: abjection in, 55, 69, 73–4, 76, 80, 81; *Allegoria del Poema*, 59; charismatic heroism in, 58–9, 60–9; civic duty in, 53–4, 55, 60–1, 68–9, 70–2, 74, 75, 76–7, 82; individual spirituality in, 55–6, 57, 58, 75, 76; intuition in, 57–9, 64–6, 69–71, 74; pleasure in, 54–6, 69, 70, 72, 78, 81; risk, as heroic, 58–63, 65, 68–9, 71, 75, 78, 81–2; romantic heroism in, 69–81

Gless, Darryl, 113, 205n15, 206–7n23, 208n38, 210–11n86

glory: affirmation of spiritual, 155, 159–60, 169, 172; critique of national/ imperial, 144, 152, 172, 175–6, 179; critique of solipsistic, 146–8, 152, 156–7, 164, 179

grace, 108, 119–26; and charisma, 127, 128, 130, 131; as irresistible, 104–5, 106–7, 108, 120, 122–3, 135, 140; as sublime, 119–20, 122, 128, 136

Graziani, Françoise, 35, 38–9

greatness of mind (poet's), 29–31, 38–9, 46–7, 48, 50, 52. See also *megalophués/ noesis*

Greenblatt, Stephen, 104

Greene, Thomas, 8, 196n6

Gregory, Tobias, 4, 182n13, 208n43, 214n30

Paul (apostle), 107

Pelagius (theologian), 135

Peri Hypsous. See Longinus; sublime

Perkins, William, 121, 135, 206n20

perturbazione, 39–41

phantasia, 25, 27, 38, 47–8, 101, 105

picturesque, 155, 157–8, 161–2

Pizzimenti, Domenico, 20, 22, 23–5

Plato, 41, 50, 185n45, 194n103, 204n5, 211n85. See also *furor*; Neoplatonism

pleasure: in the *Gerusalemme Liberata*, 54–6, 69, 70, 72, 78, 81; Longinus on, 7, 12, 43–4, 55, 168, 183n20; in *Paradise Lost*, 155, 158, 160, 163; in Renaissance literary theory, 35, 36, 37

Pléiade, 29. *See also* Du Bellay, Joachim; Ronsard, Pierre

Porta, Francesco (author of *Castel Nuovo della Gargagnana*), 37

Porter, James, 183n26

Porto, Francisco (publisher of *Peri Hypsous*), 20, 23, 33

Praz, Mario, 39, 65, 196n7, 199n33

Prescott, Anne Lake, 84, 85, 204n37

Price, Uvedale, 158, 161

prophets/prophecy (or prophecie), 52, 96, 132–4, 142, 209n103, 209n68, 211nn7–8, 211nn87–8. *See also* Ezekiel; Isaiah; Joel

Protestantism, or Protestant theology: and the affections, 107–8; the *charismata*, 14, 126–7, 132; divine sovereignty, 97, 107, 126; double predestination, 208n43; grace, 119–21, 123, 132, 135; holiness as sublime, 106–7; the invisible church, 174; irresistibility of grace/salvation, 104–5, 106–7, 108, 120, 122–3, 135, 140; judgment, 109–10, 110, 114–15, 125; Longinian scholars with connections to, 33–4; mortification, 115; and Puritanism, 205–6n18; salvation, 107; spiritual authority, 11–12;

stages of repentance, 132; stylistic connections to Longinus, 44–6, 184n33; terror, 106, 109–10. *See also* Calvin, John; Luther, Martin; Perkins, William

Puttenham, George, 47–8

Queen Elizabeth I, 104

Quint, David, 54, 169, 182n12, 216n51, 216n54

Rainolds, John, 21

rapture, 25, 27; in *The Faerie Queene*, 137; in the *Gerusalemme Liberata*, 68, 81; in *Paradise Lost*, 143, 158; perverse/distorted forms of, 90–1, 118, 154; in *Les Semaines*, 87, 91, 95, 96, 100, 101, 103. See also *ekstasis*; Longinus

Refini, Eugenio, 21–2

Reformation theology. *See* Calvin, John; Luther, Martin; Perkins, William; Protestantism

regeneration (of sublime poet), 45, 47–8, 50

religious nonconformity and the sublime, 33–4, 42, 44

Renée de France, 56

risk, as impetus to the sublime: Catholic theories of art, 58; *Discorsi del poema eroico*, 39–42; *Gerusalemme Liberata*, 58, 59–63, 64, 71, 78, 82; *Heroic Frenzies* (Bruno), 42–4; *Peri Hypsous*, 39, 41; *Paradise Lost*, critique of, 146, 156

Robortello, Francesco, 19, 23

romantic heroism, 55, 69–81

Ronsard, Pierre: *Abregé de l'art poétique françois*, 31–2; and Du Bartas, 84; *Franciade*, 10, 30–1; and Longinian influence, 29

sacrifice (or self-subordination), 52, 140, 141, 144, 165, 166; as false heroism, 145, 147, 162